New Zealand Ways of Speaking English

Multilingual Matters

Afrikaner Dissidents
    JOHA LOUW-POTGIETER
Aspects of Bilingualism in Wales
    COLIN BAKER
Australian Multiculturalism
    LOIS FOSTER and DAVID STOCKLEY
Bilingual Children: From Birth to Teens
    GEORGE SAUNDERS
Code-Mixing and Code Choice
    JOHN GIBBONS
Communication and Cross-cultural Adaptation
    YOUNG YUN KIM
English in Wales: Diversity, Conflict and Change
    N. COUPLAND in association with A. THOMAS (eds)
Language Attitudes Among Arabic-French Bilinguals in Morocco
    ABDELALI BENTAHILA
Language in Education in Africa
    CASMIR M. RUBAGUMYA (ed.)
Language and Ethnicity in Minority Sociolinguistic Perspective
    JOSHUA FISHMAN
Language in Geographic Context
    COLIN WILLIAMS (ed.)
Language Planning and Education in Australasia and the South Pacific
    R. B. BALDAUF and A. LUKE (eds)
Language Policy Across the Curriculum
    DAVID CORSON
Marriage Across Frontiers
    A. BARBARA
Minority Education: From Shame to Struggle
    T. SKUTNABB-KANGAS and J. CUMMINS (eds)
Multilingualism in India
    D. P. PATTANAYAK (ed.)
Teaching and Learning English Worldwide
    J. BRITTON, R. E. SHAFER and K. WATSON (eds)
The Use of Welsh: A Contribution to Sociolinguistics
    MARTIN J. BALL (ed.)

Please contact us for the latest book information:
Multilingual Matters,
Bank House, 8a Hill Road,
Clevedon, Avon BS21 7HH,
England

MULTILINGUAL MATTERS 65
Series Editor: Derrick Sharp

New Zealand Ways of Speaking English

Edited by

Allan Bell and Janet Holmes

MULTILINGUAL MATTERS LTD
Clevedon · Philadelphia

Library of Congress Cataloging in Publication Data

New Zealand Ways of Speaking English/Edited by Allan Bell and Janet Holmes.
p.   cm. (Multilingual Matters: 65)
1. English language — New Zealand. 2. English language — Social aspects —
New Zealand. 3. New Zealand — Social life and customs.
I. Bell, Allan. II. Holmes, Janet. III. Series: Multilingual Matters (Series): 65.
PE3602.N49   1990
306.4'4'0993 — dc20

British Library Cataloguing in Publication Data

New Zealand Ways of Speaking English (Multilingual Matters: 65)
1. English language. New Zealand usage.
I. Bell, Allan. II. Holmes, Janet.
427.993

ISBN 1–85359–083–5
ISBN 1–85359–082–7 (pbk)

Multilingual Matters Ltd
Bank House, 8a Hill Road,   &   1900 Frost Road, Suite 101
Clevedon, Avon BS21 7HH,   Bristol, PA 19007
England   USA

Cover illustration: *The Promised Land*, Oil on canvas, 1948, by Colin McCahon
(1918–1987), New Zealand. Auckland City Art Gallery, presented by the McCahon
family, 1988.

Index compiled by Meg Davies (Society of Indexers).
Typeset by Photo·graphics, Honiton, Devon.
Printed and bound in Great Britain by the Longdunn Press Ltd, Bristol.

Contents

1 Attitudes, Varieties, Discourse: An Introduction to the Sociolinguistics of New Zealand English
Janet Holmes and Allan Bell 1

ATTITUDES TO NEW ZEALAND ENGLISH

2 'This Objectionable Colonial Dialect': Historical and Contemporary Attitudes to New Zealand Speech
Elizabeth Gordon and Marcia Abell 21

3 Sociolinguistic Stereotyping in New Zealand
Graham M. Vaughan and Ingrid Huygens 49

4 'God Help Us If We All Sound Like This': Attitudes to New Zealand and Other English Accents
Donn Bayard 67

CHANGE AND VARIATION IN NEW ZEALAND ENGLISH

5 Pidgin English and Pidgin Maori in New Zealand
Ross Clark 97

6 The Rise of New Zealand Intonation
Scott Allan 115

7 A Longitudinal Study of the 'ear/air' Contrast in New Zealand Speech
Elizabeth Gordon and Margaret A. Maclagan 129

8 Minder, Mork and Mindy? (-t) Glottalisation and Post-vocalic (-r) in Younger New Zealand English Speakers
Donn Bayard 149

9 Audience and Referee Design in New Zealand Media Language
Allan Bell 165

PRAGMATIC ANALYSES OF NEW ZEALAND DISCOURSE

10 They're Off and Racing Now: The Speech of the New
    Zealand Race Caller
    Koenraad Kuiper and Paddy Austin 195

11 The Sociolinguistics of Questioning in District Court Trials
    Chris Lane 221

12 Politeness Strategies in New Zealand Women's Speech
    Janet Holmes 252

13 Politeness Revisited: The Dark Side
    Paddy Austin 276

Notes on Contributors 295

Index 297

1 Attitudes, varieties, discourse: an introduction to the sociolinguistics of New Zealand English

JANET HOLMES and ALLAN BELL

Introduction

Sociolinguistic research in New Zealand — or *Aotearoa*, to give the country its Maori name — is still a young field and this book is the first to focus on sociolinguistic research on New Zealand English (NZE). The most extensive sociolinguistic work to date is that of Richard Benton (e.g. 1978; 1979; 1981; 1983) describing the distribution and usage patterns of Maori, the indigenous language. Research on the distribution of languages other than Maori and English is minimal, as demonstrated by Walter Hirsh's (1987) useful collection documenting what is known, and revealing our current state of ignorance. Hence, perhaps appropriately, we know more about the distribution of Maori in Aotearoa than about any other language, including varieties of English.

The Maori people constitute about 12% of the New Zealand population. However only about 25% of all Maori people, and a very small proportion of younger Maori, can speak their language fluently. Though the language is now gaining increasing official recognition and use, this may well have come too late to reverse the effects of a century of neglect and opposition. Even in isolated rural areas it has been replaced by English. Attempting to remedy past omissions, the government has now established a number of official bilingual schools, but the Maori people themselves have taken the most promising initiative in attempts to revive the language. There are now over 500 *kohanga reo* or 'language nests' throughout the North Island with about 15% of Maori pre-schoolers

1

currently enrolled and plans to increase that to a majority over the next decade. It remains to be seen whether these pre-school immersion programmes can pull Maori back from the marginal position it now holds.

The British settled Aotearoa in the nineteenth century, particularly after the signing of the Treaty of Waitangi in 1840 between the Maori Chiefs and the British Crown. English is the first language of about 95% of the 3.4 million population (1986 census), most of whom are of British descent. English is also the only language spoken by some 90% of the population, making Aotearoa one of the most monolingual nations in the world. Though Maori has recently been given official status, and has been recognised as a legally protected Maori *taonga* or 'treasure', English still effectively dominates all public domains — the media, education, government and the legal system. Despite its ubiquitousness, however, no coherent sociolinguistic description of NZE yet exists. This collection of papers attempts to begin to fill this gap.

Within the confines of space, the papers in this book represent the range of sociolinguistic research in this area to date, while also making a contribution to current theory in sociolinguistics and pragmatics. All the papers provide fundamental and valuable descriptive information on the use of English in Aotearoa; some contribute new concepts and models to the development of sociolinguistic theory; still others build on and develop the standard methodology in particular areas. As the first collection of its kind, the papers we have selected and solicited include retrospectives, reviews of the state of the art in a particular area, and entirely new contributions. The revised paper from Graham Vaughan & Ingrid Huygens, for instance (originally published as Huygens & Vaughan, 1983), is now recognised as a keystone contribution in the area of attitudes to speech in Aotearoa. Another retrospective is Elizabeth Gordon's (1983) historical overview which has been revised and expanded to include an account of Marcia Abell's research findings which were not previously easily accessible. Other papers, such as Ross Clark's on the existence of a New Zealand pidgin, and Janet Holmes' article on features of New Zealand women's speech, summarise research results in an area over a period. A third group reports original research in a new area: Donn Bayard's work on post-vocalic /r/ and the distribution of glottal /t/, for instance, is pioneering stuff, as is Scott Allan's on the High Rising Terminal (HRT) in New Zealand speech. Paddy Austin's discussion of 'face attack acts' in a theory of politeness makes an original and valuable contribution to pragmatics.

The papers have been grouped in three major sections reflecting the areas of sociolinguistic research which have been most productive in Aotearoa over the last decade:

(1) attitudes to NZE;

(2) variation and change in NZE; and

(3) pragmatic analyses of New Zealand discourse.

Attitudes to NZE

In this first section we have gathered together reports on all three major studies conducted to date on attitudes towards NZE. The data come from subjects in three of the 'four main centres' (i.e. cities) in Aotearoa. Elizabeth Gordon & Marcia Abell's data were collected in Christchurch, often described as the most 'English' New Zealand city. Graham Vaughan & Ingrid Huygens worked in cosmopolitan and sub-tropical Auckland, and Donn Bayard reports from Dunedin in the south of the South Island. Small-scale unpublished studies undertaken in Wellington, the capital city, confirm and echo the patterns identified in the three studies included in this section.

Research in Britain has revealed that, despite the diversity of accents used by British people, there is a remarkably consistent pattern of accent evaluation which places RP ahead of all others on such criteria as communicative effectiveness, social status and general pleasantness (e.g. Giles & Powesland, 1975; Edwards, 1982). Perhaps surprisingly, given increasing attempts to shake free of 'Mother England', New Zealand attitude research reveals that Received Pronunciation (RP) is also the most highly rated accent in Aotearoa. Despite varying degrees of success in establishing autonomy in other areas, all three studies published here show that New Zealanders are apparently still oriented to Britain in terms of what they consider the 'best' accent. RP holds pride of place as the overtly most respected and admired accent, associated especially with high education, 'competence' and 'prestige'. Indeed, in both Bayard's and Vaughan & Huygens' work, RP was often classed as a New Zealand accent, evidence that it is regarded as part of the NZE style continuum. Interestingly, Bayard found that a North American accent ran RP a close second for status ratings.

Gordon & Abell, using the data gathered for Abell's MA dissertation, demonstrate that Christchurch teenagers share with young people from the other main South Island city, Dunedin, this attitude towards RP which Allan Bell has labelled 'linguistic colonialism' (1982). They rate RP higher than 'cultivated' NZE on a range of social prestige parameters. And Auckland university students (sampled by Vaughan & Huygens) also give RP top place on social scales, though it is closely followed in their estimation by the 'cultivated' NZE accent used by some well-educated, upper-status New Zealanders. More recent evaluations reported by Bayard, however, suggest that, at least in the conservative south, cultivated NZE may be waning both as a spoken accent and in its prestige.

Smaller scale projects by Victoria University students, Philippa Gordon (1974), Stretton Taborn (1974) and Cynthia Hamilton (1977) confirm the general pattern of these evaluations for Wellingtonians, and for a wider age range. RP was the most highly rated accent in social terms, though Taborn recorded positive attitudes to New Zealand pronunciation, and Gordon noted that the men in her sample rated the New Zealand speakers as highly as the RP speakers on a range of personality traits.

In general, the social ratings of NZE consistently reflect New Zealand social reality. Vaughan & Huygens used samples of three social classes of Pakeha speakers ('Pakeha' means a New Zealander of European ancestry). They were ranked in their class order for the prestige of their accents, upper-class speakers being rated best on status traits, and lower class worst. Bayard's findings indicate clear and consistent stigmatisation of a lower-class accent, although the individual speaker's reading skills may have played a part in this evaluation.

Bayard's title 'God help us if we all sound like this' is taken from the comments of university and school students of the 1980s on NZE. But the negative, and even apologetic, attitude it reflects has long and well-established roots, as Gordon & Abell's paper makes clear. From Gordon's historical data, drawn from periodicals and educational reports since 1880, it seems that a distinctive New Zealand accent was audible by 1900. Almost simultaneously with remarking upon the existence of the accent, writers began to condemn it — and have been doing so ever since. The New Zealand accent has been described over the past eighty years as 'indefensible', 'corrupt', 'degraded' and even 'hideous' and 'evil-sounding'. New Zealand speech has been regarded as providing evidence of carelessness, laziness and slovenliness. New Zealand children have been accused of 'murdering' the language.

Amid this cacophony of condemnation, however, there have always been a few who have fought a brave rearguard action, objecting, for example, to the adoption of imported so-called 'refined' upper-class vowels which they characterised as 'vile affectations'. Though all three of the papers in this section confirm the orientation to British RP as the 'superlect', there is some evidence that the resistance movement has survived and grown into the 1970s and 1980s. It is currently represented by responses which rate NZ accents more highly than RP on traits reflecting solidarity or social attractiveness, i.e. friendliness and sense of humour. There are also positive social ratings of high-status NZE speakers by Auckland university students, who are perhaps more cosmopolitan and less conservative than South Island secondary-school pupils. Aucklanders may be more tolerant of variation, even self-consciously assertive about the acceptability of a distinctively NZ accent. Dunedin students seem the most conservative with little evidence that the pre-eminent position of RP is likely to be challenged there for some time. Bayard's results for the rating of 'cultivated' NZE by high-school students contrast with Abell's and Vaughan & Huygens' findings. While their subjects rated it high on all traits, Bayard's downgraded it on most traits, and half his respondents rated it lower class. But these generalisations probably exceed what one can say based on reactions to just one voice.

The findings indicate also that New Zealanders have difficulty placing the origin of some accents. Bayard included Australian and North American accents among his stimulus tapes. He found that fully a third of his subjects judged the Australian accent as New Zealand. This reflects the great similarity of the two accents, and raises questions about the reliability of New Zealanders' claims that they can tell an Australian when they hear one. Bayard's subjects were still less able to identify the regional origins of the New Zealand accents they heard. This confirms linguists' assessments that there is little regional variation in NZE, despite the widespread conviction that accent can be used to differentiate people from Northland, Hawke's Bay, Auckland, Taranaki, Wellington, the West Coast, Christchurch and Southland. As yet we have no good data on the existence or otherwise of regional variation.

Nor does the attitude data resolve the controversial question of whether a distinctive Maori English exists. Vaughan & Huygens report that listeners correctly identified some, but by no means all, Maori speakers, a result confirmed in a small study by Gould (1972). These findings suggest that further research will involve careful analysis of the features of voices consistently identified as Maori.

Overall, the papers in this section provide evidence of increasing sophistication in the methodology for collecting data on attitudes to NZE. Working in a context where there was no social dialect information of any kind available on features of NZE, Gordon & Abell and Huygens & Vaughan selected their 'representative' stimulus speakers in the 1970s on the basis of informed intuition. Vaughan & Huygens' expertise as psychologists is reflected in the sophistication of their assessment scales and measuring instruments, developed in Huygens' MA research. But they do not provide information about the linguistic features characterising the different accents they selected.

New Zealand linguists have often made use of the Culti-vated–General–Broad trichotomy proposed by Mitchell & Delbridge (1965) for Australian English. In this collection, the studies by both Bayard and Gordon & Abell use the distinction for the phonetic basis of their judgements. And both studies then go on to provide information on the different vowel realisations of their speakers.

Bayard was in the fortunate position of being able to build on the social dialect research he has spear-headed in Aotearoa. He makes the important point that, though he finds the labels Cultivated, General and Broad useful for identifying broad categories, his findings suggest a continuum rather than the strict division implied by the labels. Like Gordon & Abell, he provides a linguistic analysis of diagnostic features of the accents represented on his stimulus tape, relating them to the wider context of his earlier description of linguistic features of New Zealand social dialects. His paper is marked by thorough phonetic analysis of the input materials and considerable statistical sophistication in handling the attitude data.

There is clearly plenty of scope for further research in this area of attitudes to New Zealand speech. Though one must concede that it is hard to resist the accessibility of captive audiences of school children and university students, it would be valuable, for instance, to know the views of a wider and more representative group of New Zealanders. More social dialect work is clearly needed to underpin the selection of representative speech samples. This would help in particular to resolve the issue of whether we are dealing with identifiably distinct accents of NZE, equivalent to the Australian trichotomy. Horvath's more recent study (1985) suggests a continuum is more appropriate for Australian English. NZE may be better described, as Bayard suggests, by a 'broad to cultivated' continuum. (Bayard also introduces another dimension he considers relevant, namely 'conservative'/'innovative'.)

As a final suggestion for further research on reactions to NZE, there is clearly scope for studies in this area which take account of speech accommodation theory (Giles, 1984; Giles & Powesland, 1975; Giles et al., 1987) probably the most important development in the attitudes research area in the last ten years. Allan Bell has similarly explored the implications of this approach to language attitudes, analysing how media language is accommodated on occasions to its audience and at other times to external models such as RP or American English. But there is clearly plenty of scope for further New Zealand research using this model.

Variation and Change in NZE

The section on variation and change, like the first on attitudes, opens with a paper which gives historical perspective to the section's theme. By examining the evidence for and against the existence of New Zealand pidgins, Ross Clark's paper provides an excellent historical context for studies of change and variation in NZE. Clark also tells us a great deal about attitudes to the Maori people in Aotearoa, and particularly to the pidgin English ascribed to them. He explores the evidence for a Maori pidgin and even considers the possibility of 'a single "New Zealand Pidgin"' whose lexical content varied between English-derived and Maori-derived according to the situation and the speaker's experience'.

Clark examines evidence from three different historical periods — the late eighteenth century contact between Maoris and the first European explorers, the pre-colonial early nineteenth century contacts and early twentieth century evidence. The sources of evidence are sparse, but Clark's research has turned up suggestive and thought-provoking data in the area. He concludes that there is no evidence of a fully-fledged New Zealand pidgin which became established as a language in its own right. The conditions for development of a true pidgin were lacking in Aotearoa, with its single indigenous language, Maori. There was no need for a new common language to enable communication among several language groups who could not understand each other — the situation in some Melanesian areas. But there is certainly evidence of a New Zealand jargon English — 'the local form of a widespread network of traditions' — which Clark, in his pioneering writings on other South Pacific language contact situations, has labelled South Seas jargon (Clark, 1979–80). This provides, through words shared with Melanesian Pidgin, a link between Aotearoa and Melanesia.

The increase in the English-speaking population and the spread of education ultimately guaranteed the demise of the relatively shortlived jargon English after the Treaty of Waitangi (1840) confirmed British colonisation of Aotearoa. NZE emerged from this context but Clark believes the jargon left a legacy. In the early twentieth century various literary representations of a supposed Maori English were published. Although these were rife with negative racial stereotyping, Clark argues that they may have reflected genuine features of spoken Maori English of the time.

The question 'is there a Maori dialect of English?' is clearly a contentious one. Scott Allan's analysis of the High Rising Terminal

(HRT) intonation, the next paper in this section, provides some evidence on the issue. Long stereotyped and stigmatised within Aotearoa, the rising intonation at the end of a declarative clause has more recently appeared in Australia (Guy *et al.*, 1986). Its form and function in NZE seem identical to that in Australian speech, a fact of which Guy *et al.* (1986: 50) seem unaware. In a 1987 review of sociolinguistic research on NZE (Bell & Holmes, in press), we expressed the opinion that the HRT was a feature of NZE which would repay investigation. Allan, a Scottish immigrant to Aotearoa based in Auckland, took up the challenge. The HRT is a sound pattern which has been recognised by New Zealanders as distinctive to their speech for a very long time, and it is a frequent focus of comment by new arrivals, particularly from Britain and America. Allan's paper is, however, the first published study of this feature in New Zealand speech.

Although Australian researchers appear to regard the feature as unique to Australian English, its use in Aotearoa considerably predates its identification in Australia in the past twenty years. Allan's New Zealand speakers used twice as many HRTs as the Australians recorded by Guy *et al.* (1986). He also cites evidence that its use in NZE is increasing, with younger speakers using more than older. Guy *et al.* speculated the HRT may have been brought about in response to the influx of migrants from Europe to Australia in the 1950s. But it seems more likely that it has been imported from Aotearoa, since Sydney in particular has a large New Zealand population. This speculation finds support in the recent suggestions reported by Australian sociolinguists (*The Bulletin*, 28th February 1989) that some residents of Sydney and Brisbane are adopting New Zealand vowel realisations such as a centralised /ɪ/ and very close /e/.

Returning to the Maori English issue, Allan finds, on the basis of a small but carefully matched sample, that Maori women used more HRTs than Pakeha women. But with HRTs used in an average of only 3% of declarative clauses, the feature has, as Allan observes, reached a salience far exceeding its actual occurrence. Both Bayard (1987) and Benton (in press) question the existence of a distinct Maori English. Allan's finding suggests what one might have expected: that Maori English is less likely to be identified through features unique to it than through more or less frequent occurrence of features shared with Pakeha English. Other evidence for a Maori dialect is only indirect, deriving from listeners' attempts to identify the ethnicity of taped voices. As both Gould (1972) and Vaughan & Huygens (this volume) report, Maori speakers were misclassified as Pakeha more often than correctly identified, and in neither study were the linguistic clues that listeners used to identify Maori speakers isolated. Allan's research is a first step, describing a feature which may contribute to listeners' accurate identifications of Maori speakers.

It seems likely that the major distinguishing features of the speech of those identifiable as Maori are phonological, including prosodic, perhaps also in some cases involving articulatory setting. While such features clearly do not occur in the speech of all Maori people, since many are indistinguishable on tape from Pakehas with similar backgrounds, more research of the kind which Allan has undertaken attempting to identify potentially distinguishing characteristics where they do occur is well overdue.

Whatever conclusions are ultimately reached about the existence of a Maori dialect of English, the records which Gordon & Abell unearthed and examined suggest that a distinctively New Zealand accent has been recognised since at least the beginning of the twentieth century. Moreover the features of that accent which attract comment are the same features that linguists currently identify as distinctive of NZE. The four closing diphthongs, for instance — now regarded as diagnostic of NZE — have been considered distinctive in NZ pronunciation since about 1914 when they were described as 'the four most noteworthy defects' of NZ speech.

Indeed the existence of NZE as a distinct variety is evident from the research into phonological and lexical features of NZE which has been underway for some time (e.g. Turner, 1966; Hawkins, 1973a; 1973b; 1976; Bauer, 1986). *Variation* within NZE has received very little attention, however, and the researchers represented in this collection have been the pioneers in this area. As Bayard comments, 'quantitative studies of linguistic variability are only just beginning to be carried out in New Zealand to any significant extent' (1987: 2).

One of the first such studies was Elizabeth Gordon & Margaret Maclagan's (1985) research on a feature which has been widely considered characteristic of NZE, namely the tendency for the two diphthongs /iə/ and /eə/ to merge. Interestingly Peter Trudgill (1974) noted that his working-class Norwich subjects merged these sounds. In a sample taken fifteen years after his original recordings, Trudgill (1988) found that the merger had gone to completion on the open /eə/ variant for all groups except the upper-middle class. In their 1985 study Gordon & Maclagan concluded on the basis of relatively formal speech samples from 90 adolescents that change seemed to be proceeding in a way that suggested /eə/ was the favoured variant. They noted tentatively that there was a tendency for higher-class females to use /eə/ while lower-class males converged more often on /iə/. In this volume they report in a follow up to that earlier research, that the two diphthongs are now merging more than in the previous study. However, the direction of the change they identify now appears to have reversed in the five years which have elapsed between their samples. Speakers seem to be merging the diphthongs more often on the closer variant /iə/ rather than the more open /eə/.

They also note that different pairs of words are behaving in different ways, leading them to the conclusion that the change is moving by lexical diffusion. A sample of elderly speakers, half of whom merged the diphthongs, although less often than the teenagers, shows that this change is apparently not a recent one in NZE. They note that the situation with these diphthongs is clearly very volatile.

Further potential for change in progress has been uncovered by Donn Bayard, an archaeologist by background, who in the past five years has done the most comprehensive quantitative social dialect research in Aotearoa to date. Bayard has used a representative sample in terms of age, sex and socio-economic status (Bayard, 1987). His data consisted of a four-minute tape recording of 141 informants reading a passage and a word-list and their answers to a questionnaire focusing on lexical preferences. Despite this narrow stylistic range the data clearly revealed correlations between socio-economic background, on the one hand, and phonological variables and lexical preferences on the other. Bayard's social dialect data undoubtedly confirms a view expressed by New Zealand sociologists that New Zealand society is more accurately represented by a continuum than by a socio-economic model with clear class divisions.

In this volume Bayard focuses on two particular phonological features of NZE: post-vocalic /r/, a feature which has been widely claimed as distinctive of a particular region of Aotearoa, Southland; and the increasing glottalisation of /t/ in the speech of young New Zealanders. Though the conventional lay and linguistic wisdom has always asserted the existence of 'Southland r', this study provides the first documentary evidence of the distribution of post-vocalic /r/ in the speech of New Zealanders. As well as those of Southland origin, other younger NZE speakers in Bayard's sample produced sporadic post-vocalic /r/. Bayard interprets his finding cautiously, since factors such as orthography can influence the occurrence of rhoticisation. He believes the feature may be due to the influence of American television programmes, but is unlikely to become established.

By contrast, Bayard found that glottal final /t/ is more widespread. Bayard also attributes this to media influence, this time of non-standard

British accents in television imports, and believes it is spreading rapidly among younger speakers. There is additional evidence in the form of increased glottalised /t/ over seven years in New Zealand punk pop singers' usage. The data Bayard reports in this paper, together with Bell's (1982, this volume) research on media language, constitute the first published data on the stratification of consonant variables in NZE, and this is clearly another area ripe for further work.

The final paper in this section shifts the focus from variation *between* the language of different speakers to variation *within* the speech styles of individual speakers. Bell takes up the topic of the relationship between the media and the public, examining the converse case for the audience's influence on the speech of broadcasters. He develops the framework of audience design (Bell, 1984) proposed originally to account for stylistic variation in New Zealand media English. Drawing on some fifteen years of research on the language of New Zealand media, he suggests that the range of styles used can be accounted for in terms of either audience design or 'referee' design.

In genres such as radio news bulletins, newscasters prove able to attune their speech style very finely to different audiences listening to different radio stations. The language styles of different stations in Auckland are ranked precisely according to their audience's social status, with the BBC Overseas Service acting as an external prestige norm. A far more 'initiative' use of language resources is found in television commercials, where the use of non-New Zealand accents is widespread in order to associate products with a variety of non-local stereotypes — the 'referees' — which advertisers regard as attractive to their target audiences. Bell finds that 40% of a sample of television commercials used varieties of English other than NZE. American English is frequent, especially in singing, while in spoken advertising copy, British dialects are favoured. Many of the varieties are inaccurately imitated, however, although this does not prevent them functioning successfully to evoke the intended associations in their audience.

These findings echo the research in the first section of this book on the residue of colonial attitudes which downgrade NZE and favour distant dialects as prestigious. Elsewhere Bell raises the interesting question of whether there is any realistic hope of New Zealanders developing their own distinctive linguistic identity, or whether a more likely scenario will see them falling both culturally and linguistically 'out of the British frying pan into the American fire' (1982: 254). Surveying the total picture painted by the papers in Sections 1 and 2, one might hazard that NZE is gradually forging its own identity in some areas, using Maori, British and American resources to do so. And it may even be influencing the dialect spoken in its much larger neighbour, Australia.

The extent of research on variation and change in NZE leaves plenty of scope for further work. The published research to date is largely confined to phonological variation, and there is very little at all which considers syntactic and morphological features of NZE, though Bauer (1987) and Jacob (1990) have made a start in this direction.

There is also considerable scope for further methodological sophistication in this area. New Zealand researchers have so far used early Labovian methodology, and within this they have tended to focus on eliciting relatively formal styles of speech from a rather narrow range of informants. There is little analysis of relaxed casual speech, the true vernacular. A start has been made in this direction by Jenny Jacob who has collected some excellent vernacular data (analysed by Scott Allan for HRTs) from Maori and Pakeha women in Levin, her home town and tribal area. But there is plenty of room for further research, using the kind of network approach adopted there, and focusing on the elicitation of casual speech from a wider range of speakers. There is certainly nothing approaching the community-based research using 'democratic research methods' advocated by Deborah Cameron (1985) and Ben Rampton (1988) as providing the most rewarding as well as the ethically 'proper' direction in which sociolinguistic research must develop. With the sound start that has been made by Bayard (1987) and others whose work has been represented in this section, the challenge to produce further good quality social dialect description must be taken up in the near future.

Pragmatic Analyses of New Zealand Discourse

Perhaps the most significant New Zealand contribution to the study of language in society has been in pragmatics and discourse analysis, the areas represented by the papers in the final section of the book. This research takes as its focus a genre or discourse type and uses local data for exemplification, as did Bell's chapter in the previous section, without treating it as a peculiarly New Zealand variety. The papers extend the linguistic focus from phonological and syntactic features of NZE to aspects of discourse, including oral formulae, pragmatic particles and patterns of verbal interaction. The material analysed is taken from a wide range of contexts including the racecourse and the courtroom, and a number of the papers examine aspects of 'negative' interaction which have previously received little attention in the international literature. This is 'the dark side' of interaction, to use Paddy Austin's term — the strategies used by speakers whose aims are quite deliberately unco-operative.

In this section, too, some useful theoretical concepts are introduced, developed or explored, and issues of general sociolinguistic and pragmatic interest are examined. Koenraad Kuiper & Douglas Haggo's (1985) distinction between 'play-by-play' *versus* 'colour commentary' used initially to describe ice-hockey commentary is shown to be a valuable tool in describing the speech of the (horse) race caller. Austin's notion of a 'face attack act' is a valuable contribution to pragmatic theory, in the analysis of verbal politeness. Chris Lane introduces useful apparatus such as 'elicited narrative' and 'repetitive questioning' to describe the structure of courtroom interaction. Janet Holmes provides a widely applicable model for analysing co-operative interaction, illustrating it with data on the interactive style of New Zealand women and men.

The section begins with an analysis of a genre characteristic of Aotearoa. Horse racing, and betting on horses, are a popular pastime, and the commentaries which are broadcast both on course and over the radio have a distinctive prosodic style. Koenraad Kuiper & Paddy Austin's analysis of 'race calling' provides a nice example of New Zealand-based empirical data which supports a more general theory of oral-formulaic performance. The theory was developed to account for the speech of livestock auctions in New Zealand and Canada (Kuiper & Haggo, 1984; Haggo & Kuiper, 1985), tobacco auctions in the United States (Kuiper & Tillis, 1986), and North American ice-hockey commentaries (Kuiper & Haggo, 1985). Oral-formulaic varieties develop, they suggest, in situations where fluency is paramount, such as oral poetry, auctioning and many types of sports commentaries. The requirement for fluency (race callers speak at four to five syllables per second) forces them to call on a store of formulae in order to decrease the pressure on the speaker's short-term memory.

Kuiper & Austin's data provide colourful support for the notion that there are distinctive features of oral-formulaic speech which hold over a range of contexts. It has a specific discourse structure which can be formalised; it makes use of particular lexical items from a restricted set of oral formulae; and it has distinctive prosodics. In the case of race calling these take the form of incremental increases in pitch over a well-defined interval. Using these 'droned' prosodics the race caller's pitch rises by about an octave during the race, and drops rapidly back to the initial pitch after the finish. At least one race caller believes that while New Zealand race callers use both 'drone' and 'chant' (chant being 'what happens when drone is sung'), the New Zealand indigenous tradition is chant. The nature of races and commentaries on races leads to the use of a syntactic form such as subject post-position, which gives the caller time to identify a horse before having to name it. The use of passives enables horses to be named in race order ('X is followed by Y') rather than out of order ('Y follows X').

The paper demonstrates well how the analysis of a particular variety or style can contribute to the development of sociolinguistic theory. The New Zealand features are specific realisations of more general characteristics of oral-formulaic speech. Kuiper & Austin also provide a fascinating account of language learning patterns for this style of discourse.

Chris Lane describes the courtroom as a sociolinguistic laboratory for studying the pragmatic features of certain types of interaction. Many of the variables are held constant while the witnesses are put through their pragmatic paces by the two opposing lawyers. He compares the co-operative dialogue of co-examination with the conflict inherent in cross-examination. Lane explores the function and form of lawyers' courtroom questions, which he terms 'initiations' in recognition of their distinctive function. Courtroom initiations, like classroom 'display' questions, are often intended to elicit information which the questioner, e.g. the defence counsel, already knows. Moreover, in the courtroom context, what passes as a legitimate question can become the focus of explicit dispute, a process which further illuminates the distinctive nature of this questioning. The issue of whom a witness should address also surfaces, since answers are supposed to be directed to the judge rather than the counsel who verbalises a question. Drawing on data gathered for his doctoral thesis, Lane cites extended extracts of recorded court proceedings to illustrate his analyses.

Both lexicon and syntax are involved in marking courtroom exchanges. The coercive elicitations typically used in cross-examination, for example, can be distinguished syntactically and lexically from the facilitative elicitations which tend to characterise co-examination. Lane's research demonstrates — as does that of others in this section — that judgements of politeness must always be context-relative. In cross-examination, preservation of the witness's face is not the overriding concern of the questioning counsel. The functions of the cross-examiner's language are to control, coerce and challenge. The pragmatic strategies adopted are deliberately devised to disconcert the addressee, and are thus most accurately described, as Lane points out, by the term introduced in Austin's paper — 'face attack act'.

Lane's work also demonstrates that a sociolinguistic and pragmatic approach to courtroom interaction can pinpoint potential problem areas. The situation is rife with possibilities for miscommunication especially for those who use English as a second language (Lane, 1985). The syntactic complexity of many courtroom questions is a major contributor to this difficulty.

The final two papers in the volume are concerned from different points of view with areas of high interest in sociolinguistic and pragmatic research — namely communication between the sexes and politeness strategies. Janet Holmes introduces a model of social interaction which is then illustrated with data from women's and men's verbal behaviour. She distinguishes the *referential* axis of interaction, which is concerned with the propositional content of utterances, and the *affective* axis, which focuses on the degree of social distance or intimacy of the participants. Holmes draws together a range of her own research findings of recent years in the area of sex and language (e.g. Holmes, 1984; 1986; 1988). Over a variety of contexts women's conversation, she argues, is more often affectively oriented than men's, while men tend to favour referentially oriented utterances. She shows how some devices facilitate conversation while others act to inhibit interlocutors' contributions.

Holmes' research in this area arose from scepticism at the picture of unconfident and apologetic American women painted in Robin Lakoff's description of 'women's language' (1973; 1975). Her analyses of New Zealand women's speech suggested an alternative interpretation. Holmes argues that one must examine the function of linguistic features in context. Tag-questions, and pragmatic particles such as 'you know', for instance, express different meanings depending on their position in the discourse, and the relationship between the speaker and the addressee. On closer examination many of the features regarded by Lakoff as evidence of women's lack of confidence turn out to have more positive functions.

Going further to examine the distribution of speech functions, it is apparent that women use compliments and apologies more often than men. Women clearly put a high value on verbal expressions of politeness. They consistently demonstrate explicit concern for their addressees' face needs to a greater extent than is typical of male speech. However women's concern for politeness is apparently recognised by men, since women are also complimented more often than men. Similarly, they both apologise and are apologised to more than men.

Concern for the face needs of their addressees is the unifying thread which also accounts for women's interactive patterns in other areas of interaction. Interruption patterns, the frequency of positive feedback, and concern not to dominate the available talking time are further ways in which women's talk strategies demonstrate this concern. The subordinate position of women in society provides only a partial explanation for these patterns, since some at least characterise the behaviour of women in powerful social roles. This accumulated research provides an interesting range of evidence for the different ways in which at least middle-class Pakeha New Zealand women appear to be linguistically more polite than men.

Paddy Austin's paper is also concerned with linguistic politeness. Her approach is distinctive in this section in that she focuses on how listeners interpret utterances rather than on patterns of usage. Her work has made a considerable contribution to pragmatic research (Austin, 1988), examining the implications of probably the two most influential pragmatic models currently being used in this area. She challenges the Gricean approach to politeness adopted by Brown & Levinson (1978; 1987), and shows how Sperber & Wilson's (1986) model of communication, which argues for the fundamental status of Grice's maxim of relevance, accounts more adequately for non-co-operative types of interaction. Austin focuses on situations in which the 'co-operative principle' is disputed, where in fact the interaction is deliberately and consciously non-co-operative in intent. She labels the resulting speech acts 'face attack acts'.

The maintenance of power asymmetries or social distance between participants are among the possible reasons for such face attack acts and she analyses examples of sexist language to illustrate the ways in which the process of face attack operates. The concepts of positive and negative face derived from the work of Goffman (1967), and extensively elaborated by Brown & Levinson, provide a useful descriptive framework for examining different types of face attack act. Because the underlying motivation of face attack contrasts so starkly with that of co-operative interaction, the strategies adopted provide revealing insights about the underlying assumptions that participants draw on, and it is here that relevance theory offers a valuable set of explanatory tools. Austin illustrates with detailed analyses which recover hearers' potential interpretations of face-attacking utterances. She shows that impoliteness is a phenomenon to be reckoned with in social interaction. While Holmes describes women's verbal interaction as essentially co-operative in intent, expressing solidarity rather than social distance, Austin's examples show men putting women down to maintain and reinforce the power asymmetry in a number of contexts.

The four papers in this section thus demonstrate quite clearly the importance of contextual and pragmatic factors in shaping the language appropriate to different types of interaction. Analysing language from a wide range of contexts, they draw attention to some of the less frequently examined possibilities of verbal interaction: speakers whose intention is to insult or challenge their addressee as well as speakers who attempt to facilitate contributions to a conversation. The papers represent a considerable body of work which is building up within the area of discourse analysis of NZE.

Conclusion

Most New Zealand sociolinguists have focused on issues of general sociolinguistic interest using data generalisable to other Englishes. There is undoubtedly now a pressing case for paying more attention to what makes NZE distinctive. This volume is a contribution towards that goal, in that it gathers together representative research and also attempts to point directions for future work.

There are many topics we have not had space to include in this first collection of readings on the sociolinguistics of NZE: sexist language, for instance, is receiving a good deal of attention at present with the writing, and even rewriting, of legislation and government communications in non-sexist terms. Features which distinguish the syntax and morphology of NZE from those of British and American dialects are just beginning to receive detailed attention (Bauer, 1987). The task of collecting a million words of written and a million words of spoken NZE has just begun, and New Zealand linguists are also planning to contribute to the International Corpus of English proposed by Sidney Greenbaum at University College, London.

There is much social dialect work still to be undertaken. With the support of the New Zealand Social Science Research Fund, and following a successful pilot survey (Holmes & Bell, 1988), data collection for the first extensive social dialect survey of NZ speech began in 1989. But information on rural speech and regional varieties is still sorely needed, and we know very little about the changes which have occurred in NZE over the last century.

There is also, of course, a need for sociolinguistic research on languages other than English in Aotearoa. We know little or nothing about the numbers of speakers of languages such as Tongan, Greek and Cantonese in the New Zealand community. Patterns of language maintenance and shift in such groups remain to be documented and explored.

All this presents an exciting, if somewhat daunting, blueprint for New Zealand sociolinguistic research in the next decade. There is no doubt that such research is desperately needed. Nor can there be any doubt that the information provided will be useful and interesting — not only to New Zealanders but also to the wider academic community.

References

AUSTIN, PADDY J.M. 1988, The dark side of politeness: a pragmatic analysis of non-cooperative communication. Unpublished PhD dissertation. Christchurch: University of Canterbury.

BAUER, LAURIE 1986, Notes on New Zealand English phonetics and phonology. *English World Wide* 7(2), 225–58.

— 1987, Approaching the grammar of New Zealand English. *New Zealand English Newsletter* 1, 12–15.

BAYARD, DONN 1987, Class and change in New Zealand English: a summary report. *Te Reo* 30, 3–36.

BELL, ALLAN 1982, This isn't the BBC: colonialism in New Zealand English. *Applied Linguistics* 3(3), 246–58.

— 1984, Language style as audience design. *Language in Society* 13(2), 145–204.

BELL, ALLAN and HOLMES, JANET, Sociolinguistic research on New Zealand English. To appear in JENNY CHESHIRE (ed.) *English Around the World: Sociolinguistic Perspectives*. Cambridge: Cambridge University Press.

BENTON, RICHARD A. 1978, *The Sociolinguistic Survey of Language Use in Maori Households*. Wellington: Maori Unit, New Zealand Council for Educational Research.

— 1979, *The Maori Language in the Nineteen Seventies*. Wellington: Maori Unit, New Zealand Council for Educational Research.

— 1981, *The Flight of the Amokura: Oceanic Languages and Formal Education in the Southern Pacific*. Wellington: New Zealand Council for Educational Research.

— 1983, *The NZCER Maori Language Survey*. Wellington: Maori Unit, New Zealand Council for Educational Research.

— Maori English: a New Zealand myth? To appear in JENNY CHESHIRE (ed.) *English Around the World: Sociolinguistic Perspectives*. Cambridge: Cambridge University Press.

BROWN, PENELOPE and LEVINSON, STEPHEN 1978, Universals in language usage: politeness phenomena. In ESTHER N. GOODY (ed.) *Questions and Politeness: Strategies in Social Interaction* (pp. 56–289). Cambridge: Cambridge University Press.

— 1987, *Politeness: Some Universals in Language Usage*. Cambridge: Cambridge University Press.

CAMERON, DEBORAH 1985, 'Respect please!' Subjects and objects in sociolinguistics. Mimeo. London: Roehampton Institute.

CLARK, ROSS 1979–80, In search of Beach-la-mar: towards a history of Pacific Pidgin English. *Te Reo* 22–23, 3–64.

EDWARDS, JOHN R. 1982, Language attitudes and their implications among English speakers. In ELLEN BOUCHARD RYAN and HOWARD GILES (eds) *Attitudes Towards Language Variation* (pp. 20–33). London: Edward Arnold.

GILES, HOWARD (ed.) 1984, *The Dynamics of Speech Accommodation. International Journal of the Sociology of Language* 46. Amsterdam: Mouton.

GILES, HOWARD and POWESLAND, PETER F. 1975, *Speech Style and Social Evaluation.* London: Academic Press.

GILES, HOWARD and SMITH, PHILIP 1979, Accommodation theory: optimal levels of convergence. In HOWARD GILES and ROBERT ST CLAIR (eds) *Language and Social Psychology* (pp. 44–65). Oxford: Blackwell.

GILES, HOWARD, MULAC, ANTHONY, BRADAC, JAMES J. and JOHNSON, PATRICIA 1987, Speech accommodation theory: the first decade and beyond. In MARGARET L. MCLAUGHLIN (ed.) *Communication Yearbook 10* (pp. 13–48). Beverly Hills: Sage.

GOFFMAN, ERVING 1967, *Interaction Ritual: Essays on Face to Face Behaviour.* New York: Garden City.

GORDON, ELIZABETH 1983, 'The flood of impure vocalisation' — a study of attitudes towards New Zealand speech. *The New Zealand Speech Language Therapists' Journal* 38, 16–29.

GORDON, ELIZABETH M. and MACLAGAN, MARGARET 1985, A study of the /iə/~ /eə/ contrast in New Zealand English. *The New Zealand Speech Language Therapists' Journal* 40, 16–26.

GORDON, PHILIPPA 1974, Accent evaluation: some differences between men's and women's assessments. Unpublished terms paper. Wellington: Victoria University.

GOULD, PHILIP 1972, Assessment of status by accent. Unpublished terms paper. Wellington: Victoria University.

GUY, GREGORY R. and VONWILLER, JULIA 1984, The meaning of an intonation in Australian English. *Australian Journal of Linguistics* 4(1), 1–17.

GUY, GREGORY, HORVATH, BARBARA, VONWILLER, JULIA, DAISLEY, ELAINE and ROGERS, INGE 1986, An intonational change in progress in Australian English. *Language in Society* 15(1), 23–52.

HAGGO, DOUGLAS C. and KUIPER, KOENRAAD 1985, Stock auction speech in Canada and New Zealand. In REGINALD BERRY and JAMES ACHESON (eds) *Regionalism and National Identity: Multidisciplinary Essays on Canada, Australia and New Zealand* (pp. 189–97). Christchurch: Association for Canadian Studies in Australia and New Zealand.

HAMILTON, CYNTHIA 1977, North England speech: some indications of complex attitudes and values. Unpublished terms paper. Wellington: Victoria University.

HAWKINS, PETER 1973a, A phonemic transcription system for New Zealand English. *Te Reo* 16, 15–21.

— 1973b, The sound patterns of New Zealand English. In K.I.D. MASLIN (ed.) *Proceedings and Papers of the 15th AULLA Congress* (pp. 13.1–13.8). Sydney: Australasian Universities Language and Literature Association.

— 1976, The role of NZ English in a binary feature analysis of the English short vowels. *Journal of the International Phonetics Association* 6, 50–66.

HIRSH, WALTER (ed.) 1987, *Living Languages: Bilingualism and Community Languages in New Zealand Today.* Auckland: Heinemann.

HOLMES, JANET 1984, Hedging your bets and sitting on the fence: some evidence for hedges as support structures. *Te Reo* 21, 47–62.

— 1986, Functions of 'you know' in women's and men's speech. *Language in Society* 15(1), 1–21.

— 1988, Paying compliments: a sex-preferential positive politeness strategy. *Journal of Pragmatics* 12(3), 445–65.

HOLMES, JANET and BELL, ALLAN 1988, Learning by experience: notes for New Zealand social dialectologists. *Te Reo* 31, 19–49.

HORVATH, BARBARA M. 1985, *Variation in Australian English: the Sociolects of Sydney.* Cambridge: Cambridge University Press.

HUYGENS, INGRID and VAUGHAN, GRAHAM M. 1983, Language attitudes, ethnicity and social class in New Zealand. *Journal of Multilingual and Multicultural Development* 4(2–3), 207–23.

JACOB, JENNY 1990, A grammatical comparison of the spoken English of Maori and Pakeha women in Levin. Unpublished MA Thesis, Victoria University, Wellington.

KUIPER, KOENRAAD and HAGGO, DOUGLAS C. 1984, Livestock auctions, oral poetry and ordinary language. *Language in Society* 13(2), 205–34.

— 1985, The nature of ice hockey commentaries. In REGINALD BERRY and JAMES ACHESON (eds) *Regionalism and National Identity: Multidisciplinary Essays on Canada, Australia and New Zealand* (pp. 167–75). Christchurch: Association for Canadian Studies in Australia and New Zealand.

KUIPER, KOENRAAD and TILLIS, FREDERICK 1986, The chant of the tobacco auctioneer. *American Speech* 60(2), 141–9.

LAKOFF, ROBIN T. 1973, Language and woman's place. *Language in Society* 2(1), 45–79.

— 1975, *Language and Woman's Place.* New York: Harper and Row.

LANE, CHRIS 1985, Mis-communication in cross-examinations. In J.B. PRIDE (ed.) *Cross-Cultural Encounters: Communication and Mis-communication* (pp. 196–211). Melbourne: River Seine.

MITCHELL, A.G. and DELBRIDGE, ARTHUR 1965, *The Speech of Australian Adolescents.* Sydney: Angus and Robertson.

RAMPTON, BEN 1988, Less objectivity, more commitment: a second case study. Mimeo. London: University of London, Institute of Education.

SPERBER, DANIEL and WILSON, DEIRDRE 1986, *Relevance: Communication and Cognition.* Oxford: Blackwell.

TABORN, STRETTON 1974, Social class, sex roles and linguistic attitudes in a New Zealand secondary school. Unpublished terms paper. Wellington: Victoria University.

TRUDGILL, PETER 1974, *The Social Differentiation of English in Norwich.* Cambridge: Cambridge University Press.

— 1988, Norwich revisited: recent linguistic changes in an English urban dialect. *English World-Wide* 9(1), 33–49.

TURNER, G.W. 1966, *The English Language in Australia and New Zealand.* London: Longman.

2 'This objectionable colonial dialect': historical and contemporary attitudes to New Zealand speech

ELIZABETH GORDON and MARCIA ABELL

People have been expressing opinions about spoken English in New Zealand almost from the time of the first European settlement. Writings on this subject throw an interesting light not only on the emergence of New Zealand English (NZE) as a distinct variety of English, but also on how this variety was perceived by people once they became aware of its existence. In this chapter we will begin with an account of earlier attitudes to NZE which we can deduce from written evidence. We will then give an account of a piece of research carried out in 1980 in which Marcia Abell used a subjective reaction test to investigate stereotype association with some New Zealand language varieties and Received Pronunciation, using 89 Christchurch secondary school pupils as her subjects.[1]

Written Evidence before 1900

There are various sources of written information on this subject, and no doubt more will come to light as historical research continues. Periodicals such as *The Triad* and the *NZ Journal of Education* devoted space to this topic, and from time to time the question of New Zealand speech or the 'colonial twang' as it was often called, became the subject of debate in newspapers. One of the most fruitful sources of information has been the reports written by school inspectors, published annually in the appendixes to the parliamentary debates. A number of these men had a passionate concern for language, and whenever they reported on the reading or recitation in the schools they visited, the question of pronunciation invariably also rose.

From an examination of this material a certain pattern emerges. From 1880 (when the inspectors' reports were first published) until about the turn of the century, complaints mainly concerned ordinary conversational assimilations and elisions (*compny* for 'company', *Artic* for 'Arctic', *actuly* for 'actually', *famly* for 'family' and so on) and features of pronunciation which would be associated with non-standard varieties of British English. Almost every year the inspectors complained about the omission of the aspirate and the use of the *in'* ending for *ing*.

Also at this time we find some very positive comments made about New Zealand speech. Mr Samuel McBurney, a speech and singing teacher who visited in 1887, and who had made a list of pronunciations found in different Australian and New Zealand towns, wrote an article in the *The Press* in Christchurch in which he remarked upon the surprising absence of distinctiveness in much New Zealand speech.

> I think it may be admitted that the pronunciation of the colonies as a whole, is purer than can be found in any given district at Home . . . For months after I had commenced my investigation on this subject, the unfailing answer to my enquiries in the different Australian colonies was, 'We can hear no distinction between ourselves and visitors'. It was only since coming to New Zealand that I have been able to definitely say 'There is another type here'. (*The Press*, 5th October 1887)

Three days later a leader appeared in the *The Press* congratulating its readers on the purity of their accents.

> It is satisfactory to learn that the Queen's English is well or better spoken in the colonies than in the Old Country where it had its birth. Mr McBurney . . . assures us of that. In his short but very observant paper on 'Colonial Pronunciation' which we published the other day, he shows that both Australia and New Zealand have their dialectal peculiarities, but the pronunciation of the colonies as a whole is purer than can be found in any given district at Home. . . . In the main the colonial speech flows tolerably pure from the 'well of English undefiled'. It is nearer the standard of classical English than 'English as she is spoke' in Yorkshire, or Lancashire, or Somersetshire; the astonishment of untravelled Britishers at the purity of the New Zealand accent is proverbial, and if there is merit in correct pronunciation, to a large extent we have it. (*The Press*, 8th October 1887)

By the turn of the century comments about the omission of the aspirate
and the final *in*' ending were beginning to diminish. In fact, in the case
of the aspirate, complaints began to appear that it was receiving too
much attention. In 1910 when Mr E.W. Andrews of Napier Boys' High
School was addressing the Wellington Conference of the Secondary
Schools' Assistant Teachers, he remarked:

> With regard to 'h', which is so commonly misplaced in England as
> a sin of both omission and commission, I have never come across
> a boy, born and educated in New Zealand, who had any great
> difficulty with this refractory letter. He rather overdoes the sound,
> if anything, triumphing over the obstacle so vigorously that victory
> often becomes defeat . . . It would almost make the hearers think
> that the ancestors of the New Zealander had been dropping 'h's for
> generations, and that he is now engaged in picking them up several
> at a time! (*The Triad*, 10th August 1910: 39–40)

1900: The Emergence of New Zealand Speech

It is about this time at the turn of the century, when comments on
the aspirate and final *in*' are diminishing, that we find people beginning
to comment on a distinctive variety of New Zealand speech. When
members of the Cohen Commission on Education in 1912 questioned
teachers about the pronunciation of New Zealand school children, some
replied that a distinctive New Zealand accent had been observed for
about the last ten years. Mr Augustus Heine, acting Headmaster of
Wellington College, when asked about 'this objectionable colonial dialect'
replied that it was getting worse. 'Much worse in the last ten years. I
have noticed it particularly in the last ten years' (*AJHR*, E-12, 1912:
624). A similar observation was made by Mr Andrews in 1910:

> I am just now observing that a dialect, and that not a defensible
> one, is becoming fixed in the Dominion among the children and the
> younger adults. (*The Triad*, 10th August 1910: 37)

Some people at this time had the feeling that New Zealanders were
at a linguistic crossroads. There were clear indications that a dialect would
develop in the Colony, and was in fact already appearing. But it was felt

that New Zealanders were also in a position to put a stop to this. The New Zealand teachers and pupils, if they worked hard, were in a unique position to make New Zealand a model for the rest of the Empire when it came to purity of speech. This view was strongly expressed by Mr R.N. Adams in some articles he wrote for the *Otago Daily Times* in 1904, which were later reprinted as a booklet entitled *How to Pronounce Accurately on Scientific Principles*.

> There is no good reason to prevent the hope that in these lands of the south, where we boast of such liberal systems of education, we may in the near future be recognised as the most correct speakers of the King's English of any in the wide Empire into which our people has developed. It is certainly within the power of the schools and other educational institutions to promote a system of perfect English pronunciation in these new world states.
>
> . . . It now lies with us to make our language of the future what it should be, or to neglect it very much, as we have done up to the present time. We may develop a colonialism of our own, with a variety of shades of corruption that will be as distinct from each other as have ever been the dialects of England, Ireland and Scotland; or we may set up a standard of such excellence that no-one will question that it is the purest of all the Anglo-Saxon tongue. (Adams, 1904: 30–1)

From the turn of the century onwards the school inspectors were constantly warning teachers against the impure vowels that they were hearing in the classrooms they were visiting. The variety emerging must have been distinct enough to have been given various names, some more complimentary than others — 'colonial twang' or 'colonial dialect' or even 'Austral English'.

The features of New Zealand speech which were invariably pointed to were the four closing diphthongs /ei/, /ai/, /ou/, /au/. When F. Martin Renner made a speech to the Wellington Joint Standing Committee of the NZ Educational Association, he described what he called the 'four most noteworthy defects': '"Praise" as "prise", "my" as "moi", "Mexico" as "Mexiceouw" and "shout" as "sheout"' (*Education Gazette*, 1st August 1924). The other feature to be singled out was the centralised /ɪ/. The Wellington school inspectors remarked on this in 1914: 'Carelessness or indifference on the part of the teacher is mainly responsible for such improprieties as . . . "placus" (places), "ut" for "it", "paintud" for "painted"' (*AJHR*, E-2, Appendix C, 1914: ix). One of the earliest and most perceptive comments on New Zealand vowels and diphthongs was made by Mr Andrews in his speech in 1910, though he describes them as 'eccentricities':

> The broad 'a' of 'father' and the narrow 'a' of 'fat' appear to cause great difficulty and are advanced in the mouth almost to the sound of 'e' in 'pen', so that 'last' becomes 'least', 'remark' becomes 'reme-rk', 'camp' 'kemp', and 'standard' 'standerd'. This difficulty naturally causes the broad 'a' diphthongs to diverge, 'ah-oo' into 'e-oo', and 'ah-i' into 'aw-i' so that 'noun' (nah-oon) becomes 'ne-oon' and 'mile' (mah-ill) 'maw-ill'. Ask a colonial child to say 'I went down the town to buy a brown cow', and you may almost make sausages out of that mangled beef. (*The Triad*, 10th August 1910: 40)

Mr Andrews' comments are very useful because the pronunciation of /a/ and /æ/ which he mentions and which is today a distinctive feature of New Zealand speech, is never mentioned in the school inspectors' reports. This is probably not because the features were not heard (and the comments of Mr Andrews confirms that they were) but rather that the four closing diphthongs and the centralised /ɪ/ would seem to be more prominent and noticeable, and hence always quoted as exemplifying the most 'hideous distortions' of the English tongue.

For the most part the school inspectors ascribed the impure pronunciation they were hearing to laziness. Some did attempt to ask more serious questions about language — for example, how we should establish a standard for correctness, and which speech should be taken as a model. In *Whitcombe's Graded Lessons in Speech Training* (1930), Dorothy Stewart raises the problem of finding a standard when the language is constantly changing, and eventually suggests as a model the speech of 'one who is so unmistakeably of the elect — Sir Johnstone Forbes-Robertson, so easily accessible by way of the gramophone'. This book points out the problems involved in taking orthography as a guide to correct pronunciation, a view not taken by other writers who took the written form of the word as the guide to correct pronunciation. A little booklet published in 1925 called *Do You Speak English or Only a Substitute?* written by H.T.G. (Harry Gibson) has a cover depicting a man in a bow tie and dinner jacket pointing an accusing finger at the reader. There is no explanation or discussion in the booklet — merely two columns of words, those on the left hand side of the page headed 'Do Not Say' and those on the right hand side of the page headed 'Say'. The so-called incorrect words were written in an attempt at phonetic

spelling, while the correct form was given in standard spelling: *absolootly* —
'absolutely'; *jook* — 'duke'; *evry* — 'every', etc.

The relationship between the kind of pronunciation used and the
social class of its speaker was implied on a number of occasions. John
Smith, the Inspector for the Marlborough Education Board, wrote in
1904:

> . . . children whose social surroundings are such as to familiarize
> them with the conversation and letters of well-educated persons
> require far less instruction, and benefit far more by it, than those
> less fortunately situated. These last, indeed, are constantly receiving
> at home and in the streets lessons in oral composition which they
> too readily assimilate, and the unlearning of which is one of the
> chief hindrances to even moderate proficiency in this important
> department of primary education. (*AJHR*, E1-B, 1904: 23)

The bad influence of the family was strongly stressed by Mr Louis Cohen,
a barrister-at-law, when he gave evidence before the Cohen Commission
in 1912.

> It is said that the teachers in school speak good English, that the
> good English that they speak is impaired by the baneful influences
> of home and home life, that the parents do not speak good English,
> and that that neutralises the influences of the teacher.

He then went on to suggest that only persons of 'some culture in the
speaking of English' should be employed as teachers.

> These teachers are being brought into association with children at
> the imitative age, and they will be responsible for the kind of English
> that the children will speak throughout their lives. The governesses
> in the homes of people in England are chosen with the greatest
> discrimination, chosen because of the English they speak. One
> governess, in the home in England, is preferred to another because
> of the refinement of diction. (*AJHR*, E-12, 1912: 460)

Mr Cohen's great faith in the ability of teachers to change and influence
their pupils' speech is not supported by the numerous other comments
which suggested that the teachers were fighting a losing battle against the
influence of home and street. Mr Cohen's comments about governesses
in the homes of people in England were not necessarily supported by
others. Later in his submission Mr Cohen remarked that 'you rarely find

a New Zealand man or woman who speaks English with distinction — good English' and he declared that 'the degradation of the spoken English in the Dominion is due mainly to carelessness, laziness and slovenliness' (*AJHR*, E-12, 1912: 462).

The Pestilential 'ay'

While people like Mr Louis Cohen poured scorn on the New Zealand accent, others were also complaining about the appearance of over-refined and affected speech. Mr Pirani, a member of the Cohen Commission on Education, produced his own examples of bad speech which he claimed were just as objectionable.

What hope is there for change when we find two of the Principals of the largest secondary schools in New Zealand in giving evidence, using these expressions: 'taime-table' for 'time-table'; 'Ai' for 'I'; 'may own' for 'my own'; 'faive' for 'five'; 'gairls' for 'girls'. (*AJHR*, E-12, 1912: 624)

Even Mr Heine, deputy Principal of Wellington College, who believed that the speech of New Zealand children was deteriorating badly, made the comment: 'Of course I do not believe in overdoing it, as you find in the case of some people who have been Home' (*AJHR*, E-12, 1912: 623). It was a fine line between 'pure vowels' and 'overdoing it'. These comments were supported by the editor of *The Triad*, who associated this kind of affected speech especially with people from Christchurch, and designated it 'ay-fever'.

Lots of people with the 'ay' fever speak quite good English apart from that. The 'ay' is, indeed, often a deliberate affectation that marks the incurable snob. The people in Christchurch who hold their noses up in a constant attempt to be awf'lly English are all afflicted by the pestilential 'ay'. The lady principals of secondary schools are oddly conscious of their natural superiority, and so keep on 'ay'-ing for all they are worth. (10th August 1912: 5)

There was a similar ambivalence about English dialects, described affectionately by some as 'the beautiful and sonorous dialects of the Homeland' (*The Triad*, 10th August 1910: 37) but by others less favourably. If New Zealand speech was bad, it was bad in the same way that the speech of other lower-class speakers was bad. Mr D. Petrie, Chief

Inspector of the Auckland schools, had no romantic notions about British dialects: '. . . during the past year several boys fresh from their native Yorkshire heath and Yorkshire Board Schools have passed through my hands. Their dialect was as atrociously uncouth as I remember it 35 years ago' (*AJHR*, E-1B, 1907: 2). To the Nelson Inspectors of 1912 the speech of New Zealand children was if anything rather better than that of recent British immigrants: 'The so called "colonial twang" we in no way condone, but critics are too prone to dilate upon and exaggerate this defect, which suffers little by comparison with the uncouth dialects frequently introduced by importation from the Home-land' (*AJHR*, E-2, Appendix C, 1907: xxxvii).

The connection between the variety of speech used and the social class of its speaker was often implied, but it was never examined further. The speech of the lower classes was poor, presumably because of what was considered to be the inherent laziness and decadence of the lower classes. The teachers themselves were not immune from these accusations and they too were often berated. The suggestion was made that some kind of speech test should be made compulsory for anyone wanting to become a teacher.

Throughout these reports we see the firm belief of the Inspectors that a child could only ever be in command of one variety of English at any one time. The maxim that 'bad money drives out good' is a recurring theme. If a child was to speak well it was essential that his or her way of speaking should be totally replaced by the desired variety. Impure vowels must be rooted out and pure vowels planted in their place. It was the teacher's duty to bring about this change because good speech was the mark of education. If a child was using impure vowels it naturally followed that the child in question had not been properly educated.

The Speech-Training Solution

From about 1905 onwards teachers were urged to approach this matter scientifically. They were told to study the physiology of speech so that the reasons for the impure speech could be understood. D.A. Strachan, Inspector for Marlborough, expressed his faith in the scientific principle in 1905:

It is rather their [teachers'] object to create in the pupil a scientific way of looking at things and handling them, to bring the idea of a causal connection of things above the threshold of consciousness,

and make this sense a permanent factor of his life. This is capable
of exemplification in subjects not directly scientific — e.g. in the
study of English may be noted the progression of consonants under
the influence of physiological differences. In the light of this principle
the story of Babel acquires a new significance. We see the nations
in a common family with a common tongue. Then comes a slight
change of the larynx, a thickening of the lip, a raising of the palate,
and men are divided off as if by mountain ranges. (*AJHR*, E-1B,
1905: 26)

Teachers were then encouraged to use this scientific knowledge to
teach children how to use their organs of speech, because the underlying
problem was seen as a speech defect which could be remedied. So courses
in phonic exercises were enthusiastically advocated and promoted. These
included a variety of exercises — lip movements, and breathing exercises
especially, and many specially devised rhymes for vowel practice. The
nose passages were to be kept clear with special nose-blowing jingles,
and children were warned of the perils of lazy ribs. Various booklets
were recommended. *Exercises in Phonics* by Alfred Fussell MA was
produced in Melbourne by the Victoria Education Department in 1914,
and was used in New Zealand. The New Zealand Education Department
eventually brought out its own bulletin on *Speech Training* in 1925,
prepared by 'direction of the Hon. Minister of Education', containing a
Preface by the Minister, C.J. Parr, expressing his concern about the faulty
accent and defective speech of New Zealand school children. He wrote
that 'in a democratic country such as ours it is the right of everyone to
be taught to speak in the manner that marks the educated man'. This
booklet was warmly recommended by the school inspectors, who felt that
its publication would greatly help in improving New Zealand speech.
Other books also appeared soon after this — books by Dorothy M. Stewart
who had studied phonetics in London under Daniel Jones — *Speech
Training by Phonic Methods* (1925a) and *Phonetics Practice Book* (1925b)
and *Whitcombe's Graded Lessons in Speech Training* published in 1930.
For younger children Janet McLeod, a lecturer in English at Christchurch
Training College, wrote *Rhyming Roadways to Good Speech* (1940).

These books taught the pronunciation of vowels and diphthongs as
if the learners were studying a foreign language, with detailed instructions
on articulation. The 1925 bulletin on *Speech Training*, for example, gives
a thorough account of the organs of speech. The articulation of each
sound is then described. For example /ɪ/:

This is the short vowel sound in *lip, hymn, sieve, busy, guilt*. The teeth are slightly apart; the tongue is lax and high in the palatal arch, its highest point being well towards the front. This sound is not the short form of *ee*. The lips are enough apart to partially uncover the teeth, but are not to be drawn back.

These movements were then to be practised with such sentences as: 'The little innocent soul flitted away.' and 'I', said the fish, 'With my little dish.' (NZ Department of Education, 1925: 8–9).

The results of these exercises done every day for at least five minutes would be seen not only in better vowel production but also in better health. The two were inextricably connected.

We still desire health, and health is largely dependent on a proper management of our voice and speech organs. Improper and chronic inflammation of the mucous membranes of the air passages . . . faulty methods of production, particularly the use of the nasal sounding-box, have uglified the young colonial's voice, and they are, I believe, the cause of many minor throat and chest disorders that would disappear under a proper system of breathing exercises and voice training. (*The Triad*, 10th August 1910: 39–40)

Some writers went further and claimed that poor speech was not only connected to poor health but also to poor thinking. Fundamental defects in cognition were somehow attached to impure vowel sounds. In the Foreword which he wrote for the book *Rhyming Roadways to Good Speech* by Janet McLeod (1940), Professor F. Sinclaire, Professor of English at Canterbury University wrote:

. . . debased speech — it cannot too strongly be insisted — is a symptom of general cultural debasement, of growing insensibility to values which lie at the very roots of all culture. Someone has said that people who talk through the nose will think through the nose. It is certain that if we speak badly we shall think badly and feel coarsely.

Thirty years earlier the reviewer of the Christchurch competitions had made a similar connection between speech and aesthetics:

I have been accused before now of exaggerating the importance of pronunciation. It cannot be exaggerated. It is less distressing as a fault than as a symptom. I mean, if a man or woman is content to mispronounce his or her native tongue, there is little hope of any true cultivation on the intellectual side. Mispronunciation destroys the beauty of English verse and prose. A man who mispronounces very openly cannot enjoy good literature, and most certainly cannot enjoy good verse. (*The Triad*, 11th July 1910: 8)

It is very noticeable when reading the material produced on phonics and also comments on this subject in the school inspectors' reports, that there was a regular use of technical terms and precise terminology. Teachers were expected to understand the physiology of speech and also be able to read and use phonetic script. Articulation was described in rigorous terms and without any of the apologies which seem necessary when introducing this subject to university students today. It also seems that some of the teachers at least would have been conversant with up-to-date thinking on phonetics through the works of such people as Daniel Jones and Ida Ward.

But for all this effort and attention, the 'impure vowels' did not seem to diminish, but rather to increase. The school inspectors' complaints increased accordingly. Their language became more emotive and impassioned. Children were accused of 'murdering' the language. The faulty diphthongs were described as 'hideous' and 'evil-sounding', the voices of New Zealand children compared to the noise made by a 'linen-draper's assistant tearing a sheet of unbleached calico'. The young people of New Zealand were in imminent danger of being 'swept into a flood of faulty and impure vocalisation'.

The solution was always seen to be a very simple one — five minutes of phonics every day would be sufficient to prevent this decadence. Probably the teachers in the classrooms were more realistic. Anyway, as the inspectors had so often pointed out, many of them too were suffering from these 'rasping and unlovely sounds'. Perhaps this is why they did not put the kind of effort into lip drills and breathing exercises that the inspectors were asking for.

'The Best Speakers in the Old Land'

The attitudes expressed by the school inspectors and other writers in the first part of this century show for the most part a completely unrealistic view of language and language production. Our understanding today of the processes of first-language acquisition and the influences of social motivation on sound changes makes these earlier statements about the language of New Zealand school children seem at best amusing, but more often ignorant, misguided and harmful. Yet the attitudes described here were quite consistent with the general view at that time that correct English was 'that used by people of the best education and social standing in England'. The epitome of this could be found in the speech of Their Majesties themselves, whose recorded message on a phonographic record to the children of the Empire was recommended as an excellent model of standard English for New Zealand children to copy (NZ Department of Education, 1925). The person most generally accepted as the expert on the subject of English and speech was an Englishman, Professor Arnold Wall, Professor of English at Canterbury University. In 1938 he wrote a book entitled *New Zealand English: How it Should be Spoken*. In his introduction Professor Wall made no concessions to New Zealand speech, even though he was well aware of its existence and had in fact coined the name 'Enzedic' for it.

> This book is designed for use by residents in New Zealand who wish to speak 'good' English or 'standard' English, as spoken by the 'best' speakers in the old land; it is not intended for those who wish to develop a new dialect of English for this country.

Professor Wall's attitude to New Zealand English was ambivalent. He was clearly influenced by the work of Daniel Jones. Wall's definition of 'good' and 'bad' sounds closely reflect those of Jones in his book *The Pronunciation of English* (1909): 'A clear distinction must be made between faults which are bad in themselves, and those which are "bad" in that they do not conform to a particular standard' (Wall, 1938: 15). Wall had no difficulties in determining what the standard was, and in the text of his book he describes features of New Zealand speech accurately, but always as 'essential faults'. His feelings towards this variety are summed up in his Preface: 'I remember how, at the outbreak of war in 1914, seeing that young students whose speech left much to be desired yet died gloriously at Gallipoli, I told myself that I must never criticize New Zealand speech unkindly.'

After 1930

Since the 1930s, statements and comments critical of New Zealand speech have continued to appear in newspapers and magazines. From time to time broadcast talks are given on the subject of New Zealand speech and some still complain about it. A weekly column in the *Christchurch Star* called 'Take My Word' frequently complains that New

Zealand speakers are lazy and their speech undesirable. The four closing diphthongs and the centralised /ɪ/ continue to attract adverse comments, though the effect of /l/ on the preceding vowel, and the lack of distinction between /eə/ and /iə/ are also now noticed.

From the 1930s onwards comments condemning New Zealanders who tried to adopt 'cultured middle-class British speech' also continued to appear, especially in the correspondence columns of the *NZ Listener*:

> Well educated New Zealanders speak of hospiddles, edjication, ishue (issue), New Zillan — and I repeat that this is just slovenly and without excuse. At the other extreme is that 'naiceness' which gushes hideously from a widespread inferiority complex and which is almost worse.
>
> H.M. Bracken (Auckland)
> (*NZ Listener*, 9th August 1945: 5)

The New Zealand poet, A.R.D. Fairburn wrote a series of articles on language for the *NZ Listener* in 1947. He was very critical about New Zealand speech, describing it as 'mutilations of standard English' with 'wretched consonants and mangled and telescoped vowels'. But he was also critical of the variety of New Zealand English which he labelled 'colonial-genteel'.

> Some New Zealanders have reacted sharply against the dialect I am now describing and have devised one of their own which bears the same sort of relation to standard English as 'serviette' does to a table napkin. One or two private girls' schools seem to encourage this way of speaking which we may call colonial-genteel. It borrows certain of its twists from some of the more precious and hole-in-the-corner dialects of fashionable England, but it has added a few more on its own account. The round 'o' diphthong in 'home' is pinched and drawled to make the word 'haome'. 'No' becomes 'nao' or even 'neh-oo'. The long vowel 'oo' in 'two' and 'school' is shortened to sound like the 'oot' in 'foot'. 'Culture' becomes 'cahlture' and 'love', 'lahve.' 'First' is turned into 'fust' or even 'fast' and 'persons' becomes 'pahsons.' (*NZ Listener*, 13th June 1947: 23–5)

While negative letters and comments continued to appear (and are still appearing today) occasionally writers would come to the defence of New Zealand speech. J.S. Lynch wrote this in a letter to the *NZ Listener* in 1944:

Sir — Right from your first issue various well-intentioned writers have broken out with complaints of wrong pronunciation and bad English heard over the air. I suggest it is time these people realised that English is not spoken in New Zealand. The language we speak is New Zealandese, with its own idiom and pronunciation, and is just as distinctive as the language spoken by Americans, South Africans, Australians and Canadians. All the efforts to persuade us to pronounce according to the Oxford Dictionary are doomed to failure. (16th June 1944: 2)

This received in reply a number of abusive responses in which Mr Lynch was described as an 'ardent little New Zealander'.

His letter was in the best bantam cock style. He objected to any attempt to correct mispronunciations which tend to make our speech a dialect. He was proud of his New Zealandese. The only result of this will be to encourage petty national conceit and parochialism which might end in dividing English into a number of hostile and suspicious units with a core of jealousy and bad feeling. (*NZ Listener*, 4th August 1944: 5)

Negative comments, like those of Fairburn's continued to be expressed and are still heard today. However from the 1950s onwards more tolerant views were also beginning to be heard. In the 1950s George Turner taught the language component in the Stage One English class at the University of Canterbury. Here he presented NZE as a variety in its own right and suggested that it was a fascinating subject for study. His book *The English Language in Australia and New Zealand* (1966) did much to assist the study of NZE and it has been widely used in schools and universities. The former elocution teachers who attempted to make New Zealand school children produce the vowels of Received British Pronunciation have now been replaced by members of the Speech Communication Association (NZ) Inc., whose emphasis is much more on communication — 'helping students to speak with clarity, confidence and courtesy in different situations', as one of their aims states (NZ Speech Board, 1986: 1).

That New Zealanders speak with a New Zealand accent is an established fact. But people's attitudes to this fact still vary. There are those who make fun of it in books like *Newzild* by Arch Acker (1966) or Austin Mitchell's *The Half-Gallon Quarter-Acre Pavlova Paradise* (1972). There are those whose opinions are still similar to those of the writers discussed in this chapter, who see it as a corruption of pure

English; and there are those who justify and defend it. When we compare present-day attitudes in general with those expressed in the first part of this century by the school inspectors and other writers concerned about speech, it would seem that there is now a much greater acceptance of New Zealand speech. Perhaps this can be related to other attitudes whereby Britain is no longer regarded by New Zealanders as 'Home', and there is growing confidence in and acceptance of a distinct New Zealand identity in the world.

Written Records as a Source of Data

The use of written records could be questioned as a source of data about attitudes to New Zealand speech. Strongly expressed views which appear in the current media are usually dismissed or not taken seriously. Could there be similar reservations about the earlier written comments described here? Many of the criticisms of New Zealand speech were couched in passionate and intemperate language which sometimes tells us much more about the writers than the variety they were condemning. On the other hand many writers did attempt to convey orthographically certain features of New Zealand speech and there is overwhelming evidence that the same features were being noted by commentators throughout New Zealand. The quotations given here are only representative of a much larger body of comment.

It is likely that written comments appear some time after the emergence of features of speech. The statement that the New Zealand accent first appeared at the turn of the century is probably very conservative. Such statements can, however, tell us about the time when the features were well enough established to provoke widespread comment. In 1887 Samuel McBurney commented on certain features of New Zealand speech (the /i/ ending on words like 'city', /oi/ for /ai/ and so on). He was an amateur phonetician, making it his business to observe speech in Australia and New Zealand. But it took about another twenty years before members of the general public were writing about these features. McBurney himself did not notice the /i/ ending for 'city' until someone commented on it in Brisbane. After that he heard it in every town in Australia and New Zealand that he visited. So presumably the absence of written comment before Brisbane does not mean that the feature did not exist in other places, but rather that McBurney was not listening for it. Also it is likely that writers would describe pronunciations they could represent orthographically (*ceow* for 'cow', *toime* for 'time' etc). It is much more difficult to convey a centralised /u/ or a closely rounded /ɜ/. Therefore the absence of comment about certain features may not necessarily mean that they were not there. Given these reservations the written reports do provide a large amount of very consistent evidence of changes in New Zealand speech and also of listeners' awareness of these changes.

Attitudes to New Zealand Speech in 1980: Some Contemporary Research

A piece of research which investigated more recent attitudes to NZE was carried out in 1980 by Marcia Abell, an MA student at the University of Canterbury. Following the work of Giles & Powesland (1975) she used a subjective reaction test to investigate the association of language varieties and stereotypes. Although there is a strong tendency to homogeneity and egalitarianism in New Zealand, it was felt that the earlier teaching methods and attitudes could have produced a certain amount of linguistic insecurity. Abell felt, therefore, that NZE might not be held in high esteem by many of its speakers, and that negative attitudes towards this variety would become stronger as the speech became broader.

To test this Abell (1980) used four male speakers aged between 35–50 for her stimulus material. These speakers were told that the investigation was to determine what people might think about others from their voices alone. The recorded material consisted of a word list, a reading passage and a nursery rhyme.

In order to establish the phonetic basis for the comparison of the varieties spoken by each speaker, Abell used the two diphthongs /aʊ/ and /ai/. These were chosen because they show marked variation within NZE varieties and are also two of the vowel phonemes selected by Mitchell & Delbridge (1965), whose classification of Australian English into Cultivated, General and Broad varieties was adopted by Abell for NZE.

Speaker 1 on the stimulus tape spoke the broadest of the three New Zealand varieties presented to the subjects. The diphthongs /aʊ/ and /ai/ which occur in his reading of the first passage can be illustrated on a vowel quadrilateral as in Figure 2.1. Speaker 2 who was British, used a Received Pronunciation (RP) variety. His pronunciation (Figure 2.2) of the five words under question differed markedly from that of Speaker 1. The third variety presented in the stimulus material was a Cultivated New

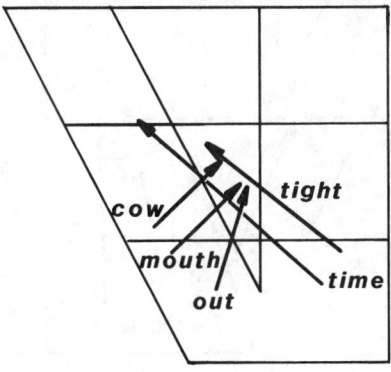

FIGURE 2.1 *Speaker 1: Broad NZE*

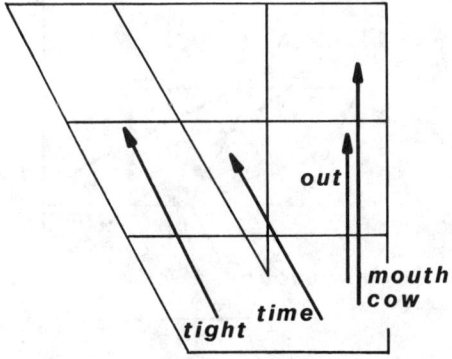

FIGURE 2.2 *Speaker 2: RP*

Zealand speech style with a slight British influence, which was most evident in the fronted /ɪ/ which contrasted with the centralised articulation of this vowel in New Zealand varieties. The phonemes under consideration can be located on a vowel quadrilateral as in Figure 2.3. Speaker 4 spoke a New Zealand variety intermediate in broadness between those of Speakers 1 and 3 which can be designated General NZE. The vowels of the words being compared are illustrated in Figure 2.4.

The subjects evaluated the speakers on eight parameters (see Table 2.1). It was recognised that for the last parameter, involving a choice of

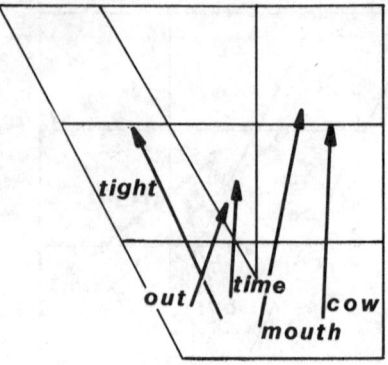

FIGURE 2.3 *Speaker 3: Cultivated NZE*

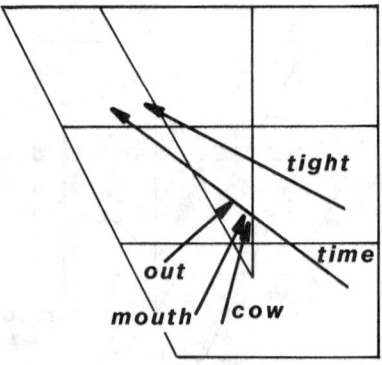

FIGURE 2.4 *Speaker 4: General NZE*

occupation, some stereotyping was involved, in that certain occupations are necessarily involved with certain personality traits, and to some extent the subjects' responses to this question are determined by the answers given to the questions about personality.

The subjects for Abell's test were 89 fourth-form pupils (aged 14–15) from three Christchurch schools. Two of the schools were single-sex private schools, and the other was a co-educational state school. The private school pupils (20 boys and 22 girls) came from higher socio-economic backgrounds than the pupils from the state school, which was situated in one of the less affluent areas of Christchurch. It was

TABLE 2.1 *Subject response sheet*

Friendly	____ :	____ :	____ :	____ :	____ :	Stand-offish
Ambitious	____ :	____ :	____ :	____ :	____ :	Easy-going
Highly educated	____ :	____ :	____ :	____ :	____ :	Poorly educated
Reliable	____ :	____ :	____ :	____ :	____ :	Unreliable
Intelligent	____ :	____ :	____ :	____ :	____ :	Stupid
High income	____ :	____ :	____ :	____ :	____ :	Low income
Good sense of humour	____ :	____ :	____ :	____ :	____ :	No sense of humour

Which of the following would you expect to be the speaker's job?
a. Doctor   b. Bank Manager   c. Bookseller
d. Bulldozer Driver   e. Farm Labourer

hypothesised that the prevalence and the nature of stereotyping applying to speech styles might be related to the socio-economic class of the judges, and that any difference in the results obtained from the private and state school responses could be attributed to this factor.

The subjects in Abell's study were told that the investigation was into 'the sort of judgement people make on the basis of another person's voice'. Pupils were reminded of situations in everyday life in which they form opinions about strangers they cannot see. People talking on the radio or on the telephone were given as examples. As there was a noticeable difference in the reading skills of the speakers who provided the stimulus material, this point was also mentioned to the subjects, who were asked to ignore this as much as possible and to concentrate on the voices alone. It was hoped that by concentrating on voice quality, attention would be diverted from pronunciation differences.

Findings

Using the figures furnished by these results, an average score to two decimal places was calculated for each parameter for each speaker. It was immediately evident that a clear distinction was being drawn between the RP speaker and the speakers of NZE. A comparison between the relative scores of RP and an average score for the three New Zealand varieties appears in the histogram in Figure 2.5. From this graph it can be seen that RP achieved higher scores than the NZ speech styles on most of the parameters investigated. The RP speaker was considered to be more ambitious, better educated, more reliable and more intelligent than the average for the NZE varieties. Corresponding to these ratings the RP speaker was considered to have a higher income and greater occupational prestige. This is consistent with the results obtained in Britain by Strongman & Woosley (1967) who found that RP speakers were rated for higher competence than speakers of non-standard dialects. Similar results have also been found in Britain by Giles & Powesland

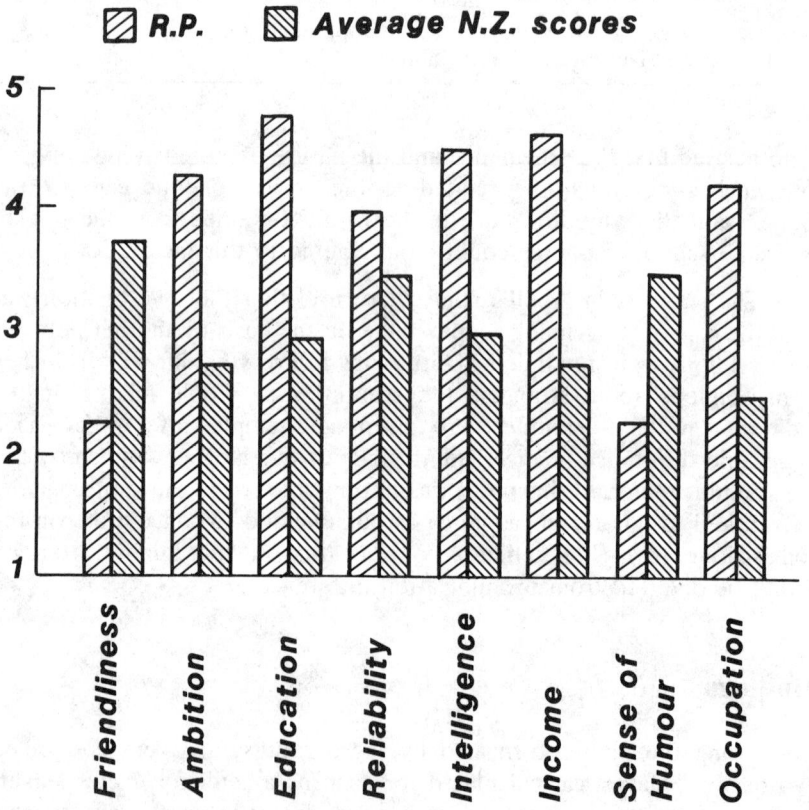

FIGURE 2.5 *RP and average scores of three NZ varieties*

(1975), in Australia (Ball, 1983) and in the United States (Stewart, Ryan & Giles, 1985). However for the two parameters in Abell's study used as indicators of social attractiveness, i.e. friendliness and sense of humour, the RP speaker was given scores considerably lower than those given to the NZ varieties overall. It appears from these results that while RP is associated with a privileged social group, even by NZ judges, its speakers are not regarded as having highly attractive personalities. Giles & Powesland's explanation for similar results in Britain was that regionally accented speakers were perhaps less concerned than RP speakers with improving their socio-economic status and more concerned with cultivating personal relationships. In the New Zealand context there is a problem with this explanation in that RP is a variety used mainly by British immigrants, and New Zealand has no autonomous regional varieties. Perhaps the explanation is a historical one, as described earlier in this chapter, whereby the attitudes revealed in these responses were imported into New Zealand from Britain from the beginning of European settlement.

An interesting difference in the results obtained by Giles and those in this study is in the RP speaker's score for reliability. Giles found that RP speakers were given lower ratings for sincerity and reliability than regional-accented speakers and he ascribed this to speakers of non-standard dialects thinking that RP speakers are hiding their regional origins and possibly their true personality. In this New Zealand study, assessments on all the parameters except reliability showed similar trends to those revealed in the study by Giles. Reliability, however, appeared to be associated with high socio-economic status in the minds of the fourth-form judges. The RP speaker was ascribed an average rating for reliability of 4.01, while the average score for the three New Zealand varieties was 3.47.

The scores for RP relative to the New Zealand varieties were also inconsistent with those reported by Huygens (1979) in her study undertaken in Auckland (see Vaughan & Huygens, this volume). While the judgements of that investigation indicated that RP was 'unambiguously prestigious', the low ratings on scales assessing elements of social attractiveness received by the RP speaker in Abell's study suggest a somewhat more ambivalent attitude towards RP amongst the subjects used in this study. In the words of one of the subjects, the RP speaker was regarded as 'snobby', and while RP is obviously considered a marker of high social status it seems unlikely that it would be adopted as a model by these subjects.

While RP was identified as a prestige speech style by the subjects of Huygens' investigation, a 'high status' New Zealand variety proved

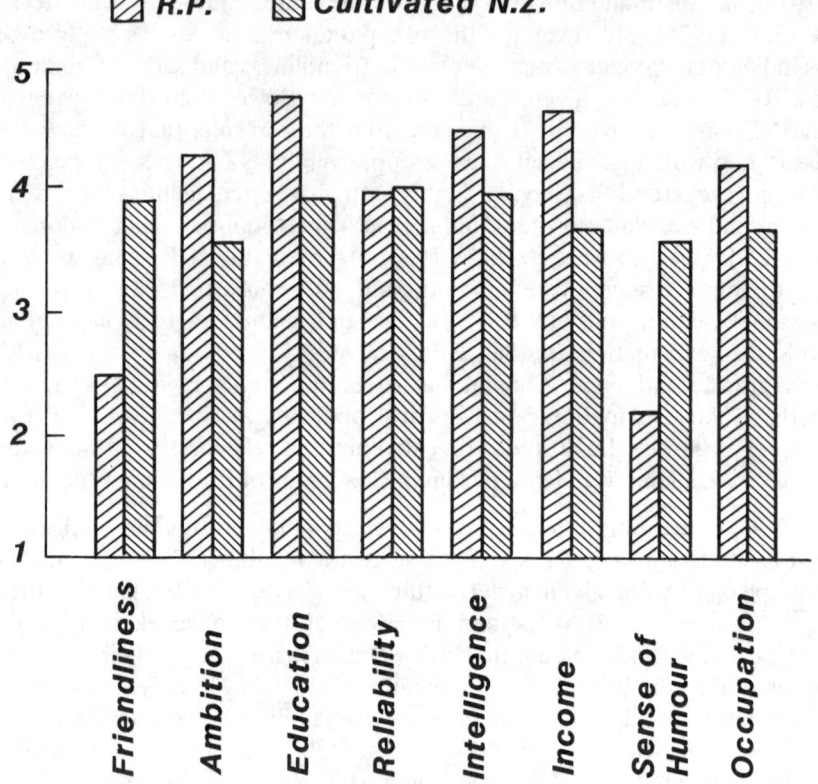

FIGURE 2.6 *RP and Cultivated NZE*

equally prestigious. This did not prove to be true in the present study. Figure 2.6 shows the average scores assigned to the RP speaker and the Cultivated NZE speaker presented side by side for comparison. On five of the eight parameters, RP was rated above the New Zealand variety. Two of the exceptions to the general assessment of RP as superior to New Zealand English have already been noted (friendliness and sense of humour) and for the third (reliability) the difference in the ratings is so small as hardly to show up on the histogram. The subjects considered the Cultivated NZE speaker to be only 0.07 of a mark more reliable than the RP speaker. On the scales which indicate the perceived social status of the speaker, the RP speaker consistently gained higher scores than the Cultivated NZE speaker. In view of the noticeable British influence on the Cultivated NZE speaker's speech style it could have been expected that differences in ratings between the RP speakers and the Cultivated NZE speaker would tend to be reduced in this study rather than increased as has actually happened. Thus it seems reasonable to assume that the different scores assigned to the two speakers represent a real difference in perceived status of the two varieties relative to each other.

The socio-economic background of the judges can be ruled out as an explanation for the differing prestige of a Cultivated variety of New Zealand English relative to RP in the two studies. Huygens' judges belonged mainly to the middle classes, and it might at first be thought possible that the presence of judges from less privileged backgrounds might account for the lower status ascribed to the Cultivated NZE speaker in this study. However, while the private school pupils showed a marked tendency to rate the Cultivated NZE speaker higher and the RP speaker lower in numerical terms than did the state school pupils, the relative perceived social status of the two speakers was still clearly maintained.

Some Explanations

Several explanations for the differences in the ratings attracted by these speakers are possible. One of these lies in the nature of the sample from which the judges for Huygens' investigation were drawn. It has been suggested that university students tend to become more liberal and tolerant during the course of their studies. If this observation also applies in New Zealand, Huygens' subjects, being second-year psychology students could possibly have undergone this change in attitude to some extent. Therefore the similarity of prestige levels associated with the two speech varieties may be due to a more liberal attitude towards New Zealand speech in general than is prevalent in the community at large. There is also the possibility that RP may have lost some of its prestige relative to a Cultivated (or 'high-status') New Zealand variety through subjects attending university having become familiar with a wider range of non-New Zealand speech styles through contact with foreign students and staff. Another possible explanation is that speakers from Christchurch (which is still recognised as the most 'English' of New Zealand cities) are still maintaining some of the earlier attitudes described in this chapter. There is also some debate about whether 14–15 year olds have yet developed an awareness of the social significance of different varieties of language (Labov, 1965; Macaulay, 1977). This could also account for the differences between Abell's and Huygens' results.

It may be, however, that the differing prestige attributed to the two varieties of English in the different studies shows a difference in attitude which is a function of the age of the subject. If this is the case, the differences may indicate a changing attitude or they may indicate that judges of the age group from which the subjects for this study were drawn are particularly sensitive to the high prestige of RP relative to New Zealand speech styles. Further research would be necessary in order to provide evidence in support of any of these explanations.

Within the three varieties of New Zealand English, some stratification was evident. The Cultivated NZE speaker rated higher on all the scales than the other two New Zealand-born speakers. For the parameters of friendliness and sense of humour, the ratings of these three speakers were most similar. Although the Cultivated NZE speaker was considered the most friendly speaker overall, gaining an average score of 3.90, the Broad and General NZE speakers were not far behind with scores of 3.74 and 3.68 respectively. Similarly, the ratings for sense of humour showed only a narrow range, the Cultivated NZE speaker having a score of 3.63, the Broad NZE speaker scoring 3.47, and the General NZE speaker achieving the lowest rating of 3.34. On the scales for ambition, education, reliability, intelligence, income and occupation, the Cultivated NZE speaker was clearly differentiated from the other two NZE speakers. The superiority ascribed to the speaker of a more Cultivated variety of New Zealand English on all the parameters evaluated suggest that this speech style is the most likely of the four presented to serve as a model for the speech community as a whole.

The high ratings given to the Cultivated NZE speaker for parameters indicating social attractiveness run contrary to the trends observed in Britain and Canada, where a speech style of high social status was associated with low personal attractiveness scores. This pattern of evaluation is also in conflict with that indicated by the subjects' attitudes towards the RP speaker. It is possible that New Zealanders are considered capable of attaining high social status without sacrificing personal relationships to the same extent as their British counterparts. If this is the reason for the uniformity of the ratings assigned to the Cultivated NZE speaker it could be a result of the greater freedom of the individual to move within the social strata of the New Zealand society compared with the greater rigidity of the British social system.

In the light of the findings for the individual New Zealand varieties, it is possible to put forward a tentative explanation for the unexpectedly high scores for reliability assigned to the RP speaker. It is clear that of the New Zealanders, the Cultivated NZE speaker was regarded as having higher social status by the subjects. His rating for reliability was also higher than those of the other New Zealand speakers, which suggests that, for New Zealand at least, there may be a tendency for perceived reliability to correlate with perceived social status. Thus, the high scores for reliability attained by the RP speaker may represent a New Zealand system of values which differs from that prevailing in Britain. If this is so, it follows that, if the characteristics ascribed to the RP speaker represented an imported set of attitudes, reliability is not included among them, and, in the event of being asked to assess a speaker's reliability, the subjects have resorted to the New Zealand system of stereotypes rather than the British one.

When the ratings given to each speaker are split into groups according to the sex of the subject, differences can be observed. However, these differences did not, in most cases, appear to be significant, as they were not associated with any parameters or any speakers on the whole. There was no general trend for subjects of one sex to assign higher scores in general than subjects of the opposite sex, nor was the relative ranking of the speakers usually affected by the sex of the judge.

In most cases, the type of school attended by the subjects did not appear to be a factor in their evaluation of the speakers. Differences between the ratings given by state and private school pupils were not associated consistently either with school or with particular parameters. The relative ranking of the speakers on five of the eight parameters was the same across the two groups of subjects. The three scales which did reveal a different ordering of the speakers according to the school attended by the judges were friendliness, reliability and sense of humour.

Private school pupils considered the Cultivated NZE speaker the most friendly, followed by the Broad NZ and the General NZ speakers respectively, with the RP speaker thought the least friendly of the four. Rather than distinguishing four different levels of friendliness as did the private school pupils, the state school pupils have made a distinction between New Zealand and non-New Zealand for friendliness. The Cultivated NZE speaker was regarded by the private school pupils as being the most reliable, followed closely by the RP speaker. The state school pupils reversed this order.

Evaluation of the speakers' sense of humour was also subject to variation according to the school attended by the subjects. The private school students identified four separate levels for sense of humour ratings. They considered that the Cultivated NZE speaker had the best sense of humour followed by the other NZE speakers, with the RP speakers being attributed with rather a poor sense of humour. This ranking was upended by the state school pupils. In their opinion, the Broad NZE speaker was blessed with the most developed sense of humour, followed by the General NZ speaker. The favourite of the private school pupils, the Cultivated NZ speaker, ranked only third when assessed by state school pupils, while the RP speaker achieved the lowest score with this group too.

There was a marked tendency among the state school pupils to reduce the differences in the scores given to the highest ranking speakers on these parameters. For friendliness, they really distinguished only two levels as opposed to the four different levels allocated by the private school pupils. Similarly the four levels of reliability identified by the private school judges were reduced to three for judges attending the state school. The similarity of the sense of humour ratings for Speakers 3 and 4 when they were assessed by the state school pupils also results in a reduction in the levels of this characteristic ascribed to the speakers.

From these results, it can be seen that the subjects clearly differentiated only three of the four speech styles presented to them for evaluation. While RP was a marker of high social status, the RP speaker had low ratings for the scales assessing friendliness and sense of humour. All three New Zealand speakers received higher scores for these parameters than did the RP speaker. To this extent, it could be said the New Zealand varieties enjoy covert prestige, at least amongst judges aged 14–15 years. That the RP speaker achieved the highest ratings for reliability is, perhaps, a reflection of a New Zealand system of values which appears to differ from that prevalent in Britain, as RP speakers in that country tend to attract low scores on this parameter.

A Cultivated New Zealand variety, while rated slightly lower than RP on social status parameters, appeared likely to serve as a model for most of the subjects in this study. This was the speech style which achieved the highest ratings for friendliness and sense of humour. In addition, the speaker of this variety was regarded as having the highest social status of the three native New Zealand speakers.

Obviously more work needs to be done using methods such as the subject reaction tests used by Marcia Abell. An omission in her research is that of Maori-accented English speech which is now being heard more and more in New Zealand. However when placed together the earlier evidence from the written records and the results of the contemporary research show interesting parallels, and the evidence from both sources of data would seem to confirm each other. The higher status ascribed to

RP by Christchurch secondary-school pupils corresponds to the attitudes towards RP promoted by schools earlier in the century. The lower ratings given to the RP speaker for friendliness and sense of humour also correspond to the derogatory references to RP which appear in the written records, suggesting that it is affected and insincere, an attempt on behalf of some speakers to appear better than they really were. The overall high ratings given to the speaker of Cultivated NZE suggest that this variety could now be taken as a standard within New Zealand. Perhaps this could also be taken as evidence that New Zealand speech is now accepted more widely within New Zealand as a variety in its own right.

Note

1. Elizabeth Gordon wrote an earlier version of the historical material in this paper which appeared as 'The flood of impure vocalisation', *The New Zealand Speech-Language Therapists' Journal*, May 1983. Marcia Abell's research was for her MA thesis which was supervised by Elizabeth Gordon.

References

ABELL, MARCIA 1980, A study of sociolinguistic stereotyping by fourth form students in Christchurch. Unpublished MA thesis. Christchurch: University of Canterbury.

ACKER, ARCH 1966, *Newzild*. Wellington: A.H. & A.W. Reed.

ADAMS, R.N. 1904, *How to Pronounce Accurately on Scientific Principles*. Dunedin: Otago Daily Times.

Appendices to the Journal of the House (AJHR).

BALL, PETER 1983, Stereotypes of Anglo-Saxon and Non-Anglo-Saxon accents. Some explanatory Australian studies with the matched-guise technique. *Language Sciences* 5, 163–84.

FUSSELL, ALFRED 1914, *Exercises in Phonics*. Melbourne: Victoria Education Department.

[GIBSON, HARRY THOMAS] 1925, *Do You Speak English or Only a Substitute?* Compiled by H.T.G. Auckland: Reliance Printery.

GILES, HOWARD and POWESLAND, PETER 1975, *Speech Styles and Social Evaluation*. London: Academic Press.

GORDON, ELIZABETH 1983, The flood of impure vocalisation: a study of attitudes towards New Zealand speech. *The New Zealand Speech-Language Therapists' Journal* 38, 16–29.

HUYGENS, INGRID 1979, Sociolinguistic stereotyping in New Zealand. Unpublished MA thesis. Auckland: University of Auckland.

JONES, DANIEL 1909, *The Pronunciation of English*. Cambridge: Cambridge University Press.

LABOV, WILLIAM 1965, Stages in the acquisition of standard English. In ROGER SHUY (ed.) *Social Dialects and Language Learning* (pp. 77–103). Champaign, Illinois: National Council of Teachers of English.

MACAULAY, RONALD K.S. 1977, *Language, Social Class and Education*. Edinburgh: Edinburgh University Press.

MCLEOD, JANET 1940, *Rhyming Roadways to Good Speech*. Christchurch: Simpson & Williams.

MITCHELL, AUSTIN 1972, *The Half-Gallon Quarter-Acre Pavlova Paradise*. Christchurch: Whitcombe & Tombs.

MITCHELL, A.G. and DELBRIDGE, ARTHUR 1965, *The Speech of Australian Adolescents*. Sydney: Angus & Robertson.

NZ DEPARTMENT OF EDUCATION 1925, *Speech Training* (Special Reports on Educational Subjects, No 14). Wellington: NZ Government Printer.

The NZ Education Gazette, Wellington: NZ Department of Education.

NZ Listener (Journal of the NZ Broadcasting Corporation), Wellington.

NZ SPEECH BOARD 1986, *Syllabus*.

STEWART, DOROTHY 1925a, *Speech Training by Phonic Methods*. Christchurch: Whitcombe & Tombs.

— 1925b, *Phonetics Practice Book*. Christchurch: Whitcombe & Tombs.

— 1930, *Graded Lessons in Speech Training*. Christchurch: Whitcombe & Tombs.

STEWART, MARK A., RYAN, ELLEN B. and GILES, HOWARD 1985, Accent and social class effects on status and solidarity evaluations. *Personality and Social Psychology Bulletin* 11, 98–105.

STRONGMAN, KENNETH T. and WOOSLEY, JANET 1967, Stereotyped reactions to regional accents. *British Journal of Social and Clinical Psychology* 6 (3), 164–7.

The Press, Christchurch.

The Triad, Wellington (1893–1927).

TURNER, GEORGE 1966, *The English Language in Australia and New Zealand*. London: Longman.

WALL, ARNOLD 1938, *New Zealand English: How it Should be Spoken*. Christchurch: Whitcombe & Tombs.

— 1952, The Way I Have Come. Broadcast Talk. Timaru: Radio New Zealand Archives.

3 Sociolinguistic stereotyping in New Zealand[1]

GRAHAM M. VAUGHAN and INGRID HUYGENS

Introduction

According to the 1976 census, New Zealand was a country of 3.1 million people, 83.7% of whom were native born. The majority of its inhabitants are of European descent and are mainly British in origin. Included in the native-born group are the Maori, New Zealand's first inhabitants, comprising 8.6% of the population at that time. Of the foreign-born inhabitants, most were British (9.5%), with some from Australia (2%), the Pacific Islands (2%) and Holland (0.7%). The British, therefore, are the largest immigrant group, while the Dutch are the only other sizeable group originating in Europe. Immigration by Pacific Islanders is still continuing and, at the time that this research was undertaken, many were not fluent in English. The British and Australians are native English speakers, while virtually all of the Dutch in New Zealand in the late 1970s were bilingual people, in Dutch and in English. Nearly all Maori speak English fluently, though there is considerable variation in their ability to speak the Maori language. Research by Benton (1979) in an outer area of Auckland (New Zealand's largest urban area, then with a population of 750,000) indicated that spoken Maori was at risk. Perhaps a half of Maori adults over twenty-five years were fluent in Maori, while less than 10% below this age were fluent. (It remains to be seen whether a move by the Maori community during the 1980s to reverse this trend by the teaching of Maori language to Maori pupils, in educational settings which cater specially for their needs, will be successful in reversing this trend.)

Regional variations in New Zealand spoken English appear to be very slight, if they exist at all (Hawkins, 1973; Trudgill & Hannah, 1982).

49

In this respect, lower prestige which can be associated with a regional accent (Edwards, 1982) in Britain is not likely to be found amongst speakers in New Zealand. On the other hand, there has been considerable interest amongst New Zealand speech-training professionals in the way in which prestige can be acquired through a cultivated speech style. Just as in Britain it has been noted (e.g. Giles & Powesland, 1975) that Received Pronunciation (RP) and certain foreign accents are accorded higher prestige (on some dimensions) than regional accents and accents from city areas, so it is argued that New Zealanders aspire towards RP to enhance their status.

Another area of interest has been the nature of English used by the Maori people. While some have argued that Maori English is distinctive (Mitcalfe, 1967), a rival view is that it differs from some New Zealand speech varieties mainly on socio-economic grounds — that it is in fact akin to New Zealand working-class English (Department of Education, 1971). Despite the interest in New Zealand language usage just described, no attempt had been made before this study to establish how accurately New Zealanders can distinguish certain speech forms, nor how these forms are evaluated.

Such questions are more than academic. Ethnic relationships in New Zealand, particularly between Maori and Pakeha (New Zealand-born person of European descent), have experienced stress, and some Maori now question the appropriateness of their status as an underprivileged minority. It is known that there are visual cues which are used by Pakeha to make social evaluations of Maori, and *vice versa* (Vaughan, 1972; 1978; 1986), but it is not known whether there are contributing linguistic cues which can also be used in this way. Likewise, the notion that RP is status-enhancing lacks an empirical base. Still other questions include: what status is accorded the accents that immigrants bring with them to this country? Should educational authorities encourage/discourage RP as a target in schools? Are there advantages in fostering the teaching of the Maori language at school? The proponents of such teaching regard it as self-evident that there are. The general lack of sociolinguistic research in this country means that opinion, rather than evidence, could guide estimates of the social impact of any planned change in language instruction in New Zealand.

Within this much broader context, the present study is a modest attempt to provide some of the basic information currently needed. There were two aims:

(1) to assess the capacity of a sample of New Zealand listeners to identify examples of speech commonly used in their own country;

(2) to have the listeners evaluate these examples.

Language varieties from four speaker groups were included: British, Dutch, Maori and Pakeha. The British and Dutch groups were represented by immigrant speakers, the former being native speakers of English, and the latter a group for whom English was a second language. The last two groups were native-born New Zealanders. All of the chosen Maori speakers spoke English fluently, though they varied in ability to use Maori from high to relatively low fluency.

Subjects

The participants were 120 Pakeha second-year psychology students. Mostly from middle-class backgrounds, they were divided into 12 groups, each group hearing a different combination of speakers on tape. Additionally, 60 second-year science students also served as subjects to provide a check on an aspect of the methodology (as noted below), though the data generated do not contribute to the main results reported.

Speech Samples

The speech used for this study consisted of samples of English which were spontaneous, though of restricted content. This decision allowed for naturally occurring variation in phonology, lexicon, syntax and fluency, while the topic remained controlled. Samples were collected on audiotape from a selection of speakers, resident in New Zealand, under the following cover story: 'I am trying to find out how different people treat strangers to this city. Please tell me how you would direct a foreign sailor from the wharf to the public library.' Transcriptions of all audiotapes were prepared to ascertain the extent to which lexical or syntactic aspects of the speech samples might be used by subjects to evaluate the speakers.

Thirty speakers were recorded. They were evenly divided by sex for each of four ethnic groups: British (six speakers), Maori (six), Dutch (six) and Pakeha (twelve). The British were all born in England and the Dutch in Holland, both groups having lived in their respective homelands for at least twenty-five years. The Maori speakers were each at least three-quarters Maori by race. Pakeha speakers were selected so that there were four each who could be classified as upper (U), middle (M) and lower (L) status in terms of occupational prestige, on a scale developed by Stewart & Gorringe (1977). Lack of a large enough pool of available speakers prevented such an evenly-distributed selection in the other ethnic groups. Amongst those chosen for the research, the approximate occupational categories represented were two upper, two middle and two lower for the British; one upper and five middle for the Dutch; and one upper, four middle and one lower status for the Maori speakers.

The speech samples were systematically combined on audiotape to make twelve tapes. Each group ($N = 10$) from the 120 subjects heard only one tape. There were two experimental conditions, single (Pakeha with one other ethnic set at a time) and combined (Pakeha with all other ethnic sets together). In the single condition, Pakeha was rotated with British, Maori and Dutch in turn. A tape always contained twelve voices, six of whom were Pakeha (two each of upper, middle and lower occupational status). There were two replications across both conditions, with one sub-group of six Pakeha speakers in the first replication and the other sub-group of six in the second. There were three replications in the combined condition. For the non-Pakeha sets, two speakers at a time were used to make three combined sets of British plus Maori plus Dutch.

An example of a single condition tape, therefore, would be Pakeha Speakers 1–6 with British Speakers 1–6. An example of a combined condition tape would be Pakeha Speakers 1–6 with British 1–2, plus Maori 1–2, plus Dutch Speakers 1–2. Finally, on each tape, any twelve speakers were randomised for serial order.

The experimental variation of two conditions was included to test the effect of changing the basis of comparison (i.e. other voices) which a subject might use in evaluating a particular speaker. It could be argued, for example, that linguistic judgements of others in a real-life context involve exposure to many speech styles, whether simultaneously present or remembered over time. If so, the combined condition could serve as a recorded analogue of the subjects' experience. Alternatively, a voice might be compared with those voices which are usually immediately available, i.e. other Pakeha voices. In this case, the single condition may better mirror reality. Both conditions, therefore, were included in the present design.

Evaluation of Speakers

At the time that this study was designed in 1979, two sets of seven-point rating scales, each containing four pairs of bipolar terms, were used as response measures. The first set was termed social scales and the second personal scales. Following Fishman (1971), Giles & Ryan (1982) have proposed other labels which we feel may be more appropriate for the two sets: status-stressing and solidarity-stressing. These are in turn seen as opposite poles on one dimension. The Giles & Ryan model also includes a second, orthogonal dimension whose poles are group-centred and person-centred. The interconnections of these dimensions with the scales of the present study are noted below.

Social scales

Four commonly-employed indicators of socio-economic status in social science research, *viz.* class, income, education and occupational status, were included in the present study:

upper class	*versus*	lower class
high income	*versus*	low income
highly educated	*versus*	poorly educated
high status job	*versus*	low status job.

These four scales are both status-stressing and group-centred in Giles & Ryan's model.

Personal scales

Lambert (1967) distinguished between scales stressing competence (e.g. intelligence, industriousness), personal integrity (e.g. helpfulness, trustworthiness), and social attractiveness (e.g. friendliness, sense of humour) which tap judges' perceptions of personality in a voice. These distinctions have been systematically explored by others (see Giles & Powesland, 1975).

In the present study, subjects were first asked to describe a sample of speakers on tape. Of the most frequently-used adjectives used by the subjects, those which corresponded to scales reported by Giles & Powesland as indicators of competence, personal integrity and social attractiveness were selected:

warm	*versus*	cold
hard-working	*versus*	easy-going
self-confident	*versus*	shy
intelligent	*versus*	dull.

All of these are person-centred in the Giles & Ryan model. However, only one of these is solidarity-stressing (warm), while three are status-stressing (hard-working, self-confident, intelligent).

Procedure

The eight social and personal rating scales were randomised for order, and for left–right position of 'positive' and 'negative' poles. After the eighth scale, the open-ended question 'what type of accent?' was included. These measures were incorporated in a booklet as eight bipolar, seven-point scales, followed by the open-ended question.

The subjects were told that the study was concerned with the impressions that New Zealanders derived from each others' speech, and that they would hear the voices of twelve speakers from the New Zealand speech environment. Their responses were to be recorded appropriately on the scales in the booklets provided. Their attention was also directed to the open-ended question: 'You may make comment on the type of accent that occurs to you, including none at all. You can complete the scales and the open question in any order, for a particular speaker.'

To distract attention from the content of the utterance, subjects were informed only that the speakers were answering an unimportant question, and that they should listen to how the utterance was delivered, not what was being talked about. They were advised to listen carefully to each voice during a first presentation, then to make their judgements quickly and spontaneously during a second presentation.

As already noted, transcriptions of all audiotapes were prepared. These were in booklet form and were presented to 60 subjects (who were not part of the experiment proper). They were asked to judge 'what the person might have been like who said these words'. The booklet also contained the same eight rating scales which were used with each of the speech samples. The aim of the procedure was to separate syntactic and lexical features from other speech cues for their effects upon the ratings of the recorded speech samples.

It could be argued that the use of the matched guise technique (see Giles & Powesland, 1975) would yield more experimental rigour than the partly content-controlled, natural speech technique used in this study. It might also at the same time remove the need for the directing question regarding accent. On the other hand, the matched guise technique is not without its critics (although see the rejoinder by Giles & Bourhis, 1976).

However, a major factor at the time of our research was that New Zealand's speech community was relatively unexplored. Consequently, we considered it premature to select explicit speech differences which could only hypothetically be ethnic- or status-dependent.

Before treating the results of the experiment proper, which deals with subjects' responses to speech samples on audiotape, we will first look at the evaluations made of the transcriptions. The 60 subjects previously referred to were asked to use the four social and the four personal scales to rate attributes of the persons responsible for the statements. This analysis showed that there were no significant effects between speaker groups on any of the scales, when only transcribed material was available. The transcriptions varied in length (number of words spoken). Likewise, the speech samples on audiotape varied in terms of time taken, with a mean utterance of twenty seconds duration. However, the factors of transcript and utterance length were randomly distributed across speaker groups. Consequently, the ratings of the speech samples referred to in the remainder of this paper must be accounted for in terms other than lexical properties, syntactic properties, number of total words or utterance length.

Results

The remaining results deal with how accurately the 120 speakers of the experiment proper were able to classify the various speakers ethnically. We shall also present the mean social and personal ratings (irrespective of individual scales) given each ethnic group. We discuss the rationale behind the analysis of variance (ANOVA) techniques employed, including the extraction of variance components. Then we examine the way in which the individual scales were applied to each ethnic group, and the relationship between accuracy of ethnic classification and evaluation.

Ethnic classification of speakers

The first results relate to the subjects' responses to the open-ended question, 'What type of accent is this?' These responses were aggregated across all conditions, all speakers and all subjects. The data are nominal; they are not independent; and the number of speakers representing the ethnic groups varies. For these reasons only a descriptive analysis is given.

The rates at which subjects attempted an ethnic classification of the speakers varied according to the speakers' ethnic group. The results in Table 3.1 are based on the subjects' responses to the question 'What type of accent is this?' Dutch speakers were most often classified by ethnicity (95%), followed by British and Maori, and then Pakeha speakers.

A more detailed analysis is given in Table 3.2. The percentages in italics show how accurate subjects were in attempting an ethnic classification of the speakers. Pakeha speakers, for example, were accurately identified 92% of the time, considered in proportion to all attempts made (59/64, with the denominator taken from Table 3.1). The corresponding accuracy percentages for the other groups were: British 71% (53/75), Maori 34% (25/74), Dutch 29% (28/95). The British were occasionally mistaken for Pakeha speakers, whereas the Maori quite often were. Dutch speakers were never categorised in this way, but were perceived often as generically foreign.

TABLE 3.1 *Percentage making ethnic referents in response to question 'What type of accent is this?'*

Ethnic origin of speaker	Ethnic referents (%)
British	75
Dutch	95
Maori	74
Pakeha	64

TABLE 3.2 *Percentage attempting an ethnic classification*

Ethnic origin of speaker	Classified as:							
	British	Dutch	Maori	Polynesian	Foreign/ European	Pakeha	Other	None
British	53	0	0	0	7	15	0	24
Dutch	0	28	0	0	48	0	19	5
Maori	0	0	25	10	0	32	7	27
Pakeha	0	0	0	0	0	59	5	36

Note: Rounding errors cause some side totals to not equal 100.

Ratings analysis: general

The overall mean scores, averaged across the four scales for each of the social ratings and the personal ratings, are shown in Figure 3.1. Scores above or below the neutral level of 4.0 are relatively more favourable or less favourable. With respect to social ratings, these results show that the British were rated more favourably, Dutch neutrally and Maori less favourably. In terms of personal ratings, both the British and Dutch were rated favourably and Maori neutrally. Status among Pakeha speakers bears a clear relationship to the favourability of ratings. The higher the status the higher the scores, on both social and personal ratings.

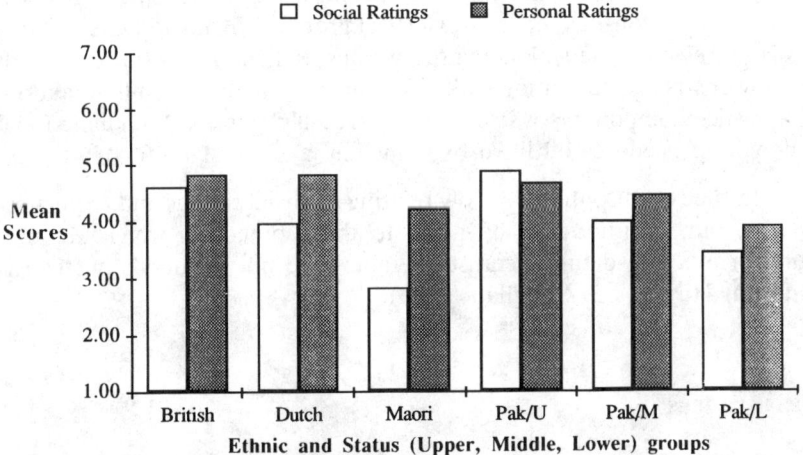

FIGURE 3.1 *Mean social and personal ratings of all ethnic and status groups*

Although the ANOVA designs used in this study force a separation of the single and combined experimental conditions, the mean scores on social ratings do not differ across these conditions. There are slight differences across conditions for some personal ratings outcomes. Further points relating to the use of ANOVA are provided in the next section.

Ratings analysis: use of ANOVA

The remaining results consist of three pairs of ANOVAs, each pair dealing first with social and then with personal ratings of the various speaker groups. The first pair uses a 3 × 2 × 4 design on each set of ratings, and deals with the single condition (British, Dutch and Maori speaker groups each on a different audiotape). The factors are ethnicity of speaker (British, Dutch, Maori), Pakeha sub-groups (Pakeha speakers 1–6, 7–12), and rating scales (four social scales, four personal scales). The last factor is a repeated measure. The second pair of ANOVAs deals with the combined condition (each audiotape with British, Dutch and Maori speakers), ethnicity of speaker (British, Dutch and Maori), and rating scales. The last two factors are repeated measures. The first and second pair of ANOVAs treat Pakeha speakers as background.

The third pair, however, treats the remaining ethnic groups as background against which to evaluate Pakeha speakers. It is a 4 × 2 × 3 × 3 design in which the last two factors are repeated measures. The first factor is non-Pakeha context (backgrounds: British, Dutch, Maori and all three combined), Pakeha sub-groups, Pakeha status (upper, middle and lower status), and rating scales. Within each analysis, a full breakdown of variance components was calculated (see Huygens & Vaughan, 1983), following procedures outlined by Vaughan & Corballis (1969).[2]

In the results outlined below relating to social ratings and to personal ratings, our attention will be given to those outcomes which are most noteworthy. The detailed statistical tables are not included, but can be found in Huygens & Vaughan (1983).

Social ratings

British, Dutch and Maori speakers

It was noted in Table 3.1 (and the left half of Figure 3.1) that ethnicity of speaker had a distinctive effect upon social ratings. The British were rated the highest, followed by the Dutch, with the Maori speakers the lowest. The mean level of these ratings did not differ from the single to the combined condition. Potentially different anchor effects implicit in these two conditions were not borne out in the results, i.e. it did not matter whether Dutch speakers, for example, were being judged against Pakeha only or against speakers from all other ethnic groups.

In the single condition, the variable 'ethnicity of speaker' accounted for 53% of total variance. In the combined condition it was still strong, accounting for 20% of total variance. Small effects were also noted in relation to uncontrolled differences between various sets of speakers: the two Pakeha combinations in the single condition (4% of variance accounted for), and the three sets of British–Dutch–Maori combinations in the combined condition (9%).

Pakeha speakers

The social ratings results for Pakeha speakers point to a strong effect (22%) attributable to Pakeha status. As was noted in Figure 3.1, upper status Pakeha speakers were rated highest, followed by middle and lower status speakers. As with the previous ANOVAs, there was a Pakeha sub-groups effect (6%), here in interaction with status, deriving from uncontrolled differences between the two six-speaker Pakeha sets. There was a smaller effect due to non-Pakeha context (3%), indicating that Pakeha speakers were judged slightly differently against varying ethnic-speaker backgrounds. Other significant F ratios observed in this analysis made no contribution to total variance and were ignored.

Status as a factor in relation to ratings of the British, Dutch and Maori groups was not examined since the lower number of subjects in these groups prevented adequate distribution by status. However, inspection of the results showed that it could be a variable of interest in subsequent research. For all groups, higher status is related to higher social ratings. In the case of the non-Pakeha groups, it did not appear to be an effect powerful enough to override the general ordering of British, then Dutch, and Maori in terms of mean ratings. Rather, its effect was within each ethnic group. Interestingly, the high scores of upper status Pakeha speakers were about equal with those of the two upper status British speakers, who in turn scored highest in the British group.

Personal ratings

British, Dutch and Maori speakers

The results in Figure 3.1 show that British and Dutch speakers were rated about the same overall, but that Maori speakers were rated less favourably. The ANOVA carried out on personal ratings in the single condition showed a strong effect for ethnicity of speaker (19% of total variance). This was less marked (3%) in the combined condition. In both conditions, ethnicity of speaker interacted with rating scales, with 14% and 6% contributions respectively. This means that the four scales were used differently to evaluate speakers according to their ethnicity.

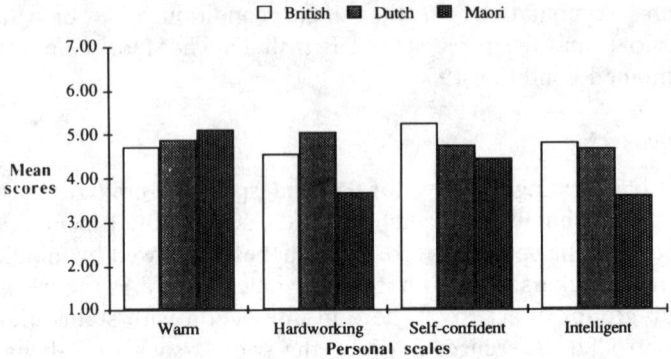

FIGURE 3.2 *Mean personal ratings on four scales for British, Dutch and Maori speakers*

Significant ANOVA effects were found in several instances. British speakers were more likely to be judged as self-confident than anything else, especially in the single condition, where they were compared with Pakeha speakers only. Maori speakers were more likely to be judged as warm than anything else, in both the single and combined conditions. There were no significant differences for the way in which Dutch speakers were evaluated on the four personal scales.

Across the three ethnic groups, significant effects were that Maori emerged as most warm in the combined condition, Dutch as hard-working in both conditions, British as self-confident in the single condition, and Maori as least intelligent in both conditions. No hypotheses had been entertained concerning specific (triple) interactions involving conditions × scales × ethnicity. Consequently, our discussion is limited to general differences between the four scales across the various ethnic groups. In fact, small variations in outcomes across the single and combined conditions did not detract from the consistency of these effects.

Overall differences in the use of the four personal rating scales were found in both the single (7%) and combined conditions (3%). In general, speakers were rated as more warm and more self-confident, rather than hard-working and intelligent. However, the way in which the four scales was used did vary according to the ethnicity of the speaker. As Figure 3.2 shows, the attributes associated with each of the following ethnic groups were:

Maori — warm, less hard-working, less intelligent

Dutch — hard-working

British — self-confident.

Pakeha speakers

The results in Figure 3.1 show that more favourable personal ratings were generally accorded upper status speakers, followed by middle and lower status speakers. The same results, broken down for the four scales, are shown in Figure 3.3. They point to a moderate effect (6%) for Pakeha status and an interaction effect of similar size between Pakeha status and the scales (hard-working goes in the opposite direction to the other three). The ANOVA tests for these effects were all significant. In summary, it was found that the attributes associated with each Pakeha status group were:

Upper — hard-working, self-confident, intelligent

Middle — warm, self-confident

Lower — warm.

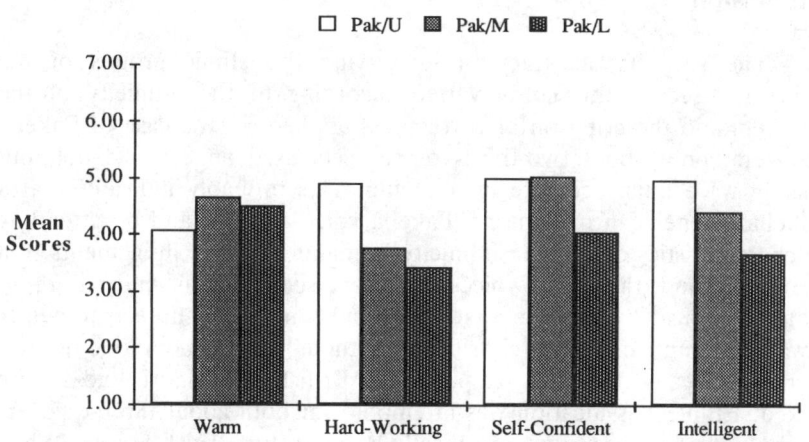

FIGURE 3.3 *Mean personal ratings on four scales for upper, middle and lower status Pakeha speakers*

Relationship between ethnic classification and evaluation

It has been noted above that some subjects were successful in making an accurate ethnic classification of speakers. The extent to which this acted as a cue for making social and personal evaluations of the speakers was also examined. In this analysis, social ratings were treated as an aggregate score, since all scales operated in the same direction for subjects, while personal ratings were treated for each scale independently. Of 18 chi square tests carried out for social ratings of the British, Dutch and Maori speakers, two were significant at the 0.05 level. One Maori speaker was given lower ratings by subjects who classified this speaker as Maori or Polynesian than by those who did not. One Dutch speaker was given higher ratings by those who classified the speaker as Dutch. There were 72 tests for the personal scales, five of which were significant. Three Maori speakers were perceived as less hard-working by those classifying these speakers as Maori. One British speaker was regarded as more intelligent when classified as British, and one Dutch speaker as more intelligent when classified as Dutch. Since the number of tests performed was large, there is the possibility that some of these outcomes are type I errors (i.e. spuriously significant results). The clustering of the results for the Maori speakers, however, suggests that this result may be replicable.

Discussion

The subjects' accuracy in identifying the ethnic groups of the speakers used in this study varied according to the ethnicity of the speakers and the criterion of correctness applied. In the case of Pakeha speakers, only about two-thirds of subjects used an ethnic label, but usually were quite accurate in so doing. This probably indicates that a Pakeha listener can recognise a Pakeha voice as such, and be attending to characteristics other than ethnicity in making further judgements. On the other hand, the Dutch voices must have seemed sufficiently different from voices usually heard in a New Zealand context for subjects to nearly always attempt an ethnic classification, though only about one-quarter were specifically accurate. Responses to British and Maori voices were mixed. Ethnic classification was attempted for both about three-quarters of the time, but was more specifically accurate for British voices. When judging Maori voices, subjects tended more often to describe them as Pakeha rather than Maori. This suggests that, even if there are characteristics of spoken English which are distinctively Maori, Pakeha listeners are generally not distinguishing them.

The results in Figure 3.1 (left half) show that the social ratings were applied more favourably to British than to Dutch or Maori speakers. Although the statistical designs did not permit a direct comparison, it is apparent that, overall, upper-status Pakeha speakers (Figure 3.1, right half) were favoured nearly as much as British speakers. Moreover, it was noted that the highest-scoring upper-status Pakeha speakers were favoured equally with upper-status British speakers. These results lend support to the view that Pakeha derive enhanced status when using a speech style approximating RP. The lower-social evaluation of Maori speakers, together with a low rate (25%) of actual classification of these voices as Maori, supports the argument that Maori voices are probably treated on non-ethnic terms, but are being evaluated as if lower-status Pakeha.

An interesting feature of the social ratings results was that subjects responded on each of the four scales in similar fashion. The categories of being upper class, highly educated, having a high status job, and high income, were treated interchangeably. From the way in which Tajfel (1978) used the term social categorisation, it seems that those cues that allow the listener to categorise (i.e. socially group) a voice in a manner which is meaningful lead to a blanket evaluation of that voice in terms of prestige. If 'prestige' is taken to mean socio-economic status, then any of the indicators (social ratings scales) used in this study appear to be an effective measure. The same applies to the personal scales hard-working, self-confident and intelligent, a finding which is consistent with Giles & Ryan's view that such scales are status-stressing.

Results for the personal ratings differed not only in terms of the ethnicity of the speaker but also in terms of the scales themselves. British and Dutch speakers were favoured about equally, and upper-status Pakeha were also placed at about this level. However, the scales were applied differently, a trend which can be chiefly accounted for in terms of an interaction with the ethnic grouping of the speaker. The British speakers emerged as the most self-confident, the Dutch as hard-working, and the Maori as least intelligent, least hard-working, and most warm. Among subjects who correctly identified a speaker's ethnicity, several of the personal ratings became more marked. For example, a Dutch speaker actually recognised as Dutch was perceived as even more intelligent.

Personal ratings of Pakeha speakers pointed to fairly clear status effects, and an interaction in the way in which particular scales were applied to speakers of different perceived status. The upper-status Pakeha is judged to be hard-working, intelligent and self-confident, and shares the last attribute with British speakers. Given their (actual) higher occupational status amongst the Pakeha speakers, it is probable that subjects detected a speech style akin to RP in these speakers. Self-confidence was also attributed to middle-status speakers, though tempered by the added judgement of warmth. Finally, only warmth was seen to be relatively distinctive in the speech style of lower-status speakers. At this juncture, it can be noted that Maori speakers were also judged to have warmth. This further supports the idea that a proportion of subjects may have judged Maori voices as being more attractive, if less competent, than RP. Although the present study was designed without the benefit of the model of speech evaluation presented by Giles & Ryan (1982) and discussed earlier, we can now note that the personal scale of warmth is the only one which is solidarity-stressing.

Some meaning can be given to the connections between social status, personal, characteristics and speech style in New Zealand by considering research in other countries. The two major evaluative dimensions of speech noted earlier; status-stressing and solidarity-stressing (Giles & Ryan, 1982) were applied by Ryan, Giles & Sebastian (1982) to a review of attitudes towards language styles in social contexts in different parts of the world. Status-stressing leads to social prestige, and is associated with a 'high' variety of a language, such as might be used on formal occasions. Socially mobile individuals in a speech community are more likely to use this variant. Solidarity-stressing enhances in-group loyalty, and can be found among 'high' or 'low' forms of a language, such as in German or Arabic. Some individuals may always use the low form, and yet others may use this form to show group loyalty. It can be the language of one's family or of intimates, and is mostly found in informal settings.

At least four patterns of high and low usage which reflect different relationships between majority and minority language groups have been distinguished. One of these is where the majority language group has social status but the minority group has solidarity. It is possible for the former to be regarded as less 'attractive', such as RP can be in Britain (cf. Edwards, 1982), or a cultivated Australian accent (nearer to RP) in Australia (cf. Eltis, 1980). Another example is provided by a 1977 study by Edwards (cited in Edwards, 1982). He found that among Irish regional accents the Donegal accent (which Edwards believes to operate in the Irish context as a received variety) was perceived to be more 'competent'. A Dublin accent was regarded as more 'socially attractive'. Such findings seem parallel to the way in which the social ratings in the present study are higher for British and for upper-status Pakeha speakers. The closer the accent is to RP the higher the social status afforded it. At the same time, the same accents are further away from the vernacular, and are regarded as less warm.

The use of different experimental conditions, single and combined, had no detectable effect on social ratings, and little that could be interpreted meaningfully on personal ratings. It is possible that whatever social anchorage cues these judges used were relatively impervious to contextual features of the specific conditions distinguished in this experiment.

Clearly, the present study is just a start for further systematic language attitude research in New Zealand. A more concerted investigation of the detectability or otherwise of Maori English amongst a wider range of speakers, including some from that shrinking minority of Maori who are bilingual, is desirable. Likewise, given the growing numbers of bilingual Pacific Islanders in the New Zealand speech community, particularly in the Auckland urban area, it would be desirable to include speech samples from these people in future research. We need to examine what are the specific advantages and disadvantages of speech styles, when these are coloured by socio-economic and/or ethnic factors. Research of this kind will provide valuable and much-needed information to policy-makers in a variety of language-related areas.

Notes

1. The data reported in this paper were first collected in 1979 by Ingrid Huygens (1979) for her Masters thesis, under the supervision of Professor Graham Vaughan. The idea for the research grew from earlier discussions which Graham Vaughan had with Howard Giles at the University of Bristol in 1976. The present paper is a revised version of that published by Huygens & Vaughan (1983).
2. The scores in Figure 3.1 to 3.3 are reversed in order from those first reported in Huygens & Vaughan (1983). High scores on the seven-point scale represent more favourable evaluations in the present paper. In the earlier paper, low scores were used for this purpose so that the presentation of the data was consistent with comparable works in the field being published at that time.

References

BENTON, RICHARD A. 1979, *The Maori Language in the 1970s*. Wellington: New Zealand Council for Educational Research, Maori Research Unit.

DEPARTMENT OF EDUCATION 1971, *Maori Children and the Teacher*. Wellington: Government Printer.

EDWARDS, JOHN R. 1982, Language attitudes and their implications among English speakers. In ELLEN BOUCHARD RYAN and HOWARD GILES (eds) *Attitudes towards Language Variation: Social and Applied Contexts* (pp. 20–33). London: Edward Arnold.

ELTIS, K.J. 1980, Pupils' speech style and teacher reaction: implications from some Australian data. *English in Australia* 51, 27–35.

FISHMAN, JOSHUA A. 1971, *Sociolinguistics: A Brief Introduction*. Rowley, Mass.: Newbury House.

GILES, HOWARD and BOURHIS, RICHARD Y. 1976, Methodological issues in dialect perception: a social psychological perspective. *Anthropological Linguistics* 18 (7), 294–304.

GILES, HOWARD and POWESLAND, PETER F. 1975, *Speech Style and Social Evaluation*. London: Academic Press.

GILES, HOWARD and RYAN, ELLEN BOUCHARD 1982, Prolegomena for developing a social psychological theory of language attitudes. In ELLEN BOUCHARD RYAN and HOWARD GILES (eds) *Attitudes towards Language Variation: Social and Applied Contexts* (pp. 208–23). London: Edward Arnold.

HAWKINS, PETER R. 1973, The sound-patterns of New Zealand English. *Proceedings and Papers of the 15th Congress of the Australasian Universities Language and Literature Association* (13/1–8). Kensington: University of New South Wales.

HUYGENS, INGRID 1979, Sociolinguistic stereotyping in New Zealand. Unpublished MA thesis. Auckland: University of Auckland.

HUYGENS, INGRID and VAUGHAN, GRAHAM M. 1983, Language attitudes, ethnicity and social class in New Zealand. *Journal of Multilingual and Multicultural Development* 4 (2–3), 207–23.

LAMBERT, WALLACE E. 1967, A social psychology of bilingualism. *Journal of Social Issues* 23 (2), 91–108.

MITCALFE, BARRY 1967, Survivals of Maori in English. *Education* 16 (8), 20–2.

RYAN, ELLEN BOUCHARD, GILES, HOWARD and SEBASTIAN, RICHARD J. 1982, An integrative perspective for the study of attitudes toward language variation. In ELLEN BOUCHARD RYAN and HOWARD GILES (eds) *Attitudes towards Language Variation: Social and Applied Contexts* (pp. 1–19). London: Edward Arnold.

STEWART, ROBERT A.C. and GORRINGE, EDITH I. 1977, Socio-economic status in New Zealand: an updated empirical index and its relationship to other New Zealand empirical and statistical indices. *The New Zealand Psychologist* 6 (1), 25–30.

TAJFEL, HENRI 1978, Social categorization, social identity and social comparison. In HENRI TAJFEL (ed.) *Differentiation between Social Groups: Studies in the Social Psychology of Intergroup Relations* (pp. 61–76). London: Academic Press.

TRUDGILL, PETER and HANNAH, JEAN 1982, *International English: A Guide to Varieties of Standard English*. London: Edward Arnold.

VAUGHAN, GRAHAM M. (ed.) 1972, *Racial Issues in New Zealand*. Auckland: Akarana Press.

— 1978, Social change and intergroup preferences in New Zealand. *European Journal of Social Psychology* 8 (3), 297–314.

— 1986, Social change and racial identity: Issues in the use of picture and doll measures. *Australian Journal of Psychology* 38 (3), 359–70.

VAUGHAN, GRAHAM M. and CORBALLIS, MICHAEL C. 1969, Beyond tests of significance: estimating strength of effects in selected ANOVA designs. *Psychological Bulletin* 72 (3), 204–13.

4 'God help us if we all sound like this': attitudes to New Zealand and other English accents[1]

DONN BAYARD

> In its context, 'rain in the elps, foin and moild alswhere' is easy enough to understand, although it may jar a sensitive ear. But such mangling of the vowels *can* cause misunderstanding. (Letter to the *NZ Listener*, 11th February 1989)

> We are not Americans, and I know I for one do not like the way this country is trying to carbon copy itself with American influence. Be it trendy or not, I totally disapprove of foreign newsreaders. Give me the warm voices and sincere faces of people like Karen Sims any day; they are New Zealand's 'real people'. (Letter to editor, *Otago Daily Times*, 12th September 1984)

> Previous radio voice work and training stood her in good stead, but she says she still had the 'usual bad New Zealand speech patterns'. (Interview with TV news presenter, *Otago Daily Times*, 26th August 1986)

Background

The pros and cons of the New Zealand accent compared with the Received Pronunciation (RP) acrolect have been debated in the written and spoken media for almost a century. Over the past decade or more the conflict has grown more confused and complex with the influx of

North American (NAm) accent programmes and news reporters on New Zealand television. It is easy to see this debate as a conflict between the slowly waning prestige of RP and the rise of NAm on the one hand, and a more domestic struggle between Kiwi loyalty and the 'cultural cringe' on the other. However, very little is known to date about the views of non-letter writers on the various accents.

Research on attitudes toward New Zealand English (NZE) as expressed in early accounts and more recent comments like those quoted above (Gordon, 1983a; 1983b; Gordon & Abell, this volume) has certainly made it clear that New Zealanders have strong feelings about their accent and its relationship to the 'Standard English' of RP. However, as Vaughan & Huygens (see this volume) pointed out some years ago, very little research has been carried out to determine just what the precise attitudes of NZE speakers are toward the range of English accents found in this country. The few studies to date have tended to focus on attitudes of NZE speakers toward 'foreign' or 'Maori' accents as opposed to 'Pakeha' NZE. Thus Hamilton, in an unpublished 1977 study, contrasted attitudes evoked by Northern English accents compared to NZE using two North English and two NZE speakers, plus a fifth matched-guise speaker employing both accents. The respondents were 30 high-school pupils. Huygens' research (1979; Vaughan & Huygens, this volume) contrasted 12 Pakeha accents with six each of 'Maori' NZE, RP and Dutch-accented English, using as subjects 120 Pakeha university students. In the only other published study of which I am aware, Watts (1981) briefly surveyed the attitudes of 124 high-school students to various foreign accents (RP, Lancashire, American, Dutch, Japanese, Polynesian, Spanish and Malaysian [Chinese]). A study by Abell (1980; Gordon & Abell, this volume), based on 89 high-school students, is the only one to date to examine specifically attitudes toward different varieties of NZE contrasted with RP. It is also the only one to provide some phonetic description of the accents employed in the experiment.

My aim in the research described here was also to investigate New Zealanders' attitudes to the range of accents found within NZE, from 'broad' to 'cultivated', and to try to ascertain how this range was viewed vis-à-vis other 'standard' accents (in this case not only to RP, but North American and Australian). It is, however, first necessary to offer some justification of my use of Mitchell & Delbridge's 'broad-general-cultivated' terminology devised for Australian English (1965). As Bauer has said,

Discussions of NZ English have tended to assume, without any empirical support, that the same kind of division is justified in New

Zealand. . . . although it is frequently useful to make reference to this rough-and-ready trichotomy, there is no evidence of which I am aware that such a stratification can be measured in phonetic or phonological terms in any kind of consistent way. (1986: 9)

Abell, following Maclagan and others, makes the reasonable but unsupported assumption that NZE can be classified into these three varieties, and provides intuitively convincing descriptions of the phonology distinguishing each variety (Abell, 1980: 7–11). However, this classification until recently lacked documentation from any reasonably large sample of NZE speakers. As a by-product of a Labovian study of phonological variation in 141 NZE speakers carried out in 1984–85 (Bayard, 1987; 1988; in press), I believe I am in a position to make at least a tentative description of a broad-to-cultivated continuum (*not* a trichotomy) for NZE, based on empirical data rather than assumptions drawn from Australian data. However, further research may well reduce the utility of the three labels as applied to arbitrary points on the continuum.

The 'Dagg-to-Dougal' Continuum[2]

The 1984–85 study provided considerable objective verification of the association of a number of phonological variables with socio-economic class (as defined along traditionally simplistic lines of educational and occupational scales). Among other variables, I studied the 'terrible diphthongs' (Gordon & Deverson, 1985: 23) (ou) (au) (ai) (ei), together with the frequently diphthongised (i) (as heard in 'Go out my gate, see?'). Predictably these were correlated to socio-economic rankings with significance levels of less than or equal to 0.01. A number of other phonological variables proved equally sensitive (merger of /el/-/æl/ and /iə/-/eə/, /-l/ vocalisation, etc.). The specific values of the phonological variables used (usually on a scale from 1 (broad) to 4 (cultivated/RP)) may be found in Bayard (1987: 32–4). The ranges of the diphthongs agree closely with those presented by Gordon & Deverson for broad and general NZE and RP (1985: 23; see also Abell, 1980: 11). Discriminant analyses proved able to classify 'lower' and 'middle-class' informants with 83% accuracy on the basis of their values of nine phonological variables alone.

Table 4.1 presents the phonetic values of broad, general and cultivated points on the NZE stigmatised vowel scale as suggested by my earlier study (see key to Table 4.2), and provides as well the values

TABLE 4.1 *Approximate broad, general and cultivated vowel foci in Australian and New Zealand accent continua (percentages are those of the total NZE sample of 141 in Bayard, 1987)*

Australia (after Mitchell & Delbridge, 1965):

	(i)	(u)	(ei)	(ou)	(ai)	(au)
Cultivated	[i]~[ii]	[u]~[ou]	[ɛɪ]~[eɪ]	[ou][a]	[aɪ]	[au]
General	[əɪ]	[əʊ][b]	[ʌɪ]	[ʌʊ]	[ɒɪ]	[æʊ]
Broad	[əˑɪ]	[əˑʊ][b]	[ʌˑɪ]	[ʌˑʊ]	[ɒˑɪ]	[æˑʊ]

New Zealand

	(i)	%	(u)	%	(ei)	%	(ou)	%	(ai)	%	(au)	%
Cultivated	[ii]~[iɪ]	10	[u]	–	[eˑɪ]	9	[əʊ]	9	[aɪ]~[ɑˑɪ]	13	[aˑʊ]	27
General	[ɨ]	57	[ɨ]	–	[ɛˑɪ] 41 [ɪˑɐ]	48	[ʌˑʊ]	75	[ɑɪ]	69	[aˑʊ]	55
Broad	[ei]~[əˑɪ]	33	[ɨ]	–	[ɐɪ]	2	[ɣˑʊ]	16	[ɒɪ]	18	[æˑʊ]	18

a. I believe that [əʊ] or [ʏʊ] would be a more representative rendering.
b. The second element might better be represented [ʉ].

originally used by Mitchell & Delbridge for Australian English. Note that while I question some of the phonetic definitions given by Mitchell & Delbridge, I would not myself wish to claim precise phonetic accuracy for my own transcriptions. These are purely auditory, and Maclagan's research has indicated some startling differences when acoustic techniques are applied to NZE (e.g. in the degree of raising of NZE /e/ and /ɔ/, Maclagan, 1982: 22).

Some further objective evidence for the 'Dagg-to-Dougal' continuum may be seen in the results of analyses of speech samples from the spoken media (including politicians as well as announcers, Table 4.2). Although the samples were only short ones (ranging from 1.5 to 5.7 min each), the continuum from broad values (1) to the cultivated/near-RP acrolect (4) is evident. The overall scalability of the table is clear, in particular the 93% consistency in Mitchell & Delbridge's six diphthongs (including fronting of (u) rather than diphthongisation, as in Australia). Hence I think it is safe to consider the continuum a fact of NZE, albeit by no means a strict trichotomy. Nor would I wish to view these points on a continuum as indicative of more or less discrete varieties (Abell, 1980: 8) or sociolects, as Horvath has done in her Sydney study (1985).

Samples and Methods

As a result of the 1984–85 study, I had access to a wide range of NZE accents reading an identical 170-word speech sample. I had also collected some 15 additional samples of non-NZE accents in the course of the research, again with the same reading passage. Hence as in Abell's study (but not Huygens') respondents heard all accents reading the same text. The accent samples used were thus uniform in length (about one minute) and in lexical and phonological content. This allowed for fairly exact categorisation of accents along the 'Dagg-to-Dougal' continuum discussed above. This contrasts with the 1979 study of Vaughan & Huygens (this volume), which controlled only for topical content of their samples, with free variation in lexicon, phonology and utterance length.

Following the advice of a psychologist colleague, I limited the number of accents presented to eight, as a larger sample might have led to a fatigue or boredom effect on how listeners scored speakers near the end of the series. Hence the samples are not balanced by sex, with one male and female speaker for each accent. But I attempted some balance in broad and general NZE by using male and female accents differing only along what I refer to below as the 'innovative–conservative'

TABLE 4.2 *Values of phonological variables in media speech samples: professional media presenters and politicians; scored 1 broad to 4 near-RP (segments analysed range from 1.5 to 5.7 min in length)*

Source	(ou)	(ei)	(au)	(ai)	(i)	(u)	(-y)	(e)	(o)	(wwh)	(-l)
Local telephone	1	1	1	(1)[a]	2	1	1	1	1[b]	1	3
Weather forecast	1–2	2	1	1–2	2	1	1	1	2	1	2
Fred Dagg[c]	2	2	2	2	3	1	1	1	1	1	3
4XO local radio	2	2	2	2	2	1	1	1	2–1	1	2
Bob Jones	2	2	2	2	3	1	1	1	2	1	4
Muldoon	2	2–3	2	3	3	1	1	3	3	1	4
Beetham	2	3	2	3	3	1	1	1	3	1	4
Lange	2	2–3	3	3	3	1	1	1	1	1	(1)
4ZB local radio	2	3	2–3	3	3	1	1	1	2	—	3
TV local news: Allan	2	3	3	3	3	1	1	3	2	3	3
TV local news: Mora	3	3–4	3–2	3–2	3	1	2	1	3	1	4
TV news: D'Audney	3	3	3	3	3	1	1	1	3	(4)	4
4ZB: RNZ News	3	4	3	4	4	1	1	3	2	—	4
TV weather: Veronica	3	4	3	4	3	1	1	3	3	—	4
TV news: Perigo	3	4	3	4	4	1	2–3	3	4	—	4
4YC: programme listing	3	4	3	4	3	1	2	4	3	4	4
TV news: Sherry	3	4	3	4	4	1	2	4	4	1	4
TV talk show: Stevenson	3–4	4	3	4	4	2	2	4	4	4	4
4YA: RNZ news	3	4	3	4	4	3	3	4	3	1	4

Variables

a. ( ) = one occurrence only; b = NORTH vowel only;
c. Source: 'Cricket' and 'Bruce's Phone Call' from *Fred Dagg's Greatest Hits*.
Total vertical scalability 86%; 9 vowels only, 88%; (ou - u) vowels only, 93%.

Key to Table 4.2: values of variables

(ou) Initial element in GOAT vowel: 1. mid-low back unrounded (ur) [ɣ⁺ʊ]; 2. mid-low back-central ur [ʌ⁺ʊ]; 3. mid-central ur [əʊ]; 4. mid-front ur [ə⁺ʊ].

(ei) Initial element in FACE vowel: 1. low mid-central [ɐɪ]; 2. low-mid, fronted slightly [ɐ⁺ɪ]; 3. mid-front, backed slightly [ɛ⁺ɪ]; 4. higher mid-front [ɛ⁺ɪ].

(au) Initial element in MOUTH vowel: 1. low mid-front [æʊ]; 2. intermediate [a⁺ʊ]; 3. low front or central [aʊ] or [a⁺ʊ]; 4. low central-back [ɑ⁺ʊ].

(ai) Initial element in PRICE vowel: 1. low back rounded [ɒɪ]; 2. low back ur [ɑ⁺ɪ]; 3. low back-central ur [ɑ⁺ɪ]; 4. low central or central-front [ɑ⁺ɪ].

(i) 1. FLEECE vowel markedly diphthongised as [əi]; 2. slight to marked diphthongisation in range [ə⁺i] to [ɨ⁺i]; 3. slight diphthongisation as [ɨi]; 4. minimal or no diphthongisation; [i] usual.

(u) 1. GOOSE vowel always centralised [ʉ] except before /-l/; 2. variably centralised or slightly centralised; 3. only occasionally centralised; 4. never centralised.

[-y] 1. HappY vowel always [-i]) 2. mostly [-i]; 3. mostly [-ɪ]; 4. always [-ɪ].

(e) 1. /e/ high, diphthongised; 3. /e/ high; 4. /e/ [ɛ⁺].

(o) 1. /ɔ/ approaching [oᵀ], diphthongised; 2. /ɔ/ high, diphthongised; 3. /ɔ/ high; 4. /ɔ/ [ɔ].

(wwh) 1. /w/ and /ʍ/ always merged as /w/; 2. usually merged; 3. often kept distinct; 4. always distinct.

(-l) 1. /-l/ always vocalised as /-ʊ/; 2. /-l/ often vocalised; 3. /-l/ reduced and sometimes vocalised; 4. /-l/ retained.

dimension. I chose the accents initially based on my subjective impressions of the stereotypes which they would (and as it proved, did) convey to NZE speakers, but as Table 4.3 shows the range of phonological values in the accents selected, ranging from 'lower-class broad' NZE to 'upper-middle-class RP', exhibit almost perfect horizontal scalability (97%). Although Huygens and Vaughan felt that at the time they carried out their study 'an explicit pre-selection of speech differences thought to be ethnic- or status-dependent was considered premature' (1983: 211), the results of the 1984–85 study mentioned above do in my view allow for a fair degree of confidence in correlating the phonological variables listed in Table 4.3 with socio-economic status. The eight speakers are described below in the order they are listed in Table 4.3 (NAm, AusE and broad NZE to RP). The speaker number refers to the order of presentation in most of the experimental sessions:

No. 4:   Male middle-class Canadian doctoral student, aged 31.
No. 6:   Male middle-class 'general Australian' speaker; university degree, business person, aged 31.
No. 2:   Female lower-class 'innovative broad' NZE speaker; school leaver, work skills trainee, aged 17.
No. 8:   Male (lower-class background) 'conservative broad' NZE speaker; doctoral degree, professional, aged 35.
No. 1:   Female lower-middle-class 'innovative general' NZE speaker; high-school education, aged 25.
No. 7:   Male middle-class 'conservative general' NZE speaker; some university, retired business person, aged 67.
No. 5:   Female middle-class 'conservative cultivated' NZE speaker; university degree, professional, aged 66.
No. 3:   Female upper-middle-class 'conservative' RP speaker taped during brief visit from England; university degree, aged 71.

'Innovative' and 'conservative' are used in the descriptions to refer to certain phonological features which are more age- than class-sensitive (e.g. /ʍ/ retention and lack of -t glottalisation in 'conservative' speakers; see Bayard, 1987: 13–16). While this dimension is at least partly independent of the 'broad-cultivated' continuum, I thought it worthwhile to include both older (Nos 7 and 8) and younger (Nos 2 and 1) speakers of broad and general NZE to investigate any possible variations in attitudes to them. I think it is of some significance that I was unable to include a younger cultivated NZE speaker to contrast with No. 5. None was present in my sample of 141, and I suspect a 'true cultivated' NZE accent (i.e. approaching RP) is very rare in New Zealanders under the age of about 40.

TABLE 4.3 Values for phonological variables of informants used in accent evaluation test, 1986 (values are those defined in Table 4.2 and Bayard, 1987: 33–4: (Y) = younger, (O) = older; horizontal scalability excluding Canadian and Australian 97%

Speaker	4 MC Can	6 Gen Aust	2 LC broad NZE (Y)	8 MC broad NZE (O)	1 MC gen NZE (Y)	7 MC gen NZE (O)	5 UMC CULT NZE	3 UMC Eng RP
			Equally or more class- than age-sensitive:					
l	3	4	1	3	4	4	4	4
ael	4	4	1	2	3	4	4	4
owen	4	1	3	1	1	4	4	4
ear	4	4	1	3	1	4	4	4
ei	4	2	2	2	2	3	4	4
i	4	1	1	2	2	3	3	4
ol	3	4	1	2	2	3	3	4
au	3	2	1	1	2	3	3	4
ai	4	2	1	1	2	2	3	3
ou	0	1	1	1	2	2	3	3
			More age- than class-sensitive:					
wwh	1	1	1	1	1	4	4	4

The speech samples admittedly have shortcomings in terms of what Giles & Powesland refer to as 'paralinguistic features' (1975: 13). As some recordings were made in the laboratory while others were done in the field, the recording quality is not uniformly good. There is clearly variation among the speakers in vocal timbre, intonation, and reading speed. For example, Speaker 2 is obviously not as fluent a reader as the rest. Such problems could have been largely eliminated by the use of the matched-guise technique widely employed overseas since its development by Lambert and others in the 1960s. However, like Abell (1980: 37) I knew of no mimic skilled enough to imitate accurately both the non-NZE accents I wished to include and also cover a range of NZE accents (e.g. 'general' Australian as well as broad and general NZE). There is also the further danger that the features employed by the mimic may either overly exaggerate or ignore the phonological features of the natural accents. As Giles & Powesland put it, this would produce 'no more than stereotyped impressions of the relevant accents' (1975: 31).

An example closer to home is provided by 'Fred Dagg' of the 'Dagg-to-Dougal' continuum. Hall interviewed John Clarke, Dagg's alter ego, and was able to contrast Clarke's natural accent with that he employed in his role as Dagg (Hall, 1976).[3] But as Hall states, Dagg's accent is 'recognised as an exaggeration of a typical New Zealander' (1976: 150).[4] Hence, while the eight samples employed are far from equal in paralinguistic features, they are at least natural stereotypes with more or less precisely defined phonetic features rather than exaggerated caricatures. Like Huygens, I feel that 'natural speakers can be seen as equally suitable stimuli for the initial triggering of stereotypes' (1979: 27). I think the results presented in Tables 4.4 and 4.5 support this conclusion.

It is also worth noting that previous studies employing more subtle techniques by directing respondents' attention toward something other than the accents used in the experiment have arrived at results similar to more direct tests. For example, subjects were completely unaware of their participation in Bourhis & Giles' Welsh theatre experiment, but this produced results which were similar to matched-guise experiments (Giles & Bourhis, 1976: 297). This strongly suggests that views held about different sorts of accent colour impressions both consciously/attitudinally and consciously/behaviourally, although it is obviously the first area which we are investigating here.

The questionnaire administered to subjects followed the form usual for this sort of study. Respondents were asked to listen to and rank each of the eight speakers on a scale of 1 (++) to 5 (−−) for eleven traits:

Pleasantness of accent
Reliability
Ambition
Sense of humour
Leadership ability
Likely annual income (less than $10,000 to over $35,000)[5]
Educational level (from school leaver to advanced university degrees)
Self-confidence
Intelligence
Likeability
Acceptability ('exclude from NZ', 'visitor to NZ', 'workmate', 'neighbour', 'close friend', 'family member'. As several subjects pointed out, 'workmate' and 'neighbour' should perhaps have been reversed.)

Respondents were then asked to assess the speaker's nationality, social class and likely type of job. While this last section was necessarily more subjective than the eleven scaled traits, it was still relatively simple in almost all cases to assess respondents' opinions on socio-economic level (1 lower class, 2 upper-lower class, lower-middle class, 3 middle-middle class, 4 upper-middle class, 5 upper class). Ambiguous responses were of course not scored. Nationality opinions were similarly scored: 0, Maori/ Polynesian; 1, NZ (although unmarked, presumably Pakeha New Zea- lander, at least for those respondents contrasting it with 'Maori/ Polynesian'); 2, Australian; 3, British; 4, Canadian/North American; 5, American/United States. This was done only to provide some overall indication of the accuracy of subjects' attributions. Obviously the values are strictly nominal rather than ordinal. Subjects were finally asked to supply their own birth year, sex, foreign language knowledge and place(s) and amount of time spent overseas (this last to eliminate non-NZE speakers).

The overall sample of respondents consisted of 17 first-year, 65 second-year and 8 postgraduate students, for a total of 86 after the elimination of 4 apparently non-NZE speaking subjects. Ages ranged from 18 to 41, with a mean of 21.7. Subjects first listened to a ten-second sample of all 8 accents, then to each accent sample in full (about one minute each), pausing between each accent to tick their responses to that speaker on the 11 scales provided. The ten-second sample was then played again while subjects completed the section on nationality, class, and occupation of each speaker. Nineteen of the subjects heard the accents in reverse order, to test for fatigue or boredom affecting feelings toward the final speaker in the series. Groups t-tests comparing the scores of these 19 to the main body of respondents suggest little significant effect.

To check the consistency of the overall results and test for significant differences between university students' evaluations and those of a second group of New Zealanders, I administered the same set of accents and questionnaire to 47 fourth-form students (aged 14 and 15) at a Dunedin state boys' high school. Pupils came predominantly from lower- and middle-class backgrounds. The test was administered in two groups, and one possible non-NZE subject was excluded to give a final total of 46. As will be seen below, the second series produced general confirmation of the university results, but with some interesting specific differences.

Results: the University Sample

I first investigated possible significant variation in attitude between first-year and postgraduate students using groups t-tests contrasting mean scores for each of the 13 traits for each of the eight speakers. Only four of the 104 t-tests were significant at the 95% level, although it should be noted that the sample size for both groups was of course very small. Groups t-tests contrasting male ($N = 28$) and female ($N = 58$) respondents produced a number of significant differences, but these will be discussed later in terms of the total sample of 132, which exhibits a very similar pattern and offers a more even balance between the sexes (74 male *versus* 58 female).

Pairs t-tests examining variation in scores of all respondents for each of the 13 traits between each pair of speakers (e.g. Speaker 1's sense of humour compared with Speaker 2's) proved considerably more valuable. Eighty of the 104 pairs tested had significance levels of less than 0.05. Rather than present a lengthy table of F values and significance levels, I have summarised the results for the university sample in Figure 4.1, ranking the mean scores of each speaker for the 12 traits (excluding nationality).

I have ordered the 12 traits along what is generally an 'overt' to 'covert prestige' axis, although I prefer to use Brown & Gilman's (1960) terms 'power' and 'solidarity'. This obviously equates with Bell's 'prestige norm' *versus* 'group solidarity' contrast in his discussion of variation in the broadcast media (1983: 36). The eight traits from self-confidence through educational level tend to relate more to power and overt prestige,

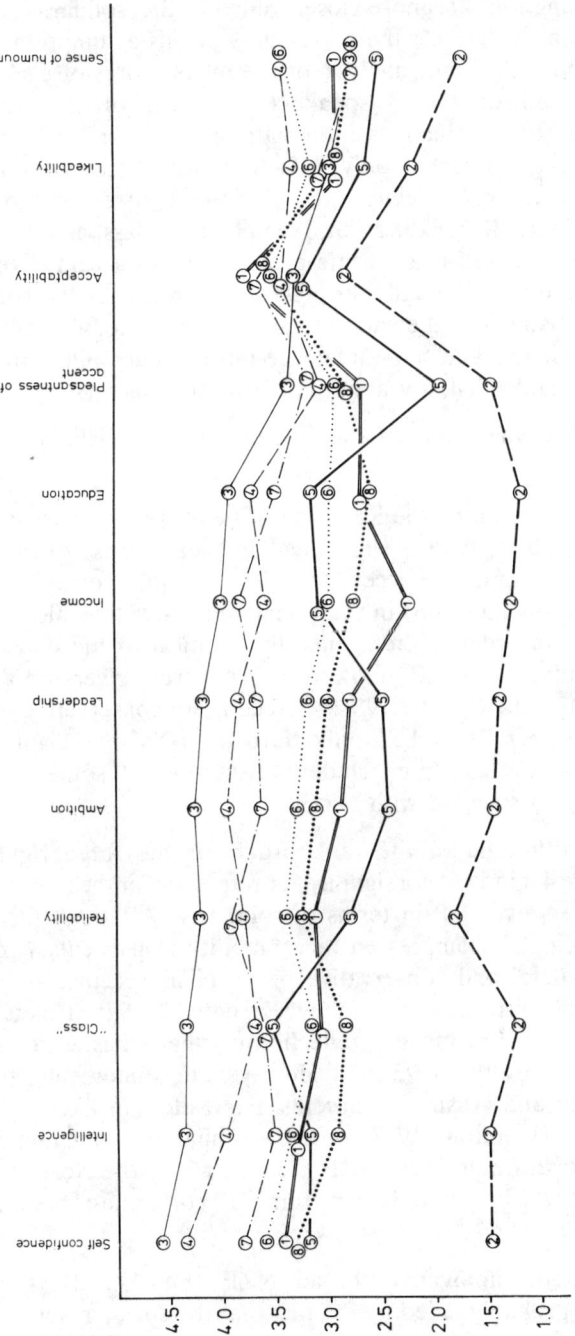

FIGURE 4.1 *Mean scores for accent evaluation variables: 86 university students* (1=, Young MC general NZ; 2— — —, LC broad NZ; 3———, UMC RP; 4 – – –, (U) MC Canadian; 5———, cultivated (UMC) NZ; 6 ···, UMC general Aust.; 7– · – old (U) MC general NZ; 8 ····, (U) MC broad NZ)

while the remaining four are more closely allied to the 'solidarity' of local New Zealand identity. To test the correctness of this assumption, I used a principal components factor analysis of the mean scores of each of the 86 subjects for all of the 8 speakers for each of the 12 traits (again excluding the nominally scored nationality variable).[6] Principal components analysis extracted only 2 factors (together accounting for 53% of the variance), and it seems likely that these correspond to power and solidarity (Figure 4.2). Education, income, and 'class' are clearly the major power variables (F1 axis), while pleasantness of accent, likeability and sense of humour are equally strongly associated with the solidarity axis (F2). The remainder of the variables are intermediate, with ambition, leadership, intelligence, and self-confidence more closely allied to power, and acceptability and reliability about equal in both factors.

The results shown in Figure 4.1 allow a number of specific conclusions to be drawn:

1. Perhaps predictably, the RP accent (Speaker 3) is the clear leader in the power variables, with a slight lead in pleasantness of accent as well. However, the Canadian accent (Speaker 4) ranks second in six of the eight power traits and third in the remainder, as well as pleasantness of accent. The rank order is thus generally identical to the outcome of Watts' earlier study, where RP followed by NAm were given top ranking by 'academic achievers' (Watts, 1981: 4). The more conservative general NZE accent (Speaker 7) ranked only third in six of the eight power variables, and it seems safe to conclude that there is still some degree of colonial inferiority associated with NZE.

2. On the other hand, the rank order for the three right-hand variables in Figure 4.1 indicates a significant preference for the Australasian and NAm speakers over RP in terms of solidarity. Although the range of solidarity rankings is compressed (acceptability in particular) relative to power, the general and conservative broad NZE accents, as well as the Canadian and Australian, rank above or equal to RP. This is to be expected for the NZE accents as a reflection of what Giles & Powesland refer to as 'accent loyalty' (1975: 67). However, it is interesting to note that the Canadian and Australian accents are leaders in likeability and sense of humour. Hamilton (1977) noted a similar phenomenon in her comparison of North English and NZE accents, where the North English and NZE accents which deviated most from RP 'correctness' were highly ranked in covert prestige.

3. Uneducated, 'innovative' broad NZE (Speaker 2) is clearly stigmatised, very probably aided by the fact that the speaker was a rather

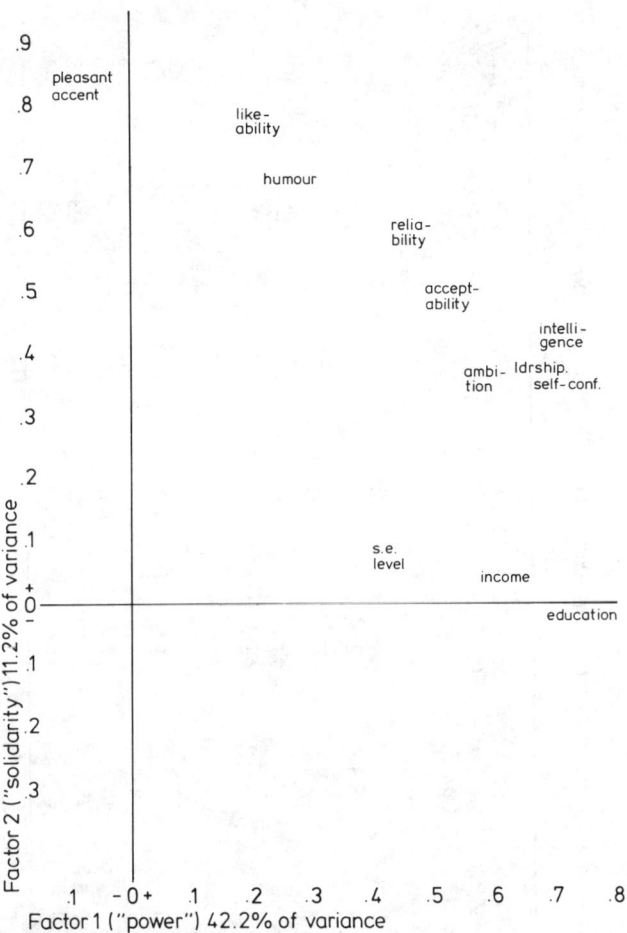

FIGURE 4.2 *Two-factor analysis of average scores for each of 86 university students for all eight speakers*

hesitant reader. The stigma found overt expression in many comments by respondents on this speaker, among them the title of this article. The fact that 10.5% of the university subjects assumed that the speaker was a low-paid or unemployed ethnic Maori or Pacific Islander (Table 4.4) is a depressing but sadly realistic reflection of ethnic stereotypes in contemporary New Zealand.[7] A slightly greater percentage of subjects assumed that this speaker was non-RP British ('Cockney', 'Soho', etc.). This is almost certainly due to the high degree of -t glottalisation present

TABLE 4.4 *University students' perceptions of speakers' national origin and social class (majority/plurality for each speaker in italics; Y = younger, O = older)*

	Spkr 1 MC NZE Y Gen.	Spkr 2 LC NZE Broad	Spkr 3 UMC RP Cons.	Spkr 4 MC Can NAm.	Spkr 5 UMC NZE Cult.	Spkr 6 MC Aust Gen.	Spkr 7 MC NZE O Gen.	Spkr 8 MC NZE Broad
Maori/PN	—	10.5	—	—	1.2	—	—	—
NZ	*93.0*	*74.4*	16.3	2.3	*43.0*	33.7	*66.3*	*91.9*
Australian	1.2	1.2	—	—	1.2	*64.0*	18.6	5.8
British	4.7	11.6	*80.2*	—	*47.7*	—	9.3	—
Canada/NAm.	—	—	—	27.9	—	—	—	—
American	—	—	—	*65.1*	—	—	—	—
Other	—	—	—	2.4	—	—	—	—
LC	2.3	*75.6*	1.2	—	3.5	2.3	1.2	5.8
ULC/LMC	9.3	14.0	—	1.2	7.0	10.5	2.3	22.1
MC	*57.0*	3.5	8.1	32.6	19.8	*46.5*	30.2	*43.0*
UMC	15.1	—	40.7	*47.7*	*36.0*	23.3	*47.7*	18.6
UC	2.3	—	*45.3*	7.0	10.5	2.3	9.3	1.2
No data	14.0	7.0	4.7	11.6	23.3	15.1	9.3	9.3

in her speech (see Bayard, this volume). Despite this, the stigma is less pronounced in the solidarity scores (particularly in acceptability).

4. Cultivated NZE (Speaker 5) received little favour from the university respondents in either power or solidarity categories, consistently ranking low in all variables save class, income and education. Comments by subjects indicated that many of them (43%) judged that the speaker was a New Zealander, assuming (incorrectly) that she was trying to put on a 'posh' accent, and they clearly resented it (cf. low rank in pleasantness of accent).[8]

5. Acceptability exhibits the least variation of any of the variables, with all speakers except the uneducated broad NZE speaker forming a fairly tight group. Predictably, the other NZE accents (except cultivated) are on top, but Canadian and Australian rank just below them, and above RP.

6. Tables 4.4 and 4.5 present the perceptions of both the university and high-school groups of the speakers' national origin and social class. In general, the university subjects were quite accurate in estimating socio-economic level with the exception of the conservative broad NZE speaker (Speaker 8), who was ranked lower-middle to middle-middle class rather than professional/upper-middle class. This is in fact a fair assessment, as the speaker in question is quite conscious of his broad accent and prefers to retain it.

7. Predictably only a minority of university subjects were able to identify the North American accent as Canadian rather than American, even with North American counted as Canadian in scoring.

8. Perhaps equally predictably, a narrow plurality of the university group described the cultivated NZE speaker as British rather than New Zealand (48% versus 43%). Some 16% also took the RP speaker for a New Zealander, a figure closely comparable to the 15% result obtained by Huygens (1979: 43).

9. Surprisingly, however, 34% identified the general Australian speaker (Speaker 6) as a New Zealander, although his accent seemed to me a clear example of Mitchell & Delbridge's general Australian.[9] This suggests that Australian accents are not as perceptually distinct from NZE as most New Zealanders believe (a suggestion supported by the fact that many television commercials screened here are in fact made in Australia; Bell, 1987).

10. Finally, the results allow a few remarks about the oft-debated question of regional variation in NZE. As Bauer says,

TABLE 4.5 *High-school students' perceptions of speakers' national origin and social class (majority/plurality for each speaker in italics; Y = younger, O = older)*

	Spkr 1 MC NZE Y Gen.	Spkr 2 LC NZE Broad	Spkr 3 UMC RP Cons.	Spkr 4 MC Can NAm.	Spkr 5 UMC NZE Cult.	Spkr 6 MC Aust Gen.	Spkr 7 MC NZE O Gen.	Spkr 8 MC NZE Broad
Maori/PN	—	17.4	—	—	2.2	—	—	—
NZ	50.0	41.3	2.2	21.7	23.9	52.2	41.3	69.6
Australian	6.5	4.3	—	10.9	2.2	23.9	19.6	2.2
British	28.3	13.0	76.1	2.2	37.0	4.3	13.0	2.2
Canada/NAm.	2.2	—	—	8.7	—	—	2.2	2.2
American	2.2	—	2.2	34.8	2.2	—	4.3	2.2
Other/no data	10.9	23.9	19.6	21.8	32.6	19.6	19.6	21.7
LC	10.9	82.6	—	8.7	45.7	13.0	4.3	8.7
ULC/LMC	—	—	—	—	8.7	8.7	8.7	6.5
MC	69.6	10.9	6.5	39.1	19.6	45.7	39.1	43.5
UMC	10.9	—	13.0	28.3	4.3	21.7	30.4	23.9
UC	6.5	—	76.1	19.6	4.3	6.5	8.7	4.3
No data	2.2	6.5	4.3	4.3	17.4	4.3	8.7	13.0

TABLE 4.6 *University respondents' regional attributions of NZE speakers' accents (All NZE informants were raised in Dunedin)*

Speaker	N. Is.	S. Is.	Urban	Small town	Rural
UMC Cult NZE	4	—	1	—	—
MC Gen NZE (older)	2	2	1	—	—
MC Gen NZE (younger)	2	2	—	1	—
MC Broad NZE (older)	—	8	1	—	8
LC Broad NZE (younger)	4	4	4	1	3

N. Is. *versus* S. Is. mean correct = 57%; urban *versus* rural mean correct = 45%.

> Linguists have been very reluctant to allow any kind of regional variation within New Zealand except for the celebrated Southland /r/. . . . This might not be surprising, were it not for the fact that the vast majority of New Zealanders appear to be convinced that there are regional dialects . . . marked by pronunciation and not just by lexis. (1986: 10)

About one-half of the university respondents offered opinions on the region of origin of one or more of the speakers, and these are summarised for the NZE speakers in Table 4.6. The guesses for the two general NZE speakers (Speakers 1 and 7) are equally distributed across the North and South Islands, as they are with the innovative broad NZE accent (Speaker 2). The conservative broad NZE accent (Speaker 8) was viewed as South Island rural by most of those hazarding a guess. In fact, all five NZE speakers were raised in Dunedin, and the figure of only 57% correct for North compared with South Island and 45% for urban compared with rural suggests that the linguists are perhaps right and lay persons wrong in this case. I would suggest instead that the stereotypes that NZE speakers attribute to regional variation are social in origin (cf. Durkin, 1972, as summarised in Gordon & Deverson, 1985: 61). Despite this, I continue to have a tentative and unsupported impression that certain of the features I referred to as 'innovative' above are more widespread in North Island urban areas (Bayard, 1987: 19–20).

Results: the High School Sample

The questionnaires answered by the 46 high-school boys (mostly aged 14) were analysed using the techniques employed in the university sample, and produced a generally similar overall pattern (shown in Figure 4.3). However, there are a number of interesting specific differences between the two samples.

1. The RP accent is still the clear leader in power traits, but the gap between it and Canadian in second place is markedly narrower for most traits. The chief exception is class, where the high-school students made a very wide separation between the RP speaker and the five other preferred accents. However, the RP accent was equally clearly not liked, as indicated not only by its low ranking (sixth and seventh place in the solidarity variables), but by the many derisory comments supplied by the students. Abell's 1980 study, coincidentally also using fourth-form students, produced broadly comparable results in terms of the very similar variables employed in her questionnaire (six power and two solidarity variables). RP ranked highest in power variables, but well below all three NZE accents in friendliness and sense of humour. The high-school students appeared more conscious of the 'foreignness' of the RP accent. Only 2.2% assumed that the speaker was a New Zealander, as opposed to 16.3% of the university students.

2. The North American accent ranks highest in three of the four solidarity variables, although the slight difference between Canadian, Australian, and the upper three NZE accents is not significant (nor is the second-place acceptability ranking of Canadian closely behind the innovative general NZE and conservative broad NZE, tied for first place). The high ranking of the North American accent by high-school students may be a reflection of the tendency for the academically more able students (in the present case the university sample) to favour RP over American (Watts, 1981: 4). I could have tested this in more detail with the high-school group alone by requesting students' names for later assessment of their academic abilities. However, I chose not to do so, as I did not wish to inhibit spontaneous comments or judgements on the questionnaires. Obviously the question would merit further investigation.

3. In contrast to the university sample, the conservative educated broad NZE and younger general NZE accents rank alongside the older general NZE speaker rather than below him. In the case of acceptability, the first two accents have a slight (but not significant) hold on first place.

4. Although the Australian accent ranks only in the middle range of the power variables, it ranks second in sense of humour and pleasantness of accent (only fourth in the latter trait in the university sample), and is tied for third place in acceptability.

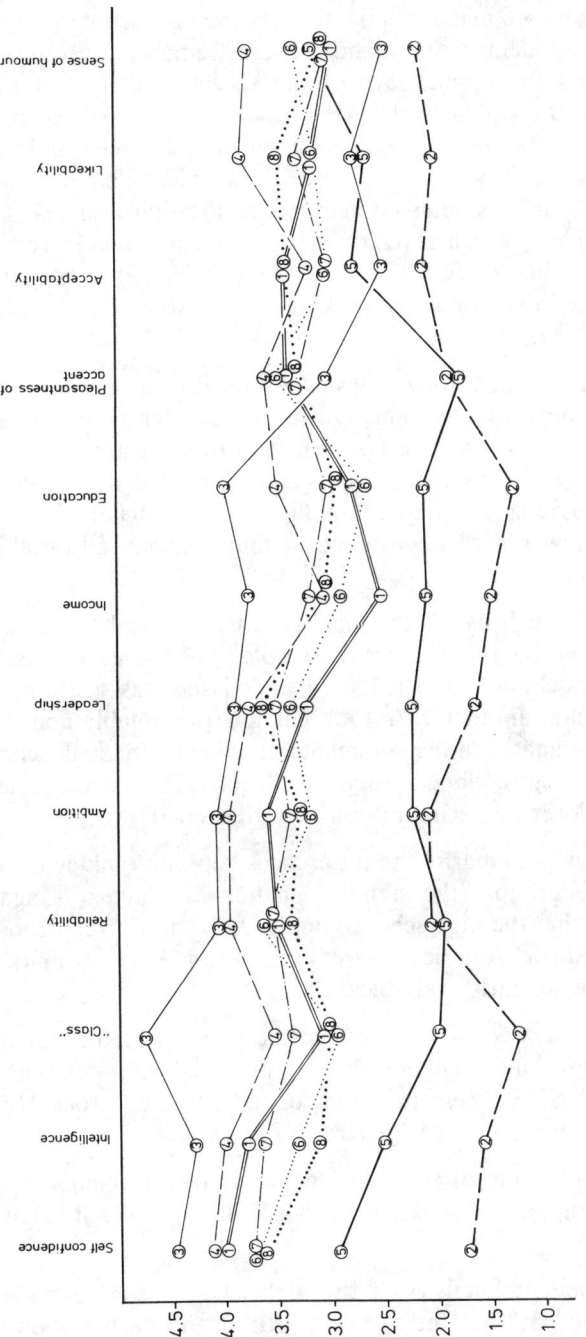

FIGURE 4.3 *Mean scores for accent evaluation variables: 46 fourth-form high-school students* (1 ═══, Young MC general NZ; 2— — —, LC broad NZ; 3 ────, UMC RP; 4 - - -, (U) MC Canadian; 5 ────, cultivated (UMC) NZ; 6 ···, UMC general Aust.; 7 - · - · -, old (U) MC general NZ; 8 ····, (U) MC broad NZ)

5. Tables 4.4 and 4.5 make it apparent that the high-school students are clearly less able to identify origin and class, presumably because their preconceptions about the implications of the accents are not yet fully developed. In marked contrast to the RP speaker, almost 33% assumed that the Canadian speaker was a New Zealander or Australian, and over half the group took the Australian as a New Zealander. This replicates the results of Giles' earlier studies on accent identification using 12- and 17-year-old respondents, which revealed a significant increase in correct accent identification with age (Giles & Powesland, 1975: 29). It may also be a reflection of the high solidarity rankings awarded to the Canadian and Australian speakers.

6. In startling contrast to Abell's 1980 results, it appears that cultivated NZE has obviously lost much of its mana as far as the present sample of high-school students are concerned. Although a plurality of 37% assumed Speaker 5 was British, almost half ranked her as lower class, and only 28% judged her to be middle class or higher. She was ranked consistently lower by the high-school sample in almost all variables save sense of humour.

7. The uneducated broad NZE speaker (2) kept the bottom-rung position assigned her by the university sample, but an even greater number of the high-school group (17%) assumed she was a Maori or Pacific Islander. Again, another 13% took her for (presumably non-RP) British. The negative images in the comments supplied by the high-school sample make depressing reading: 'dropout . . . slave . . . on the dole[10] . . . street kid . . . loser . . . scummy job . . . glue smeller'.

8. In Figure 4.4 I summarise the differences between ranking of the accents by the two groups (the nominal 'nationality' index is again omitted). It is clear that the high-school sample shows an overall drop in RP and rise in North American ranking, due mainly to marked discrepanciecs in the solidarity variables.

9. There is also a very marked drop in the power variables for the cultivated NZE accent, and a general drop in all variables for the older conservative general NZE accent in favour of the educated broad NZE and (except for solidarity) younger general NZE accents.

10. Finally, application of the same factor analysis technique used for the university sample produced a significantly different result (Figure 4.5).

Principal components analysis of the high-school means extracted three factors involving 66% of the variance. Although interpretation of

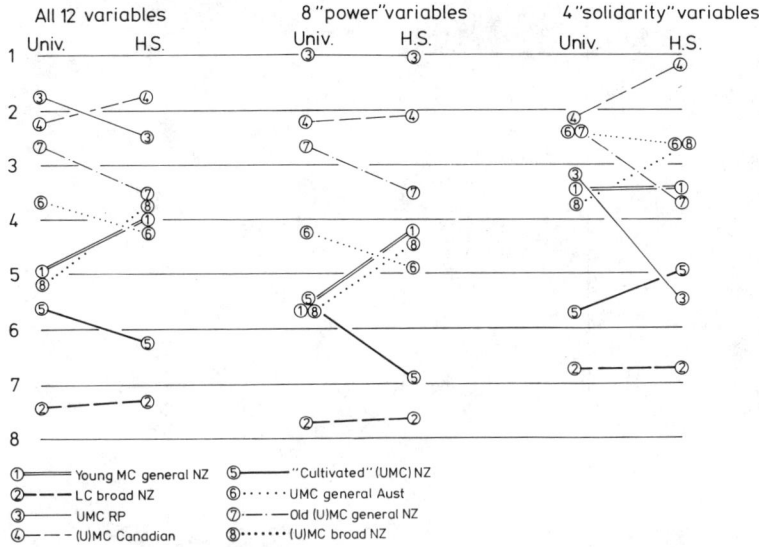

FIGURE 4.4 *Changes in average rank of speakers: university versus high-school students ('nationality' excluded)*

the factors is of course subjective, the vertical F2 axis here appears to be more purely economic (income and education) rather than socio-economic; the horizontal F1 axis encompasses most of the solidarity variables, plus what the students may view — however incorrectly — 'as the 'manly' traits of reliability, self-confidence, ambition, leadership and intelligence.[11] Pleasant accent is also far to the right, but negative in F2. F3 shows high loadings for likeability, acceptability and the class variable, which may perhaps be interpreted here as middle-classishness; i.e. non-poshness. In other words, the three positive poles of the factors may represent good personality (F1); good economic position (F2); and middle-classishness as opposed to being perceived as either 'posh' or a 'slave' (F3). Obviously this analysis requires further objective verification!

Conclusions

1. The two samples taken as a whole show a high measure of agreement in their attitudes toward the eight accents. The rank-order correlation between mean university scores and mean high-school scores for all 13 variables for each of the eight accents is $+0.80$ ($p < 0.001$).

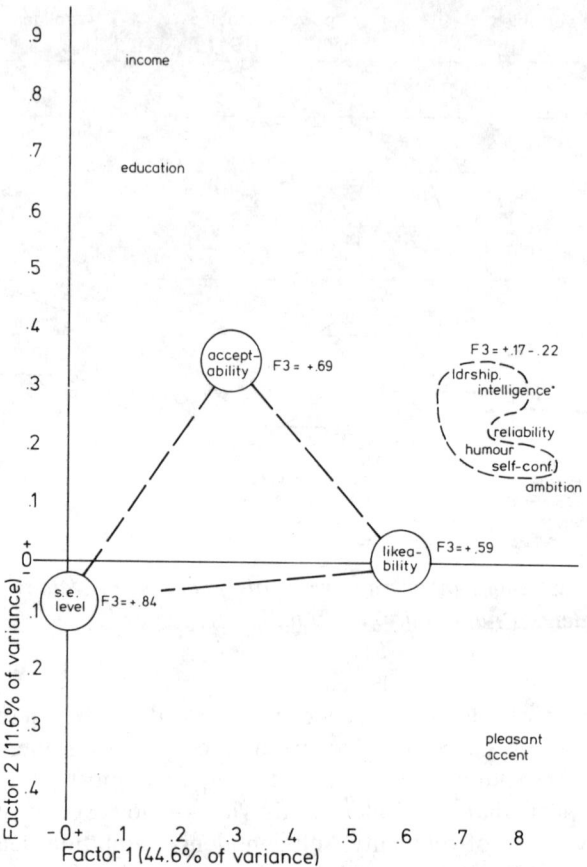

FIGURE 4.5 *Three-factor analysis of average scores for each of 46 fourth-form high-school students for all eight speakers. Factor 3 = 10.2% of variance (uncircled variables are not weighted in factor 3)*

This agrees well with similarly highly correlated evaluations of British and 'foreign' accents by differing age groups, based on both matched-guise speech samples and on accent names alone, carried out by Giles (summarised in Giles & Powesland, 1975: 28–32). Correlations of mean scores of university and high-school groups for the eight power variables averaged +0.84 ($p < 0.005$). As in Giles' British studies, the figure is predictably lower for the four 'solidarity' variables (+0.63, or +0.69 if nationality is included as well). The correlation between mean scores of the two groups of students for the eight accents is about the same (+0.603,

$p = 0.01$). The two groups were nearly unanimous in their evaluation of the RP and uneducated broad NZE accents (positive and negative respectively), and agreed closely on educated broad NZE as well. On the other hand, they differed very widely in their views of the Canadian and cultivated NZE accents, with the high-school students more strongly favouring the first and disliking the second.

2. The narrow age range in both samples precludes any investigation of its effect, although I feel certain that responses of older New Zealanders would contain significant differences.[12] However, some interesting sex differences were present in the evaluations. Within the university sample (heavily biased toward women, with 58 as opposed to 28 men), men ranked the pleasantness of accent of the younger innovative general NZE speaker significantly higher than women. With both broad NZE accents, cultivated NZE, and Canadian, women were significantly more sympathetic in their scoring of variables like leadership, intelligence, class and education. This trend is apparent even when both university and high-school samples are combined to produce a more even sex ratio. When the overall mean ratings (be they high or low) are dissected by respondent's gender, ANOVA analyses of mean scores show that female respondents are significantly *relatively* more favourable toward the cultivated NZE accent (and toward the conservative general NZE accent), while men rank the innovative general NZE accent relatively higher. Women also awarded significantly higher scores overall to income, education, acceptability and class variables. Of course it remains to be seen whether this trend holds true with more or less equal samples of both sexes from the same age and educational background.

3. It is difficult to make extensive specific comparisons between these results and those of earlier attitudinal studies in New Zealand due to the differences in emphasis and method mentioned in the first section of this article. Abell's 1980 study is certainly the closest, and her results will be referred to in some detail below. Huygens' 1979 study is less similar, as it relied on speech samples of highly variable length and phonological-lexical content, and was concerned with ethnicity as much as status. Although she also investigated 'social' *versus* 'personal' rankings (roughly paralleling the 'power/solidarity' axes used here), three of the four personal variables ('hard-working *versus* easy-going', 'self-confident *versus* shy', 'intelligent *versus* dull') appear to me to be more closely tied to the power axis, as shown in the factor analysis presented in Figure 4.2 above. Only the 'warm *versus* cold' variable would seem to relate more to solidarity (roughly equating with this study's 'likeability' variable). Nonetheless, there are some general similarities in the results of her study

and this one. Upper-status English accents (= RP) scored highest in social ranking, but unlike this study near-RP Pakeha accents (= my cultivated NZE) scored equally high, although the absence of any phonetic description of the accents in the earlier study makes more detailed comment difficult. 'Maori' and 'lower-class Pakeha' accents rated lowest in social ratings, but somewhat above 'lower-class Pakeha' in personal ratings. Judging from Vaughan & Huygens' mean ratings (this volume, Figure 3.1), rankings in the personal scale were much more closely spaced over a narrow range, similar to the narrower spread encountered with solidarity variables in this study.

There are several more general conclusions that I think can be drawn from the results of the present study:

1. Despite my earlier statement that 'RP will continue to command more prestige here than NAm [North American] *relatively speaking*, but will continue an overall decline *vis-à-vis* the local accent' (Bayard, 1987: 25), it seems clear that RP continues to have the considerable overt prestige in New Zealand evidenced in Huygens' and Abell's earlier studies. However, it seems equally clear if these two samples are any guide that North American accents command almost as much overt prestige as RP, and more than any NZE accent. In terms of covert prestige or solidarity, North American accents rank over RP and most NZE accents.

2. It is obviously plausible to assume that the high ranking of the North American accent is largely due to media influences, television in particular. I have argued this elsewhere (Bayard, 1987: 21–5), but it is devilishly difficult to establish firm objective evidence for causality (see Chambers, 1981 for a careful but inconclusive attempt to do just this for a phonetic change taking place in 'Canadian raising'). There are certainly signs — as yet sporadic — that American influence is being reflected in the orthography of written English here. I have encountered advertisements for 'color' prints, and local primary school teachers have told me they no longer bother to correct ⟨-or⟩ spellings. Whatever the causes, there seems a fair chance that North American will equal or even exceed the prestige currently held by the RP accent in a decade or two, although I would not like to gamble a large sum on the outcome.

3. It seems quite clear that some amount of negative prestige or 'colonial inferiority' still attaches to even general NZE as far as overt prestige or power is concerned, rather as with Canadian French *vis-à-vis* both English and Continental French (see Giles & Powesland, 1975: 55 ff). Moreover, both North American and Australian accents rank as high as

'approved' NZE accents in the solidarity variables. Apparently disparaging attitudes toward NZE find overt expression in comments on the NZE accent recently extracted from seventh-form examination scripts of high-school students aged 17–18 by Deverson (1988). Indeed, contrary to Huygens' findings (1979: 44), only a very few respondents took the broad NZE accents to be Australian (1.2% and 4.3% for the uneducated speaker, and 5.8% and 2.2% for the educated; see Tables 4.4 and 4.5). It thus appears likely that NZE speakers are still looking abroad for prestige models rather than to their own accent. It remains to be seen if New Zealand can adopt its own *overtly* standard accent as appears to have happened in Australia, or whether, as Bell succinctly put it, NZE speakers will simply fall 'out of the British frying pan into the American fire' (1982: 254), retaining the NZE accent as a covert standard only.

4. Cultivated NZE among at least these two groups appears not to have the prestige usually claimed for it (e.g. by Gordon & Deverson, 1985: 57). Forty-six per cent of the high-school sample identified it as lower class. This possible trend away from an RP acrolect is also suggested by the replacement in the 1970s of RP-like accents for a general NZE-RP compromise on television and many radio stations (Table 4.2; Bayard, 1987: 24).[13] This seeming decline in the prestige of cultivated NZE (despite its continuing use — rather than RP — by many national newsreaders) is clearly the most striking difference between my findings and Abell's 1980 study, and could be due to several factors. First, there was obviously some degree of paralinguistic variation in the speakers used in both studies: e.g. my hesitant Speaker 2 and the greater fluency of Abell's broad NZE speaker *vis-à-vis* the apparently nervous general NZE speaker (1980: 59). This latter may well account for the surprising lack of any significant differences in the ranks assigned them by Abell's informants. Both were equally well below the cultivated NZE speaker in the power variables. Secondly, while my sample was entirely made up of state-school students, Abell's sample included 42 students from single-sex private schools as well as 47 state-school pupils. However, given the very slight differences present in her two sub-samples (1980: 64–7) this is not a likely explanation. Finally, there is the distinct possibility that attitudes have shifted among this age group during the eight years or so which separate the two studies. However, further testing would certainly be necessary to confirm this.

5. Uneducated broad NZE accents or registers appear to be the most highly stigmatised, and appear to be associated by a significant minority of respondents in this study with a stereotype of lower-class Polynesians, either unemployed or employed in menial jobs.

Unfortunately, as a social anthropologist colleague remarked to me, the stereotype is a widespread reality in contemporary New Zealand society. On the other hand, the incorrect assumptions that this speaker was ethnically Maori or Polynesian, coupled with Huygens' earlier findings that only 25% of her respondents could identify speakers as specifically Maori (1979: 43), cast some doubt on the existence of a clearly definable 'Maori' variety of NZE.

6. Finally, looking to the future, one might ask if a specifically Australasian 'Pacific English' is currently developing under the heavy and constant influence of *Pax Americana*, or whether such influence is a worldwide occurrence. I would guess that from what little I know of the British situation that the second alternative is the more likely, at least as far as lexicon is concerned. One of my non-NZE reference samples is an RP-speaking English 'public' schoolboy who says LOOtenant, SKEDule, MYgraine, and med-i-cine, in marked contrast to my older RP samples.

However, the results of this study cannot begin to answer such questions, and a great deal of work remains to be done with further samples to arrive at definitive answers. I look forward to seeing the results of similar studies carried out with a wider age range of Pakeha, Maori and Pacific Island New Zealanders in the northern urban centres. I suspect that even my younger Dunedin respondents may be fairly conservative when compared with Auckland, Wellington and Christchurch.

Notes

1. I am grateful to Paul Armfelt and my wife, Daisy N.H.L. Bayard, for their help in administering the tests, and to Martin Fisher for providing the illustrations. I would also like to express my gratitude to the teacher, Mr John Cox, for allowing me to carry out the high-school tests, and of course to all the high-school and university students who agreed to participate.
2. 'Fred Dagg' as portrayed by entertainer John Clarke was a popular comic television character of the 1970s, representing the archetypal broad-NZE-speaking farmer; Dougal Stevenson is a television personality and former TVNZ newsreader whose accent approximates RP (see Table 4.2).
3. I must admit to a measure of difficulty in interpreting some of Hall's phonetic descriptions.
4. In Clarke's recent portrayal of another archetypal rural NZE speaker in the film *Footrot Flats*, his residence in Australia over the last decade also occasionally shows in his accent.
5. In the 1986 census the median income in New Zealand was $10,663 (male $15,119; female $7,575); mean figures were not available (Department of Statistics, personal communication).
6. This technique, widely used in the social sciences, attempts to fit the matrix

of correlations present between the different variables into a number of vectors, or 'factors', which best explain their overall relationships to each other. I am particularly grateful to Dr S.H. Ng of the University of Otago Psychology Department for suggesting this approach, and for valuable help in designing the questionnaire and test routines.

7. Interestingly, the speaker in question is physically Polynesian in appearance, but is the adopted child of Pakeha parents and ethnically Pakeha. Respondents were of course not aware of her physical appearance.

8. Having known this particular speaker for twenty years, I can state that this is definitely not the case. Instead, the speaker had very successfully assimilated the rules of 'proper' speech in vogue here during the pre-war years as expressed in prescriptive texts like that of Wall (1941). Very few NZE features are present in her accent aside from a slightly raised /e/ and final /-i/ in about one-half of *happY* contexts; however, these traces were apparently enough to enable 43% of the university subjects to identify her as a NZE speaker.

9. I am grateful to Margaret Maclagan for confirming this evaluation for me.

10. As far as the students' teacher could ascertain, 'slave' derives from the *Roots* television series, and was apparently a current slang term for a powerless no-hoper. I should also note parenthetically that in the comments 'dole' was almost always spelt 'doll', a probable sign that this merger (Bayard, 1987: 5) is alive and well in this group of young NZE speakers.

11. Unfortunately, considerable sexism is evidenced by the many deprecatory remarks made about Speakers 2, 3 and 5, ('snobby housewife, prostitute, gutter sweep', etc.) and guesses on the occupation of all four of the female speakers.

12. A sampling of opinion obtained from a group of older NZE speakers obtained while carrying out final editing of this paper confirms this assumption; results will be discussed in a subsequent paper.

13. See also Bell (1982; 1983; 1985) for RP-like/NZE contrasts in radio styles and some US stylistic influences on New Zealand newspapers.

References

ABELL, MARCIA 1980, A study of sociolinguistic stereotyping by fourth form students in Christchurch. Unpublished MA thesis. Christchurch: University of Canterbury.

BAUER, LAURIE 1986, Notes on New Zealand English phonetics and phonology. Expanded version of paper published in *English World Wide* 7 (2), 225–58.

BAYARD, DONN 1987, Class and change in New Zealand English: a summary report. *Te Reo* 30, 3–36.

— 1988, Variation in and attitudes toward New Zealand English: a quantitative approach. *New Zealand English Newsletter* 2, 13–16.

— Social constraints on the phonology of New Zealand English. In JENNY CHESHIRE (ed.) *English Around the World: Sociolinguistic Perspectives.* Cambridge: Cambridge University Press. To appear.

BELL, ALLAN 1982, This isn't the BBC: colonialism in New Zealand English. *Applied Linguistics* 3 (3), 246–58.

— 1983, Broadcast news as a language standard. *International Journal of the Sociology of Language* 40, 29–42.

— 1985, One rule of news English: geographical, social, and historical spread. *Te Reo* 28, 95–117.

— 1987, Responding to your audience: taking the initiative. Paper presented at the 7th New Zealand Linguistics Conference, Dunedin.

BROWN, ROGER and GILMAN, ALBERT 1960, The pronouns of power and solidarity. In THOMAS SEBEOK (ed.) *Style in Language* (pp. 253–76). Cambridge, Mass.: Massachusetts Institute of Technology Press.

CHAMBERS, J.K. 1981, The Americanization of Canadian Raising. In CARRIE S. MASEK, ROBERTA A. HENDRICK and MARY FRANCES MILLER (eds) *Papers from the Parasession on Language and Behavior* (pp. 20–35). Chicago: Chicago Linguistic Society.

DEVERSON, TONY 1988, Editor's note: 'A rather funny accent'. *New Zealand English Newsletter* 2, 2–3.

DURKIN, MARY 1972, A study of the pronunciation, oral grammar and vocabulary of West Coast school children. Unpublished MA thesis. Christchurch: University of Canterbury.

GILES, HOWARD and BOURHIS, RICHARD Y. 1976, Methodological issues in dialect perception: some social psychological perspectives. *Anthropological Linguistics* 18 (7), 294–304.

GILES, HOWARD and POWESLAND, PETER F. 1975, *Speech Style and Social Evaluation*. London: Academic Press.

GORDON, ELIZABETH 1983a, New Zealand English pronunciation: an investigation into some early written records. *Te Reo* 26, 29–42.

— 1983b, 'The flood of impure vocalisation' — a study of attitudes towards New Zealand speech. *New Zealand Speech-Language Therapists Journal* 38 (1), 16–29.

GORDON, ELIZABETH and DEVERSON, TONY 1985, *New Zealand English: an Introduction to New Zealand Speech and Usage*. Auckland: Heinemann.

HALL, MOIRA 1976, An acoustic analysis of New Zealand vowels. Unpublished MA Thesis. Auckland: University of Auckland.

HAMILTON, CYNTHIA 1977, North England speech: some indications of complex attitudes and values. Unpublished term paper. Wellington: Victoria University.

HORVATH, BARBARA M. 1985, *Variation in Australian English: the Sociolects of Sydney*. Cambridge: Cambridge University Press.

HUYGENS, INGRID 1979, Sociolinguistic stereotyping in New Zealand. Unpublished MA thesis. Auckland: University of Auckland.

HUYGENS, INGRID and VAUGHAN, GRAHAM M. 1983, Language attitudes, ethnicity and social class in New Zealand. *Journal of Multilingual and Multicultural Development* 4 (2–3), 207–23.

MACLAGAN, MARGARET 1982, An acoustic study of New Zealand vowels. *New Zealand Speech Therapists Journal* 37 (1), 20–6.

MITCHELL, A.G. and DELBRIDGE, ARTHUR 1965, *The Speech of Australian Adolescents: a Survey*. Sydney: Angus & Robertson.

WALL, ARNOLD 1941, *New Zealand English: a Guide to the Correct Pronunciation of English with Special Reference to New Zealand Conditions and Problems* (2nd edn). Christchurch: Whitcombe & Tombs.

WATTS, NOEL 1981, The attitudes of New Zealanders to speakers with foreign accents. *Rostra* 16 (1), 3–5.

5 Pidgin English and Pidgin Maori in New Zealand[1]

ROSS CLARK

Is there, or was there once, a distinctive New Zealand form of 'Pidgin English'? A recent survey of pidgin and creole languages contains a reference to 'New Zealand P[idgin] E[nglish]', as well as to a 'Maori Pidgin English, no longer spoken, similar to Neo-Melanesian' (Romaine, 1988: 94, 318, 321). Another such book (Mühlhäusler, 1986) uses as its cover illustration a drawing, from Cook's first voyage, of a Maori and an Englishman exchanging a crayfish for a handkerchief, thus at least implying that pidgin was present in the earliest Maori–European contacts. Neither of these books is a primary source, however, and it appears that all recent references to New Zealand pidgin ultimately trace back to Sidney J. Baker's book *New Zealand Slang* (1941) and its ninth chapter, entitled '"Pidgin" English in New Zealand'.

Baker's chapter is largely devoted to English loanwords in Maori. These have nothing to do with 'pidgin', except in so far as the term is used disparagingly by non-linguists to refer to a wide variety of types of language 'mixing' and 'corruption'. Regarding pidgin in the sense of a simplified contact language, Baker states:

> . . . this sort of speech has never had currency in New Zealand. We have a few examples recorded in the early days, it is true, but since the Maori has been quick to master the complications of English syntax he has rarely had to adopt the circumlocutions of Pidgin to make himself understood. When circumlocutions have been adopted they cannot be regarded as having assumed the status of a more or less standardized jargon between native and white man. (Baker, 1941: 73)

Baker's 'few examples recorded in the early days' are taken from the narrative of J.L. Nicholas (1817), the only primary source which has

97

hitherto been noted in the literature. It is clear, however, that Baker is anxious to minimise the prevalence of pidgin in New Zealand, out of what he terms 'natural respect for the intelligence of the Maori race' (Baker, 1941: 73).

In the present paper, we will not be encumbered by the assumption that the use of pidgin is an indication of defective intelligence. In the following discussion, 'pidgin' will broadly mean any simplified language used in contact between speakers of different languages. Later I will consider a more restricted sense of the term and whether it can be applied to the New Zealand case.

An examination of accounts of Maori–European contact in the late eighteenth and early nineteenth century shows that the speech recorded by Nicholas was not some brief and local aberration, but part of a general pattern of language use, involving pidginised varieties of both English and Maori, throughout the first century of European involvement in New Zealand. This pattern in turn parallels the history of language contact documented in other parts of the South Pacific at the same period (Clark, 1979–80). This study will deal primarily with the evidence from the time of the first European visitors (1769–77) and the pre-colonial period (1790–1840), when pidgin is most abundantly documented. I will conclude with some more speculative ideas about its subsequent history.

The First European Visitors

The Dutch navigator Abel Tasman was the first European known to have sighted New Zealand, in 1642, but he never went ashore. His contact with the Maori at sea was brief and ended in violence; nothing of linguistic interest is recorded. Our history of language contact begins, therefore, with the three voyages of the Englishman Captain James Cook, from 1769 to 1777. During the same period there were two groups of French visitors, under Jean de Surville in 1769 and Marion du Fresne in 1772. From scattered comments in the journals and published narratives of the explorers, we may reconstruct the main features of the language situation during these early contacts.

Non-verbal communication

Certain types of action, such as a physical threat (with or without a weapon), beckoning to 'come here', presentation of a gift, and so on, were probably universal enough to be clear to both sides even without any understanding of the accompanying words. The full possibilities of pantomime would also have been exploited. Maoris are often reported to have imparted some message by signs:

> When we took leave they followed us to our boat, seeing the musquets lying a Cross the stern they made signs for them to be taken away which when done they came along side and even assisted us to launch her. (Cook, II: 125)

Likewise, expressions such as 'made them understand' in the following suggest a difficult and largely non-verbal mode of communication:

> The natives came and took us into a ravine where they showed us trees which were nowhere near the size we required. We made them understand that they were not nearly long enough. One of the natives promised to take us another day to a place where there were finer ones, making signs that it was in the spot that they got wood for their beautiful canoes. (Marion, n.d.: 151)

At times more elaborate aids to communication were devised:

> We made two pieces of paper, to represent the two ships, and drew the figure of the Sound on a larger piece; then drawing the two ships into the Sound, and out of it again, as often as they had touched at and left it, including our last departure, we stopped a while, and at last proceeded to bring our ship in again; but the natives interrupted us, and taking up the paper which represented the Adventure, they brought it into the harbour, and drew it out again, counting on their fingers how many moons she had been gone. (Cook, II: 576, n. 5)

When in Rome

In order to make themselves more fully understood, the Europeans took it for granted that they would have to speak Maori, the language of the country. There are no references in these early accounts to any Maoris encountered who could speak English or French (whether pidgin or otherwise), nor to Europeans speaking to them in these languages.[2] This generalisation needs to be qualified by two documented exceptions; but these exceptions, taken with the general case, will illuminate the implicit rule of language choice, which might be termed the 'When in Rome Principle'. New Zealand was a Maori domain, and Europeans accepted the need to learn the Maori language while visiting there. Maoris who sailed away in European ships, on the other hand, became visitors in a European domain, and it is in just these cases that we have the earliest evidence of their learning European languages.

On 31st December 1769, at Doubtless Bay, de Surville took a Maori man, 'Naquinovi', prisoner in reprisal for the theft of a French boat. The *St Jean Baptiste* sailed away the same evening, and this man remained on the ship until his death a few months later. Little is recorded about him, but there is some evidence that he began to learn French (Surville, n.d.: 85, 132, 173). Two Maori youths, 'Tiarooa' and 'Coaa' were 'bought' by the Tahitian Omai at Queen Charlotte Sound in February 1777. They accompanied him when he left the ship in November of that year, at Raiatea in the Society Islands, by which time it was noted that they 'had already learned to speak English so as to be able to express their hopes and fears' (Rickman, 1781: 184; Cook, III: 292n.).

Pakeha Maori

The European visitors recorded various Maori words, and occasionally phrases or sentences.[3] This gives us some idea of how they perceived the language; and, by inference, of how they spoke it. The explorers' Maori deviated lexically and grammatically from normal Maori in certain ways which are characteristic of pidgins.[4]

The number of words used was very limited: du Clesmeur gives a list of 23 Maori words which he says 'are the only ones we understood the meaning of' (Marion, n.d.: 35). While this may be an exaggeration, the total number of words recorded by all the early visitors is less than 200.

Meanings of words were sometimes distorted, presumably as a result of misunderstanding in a particular situation where two or more different meanings would be appropriate. For example, Maori *pai* 'good, to be pleased' and *kino* 'bad, to dislike' are recorded by the French as *pays* 'friends', *paye* 'peace', and *quinos* 'enemies'. In the same vocabularies we find *éouaye* 'to drink' and *taro* 'to eat' from Maori *wai* 'water' and *taro* 'taro (Colocasia esculenta)' (Marion, n.d.: 35, 339).

The particles which mark grammatical categories and relations in Maori are commonly omitted. If present, they are most often misinterpreted as part of the noun or verb with which they are associated. Thus

Cook's frequently used *hippa* 'fortified village' derives from Maori *paa* with agglutination of the nominal specifier *he*. (*He paa* would be a complete sentence meaning 'It is a fortified village'.) Stative verbs are often combined with the particle *ka* as in *carreca* 'good' from *Ka reka* 'It is sweet' (Marion, n.d.: 35).

The few examples of phrases and sentences recorded in these early sources also show deviations from normal Maori syntax. Sometimes they are telegraphic juxtapositions, with no explicit connection between the elements: *A popo ica* 'tomorrow — fish' (Marion, n.d.: 295). More clearly connected sentences sometimes have subject-first word order, where the normal Maori sentence is verb-first. One example is unusually well documented, since it relates to the death of Marion du Fresne:

> As I got nearer I saw that he was crying as he said: *Tacoury maté Marion*, which meant 'Tacoury has killed Marion'. I did not understand what he was saying at first because I was persuaded that Mr Marion was on board the vessel, however he repeated the same words several times so that I thought that the chief was trying to warn me that Tacoury planned to kill Mr Marion. (Marion, n.d.: 179)

Note that the sentence was repeated several times, which makes it unlikely that it was misheard. Subject and object are indicated by position relative to the verb, as in French or English, rather than by case-marking prepositions as in Maori. The verb *mate* 'die, dead' is used as a transitive 'kill'; and the verb is unmarked for tense, aspect or mood, which makes it impossible, as the writer notes, to tell whether the speaker is reporting a past event or warning about a future one.[5]

A final pidgin feature found in these early European records of Maori is reduplication. The use of reduplicated forms in contact situations may arise from a universal tendency to repeat things for greater certainty of understanding (Ferguson & DeBose, 1977: 106). While reduplication plays some part in Maori grammar, the European writers reduplicate forms which are not (or cannot be) reduplicated in Maori. Thus Maori *paakee* 'rough outer cloak', *patu* 'weapon' and *puu* 'tube, gun' are found in Cook's journals as *buggy-buggy*, *patoo-patoo* and *poupou*.

The Pre-Colonial Period

After Cook's third visit, there was a hiatus of about fifteen years before outside contact with New Zealand was established again. The next period of language contact begins with the resumption of visits in the early 1790s and ends in the 1840s, when a British colony was proclaimed and large-scale white settlement began.

Europeans visited New Zealand during this period to hunt seals and whales, to gather flax and timber, and to provision ships with fresh water, pork and potatoes. Maoris in the Bay of Islands and other areas of frequent contact traded these commodities for muskets, tobacco, cloth and tools. Only a few scattered foreigners settled ashore in New Zealand, but the first European 'town' at Kororareka in the Bay of Islands, grew up in the 1820s, principally as a shore station for transient whalers. These decades also saw the arrival of the first missionaries (1814), who would eventually establish a standard written form of Maori and publish grammars, dictionaries and other books.

New Zealand during this period was still overwhelmingly a monolingual Maori-speaking country, and the use of more or less pidginised Maori by Europeans continued (Savage (1807) is a particularly rich source). From the earliest years, however, we read of Maoris who could speak English to some degree. This was an unusual enough accomplishment that a note of explanation is often added. Sailing on European ships continued to be the most common way in which Maoris learned English, but now they might also acquire the language in the linguistic enclaves established by missionaries and whalers:

['Mrs Goshore'] From the circumstance of having cohabited with a Captain Jones, the master of a vessel from Port Jackson, who had her on board with him for some weeks, she had picked up a good deal of our language, and become much attached to Europeans. (Nicholas, 1817: I, 211)

['George'] . . . had lived as servant with the missionaries, and understood English pretty well . . . (Cruise, 1824: 122)

['Nayti', interpreter aboard the *Tory*] . . . a Maori who had been taken to Europe in the French whaler *Mississippi*, after whaling in Cloudy Bay in 1836. (McNab, 1913: 347)

The earliest documented case is that of 'Toogee' and 'Hoodoo', two men abducted off the Northland coast in 1793, with the intention that they would teach the English at Norfolk Island how to work flax. Governor King, who accompanied them on their return to New Zealand, comments:

> It may be expected . . . that after a six months acquaintance between us and the New Zealanders, we should not be ignorant of each other's language. Myself and some of the officers . . . could make our ideas known and tolerably well understood by them. They too, by intermixing what English words they knew with what we knew of their language, could make themselves sufficiently understood by us. (Collins, 1798: 525)

The lexically mixed nature of the language described here is illustrated in the speech of 'Toogee', as given by King: *etiketica no eteka* 'a chief never deceives' (Collins, 1798: 528). The first and last words can be explained as Maori *tiketike* 'high, important'[6] and *teka* 'lie, deceive', with agglutinated particles; but the negative can only be English. As with other short utterances in the literature, we are unsure here whether to classify this as pidgin English or pidgin Maori.

The question might be raised whether such a distinction needs to be made. Perhaps we should really be talking of a single 'New Zealand Pidgin' whose vocabulary could be either English-derived or Maori-derived according to the situation and the speaker's experience. But there are some cases where speakers are quite sure what they are speaking. Savage, for example, thinks himself a 'tolerably apt scholar' of Maori (Savage, 1807: 73), yet he has his Maori companion, 'Moyhanger', saying things like *Tungata nue nue kikie* 'That man has plenty to eat', (Savage, 1807: 109). Moyhanger's language is lexically pure Maori, but radically pidginised in its grammar.[7] We must assume that Savage himself spoke this way, and believed he was speaking Maori. On the other side, there are cases where the speaker is manifestly speaking English:

> Then . . . why you not hang Captain —— ? . . . Captain, he come to New Zealand, he come ashore, and *tihi* all my potatoes — you hang up Captain ———. (Nicholas, 1817: I, 11)

Here the Maori speaker, in the midst of an English discourse, has recourse to a single Maori word (*taahae* 'steal') to supplement his English vocabulary. Given the possibility of this type of code-mixing (*ad hoc* transfer of a single word), as well as code-switching (shifting from one language to the other over longer stretches) and lexical borrowing (permanent transfer), it is to be expected that short quotations may sometimes be difficult to assign to the English or the Maori side, even if speakers were always sure at any given moment which language they were trying to speak.

Maori English

Although Nicholas is the best single source, there is in fact quite a lot of Maori English recorded by writers of this period. Whereas examples of pidgin Maori rarely extend beyond three or four words at a time, pidgin English is sometimes quoted at paragraph length. Lexically and grammatically, it deviates from standard English in certain ways that parallel the deviations of Pakeha Maori.

The vocabulary appears to be very small, though it is hard to be precise about its size, since no lists are provided corresponding to the Maori vocabularies of the early writers. The total number of different words in the early English texts is well under 200.

Meanings of individual words may be distorted. A particularly well attested example is English *cook*, which in New Zealand pidgin assumes the meaning of 'slave, person of low status':

> He assisted us in rowing the boat; but reflecting at intervals on the rank he held among his countrymen, . . . he would several times shake his head, and cry out against this indignity, by saying that he was 'rungateeda [Maori *rangatira* 'noble'], and that workee workee was no good for rungateeda, only for cookee cookee . . .'. (Nicholas, 1817: 227)

D'Urville in 1824 gives a clear explanation of the origin of this word:

> In the language of the New Zealanders the real word for a slave or prisoner was *tao reka-reka* and for a servant *wari*. Nowadays they are more frequently known by the name of *kouki*, which is a corruption of the English word *cook*, because the chief work of the slaves is to prepare their masters' food and to cook dishes for them. (Sharp, 1971: 38)

The grammatical apparatus of English, including both inflections (for number, tense, etc.) and independent words such as copula, auxiliaries, prepositions and conjunctions, is largely dispensed with, and we find the typical pidgin concatenation of invariant lexical morphemes:[8]

> English man swear much. (Havard-Williams, 1961: 41)

> Mr Nicholas no good, no good, shoot Mr Kora-kora. (Nicholas, 1817: 423)

Good-bye, father, me no see you again. (Barton, 1927: 306)

Me gentleman! (Cruise, 1824: 164)

Word order in pidgin English does not seem to have been influenced by Maori in the same way that pidgin Maori was influenced by English. Subject–verb–object is the normal order in the sentences documented. However, there may possibly be a reflection of the sentence-initial position of negatives in Maori in the following:

no more tiki tiki 'we shall not see him again'. (Barton, 1927: 312)

no Mr Butler go back to New Zealand, very bad. (Barton, 1927: 372)

Finally, reduplication occurs in pidgin English as well as pidgin Maori. English *cook* and *work* are shown in reduplicated forms in the above examples, and we may also note a few words which have become established in standard Maori in this form: *pukapuka* 'book', *rakiraki* 'duck' and *nanenane* 'goat' (*nanny*).

Broken, Jargon, Pidgin

Having used the term 'pidgin' rather casually up to now, I would like to consider how the New Zealand case fits into a more precise terminology for contact languages. The word 'broken' is commonly used for language which is seriously and persistently deviant from the standard in lexicon and grammar. Such 'broken English' or 'broken Maori' is typical of the earliest stages of second-language learning. It may sometimes happen that a 'broken tradition' develops — one learner may pass on deviant features to another, and access to the standard language may be limited enough that this is not corrected. Correction is even less likely if native speakers themselves adjust to the broken language of the learners and speak it back to them.

If such a tradition develops we may speak of a 'jargon'. Such a system is perceived differently by the two sides. Learners may not be aware that what they are speaking (and hearing) is non-standard, as with Savage's version of Maori mentioned above. Native speakers, on the other hand, will think of the jargon as 'foreigner talk', a special style or register appropriate for communication with alien peoples (Romaine, 1988: 76ff).

The term 'pidgin' is reserved by some linguists for a language which has undergone a further development. As first suggested by Whinnom (1971), if a jargon becomes the regular means of communication *used by non-native speakers among themselves*, it will achieve a new degree of coherence and stability, a stage at which it must be recognised as a new language. Such a situation existed on the plantations of the southwest Pacific (Queensland, Samoa, Fiji) in the late nineteenth century when plantation workers from many different language areas of Melanesia found themselves with no other common language but jargon English. From this situation developed Melanesian Pidgin, which continues to function as the *lingua franca* of multilingual Vanuatu, the Solomon Islands and Papua New Guinea. In New Zealand and the rest of Polynesia, by contrast, there was only a single indigenous language in each group of islands. While jargon English was used everywhere that whalers and traders went, the indigenous people had no reason to use it among themselves. Whinnom's theory thus accounts for the fact that (with the historically unique exception of Hawaii) nothing comparable to Melanesian Pidgin developed in Polynesia.

In this strict sense, therefore, New Zealand never had a pidgin. There is ample evidence, however, that for both Maori and English there was a jargon tradition in which speakers on both sides participated. We have seen that a jargon Maori was spoken by the earliest explorers and continued in use well into the nineteenth century. Almost all the quoted examples, however, are represented as spoken by Maoris. If a writer (such as Savage) represents Maoris as speaking jargon Maori, we can be quite sure that what he spoke to them was least as deviant. But how do we know that the Maoris were not actually speaking fully grammatical Maori, which has been misrepresented by the Pakeha writer as jargon? Fortunately we have explicit comments on this point by a few writers, William Richard Wade observed in 1838 that:

> The Ngapuhi, or Bay of Islands Natives, who live with the Missionaries in the northern stations, too commonly fall into the lazy habit of speaking to you after your own fashion, rather than be at the trouble of constantly correcting you. (Wade, 1842: 102)

The same complaint is made by William Mortimer Baines, who arrived in 1850:

> One trouble for the learner is that the natives will persist in talking easy 'pigeon' Maori to new 'pakehas'; perhaps that is one reason

why so few Europeans talk Maori well, though many know enough of the language for ordinary purposes, such as buying and selling. (Baines, 1874: 115)

Still later, the printer and lexicographer Colenso, with half a century's experience in the colony, made the more general statement:

> Several Europeans now speak the New Zealand language; few, however, correctly; still fewer idiomatically; and scarcely any in such a way as to be wholly grateful (*reka*) to a native's ear . . . It is also remarkable how very soon natives get to know the true mental calibre of a white man; to gauge, as it were, his knowledge of their language and of themselves, and to say and act accordingly; setting aside for the time, with him, their own true grammar, pronunciation and idiom, while he does not perceive or suspect it. Not a few of our old missionaries, officials and settlers, are thus continually being politely treated by them . . . (Colenso, 1868: 392)

It is clear, then, that Maoris participated in the jargon situation by using a simplified, foreigner-talk version of their own language, at least with Pakehas whose linguistic skills they believed required it.

With jargon English, likewise, most of the quoted speakers are Maoris. (All the books were written by Pakehas, who usually do not quote their own speech directly.) But it can hardly be doubted that with Maoris who spoke some English, Europeans adjusted to some of their errors, as well as making use of any Maori words they might happen to know. D'Urville refers on three occasions to conversing with Maoris in 'a mixture of New Zealand and debased English' (D'Urville, n.d.: 117, 145, 201). And in the following we have at least a rough sketch of a conversation:

> . . . I told him in the language of vulgar ridicule, that the taboo taboo was all gammon . . . he replied that 'it was no gammon at all; New Zealand man' said he, 'say that Mr Marsden's *crackee crackee* (preaching) of a Sunday, is all *gammon*.' 'No, no,' I rejoined, 'that is not *gammon*, that is *miti*,' (good.) 'Well then', retorted the tenacious reasoner, 'if your *crackee crackee* is no gammon, our taboo taboo is no gammon'. (Nicholas, 1817: I, 274)

The New Zealand jargon English tradition was the local form of a widespread network of traditions which I have termed South Seas Jargon

(Clark, 1979–80). Related forms are well documented in the early nineteenth century literature from such places as Hawaii, eastern Micronesia, Tahiti and Fiji. South Seas Jargon spread to southern Melanesia with the sandalwood trade about 1840, and eventually provided the raw material from which Melanesian Pidgin was constructed. New Zealand's connections with these other areas can be seen in a number of jargon words and phrases documented here by the 1840s:

> *all same* 'like' (Barton, 1927: 372)
> *by and by* 'in the future' (Barton, 1927: 372; Heaphy, 1959: 193)
> *gammon* 'lies, nonsense' (Nicholas, 1817: I, 274)
> *kaikai* 'eat, food' (Savage, 1807: 75, 109; Hempleman, 1910: 143)
> *kill* 'beat' (Barton, 1927: 314)
> *man o' war* 'warship' (Taylor, 1966: 383)
> *moon* 'month' (Markham, 1963: 40; Barton, 1927: 426; Cruise, 1824: 248; Wakefield, 1845: I, 285)
> *no good* 'bad' (Nicholas, 1817: I, 12 etc.; Barton, 1927: 167; Cruise, 1824: 9, 70; McNab, 1907: 283; Polack, 1838: II, 162)
> *oui-oui* 'Frenchman' (Wakefield, 1845: I, 94)
> *piccaninny* 'child' (Nicholas, 1817: I, 280; Marshall, 1837: 6)
> *plenty* 'much, many' (Barton, 1927: 372; McNab, 1913: 487; Marshall, 1837: 7)
> *something* 'thing' (Polack, 1838: I, 199)
> *suppose* 'if' (Kenny, 1956: 108)
> *too much* 'very' (Heaphy, 1959: 193)
> *very good* 'good' (Barton, 1927: 61, 372; Kenny, 1956: 108; Marshall, 1837: 6)

Most of the above are well attested from various early Pacific sources and survive in present-day Melanesian Pidgin. *Kaikai* may actually be of Maori origin, but had become part of South Seas Jargon by mid-century.

What Became of New Zealand Pidgin?

The evidence presented in the preceding sections shows that while 'pidgin' in the strictest sense has never existed in New Zealand, at least up to the 1840s there were jargon versions of both Maori and English which were used in communication between the two peoples. In this section I will consider the subsequent history of this jargon tradition.

This account is fairly speculative, and a proper linguistic history of the period since the 1840s will require much further research.

The Treaty of Waitangi in 1840 opened the way for large-scale European settlement of New Zealand. Within a decade or two the population balance had radically shifted so that Maoris were a minority in their own country. Geographically and socially separate European communities grew up, within which it was possible for Pakehas to live out the course of their lives without any significant contact with the native people. Thus whereas all early writings contain some mention of meetings and dealings with Maoris, in the later nineteenth century many New Zealand journals, biographies, letters and the like refer to a completely European world.

Among the minority of Europeans who spoke Maori, we have Colenso's testimony (quoted above) that a jargon version of the language was widely used at least through the 1860s. On the other hand, there was now a normalised written Maori. Dictionaries and grammars of the language were available, at least to editors and publishers, with the result that very little non-standard Maori found its way into print. Such books, indeed, could hardly have helped but improve the average level of competence among those Pakehas who did try to learn Maori.

On the Maori side, a similar range of linguistic performance presumably existed. The gradually increasing accessibility of native English speakers, books in English, and formal schooling would have brought about a corresponding improvement in the overall level of competence in the language. By the early twentieth century, there were substantial numbers of Maoris who spoke educated standard English.

At the same time, however, there appears in print a 'Maori Pidgin English' in the form of a stereotyped literary dialect, exemplified in the comic anecdotes of A.A. Grace (1910) and J.C. Fussell (1917)[9]:

> My Korry! t'e train late . . . We miss t'e firs' race, I t'ink. I no able to put my money on King Teddy. I run all t'e way from Cummin' Hotel to ketch t'e train — I get here plenty time, but t'e train late. My wurra! too slow, too much t'e taihoa belonga t'e train. (Grace, 1910: 8)

The racial attitudes implicit in these stories are so offensive to most modern readers that they may be tempted to dismiss the language as nothing but a Pakeha fabrication. On careful examination, however, many of its phonological and grammatical features are just those one would expect to find as interference effects in the English of native Maori speakers. Some other features have been inherited from the jargon of the early nineteenth century, but a number of highly deviant features have been eliminated (e.g. 'I' replaces 'me' as subject pronoun). The result is close enough to standard English that 'dialect' seems a more appropriate term than 'jargon'. Allowing for embellishments by the writers for literary effect, it seems at least possible that this dialect is based on the English of uneducated Maori speakers around the turn of the century.

Whether 'jargon', 'pidgin' or 'dialect', however, this type of language still bears a heavy stigma, and twentieth-century writers often appear to wish it did not exist. At the beginning of this paper I noted Baker's effort to minimise the prevalence of pidgin in early New Zealand history. The same well-meaning view is expressed by Arnold Wall, writing at about the same time, when he deplores

> our habit of ascribing to the Maori a kind of 'pigeon' English which has no existence in fact. I . . . regard this as an undeserved aspersion upon our Maori fellow-citizens, whose English, in my experience, is at least as good as our own, and in many cases a great deal better than that of the average 'New Zealander'. (Wall, 1936: 86)

One may question whether Wall's 'experience', as a university professor, would have acquainted him with the full range of English spoken by Maoris. Even more recently, G.W. Turner flatly denies any factual basis to the pidgin used by Grace and Fussell:

> The literary convention of Maori English interlarded with *plurry* and sentences like 'Py korry, that the nice baby, eh?' belongs to the language of journalists rather than the language of Maori. (Turner, 1972: 203)

In one sense Turner is probably correct, since the 'literary convention' he refers to, as we have seen, was established at least 60 years earlier. It is unlikely that anyone still spoke that way in 1972. But in their anxiety to defend 'the Maori' from the opprobrium of using 'pidgin', Turner, Wall and Baker are forced to ignore not only the considerable documentary evidence of the nineteenth century, but the variability that must have existed within 'Maori English' from the earliest times.[10] The mixed language of 'Toogee' and 'Hoodoo' and the jargon recorded by Nicholas are part of that historical and social continuum, just as much as the English 'at least as good as our own'.

Notes

1. This is an extensively revised version of a paper originally presented at the Second New Zealand Linguistics Conference, Wellington, 1978.
2. Of course, it is almost certain that Maoris on shore who traded with the Europeans would have learned some European personal names, as well as European words for some novelties such as tobacco. But even this cultural borrowing may have been less extensive than we assume. Several examples are documented of Maori words which were immediately extended semantically to cover new artifacts: *puu* 'trumpet, wooden tube' was applied to guns, and *whao* 'chisel' to nails.
3. A complicating factor was the fact that both English and French visitors had some previous acquaintance with Tahitian, which is closely related to Maori. Cook's first expedition made extensive use of a Tahitian interpreter, Tupaia, which resulted in a few Tahitian words being introduced into the jargon under the misapprehension that they were the same in Maori — e.g. *'ahu* 'clothing' (Maori *kaakahu*) and *muita'i* 'good' (Maori *pai*).
4. Modern readers are most often struck by the spellings, which sometimes bear little resemblance to the modern standard orthography. (For example, Maori *ihu* 'nose' is spelled *ahewh* by Cook and *aéiou* by Marion.) But when one takes into account traditional English and French spelling, the dialects spoken by the explorers, and certain historical and geographical variations in Maori itself, these transcriptions turn out to be more systematic and accurate than at first appears (see Pearce, 1976 for some analysis). Although European pronunciation of Maori must often have been very bad, this is not generally reflected in the documents, and therefore will not be further discussed in connection with the jargon.
5. The closest grammatical approximation to the quoted sentence would be the actor-emphatic *Naa Te Kurii i mate ai a Marion* 'It was Te Kurii who was responsible for Marion's death'.
6. Alternatively, this may be a reduplicated derivative of *ariki*, a more common word for 'chief'.
7. The Maori words are *tangata* 'person', *nui* 'big, much' and *kai* 'food, eat'.
8. The English article *the* may be an exception to this, owing to its considerable similarity in form and function to Maori *te*, so that the two might be equated in a cross-linguistic situation. Certainly over-generalisation of *the/te* (for instance to indefinite and generic noun phrases) is a recurrent feature of New Zealand pidgin:

give it the wow 'give me a nail' (Nicholas, 1817: 33)

he replied that the people at the Waree Karrakeeah are bad, and the

Karrakeeah itself, was no good for the New Zealand man. (Barton, 1927: 167)

(*karakia* 'prayer, preaching, Christianity', *whare karakia* 'church')

9. These are the main examples known to me, but I suspect that a search of newspaper and magazine humour from this period would turn up much more of this dialect. See Pearson (1958) for a discussion of Grace and Fussell in the context of Pakeha fiction about Maoris.
10. It should be noted that the 'natural respect for the intelligence of the Maori race' expressed by Baker and Wall goes along with a contempt for pidgins in other parts of the Pacific (and implicitly for their speakers). The New Zealand situation is contrasted by Wall with 'the "pfeller" and the "mine gibbit" of the Australian black as presented in the "Bulletin"' (Wall, 1936: 86). Baker is anxious to distance the Maori from 'Chinese corruptions of English' as well as from 'Beach-la-Mar' (Melanesian Pidgin). To be fair, neither writer considers the inferior intelligence of the native entirely responsible for the corruption of the pidgin. Both assign at least part of the blame to journalists and depraved whites, 'the veriest scum of the earth' (Baker, 1941: 71–4).

References

[BAINES, WILLIAM MORTIMER] 1874, *The Narrative of Edward Crewe, or Life in New Zealand*. London: Sampson Low.

BAKER, SIDNEY J. 1941, *New Zealand Slang: A Dictionary of Colloquialisms*. Christchurch: Whitcombe & Tombs.

BARTON, R.J. 1927, *Earliest New Zealand: The Journals and Correspondence of the Rev. John Butler*. Masterton: Palamontain & Petherick.

CLARK, ROSS 1979–80, In search of Beach-la-mar: towards a history of Pacific Pidgin English. *Te Reo* 22–23, 3–64.

COLENSO, WILLIAM 1868, On the Maori races of New Zealand. *Transactions and Proceedings of the New Zealand Institute* 1, 339–424.

COLLINS, DAVID 1798, *An Account of the English Colony in New South Wales*. London: Cadell & Davies.

[COOK I, II, III] *The Journals of Captain James Cook on his Voyages of Discovery. Volume I: The Voyage of the* Endeavour *1768–1771. Volume II: The Voyage of the* Resolution *and* Adventure *1772–1775. Volume III: The Voyage of the* Resolution *and* Discovery *1776–1780* (ed. J.C. BEAGLEHOLE). Cambridge: Published for the Hakluyt Society at the University Press (1955, 1961, 1967).

CRUISE, RICHARD A. 1824, *Journal of a Ten Months' Residence in New Zealand*. London: Longman.

[D'URVILLE] n.d., *New Zealand 1826–1827, from the French of Dumont D'Urville* (Translated by OLIVE WRIGHT). Wingfield Press.

FERGUSON, CHARLES A. and DEBOSE, CHARLES E. 1977, Simplified registers, broken language, and pidginization. In ALBERT VALDMAN (ed.) *Pidgin and Creole Linguistics* (pp. 99–125). Bloomington: Indiana University Press.

FUSSELL, J.C. 1917, *Letters from Private Henare Tikitanu*. Auckland: Worthington.

GRACE, A.A. 1910, *Hone Tiki Dialogues*. Wellington: Gordon & Gotch.

HAVARD-WILLIAMS, P. (ed.) 1961, *Marsden and the New Zealand Mission: Sixteen Letters*. Dunedin: University of Otago Press.

HEAPHY, CHARLES 1959, Account of an exploring expedition to the south-west of Nelson. In NANCY M. TAYLOR (ed.) *Early Travellers in New Zealand*. Oxford: Clarendon Press.

[HEMPLEMAN] 1910, *The Piraki Log or Diary of Captain Hempleman*. London: Henry Frowde, Oxford University Press.

KENNY, ROBERT W. (ed.) 1956, *The New Zealand Journal, 1842–1844 of John B. Williams of Salem, Massachusetts*. Salem, Mass.: Peabody Museum of Salem and Brown University Press.

McNAB, ROBERT 1907, *Murihiku and the Southern Islands*. Invercargill: William Smith.

— 1913, *The Old Whaling Days*. Christchurch: Whitcombe & Tombs.

[MARION] n.d., *Extracts from Journals relating to the visit to New Zealand in May–July 1772 of the French ships* Mascarin *and* Marquis de Castries *under the command of M.-J. Marion du Fresne*. Wellington: Alexander Turnbull Library Endowment Trust (1985).

MARKHAM, EDWARD 1963, *New Zealand or Recollections of It*. Wellington: Government Printer.

MARSHALL, WILLIAM BARRETT 1837, *A Personal Narrative of Two Visits to New Zealand*. London: James Nisbet.

MÜHLHÄUSLER, PETER 1986, *Pidgin and Creole Linguistics*. Oxford: Blackwell.

NICHOLAS, J.L. 1817, *Narrative of a Voyage to New Zealand*. London: James Black & Son.

PEARCE, G.L. 1976, Captain Cook's spelling of English and Polynesian vowels. *Te Reo* 19, 67–82.

PEARSON, W.H. 1958, Attitudes to the Maori in some pakeha fiction. *Journal of the Polynesian Society* 67, 211–38.

POLACK, J.S. 1838, *New Zealand: Being a Narrative of Travels and Adventures*. London: Richard Bentley.

[RICKMAN] 1781, *Journal of Captain Cook's Last Voyage to the Pacific Ocean on Discovery*. London: Newbery.

ROMAINE, SUZANNE 1988, *Pidgin and Creole Languages*. London: Longman.

SAVAGE, JOHN 1807, *Some Account of New Zealand*. London: John Murray.

SHARP, ANDREW (ed.) 1971, *Duperrey's Visit to New Zealand in 1824*. Wellington: Alexander Turnbull Library.

[SURVILLE] n.d., *Extracts from Journals Relating to the Visit to New Zealand of the French Ship* St Jean Baptiste *in December 1769 Under the Command of J.F.M. de Surville*. Wellington: National Library of New Zealand (1982).

TAYLOR, NANCY M. (ed.) 1966, *The Journal of Ensign Best, 1837–1843*. Wellington: Government Printer.

TURNER, G.W. 1972, *The English Language in Australia and New Zealand*. London: Longman.

WADE, WILLIAM RICHARD 1842, *A Journey in the Northern Island of New Zealand*. Hobart: George Rólwegan.

WAKEFIELD, E.J. 1845, *Adventures in New Zealand*. London: John Murray.
WALL, ARNOLD 1936, *The Mother Tongue in New Zealand*. Christchurch: Whitcombe & Tombs.
WHINNOM, KEITH 1971, Linguistic hybridization and the 'special case' of pidgins and creoles. In DELL HYMES (ed.) *Pidginization and Creolization of Languages* (pp. 91–115). Cambridge: Cambridge University Press.

6 The rise of New Zealand intonation

SCOTT ALLAN

Introduction

The question most often asked by New Zealand students when the topic of intonation is introduced is, 'Why do we raise the pitch of our voices at the end of everything we say?' It is certainly not the case that every utterance made by a speaker of New Zealand English (henceforth NZE) ends with rising pitch, but rising pitch contours do occur on the final element of declaratives, as shown, e.g.[1], in Example 1.

EXAMPLE 1

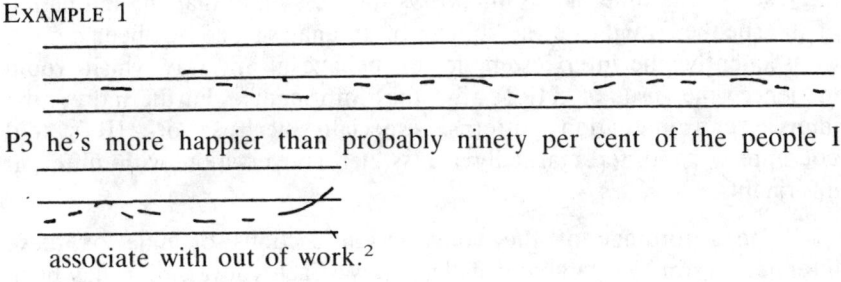

P3 he's more happier than probably ninety per cent of the people I

associate with out of work.[2]

This phenomenon is not peculiar to NZE and has already been well documented in other dialects of English. K. Allan (1984), Guy & Vonwiller (1984) and Horvath (1985) all discuss both the frequency of occurrence and meaninng of what they call the high-rising terminal tone (henceforth HRT) in Australian English. Jarman & Cruttenden (1976), and Pellowe & Jones (1978) report the occurrence of HRT in various dialects of British English, while Cruttenden (1986) discusses the phenomenon in General American. However, despite the occurrence of the HRT in NZE there has been no published study of the phenomenon.

Methodology

ethnicity not held constant (handwritten marginalia)

In this study I will document the frequency of occurrence and the function of the HRT in the speech of nine NZE speakers who live in Levin, a town north of Wellington. I will also compare the findings of this study with those of Horvath (1985). The speakers who provide the database are matched for major demographic variables except ethnicity. They are all female, all of the same age group, 25–35, and all from the same socio-economic group. This matching allowed a direct comparison to be made between Maori and Pakeha speakers of English.[3] In this study five of the informants are Pakeha, while the remaining four are Maori. All the informants were interviewed in their own homes by an interviewer who is a member of the community. Given the small number of informants it is clear that this is only a pilot study.

Each interview involved a number of tasks designed to elicit a range of speech styles. These tasks included questions concerning the regional identification of a speaker from his or her speech, gap filling, word lists and a reading passage. The most difficult task faced by the interviewer was eliciting informal speech or casual conversation. This was achieved through Labovian interview techniques (Labov, 1984). The interviewer would ask a number of questions and, through careful listening, prompt the informants to follow through those topics which provoked the most interest. At the time of the interviews the possibility that the intonation of the speakers might be the subject of an analysis had not been raised. Consequently, the interviewer did not behave in any way which would influence the use of HRTs by the informants. Furthermore, the interviewer's intonation patterns, especially her use of HRTs, did not appear to differ markedly across her conversation with different informants.

The recordings of the conversation sections of nine of these interviews form the database of this study. Each conversation has been transcribed and the intonation has been analysed. In this analysis I have not attempted to identify tone groups, but have analysed each text into 'pause defined units'. My justification for taking this approach is exactly the same as that proposed by Brown, Currie & Kenworthy (1980: 40–7). They found that speakers often paused in the middle of noun phrases, extended their pitch span on non-contrastive elements, and changed both pitch height and direction on fillers which function only to maintain the speaker's right to speak while planning his or her utterance. Furthermore, neither syntactic nor semantic criteria permitted them to make a principled decision on the placement of a tone group boundary, as shown, for example, in Example 2.

EXAMPLE 2 *Taken from Brown, Currie & Kenworthy (1980: 42)*

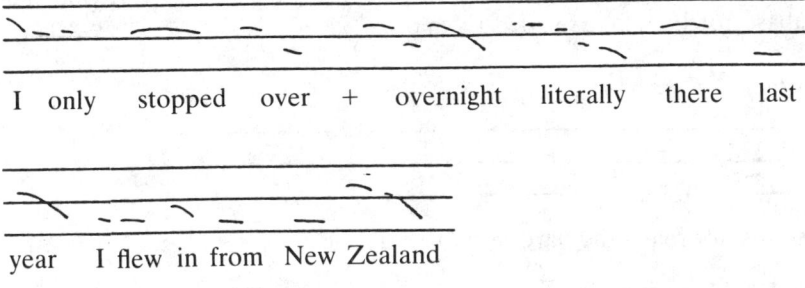

I   only   stopped   over   +   overnight   literally   there   last

year   I flew in from New Zealand

Brown, Currie & Kenworthy claim that the problem with this example is 'last year' and what it modifies. Does it occur with the first phrase, giving 'I only stopped overnight there last year', or does it modify the second, giving 'last year I flew in from New Zealand', or is there a separate tone group 'last year'? They claim that this problem arises because the speaker is experiencing planning difficulties. The result of these difficulties is that it is difficult to decide what 'last year' is modifying when listening to the tape recording of the interview.

The occurrence of pauses which do not coincide with the boundaries of other units which Brown, Currie & Kenworthy would like to identify as tone groups on other criteria also pose problems, as, for example, in Example 3.

EXAMPLE 3 *Taken from Brown, Currie & Kenworthy (1980: 43)*

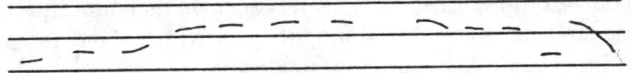

was the bad natured daughter + + beautiful as well

Despite the double plus which indicates a fairly long pause, the pitch contour continues through this pause, suggesting that there is a single tone group. However, the pause falls in the middle of this 'tone group' disrupting both the semantic and syntactic coherence of the group. This is problematic if tone groups are defined as having coherent internal syntactic and semantic structure (see Halliday, 1963). Furthermore, if pauses are one of the criteria used to identify tone group boundaries then this utterance must contain two tone groups. Given these problems and the frequency with which they recur, Brown, Currie & Kenworthy abandon the notion of tone group in favour of the pause defined unit (henceforth PDU).

These same problems occur in the recordings which provide the database for this analysis, see Example 4.

EXAMPLE 4

P3 no it's not really the hardest part would be

just doing his leg exercises

P5 after a few little + sort of tests and things like that

The first of these two examples parallels the first example from Brown, Currie & Kenworthy. It is not obvious what tone group 'really' belongs to. The question is whether 'really' modifies what precedes it or what follows it. The tape does not provide sufficient clues to resolve this ambiguity. The second example raises the same issues as its counterpart from Brown, Currie & Kenworthy. Despite the plus which indicates a pause the pitch contour continues through this pause, suggesting that there is a single tone group. However, the semantic and syntactic coherence of the group is disrupted by the occurrence of this pause. Again this is problematic if tone groups are defined as having a coherent internal semantic and syntactic structure. Furthermore, if pauses are one of the criteria used to identify tone group boundaries then, as with the example above, this utterance must contain two tone groups.

The problems raised by these examples for the placement of tone group boundaries, and the frequency with which such examples recur are identical with those outlined above in the discussion of Brown, Currie & Kenworthy (1980). Given such similarities, I have adopted their solution and analysed each text into PDUs.

According to Brown, Currie & Kenworthy (1980: 47) the pause is the only signal which can be relied on to occur frequently in spontaneous speech and texts which are read aloud. Pauses may be identified instrumentally and the instrumental readings Brown, Currie & Kenworthy arrived at corresponded closely to perceived pauses. Although I was not able to identify pauses instrumentally, each text was divided into PDUs based on perceived pauses. The total number of PDUs for each interviewee was calculated. Any PDUs which corresponded to interrogatives were removed from the total. Each text was then reviewed and PDUs which ended in a high rise were counted. Any remaining PDUs which ended with a HRT but corresponded to an interrogative were excluded from the total. This gave for each speaker a ratio of HRT PDUs as a proportion of all declarative PDUs. This was then expressed as a percentage.

Results

The results of these calculations are set out in Table 6.1. Only 3.00% of all non-interrogative PDUs end with a HRT, and it is clearly the case that this feature of NZE has achieved salience beyond its statistical frequency. However, this study shows it to be more frequent than its Australian counterpart. Horvath (1985: 121) found that out of 107,685 non-interrogative tone groups only 1,724 or 1.6% contained a HRT. The study of HRTs in the speech of 30 Auckland males, grouped by age (Kaiser et al. 1987), found that 135 of 3,104 or 4.35% of declarative tone units ended with a HRT.[4] This is higher than the present study but Kaiser et al. conclude that their results were probably skewed by two extremely nervous speakers.

The Pakeha women had an average of 2.33% of PDUs ending with a HRT, while the Maori women averaged 3.58%. Of the 120 HRT PDUs, the Pakeha women produced 44 or 35.77%, while the Maori women produced 79 or 64.23%. Maori women use HRTs more frequently than their Pakeha counterparts by a factor of 1.8, i.e. if a Pakeha woman uses 10 HRTs then her Maori counterpart is likely to use 18.

Kaiser et al. (1987) suggest that age is a factor in the occurrence of HRTs, with younger speakers more likely to use HRTs than older speakers. The present study suggests that ethnicity also plays a role.

TABLE 6.1 *Distribution of HRT over informants*

	Pakeha				Maori		
Interviewee	*HRT*	*PDU*	*%HRT*	*Interviewee*	*HRT*	*PDU*	*%HRT*
P1	5	531	0.94	M1	14	584	2.39
P2	6	441	1.36	M2	25	583	4.28
P3	16	296	5.40	M3	11	495	2.22
P4	5	173	2.89	M4	29	539	5.38
P5	12	446	2.69				
Total: Pakeha:	44	1,887	2.33	Maori:	79	2,201	3.58

Overall total of HRTS	123
Overall total of PDUs	4,088
Overall percentage	3.00

However, this could be an artifact of the small data base or it is possible that the ethnic division disguises variation between different socio-economic groups. Both age and ethnicity are identified by Horvath (1985) as factors which determine the frequency of occurrence of HRTs in Australian English. In Australian English HRTs are associated with teenagers, females, people of lower-working-class background and either Greeks or Anglos (Horvath, 1985: 122). Although HRTs occur more frequently in NZE than in Australian English, it is clearly the case that, like Australian English, age and ethnicity play a role in determining frequency of occurrence.

Text Type and Length of Turn

It is certainly the case that social factors play a role in determining the distribution of HRTs, but it is also possible that linguistic factors might play a role. HRTs may be more likely to occur in certain linguistic environments than others. Horvath (1985: 121–2) found that there was a relationship between both text type and length of turn. She classified texts into the following types:

Description (text following a 'how' question)
Opinion ('What do you think?')
Explanation ('Why?')

Factual ('What?')
Narrative ('Tell me')   Horvath (1985: 121)

Although this division seems, in principle, to be quite straightforward, when I applied it to the texts under discussion I soon ran into problems. The major problem arises when an attempt is made to divide a text into various types. The interviewer may ask a question which should, and does, elicit an opinion, but very quickly this develops into a narrative. Consequently, I assigned each occurrence of a HRT to a particular text type not on the basis of the question the interviewer used to initiate the text, but on the function within the text of the PDU containing the HRT. If the interviewer asked a question designed to elicit an opinion, and that opinion is supported through a narrative which contains an instance of HRT, then the PDU containing that HRT is labelled 'narrative', rather than 'opinion'. For each text type this gave a ratio of HRT PDUs as a proportion of the total number of all HRT PDUs, which was then expressed as a percentage. The results are shown in Table 6.2.

TABLE 6.2 *Distribution of HRTs over text types*

	No. of HRTs	%
Description	6	4.9
Opinion	10	8.1
Explanation	2	1.6
Factual	16	13.0
Narrative	89	72.4
	$N = 123$	100.0

These results are not directly comparable for a number of reasons with those in Horvath (1985). Firstly, whereas the percentages in Table 6.2 are based on the ratio of HRT PDUs for a particular text type as a proportion of the total number of all HRT PDUs, those given in Horvath (1985: 122) are calculated on the ratio of HRT tone groups of a particular text type as a proportion of the total number of all tone groups for that text type. Secondly, when the data discussed here were collected, no consideration was given to an intonational analysis. Consequently, no attempt was made to elicit instances of each text type from each informant. A direct comparison between the two analyses would only be possible if each database contained relatively the same proportion of each text type. Finally, there is no variable rule analysis of the data.

There are a number of differences between the figures presented here and those in Horvath (1985). Horvath found that narratives and descriptions favoured HRTs, opinions and factual texts disfavoured HRTs, while explanations neither favoured nor disfavoured HRTs. This leads to the following hierarchy: HRT in factual texts ⊃ opinion ⊃ explanation ⊃ description ⊃ narrative. In NZE it would appear that HRT in explanation texts ⊃ description ⊃ opinion ⊃ factual ⊃ narrative. These differences may well be a result of either the relatively small database, different relative proportions of each text type in the database or the differences in analysis. However, it is clear in both samples that narrative texts favour HRTs.

Horvath also considered length of turn as a possible influencing factor. She considered four categories of turn: (1) one word, (2) an elliptical clause, (3) a single clause and (4) multiple clauses. Her results showed that multiple and elliptical clauses favoured HRTs, while single clauses and one word texts did not. In analysing length of turn for the texts under discussion here, I identified one word, single clause, and multiple clause turns. This produced the results in Table 6.3. It appears that multiple clause texts favour the occurrence of HRTs, while both one word and single clause texts do not.

TABLE 6.3 *Distribution of HRTs over length of turn*

	No. of HRTs	%
One word	5	4.0
Single clause	13	10.6
Multiple clause	105	85.4
	N = 123	100.0

Despite differences between this study and that of Horvath (1985) in the distribution of HRTs through text types, it appears that narrative texts in both Australian English and NZE favour HRT and the implicational hierarchy, based on length of turn, set up by Horvath (1985: 125) for Australian English, i.e. HRT in one word texts ⊃ single clause ⊃ multiple clause, applies to NZE. It would also appear that ethnicity and age are important factors. The Kaiser *et al.* (1987) study shows that younger age groups are more likely to use HRTs than older ones, while the present study shows that Maori women are 1.8 times more likely to use HRTs than Pakeha women. Perhaps an explanation for these results may be found in the functions of HRT.

Function of HRT

The meaning or function of the HRT has been discussed by a number of linguists. Cruttenden (1986: 142) states that the high rise is becoming more frequent in General American and is a marker of casualness. Lakoff (1975) claims that HRT is used to show deference on the part of the speaker towards the hearer. Women show deference to men, wives to husbands, and children to parents and teachers. In each case the speaker is in a position of powerlessness toward the hearer.

However, a number of problems arise with this explanation for the occurrence of HRTs in the texts under discussion here. The interviewer is a member of the community from which the informants were selected. She is known personally to most, if not all, the informants; is younger than all the informants; belongs to the same social group; and is of the same gender as the informants. Furthermore, Holmes & Bell (1988) state that although the interviewer is blond and fair skinned, she is actually Maori and plays an active role in the local Maori community. Consequently, she appears Pakeha to the Pakeha informants, but is known to be Maori by the Maori informants. There would appear to be no reasons for assuming that the informants considered themselves to be in a position of powerlessness towards the interviewer. Deference may explain some occurrences of HRTs but it does not provide a sufficient explanation for the occurrence of HRTs in the texts under discussion here.

Horvath (1985: 127) cites two pieces of evidence which led her to conclude that the deference explanation did not account for the occurrence of HRTs in the texts she collected. Firstly, the Sydney evidence shows that factual and opinion texts do not favour HRT. Deference is most common when the matter under discussion is factual. If deference were a sufficient explanation then we would expect factual texts to display a greater proportion of HRTs. Secondly, she cites a piece of anecdotal evidence. She states that having listened to conversations between teenagers on trains and her own teenagers and their friends, she could only conclude that HRTs are a regular feature of conversation.

Similar points may be made concerning the distribution of HRTs in the NZE texts. The majority of HRTs do not occur in factual texts but in narrative texts. We would not expect to find speakers showing deference to hearers in narratives. Having observed my colleagues, students, neighbours and their children in conversation, it is certainly the case that, as in Sydney, HRTs are a regular feature of conversation. This raises the question of what the function of a HRT is in a narrative.

Brown (1977: 136) states that in English the unmarked pitch movement is the fall. The rise issues a challenge and demands a response. She regrets that the rise has been linked to the asking of questions and that statements such as 'a rising intonation can turn a statement into a question' have been made. A statement marked by rising pitch does not carry the same meaning as the formal question and is not appropriate to the same situation. Brown illustrates this with the following example:

EXAMPLE 5

> **Statement:**   The doctor's coming.
> **Question 1:** Is the doctor coming?
> **Question 2:** The doctor's coming?

The second question can only be uttered as a response to the immediately preceding statement. It queries the correctness of the assertion made in the previous statement and is an example of the challenging use of the high rise.

The HRTs in the NZE texts never signal a challenge but they do in many instances require a response from the hearer. The speaker creates the narrative for the benefit of the listeners and must always take account of the audience: what the listeners already know or want to know, and whether or not they have followed or understood what has been said. One function of the HRT in narratives is to check whether or not the audience understands or has followed the narrative up to that point. It requires a minimal response from the listener(s). This interactional function of HRT is identical to the function of what Guy *et al.* (1986) call Australian Questioning Intonation. The following examples of HRT from NZE illustrate this interactive function:

EXAMPLE 6

> **P3:**   well he used to do a lot of running and rugby for into his rugby and that ↑ [5]
> **I:**   +yeah
> **P3:**   +and then you know he even says now and that like sort of . . .
>
> **M4:**   bloody fair skin with freckles and red hair ↑
> **I:**   yeah + yeah
> **M4:**   you know I think you poor little . . .

M2: +it's just um + saves on the wear and tear of all the other clothes ↑

I: yeah

M2: I mean if you got a set + a set you know garment . . .

In each of the above examples the informant uses a HRT at the end of her first turn. This demands a response from the interviewer and in each case gets one. The response of the interviewer is minimal — 'yeah' or 'yeah yeah' — showing that she understands the function of the HRT. Other minimal responses could be 'mmm', 'uh huh', 'mm hmm', or even just a nod. This function of the HRT may also be performed lexically. This is illustrated by the following examples:

EXAMPLE 7

P2: an they say oh you know

I: yeah

P2: I didn't feel anything it didn't feel like I did anything

P3: no I do it | oh I do it with different parts of his legs and that

I: oh I see

P3: and he does weights in the afternoon for his arms

P5: . . . an that little bridge down by Totem park there you know/ the one/

I: /yeah/

P5: the little narrow one

In the first example the informant P2 uses 'you know' to elicit a response from the listener, while in the second P3 uses 'and that'.[6] Both of these items elicit a minimal response. The listener does not go beyond a minimal response in each of the above examples and clearly understands the function of the items. It would appear that the HRT and items like 'you know' or 'an(d) that' have similar functions in certain environments. Speakers may, in fact, combine the HRT with one of the lexical items which requires a response, e.g.

functional equivalence of HRT and you know etc.

EXAMPLE 8

P5: they've like ye- four five six in a car you know ↑

I: yeah

P5: they overtake on corners

In the above example P5 ends her turn with a HRT on 'know'.

Of the 123 HRTs in the texts, 41 or 33.33% were followed by a minimal response from the listener. This minimal response was usually 'yeah'. There were 28 instances or 22.76% of HRTs where the listener agreed with the speaker but gave more than a minimal response. This longer response often took the form of endorsing what the informant had just said, e.g.

EXAMPLE 9

> **M4**: . . . + + and it's very very rarely we get traffic round here ↑
> **I**:   yeah that's right too

M4 ends with a HRT on 'here' and the interviewer responds by endorsing what has been said. Other instances of the longer response show that the interviewer agreed with the speaker and had first hand knowledge of the topic, e.g.

EXAMPLE 10

> **M2**: +the next day we went into market+Paddy's /Market ↑ /
> **I**:   /oh/ yeah you can pick up some good things eh

The informant did not change the topic of her narrative after any of the interviewer's longer responses, unless it contained a question which introduced a new topic. The speaker interpreted these longer responses as showing not just an endorsement of what had been said but also as showing that the hearer had understood the narrative up to that point.

On 52 occasions the HRT received no verbal response from the listener. However, it is possible that a non-verbal response was given. In each of these cases the speaker continued with her narrative. However, it is possible that the HRT which is not followed by any verbal response has another function.

All conversations occur in real time and are the product of social interaction between at least two people, i.e. they are not prepared or planned and require co-operation. Quite often speakers require time to organise their next utterance but do not wish to surrender their turn. In these instances it is possible that the HRT is used, at a point where a structural unit terminates and the hearer might be expected to contribute, to hold the floor or request permission to continue.

This function gains support from the distribution of HRT over length of turn. It was stated above that 85.36% of HRTs occurred in multiple clause units. Clearly, the speaker is aware that she is talking more than the other participant and uses the HRT to request permission to continue or forestall participation of the hearer while she organises her next utterance. Supporting evidence may also be seen in the unmarked use of falling and rising tones. If I answer a question with a falling tone, then the hearer will interpret this as a desire on my behalf not to discuss the matter which produced such a response. The use of a rise, however, will suggest that the matter may be pursued.

It would appear that the distribution of HRTs across text types and length of turn does not support the deference function. This is not to suggest that one of the functions of HRT might not be to signal deference. However, it is difficult to see that it has that function in these texts. It would appear that the HRT is a feature of narrative texts, which are the most common text type in conversations and the least likely text type to favour deference. The interaction between the participants, and the interviewer's response to the speaker's use of HRT, only undermines the deference function of HRT. The above interpretation of the twin discourse functions of the HRT, i.e. requesting a response from the hearer and requesting permission to continue or hold the floor, gains support from the distribution of HRTs over the different text types, length of turn and the hearer's response to them.

no support for the deference function of HRT.

Conclusion

Although this is only a pilot study, it does raise some interesting points. The data suggest that HRT is more common in NZE than in Australian English. However, it would appear that narrative texts in both dialects favour HRTs, and its distribution over length of turn is identical in both NZE and Australian English. The same social characteristics that play a role in its distribution in Australian English also play a role in its distribution in NZE. Furthermore, as with its Australian counterpart, it has achieved salience beyond its statistical occurrence. Nevertheless, despite its low frequency, it deserves a more detailed study in which a greater range of sociolinguistic variables may be taken into account and its function in texts may be more decisively defined.

HRT more common in NZ

Notes

1. I would like to thank the interviewer, Jenny Jacob, for collecting the data and giving me permission to work on it. Thanks go also to Harriet who not only told me that the impossible was possible but made me believe it.
2. The intonation transcription system used here is identical to that used in Brown, Currie & Kenworthy (1980). The space between the top and bottom lines of the stave represents the top and bottom of the speaker's pitch span. The marks on the stave represent the perceived pitch. If the pitch moves up, the line moves up, if it moves down then the line moves down. The length of

a line is in direct proportion to the length of the syllable associated with it. The longer a line, the longer the syllable. Lines associated with stressed syllables are placed, in general, above the middle line, while those associated with unstressed ones falls, in general, below the middle line.

3. The methodology behind the project and data collection was designed by Janet Holmes and Allan Bell, and is discussed in Holmes & Bell (1988).

4. Kaiser et al.'s 30 male informants were divided into five groups of six, according to age. The groups were (a) 'child', < 12; (b) 'adolescent', 13–20; (c) 'young adult', 21–30; (d) 'adult', 31–50; and (e) 'mature adult', 50+.

5. In the orthographic transcriptions of the texts the following conventions are used: (a) ↑ marks a high rise; (b) + signals a pause and + + an extended pause; and (c) / / indicates an overlap between the two speakers.

6. On the uses of 'you know' see Holmes (1986).

References

ALLAN, KEITH 1984, The component functions of the high rise terminal contour in Australian declarative sentences. *Australian Journal of Linguistics* 4 (1), 19–32.

BROWN, GILLIAN 1977, *Listening to Spoken English*. London: Longman.

BROWN, GILLIAN, CURRIE, KAREN and KENWORTHY, JOANNE 1980, *Questions of Intonation*. London: Croom Helm.

CRUTTENDEN, ALAN 1986, *Intonation*. Cambridge: Cambridge University Press.

GUY, GREGORY and VONWILLER, JULIA 1984, The meaning of an intonation in Australian English. *Australian Journal of Linguistics* 4 (1), 1–17.

GUY, GREGORY, HORVATH, BARBARA, VONWILLER, JULIA, DAISLEY, ELAINE and ROGERS, INGE 1986, An intonational change in progress in Australian English. *Language in Society* 15 (1), 22–52.

HALLIDAY, MICHAEL A.K. 1963, The tones of English. *Archivum Linguisticum* 15, 1–28.

HOLMES, JANET 1986, Functions of 'you know' in women's and men's speech. *Language in Society* 15 (1), 1–22.

HOLMES, JANET and BELL, ALLAN 1988, Learning by experience: notes for New Zealand social dialectologists. *Te Reo* 31, 19–49.

HORVATH, BARBARA M. 1985, *Variation in Australian English*. Cambridge: Cambridge University Press.

JARMAN, ERIC and CRUTTENDEN, ALAN 1976, Belfast intonation and the myth of the fall. *Journal of the International Phonetic Association* 6, 4–12.

KAISER, JULIA, MUNROW, ALISON, PIDWELL, RUTH, TUBBY, JUDITH and WHITE, JILL 1987, Final high-rising tones in declarative utterances. Unpublished research project. Auckland: University of Auckland.

LABOV, WILLIAM 1984, Field methods of the project on linguistic change and variation. In JOHN BAUGH and JOEL SHERZER (eds) *Language in Use: Readings in Sociolinguistics* (pp. 28–53). Englewood Cliffs, New Jersey: Prentice-Hall.

LAKOFF, ROBIN 1975, *Language and Woman's Place*. New York: Harper and Row.

PELLOWE, JOHN and JONES, VAL 1978, On intonational variability in Tyneside speech. In PETER TRUDGILL (ed.) *Sociolinguistic Patterns in British Speech* (pp. 101–21). London: Edward Arnold.

7 A longitudinal study of the 'ear/air' contrast in New Zealand speech

ELIZABETH GORDON and MARGARET A. MACLAGAN

Background

Our attention was drawn to the contrast between the two diphthongs represented by the words 'ear' and 'air' when we both started to teach phonetics to first-year students. Many students have trouble with these two sounds in transcription. We have found that some of our students can hear a difference between these two front centring diphthongs and others cannot — and it is almost impossible to train those students who do not hear the distinction to do so.[1]

This lack of contrast between /iə/ and /eə/ is now attracting wider attention. A letter to the Editor of the *NZ Listener* in 1983 complained

. . . our 10-year-old came home from school one day almost in tears. Her teacher had told her class that they had to be careful of four English words which were all pronounced the same but had different spellings, each with a different meaning. The four words? *Hare, here, hair* and *hear*.

The letter writer concluded, 'Communication?' (*NZ Listener* 12th March 1983: 10–11)

The writer to the *Listener* did not indicate how the four words in question were pronounced. All four could be pronounced /hiə/ to rhyme with the traditional pronunciation of 'here' or they could all be pronounced /heə/ to rhyme with the traditional pronunciation of 'hair'. If a simple across-the-board sound change is taking place involving the diphthongs /iə/ and /eə/ we could expect that all words containing /iə/

129

and /eə/ would be pronounced in similar ways. Informal observation and a check through the literature indicated that such a simple solution was far from reality.

Since the end of the last century many people have commented on the characteristics of New Zealand pronunciation (Gordon, 1983). However the lack of contrast between /iə/ and /eə/ referred to by the letter writer is not one of the features singled out for comment. It is not mentioned by Arnold Wall in his list headed 'Essential Faults in New Zealand Speech' which appeared in 1938 in his book *New Zealand English*.

We would assume that if Arnold Wall had noticed such a merger, he would have mentioned it, and therefore the conclusion could be drawn that the merger of these diphthongs is a more recent development. George Turner in 1966 also failed to mention the merger, although there is a hint of it in his comment that the first element in the word 'there' is close in Australia, and may be close in New Zealand speech. 'It would be interesting to discover whether a very close pronunciation of /ɛə/ occurs along with a centralised first element of /iə/ in New Zealand, or how otherwise the phonemes are kept distinct, if they are kept distinct' (Turner, 1966: 103). An early auditory study was carried out by one of our MA students, Mary Durkin. She studied the speech of a sample of 75 West Coast school children in the 10–12 year-old age group. She included several iə/eə word pairs and found that: 'When the phonemes occurred in the list of words a high proportion of the pupils tested (72%) made absolutely no distinction between them, realising either [ẹə]/[ẹə] or [eə]/[eə]' (Durkin, 1972: 78).

Recent books have commented on the merger. John Wells in *Accents of English* (1982: 608) states that some New Zealand speakers, particularly children, have merged the two front centring diphthongs, so that 'fair' and 'fear', 'bear' and 'beer', 'share' and 'sheer' are homophonous. He quotes Peter Hawkins, '. . . the sounds in this area are undergoing significant changes at present, and the patterns that will eventually emerge are by no means certain'. Other people who have referred to this diphthong merger are Trudgill & Hannah (1982: 19) who say: 'There is a strong tendency in New Zealand English for /ɪə/ and /ɛə/ to merge; thus 'beer' and 'bare' are [bẹ:].'

By contrast in the Australian edition of *An Introduction to Language* by Fromkin *et al.* (1984: 257) it is stated that the centring diphthong /ɛə/ has a higher starting point in New Zealand English (NZE) so that for many New Zealanders 'rare' and 'rear', 'pear' and 'peer', 'bare' and 'beer' are homophonous, pronounced [rɪə], [pɪə] and [bɪə] respectively. In another passage in their book, Fromkin *et al.* (1984: 285) write:

> If you visit Wellington in July, you'll no doubt hear references to the cold winter 'ear' and to the 'beer' branches on the trees. What you are hearing is a dialect difference, sometimes called an 'accent'. Remarkably enough, those New Zealanders who speak this dialect pronounce *all* words like *air, bare, mayor, stair, share* and so on as 'ear', 'beer', 'mere', 'steer', 'sheer'. Wherever an Australian, say, pronounces /ɛə/ at the end of a word, speakers of this NZ dialect pronounce /ɪə/.

From our observation, we felt that the situation with these diphthongs in New Zealand was complex. Firstly we questioned whether the sound change was right across the board as these writers suggested. Secondly, we questioned whether the merger necessarily always involved the same starting point of the diphthong for all speakers. And thirdly we wondered which starting point, higher or lower, speakers actually chose, and whether the choice correlated with factors such as the social class, age or sex of the speaker. When one of our children was recounting a story where a knight had to return to his castle for his 'spare spear', he pronounced this /spɪə spɪə/. His cousin, a girl a few years older than he was, immediately corrected him and said it should have been pronounced /speə speə/. This gave us the idea that further investigation was definitely indicated.[2]

The merger between the two front centring diphthongs is one which has also occurred in other varieties of English. Labov reports this merger in New York City (Labov, 1966). It has also occurred in South Carolina (Kurath & McDavid, 1961) and in the West Indies (Cassidy & Le Page, 1980). It is one of the variables Trudgill included in his study of speech in Norwich (1974). He says that /ɪə/ and /ɛə/ are generally not distinguished in Norwich, and that the merger is prevalent in East Anglia, although not so fully carried out in Suffolk, especially when compared with Norwich. He found that, in Norwich /ɪə/ was merged with /eə/, so that *here* was pronounced /heə/, but that /eə/ was not merged with /ɪə/ (Trudgill, 1974: 121). Trudgill found that the more open form of the diphthong /eə/ carried more prestige than the closer form /ɪə/. The more open form was therefore used by speakers from higher social classes, by women rather than men, and by most speakers in more formal contexts, which in Trudgill's research included reading lists and word passages. Trudgill comments that the /ɪə/~/eə/ merger is one of the places where

Norwich English pronunciation differs from Received Pronunciation (RP). He says that the merger is not surprising in view of the small functional load carried by the distinction. Fry (1947) has calculated that /ɛə/ and /ɪə/ are respectively seventeenth and eighteenth in order of frequency of the 20 RP vowel phonemes and between them account for only 0.55% of the total number of phonemes occurring.

Although New Zealand pronunciation has often been criticised (see Gordon & Abell, this volume) and does in fact differ from RP at several points, the potential merger of /ɪə/ and /eə/ is the only point at which the New Zealand vowel system actually differs phonemically from that of RP. This makes the iə/eə contrast especially interesting. Trudgill appears to assume that, when the merger occurs, it will affect all words involving /ɪə/ and /eə/. Jean Aitchison (1981) however, suggests that a more piecemeal method of change known as lexical diffusion is equally likely. She says:

> Once a change has gained a foothold in a few common words, or group of words important to a particular subculture, it is likely to start moving through the vocabulary. This is a messy business, with different words affected at different times. Amidst general fluctuation, change spreads gradually through the lexicon (vocabulary) of the language, one or two words at a time. This word-by-word progress is known as lexical diffusion. (Aitchison, 1981: 95)

We thought that there was a strong possibility that the changes we were studying could be coming about through lexical diffusion.

Other investigators have found correlations between sound changes and social class (Labov, 1972a; 1972b; Macaulay, 1977; 1978). The comments that have traditionally been made about NZE have always indicated that social class is a factor in the changes observed (see Gordon & Abell, this volume). We therefore decided to include this factor in our investigations.

The Study

This paper presents the results of two investigations carried out on the iə/eə contrast in NZE. The first investigation was carried out in 1983 (Gordon & Maclagan, 1985) and the second follow-up study five years later in 1988. If we also include the research of Durkin in 1972 and an

[handwritten margin note: lexical diffusion hypothesis.]

acoustic study of New Zealand vowels carried out by Maclagan in 1978 (Maclagan, 1982), we have data on these diphthongs which go back sixteen years.

Hypotheses

In our investigation of the current state of the /iə/~/eə/ contrast in New Zealand speech, we set out six hypotheses to test.

(1) That for some New Zealand speakers, /iə/ and /eə/ have merged.
(2) That this merger is a fairly recent development and would therefore not be found in the speech of older New Zealand speakers.
(3) That some speakers who have merged these diphthongs use a closer starting point, [iə], and others use a more open starting point, [eə].
(4) That the change in pronunciation of /iə/ and /eə/ is affecting New Zealand speech by lexical diffusion. We expected that some pairs of words would be more likely to have merged, while in other pairs the contrast would be still maintained.
(5) That there would be a male/female difference both in the number of mergers, and in the type of mergers.
(6) That the position of the starting point of the merged diphthongs might be related to socio-economic class and/or accent.

Method

In 1983 with the help of two research assistants, interviews were tape-recorded with 160 Christchurch fourth-form students and about 20 elderly New Zealand speakers. In 1988, interviews were recorded with a further 118 fourth-form students.

In order to investigate the relationship between pronunciation and social class, we recorded students from four Christchurch secondary schools: a private boys' school, a private girls' school, a co-educational state school whose catchment area included more affluent suburbs and a co-educational state school whose catchment area included less affluent areas. We used the same state schools and private boys' school in both 1983 and 1988.[3] This design enabled us to compare social class differences between the private schools and the state schools, with reasonable balance between male and female speakers in each.[4]

Unfortunately, through a series of misadventures, we were unable to include the 1983 recordings from the private boys' school. In 1983, we were therefore left with recordings from 120 informants from three schools. We were able to use material from 105 of the 120 interviews obtained. In 1988 we were able to use material from 113 of the 118 interviews obtained.[5] The pupils interviewed were all in the fourth form, aged 14 or 15, and were of middle ability. Neither the highest nor the lowest ability classes in the schools were used in this project.

The interviews with the elderly informants were carried out in two Christchurch old people's homes. The interviews varied considerably in length. As well as reading the structured material, the speakers were invited to talk about their childhood and, where possible, to remember what they did in school English lessons. The interview with a 100-year-old woman petered out when she fell asleep. Other interviews were terminated with difficulty and the informants were overjoyed at being asked to assist with the project. Recordings from only 11 of these interviews have been used in the current analysis. The youngest of the speakers was 73 and the oldest 97. The average age was 84 years 6 months.

During the interviews with school pupils (which lasted about five minutes) informants in both 1983 and 1988 were asked to read sentences containing the /iə/~/eə/ diphthongs. Table 7.1 lists the recorded material that is relevant to the analysis described in this paper. We tried to ensure that the words being tested were in a stressed position, except for the 'air' in 'Air New Zealand' which we wanted to compare with 'air' on its own. 'Careful' and 'tearful', 'rarely' and 'really' were included as examples where the diphthongs were in a different phonetic context, *viz.* the stressed syllable of a disyllabic word. The pair 'kea' and 'care' was included as one where we thought that the merger was less likely to take place, 'kea' being the name for a New Zealand native parrot.

An unexpected and disquieting aspect of the study was the extent of the reading difficulties experienced by the fourth-form pupils. In addition, diminished sight made reading impossible for some of the older informants. The research assistant working with the elderly informants reported an unexpected reluctance, and in one case an outright refusal, to read the sentence 'The big brown bear was drinking beer'. We therefore agreed to omit that sentence in later interviews, and that word pair is not included in the data from the older speakers.

In order further to assess the relationship between social class and pronunciation, each school pupil was classified according to social class

TABLE 7.1 *Reading materials*

Test sentences containing /iə/ and /eə/

1. Come *here* and I'll brush your *hair*.
2. The big brown *bear* was drinking *beer*.
3. He sat on a *chair* and gave a loud *cheer*.
4. Can I have a word in your *ear*? I have *fears* that *Air* New Zealand is going to put up *fares*. Do you think it's *fair*? I think it's an insult. The result will be that we can't travel by *air*.
5. He would have known that he would lose the fight and that he would need his *spare spear*.

Word list
see, Sue, fall, bed, shed, ten, yes, grown, *shear*, poor, feel, *share*, bad, end.

Word pairs (part of a longer list of pairs)
careful/tearful   really/rarely   kea/care

From these recordings, the following word pairs were available for investigation:

1.	here/hair	7.	spear/spare
2.	beer/bear	8.	shear/share
3.	cheer/chair	9.	tearful/careful
4.	ear/air	10.	really/rarely
5.	fear/fare	11.	kea/care
6.	fear/fair		

---

using the revised Elley–Irving socio-economic index (1985). In this index occupations are ranked on six levels with Level 1 being the highest and Level 6 the lowest. Where both parents' occupations were given, the higher ranking occupation was used in the classification. In studies of Australian English, following the work of Mitchell & Delbridge (1965), speakers have been classified according to accent. Accent is assessed on the basis of the pronunciation of the long vowels and closing diphthongs in six key words: 'beat', 'boot', 'say', 'so', 'high' and 'how'. We classified all our school-aged speakers according to accent in order to see whether accent might be a relevant variable, using Mitchell & Delbridge's classification of Cultivated, General and Broad varieties.

Analysis

A close phonetic transcription was made of the data. The hypothesis being tested was that the two sounds /iə/ and /eə/ have merged for some speakers in some words. In transcription, the pairs of words were marked as distinct if any difference between them was audible. The results presented here will therefore *underestimate* rather than *overestimate* any trends towards diphthong merging in the data. The data were coded and fed into a computer for sorting and analysis. For final analysis, a judgement was made whether or not a speaker used the same diphthong in the two words belonging to a given pair. If the same diphthong was used, it was analysed as /iə/ or /eə/ as appropriate. If the two words remained distinct, this was noted.

The results were calculated separately for individual speakers and then summed across the various categories of interest (male, female, different schools, etc). Three figures were calculated for each speaker: the number of word pairs where both words were pronounced with /iə/, the number of word pairs which were kept distinct, and the number of word pairs which were both pronounced as /eə/. There was a total number of 11 pairs for each speaker. Adding the number of word pairs pronounced as /iə/ and the number pronounced as /eə/, gives the total number of pairs where the distinction is collapsed by a given speaker. A comparison can therefore be made between those speakers who show a trend towards collapsing the diphthongs (whatever the actual vowel chosen) and those who keep them apart. The probability of the various results happening by chance was calculated. In the tables, only those results are presented that would be extremely unlikely to have occurred by chance. Results are presented at both the 1% and the 5% levels of confidence.

Results

The results are presented in terms of the six hypotheses we set out to test.

First hypothesis

The first hypothesis was that /iə/ and /eə/ would have merged for some speakers. Table 7.2 presents the overall results for our school-aged speakers in 1983 and 1988. While patterns are not yet clear (at least 60% of subjects in each sample showing no statistically significant trends in their data), more subjects collapse the distinction than maintain it, and relatively more collapse the distinction at the higher level of confidence. A trend towards collapsing the distinction certainly seems indicated.

TABLE 7.2 *Comparison of 1983 and 1988 results: number of subjects who maintain or collapse the distinction between /iə/ and /eə/ a significant number of times*

		Subjects who maintain iə/eə	Subjects who collapse iə/eə	Subjects who show no trend
5% level of confidence	1983	14 (13.5%) n = 105	26 (24.8%)	65 (62.0%)
	1988	3 (2.6%) n = 113	37 (32.7%)	73 (64.6%)

The difference between the 1983 results and the 1988 results is significant. $p < 0.25$, $\chi^2 = 9.15$, 2 d.f.

1% level of confidence	1983	6 (5.5%) n = 105	17 (16.2%)	82 (78.0%)
	1988	2 (1.8%) n = 113	25 (22.1%)	86 (76.1%)

The difference between the 1983 results and the 1988 results fails to reach significance. $\chi^2 = 3.42$, 2 d.f.

In 1988 the trend towards collapsing the diphthongs is even clearer than in 1983. Only three subjects actually keep the diphthongs separate and relatively more speakers than in 1983 collapse the distinction (33% compared with 25%). Even though at least 60% of the subjects still show no statistically significant trend towards collapsing or maintaining the difference, this number may mask a movement towards collapsing the word pairs that is even greater than the results indicate. Although we are dealing with similar aged subjects in 1983 and 1988, we are not actually dealing with the same speakers in the two studies. It is possible that speakers who would have kept the diphthongs separate in 1983 have, by 1988, started to collapse them, but are not yet collapsing them a significant number of times. Similarly, speakers who would have showed no significant trend in 1983 may, by the 1988 study, be collapsing the diphthongs a significant number of times.

In spite of the number of subjects who show no clear trends, it would seem that the trend towards collapsing the diphthong pairs is stronger in 1988 than it was in 1983. A chi-squared test was used to see whether the greater number of speakers who collapsed the diphthongs was statistically significant or whether it could have happened by chance. Although the differences between the 1983 results and the 1988 results are not statistically significant at the 1% level, at the 5% level of confidence, the differences between the 1983 results and the 1988 results gives a chi-squared of 9.15 with 2 d.f. and $p < 0.025$. The increase in the number of speakers who collapse the diphthongs is therefore unlikely to have occurred by chance, and the extent to which /iə/ and /eə/ are being merged therefore seems to be increasing and may be increasing even more than these results indicate.

Second hypothesis

The second hypothesis was that the /iə/~/eə/ merger is recent and would not be found in the speech of our older speakers. To our surprise, five of the eleven older speakers did in fact collapse some of the pairs of words. Two women (ages 78 and 80) collapsed 'cheer' and 'chair' as /tʃeə/, and a woman (age 83) and a man (age 84) both produced 'sheer' and 'share' as /ʃeə/. The fifth speaker, a man aged 75 collapsed 'sheer' and 'share' on /ʃiə/ and also 'here' and 'hair' on /hiə/. The numbers are not large enough to draw conclusions from, and the trend is weaker than for the younger speakers, but, contrary to predictions, the merger does occur. Even though it has not been commented on by earlier writers, this merger may, in fact, have been present in New Zealand speech for longer than we realise.

Third hypothesis

The third hypothesis was that some speakers would collapse the distinction between /iə/ and /eə/ on /iə/ and others would collapse it on /eə/. Table 7.3 shows the way in which the speakers collapsed the diphthongs in 1983 and 1988. In 1983 slightly more speakers collapse the diphthong pairs on the open vowel than on the close vowel, and considerably more speakers consistently collapse the diphthong pairs than consistently keep them apart. In 1988, considerably more speakers again collapse the diphthong pairs than keep them apart — in fact, in 1988, only three speakers actually kept the diphthong pairs distinct a statistically significant number of times. Some speakers chose the lower /eə/ starting point for their collapsed diphthongs, but the great majority of speakers chose the higher /iə/ starting point. A chi-squared test indicates that the differences between the 1983 and 1988 results are highly unlikely to have

TABLE 7.3 *Comparison of 1983 and 1988 results: number of subjects who collapse or maintain the diphthong distinction a significant number of times, according to the choice of diphthong used*

		iə/iə	iə/eə	eə/eə
5% level of confidence	1983	10 (9.0%) n = 105	14 (13.3%)	16 (15.0%)
	1988	31 (27.4%) n = 113	3 (2.6%)	6 (5.3%)

The difference between the 1983 results and the 1988 results is significant. $p < 0.005$, $\chi^2 = 23.55$, 2 d.f.

		iə/iə	iə/eə	eə/eə
1% level of confidence	1983	8 (7.5%) n = 105	6 (5.5%)	9 (8.0%)
	1988	23 (20.3%) n = 113	2 (1.8%)	2 (1.8%)

The difference between the 1983 results and the 1988 results is significant. $p < 0.005$, $\chi^2 = 13.64$, 2 d.f.

occurred by chance ($p < 0.005$ at both the 5% and the 1% levels of confidence). When we first interpreted the 1983 results, it seemed to us that our third hypothesis was supported: speakers varied in the starting point they chose for the merged diphthongs. When we examine the 1988 results, the hypothesis is again supported, but many more speakers are choosing the higher starting point than the lower one. Although speakers still vary in their choice of starting point for the merged diphthongs, there now seems to be pressure towards the closer position.

Fourth hypothesis

The fourth hypothesis was that the trend towards collapsing the difference between /iə/ and /eə/ is proceeding through the lexicon by lexical diffusion. This hypothesis is clearly upheld in that different pairs of words are treated differently, but the progress of these changes supports Jean Aitchison's comment that lexical diffusion can be a messy business. Trends that appeared to be established in 1983 have been reversed in

1988. Table 7.4 presents the word pairs that were collapsed on /iə/, those that were collapsed on /eə/ and those that were kept distinct at the 1% level of confidence. The difference in pattern is immediately apparent: in 1983 two pairs were collapsed on /iə/ and five pairs were collapsed on /eə/, whereas in 1988 five pairs were collapsed on /iə/ and only one pair, 'cheer' and 'chair' remained collapsed on /eə/. To add to the confusion, different pairs of words are collapsed or kept distinct in the two studies.

'Really' and 'rarely' and 'kea' and 'care' are collapsed on /iə/ in both studies and it would seem that the merger has worked right through with these pairs. 'Kea' and 'care' were included in the original study because we did not expect them to be merged. The results overwhelmingly indicate that 'care' is pronounced as /kiə/, thus becoming merged with 'kea'. We expect that a general movement towards a closer pronunciation of the front centring diphthongs would happen faster in words where there is not a meaningful contrast between /iə/ and /eə/ in a word pair. We therefore wonder if 'kea' and 'care' are *not* regarded as a pair, so that 'care' was able to change in pronunciation to /kiə/ unhindered by pressure from an /eə/ pair word. The /kiə/ pronunciation for 'care' has, in fact, rendered it identical with 'kea'. This also suggests that further study of these diphthongs should include words where there are no minimal pairs.

TABLE 7.4 *Trends according to word pairs in 1983 and 1988*

	1983	1988
Collapsed on /iə/	really/rarely	really/rarely
	kea/care	kea/care
		hear/hair
		spear/spare
		shear/share
Remain distinct	fear/fare	fear/fare
	fear/fair	fear/fair
	tearful/careful	tearful/careful
	here/hair	ear/air
Collapsed on /eə/	cheer/chair	cheer/chair
	beer/bear	
	ear/air	
	spear/spare	
	shear/share	

'Spear/spare' and 'shear/share' were merged on /eə/ in 1983. They have moved to being merged on /iə/ in 1988. A possible explanation for this is that the closer diphthong may have been stigmatised in 1983 as the merger started to become apparent. The more open pronunciation for these two merged pairs could have been caused by an attempt to avoid the stigmatised closer diphthong. By 1988 the merger seems to be becoming more readily acknowledged and the closer pronunciation may no longer be stigmatised. Thus it could be now following the general trend towards the closer pronunciation.

This hypothesis is strengthened by the treatment of 'here' and 'hair' which were kept separate in 1983 but merged on /iə/ in 1988. In 1988 female and lower social class speakers merge the two words (see below), whereas males keep them distinct. 'Beer' and 'bear' went from being merged on /eə/ in 1983 to showing no clear pattern in 1988. Nevertheless, in 1988 some of the female speakers have moved to using the closer diphthong a significant number of times for this pair. It would seem that as with 'spear/spare' and 'sheer/share' the closer diphthong no longer has any social stigma attached to it, and contrary to expectations, it is the females who are leading the trend toward the closer pronunciation.

'Tearful' and 'careful' were kept distinct in both studies. So were 'fear' and 'fare' and 'fear' and 'fair'. There is no *a priori* reason why these two pairs should be treated in similar ways, or why 'fair' and 'fare' should now receive the same pronunciation. In 1983 'fare' and 'fair' were both overwhelmingly pronounced with the open diphthong. In 1988 'fair' but not 'fare' is pronounced with the closer diphthong by a significant number of female speakers. Again lexical diffusion seems to be operating, led by the female speakers, and this time it is separating two words, 'fair' and 'fare' that have always before been identical in pronunciation.

Fifth hypothesis

The fifth hypothesis was that males and females might treat the word pairs differently. In 1983, there was slight evidence that girls preferred the lower starting point, collapsing the diphthongs on /eə/ for 'beer/bear' and for 'spear/spare'. The boys, by contrast seemed to prefer the higher starting point, collapsing 'spear/spare' on /iə/. The pattern was not completely clear, in that the girls, but not the boys, collapsed 'really/rarely' on /iə/. These results are set out in Table 7.5.

In 1988, the results were different. The preference for /eə/ shown by the girls in 1983 has disappeared and the girls seem, in fact, to be

TABLE 7.5 *Male/female differences in the treatment of the word pairs in 1983 and 1988*

Female speakers					
1983	/iə/			really/rarely	
	/eə/	spear/spare	beer/bear		
1988	/iə/	spear/spare	beer/bear	really/rarely	fear/fare
	/eə/				
Male speakers					
1983	/iə/	spear/spare			
	/eə/			really/rarely	
1988	/iə/	spear/spare		really/rarely	
	/eə/				

leading the trend towards the closer pronunciation of the diphthongs. They no longer collapse 'bear/bare' on /eə/. Instead there is an, as yet non-significant, move towards collapsing this pair on /iə/, a move that is not shared by the boys in the 1988 sample. Everyone collapses 'spear/ spare' on /iə/ and the boys have joined the girls in collapsing 'really/ rarely' on /iə/. The girls but not the boys collapse 'fear/fair' on /iə/. (As noted above, neither group collapses 'fear/fare'. At present 'fair' appears to be affected by the sound change, but 'fare' is not.)

We had expected that the more open pronunciation would be the more conservative pronunciation (see Trudgill, 1974) and that the girls would retain this more open pronunciation more often than the boys. The 1983 results seemed to support this hypothesis, even though we indicated that they needed to be treated with caution. We now suggest that the apparent reversal of trend is compatible with a suggestion that the sound change must have still been stigmatised in 1983. The more open pronunciation retained by the girls at that time probably was, in fact, the more conservative hypercorrected pronunciation. By 1988 the change seems to have become accepted and the girls, as well as the boys, use the closer pronunciation.

Sixth hypothesis

The sixth hypothesis was that social class and/or accent as defined by Mitchell & Delbridge (1965) might affect the starting point of the diphthongs. In 1983 we suggested that there was an interaction between social class and sex in the trends observed. In 1988 we still consider that this is the case.

In 1983 there is a slight trend for speakers who were from lower social classes as measured on the Elley–Irving scale to prefer a higher starting point for the diphthongs whereas those who were from higher social classes preferred a lower starting point. More lower-class speakers collapsed 'spear/spare', 'really/rarely' and 'kea/care' on /iə/ and more upper-class speakers collapsed 'beer/bare' and 'spear/spare' on /eə/ and kept 'really/rarely' and 'kea/care' distinct.

No clear trends emerged in the preferences of speakers with different accents. Some Cultivated speakers kept more pairs distinct, but there was no parallel trend for General or Broad speakers to collapse more pairs than the overall average. In 1988 there were so few Cultivated and Broad speakers in our sample that we did not analyse the data according to accent. This trend towards a greater number of General speakers is similar to one noted by Horvath in her samples of Australian English (Horvath, 1985: 91).

In both studies we used the differences between the schools in order to investigate the effects of social class on diphthong pronunciation. In 1988 the only differences between the private and state schools was that the state-school students merged 'here/hair' on /iə/ while the private-school speakers kept them distinct, and the private-school speakers merged 'beer/bear' on /iə/ while the state-school speakers showed no trend.

In 1988 we decided to check the results for social classes summed across all schools. Because of the very small number of pupils in some levels we conflated the six categories on the Elley–Irving socio-economic index into three groups, representing higher, middle and lower socio-economic groupings. Table 7.6 presents the results for the numbers of speakers who collapse the diphthongs on /iə/, those who keep the pairs distinct and those who collapse them on /eə/ for the three social class groupings in 1988. Although the numbers are small and the differences that show up are not, in fact, statistically significant, as the social class becomes lower there is a trend towards a closer pronunciation for more pairs of the diphthongs. This trend is shown more clearly when percentages, rather than raw scores, are used as in Table 7.7.

For the individual word pairs, the only significant difference was for 'here/hair' with the higher grouping keeping them distinct while the other two groupings merged them on /hiə/. When male and female speakers are considered separately even the higher grouping females

TABLE 7.6 *Numbers of speakers who collapse and maintain the distinction between diphthong pairs according to social class and diphthong starting point in 1988*

		Collapse on iə	Maintain the distinction	Collapse on eə
(higher) Classes 1 and 2	5% level	9	2	5
n = 36	1% level	8	1	2
(middle) Classes 3 and 4	5% level	16	1	5
n = 60	1% level	11	1	4
(lower) Classes 5 and 6	5% level	6	—	1
n = 17	1% level	4	—	—

TABLE 7.7 *Percentages of speakers who collapse and maintain the distinction between the diphthong pairs at the 5% level of confidence according to social class and diphthong starting point in 1988*

	Collapse on iə (%)	Maintain distinction (%)	Collapse on eə (%)
Classes 1 and 2	25.0	5.5	14.0
Classes 3 and 4	26.0	1.5	8.0
Classes 5 and 6	35.0	—	5.0

merge these two words. The higher grouping males merge 'tearful/careful' on /eə/ (the only group to do this in the two studies) and fail to show any trends for 'spear/spare' and 'sheer/share'. The higher grouping females keep 'tearful/careful' distinct and merge 'spear/spare' and 'sheer/share' on /iə/. The middle grouping males are relatively conservative, keeping 'here/hair' distinct and merging 'shear/share' on /eə/. The middle grouping females merge 'here/hair', 'fear/fair' and 'shear/share' on /iə/. There are relatively fewer speakers in the lower social class groupings so the results for this grouping must be treated more cautiously than the results for the other groupings. The males, but not the females, merged 'fear/fare' on /iə/ (the only group to do so) and the females, but not the males, merged 'fear/fair' on /iə/. The males, but not the females, merged 'sheer/share' on /iə/.

There thus seems to be a trend in the two higher social class groupings for the females to use /iə/ diphthongs more often than the male speakers. This trend does not appear in the lower social class grouping but the numbers are too small for any conclusion to be drawn about this grouping. Nevertheless, it would appear that the social classes are treating the diphthongs differently, with more speakers from lower classes using the closer diphthong. It also appears that, within social classes, male and female speakers are behaving differently, with female speakers leading the movement towards the closer pronunciation.

Conclusions

Mary Durkin's conclusions from her 1972 study were that the diphthongs were merging on the more open variants. However her phonetic transcriptions of [ɛ̣ə]/[ɛ̣ə] and [eə]/[eə] indicate that what she describes as an 'open' variant is auditorily relatively close.

As a result of acoustic analysis of data recorded in 1978, one of the current authors wrote: 'In the present study, the starting points for the diphthongs are closer rather than open, so that a transcription of /iə/ would be more appropriate than /ɛə/ [Maclagan, 1982: 24).

As a result of our 1983 study, we wrote: 'Most of those who have commented on the /iə/~/eə/ merger indicate that the two diphthongs are merged with a close starting point, i.e. that they merge on /iə/. In this study there is a small but consistent overall trend towards preferring the more open starting point /eə/' (Gordon & Maclagan, 1985: 25). In our 1988 study, there was a clear move towards the closer starting point, /iə/.

On the surface these results are difficult to explain. Most commentators (with the exception of Trudgill & Hannah, 1982) claim that /iə/ and /eə/ are merged on the closer diphthong in NZE, and yet our 1983 data, in contrast to Maclagan's limited 1978 acoustic data and our 1988 data, had many more word pairs merged on the more open diphthong. We would speculate that our samples have spanned a period during which awareness of the diphthong merger increased. As people became aware of the potential merger (as indicated by the letter to the *Listener* quoted in the introduction to this chapter), the closer pronunciation became stigmatised and the more open pronunciation became desirable. Our 1983 results, with the female speakers and those from higher social classes showing a slight preference for the more open vowel would support the greater prestige of the /eə/ pronunciation.

As the merger of /iə/ and /eə/ became more common and less stigmatised, the pressure towards the more open pronunciation became less. Words containing /eə/ were then free to continue to move towards the closer pronunciation, and words containing /iə/ were no longer hypercorrected towards the more prestigious open pronunciation. Word pairs that had been collapsed on /eə/ in 1983 were free to move towards /iə/, a movement that some of them may have already started before the 1983 study was undertaken. Perhaps this was interrupted as people became more conscious of potential confusions and hypercorrected their pronunciations. The fact that in 1988 the female speakers used more closer pronunciations than the male speakers supports our contention that in general the closer pronunciation of the diphthongs is no longer stigmatised. However the fact that the higher social classes are still using more open pronunciations than are the lower social classes may indicate that some stigma still remains on the closer diphthongs for some speakers.[6] If we are correct in our assumption that 'kea' and 'care' are not seen as a minimal pair we could also hypothesise that words containing /eə/ which are not part of a pair would be more likely to move to /iə/ than those in a pair where a potential distinction can be made. In the 1988 study, the pair 'cheer/chair' are still collapsed on /eə/. We would suggest that this pair may eventually also move towards the closer pronunciation and collapse on /iə/.

The nature of this piece of research is such that a conservative result could be expected. It is well known that people reading sentences or word lists aloud will produce more careful speech than they would use in spontaneous conversations. So it is possible that some of our informants took extra care to differentiate words spelt differently in our word lists and thus produced a greater differentiation of the diphthongs we were investigating. It is possible that if the data had come from spontaneous spoken English there might have been an even greater incidence of the merging of these two diphthongs.

After our 1983 study we wrote: 'In conclusion, we would agree with Peter Hawkins that "the sounds in this area are undergoing significant changes at present"' (1985: 24). We also wrote that the situation involving the front centring diphthongs in NZE is not as simple as most commentators have contended. We would still stand by these statements. The sound changes involving /iə/ and /eə/ are still in progress and the final pattern may well not yet be apparent. At this stage, it seems that the closer /iə/ pronunciation is becoming established, but further study is necessary to check the movement and to investigate further the effects of sex and social class on the diphthong movement.

Notes

1. We would like to acknowledge the help given to us in this research by our research assistants Shirley C'Ailceta, Kathryn Yeadon and Gillian Lewis. We would also like to thank Derry Gordon who wrote the computer program used for the analysis of the data and Robert Maclagan who helped with the analysis of the data. Special thanks are due to the older New Zealand speakers and the teachers and pupils in the schools who participated in this study. We also acknowledge our gratitude to the University of Canterbury for funding the research project. An earlier version of this paper appears in the *Australian Journal of Linguistics*, December 1989.
2. We consider that Holmes & Bell are over-simplifying when they state, 'if they do not make the distinction when faced with *beer* and *bear* side by side, we can be reasonably confident this distinction has disappeared from their speech' (1988: 24). Holmes & Bell do include other iə/eə pairs in their word list, but we do not think it is adequate to test for this phoneme difference on the basis of one pair alone as the text of their article seems to indicate.
3. Although a different private girls' school was used for the second study a 1988 analysis of both schools using the Elley–Irving Socio-Economic Index (1985) showed them to be almost identical.
4. In order to disrupt schools as little as possible, we used complete classes. The balance between male and female speakers in the co-educational schools therefore relies on the extent to which classes were balanced in the schools concerned. (There are, in fact, more female than male speakers in the study.) The design also enabled us to compare male and female speakers across all schools, and hence across social classes.
5. In both studies we removed recordings where there were technical difficulties or where the speakers were not native New Zealanders.
6. We would like to thank David Bradley for his support of our theory of hypercorrection (personal communication).

References

AITCHISON, JEAN 1981, *Language Change: Progress or Decay?* London: Fontana.
CASSIDY, FREDERIC G. and LE PAGE, ROBERT 1980, *Dictionary of Jamaican English.* Cambridge: Cambridge University Press.
DURKIN, MARY E. 1972, A study of the pronunciation, oral grammar and vocabulary of West Coast schoolchildren. Unpublished MA thesis. Christchurch: University of Canterbury.
ELLEY, W.B. and IRVING, J.C. 1985, The Elley–Irving Socio-Economic Index: 1981 Census Revision. *NZ Journal of Educational Studies* 20 (2), 115–28.
FROMKIN, VICTORIA, RODMAN, ROBERT, COLLINS, PETER and BLAIR, DAVID 1984, *An Introduction to Language* (Australian edn). Sydney: Holt, Rinehart & Winston.
FRY, D.B. 1947, The frequency of occurrence of speech sounds in Southern English. *Archive Néerlandaises de Phonétique Expérimentale* XX, 103–6.
GORDON, ELIZABETH 1983, New Zealand pronunciation: an investigation into some early written records. *Te Reo* 26, 29–42.

GORDON, ELIZABETH and MACLAGAN, MARGARET A. 1985, A study of the /iə/~ /eə/ contrast in New Zealand English. *The New Zealand Speech-Language Therapists' Journal* 40 (2), 16–26.

HAWKINS, P.R. 1973, The sound-patterns of New Zealand English. In *Proceedings and Papers of the 15th Congress* (13/1–8). Sydney: Australasian Universities Language & Literature Association.

HOLMES, JANET and BELL, ALLAN 1988, Learning by experience: notes for New Zealand social dialectologists. *Te Reo* 31, 19–49.

HORVATH, BARBARA M. 1985, *Variation in Australian English.* Cambridge: Cambridge University Press.

KURATH, HANS and McDAVID, RAVEN I. 1961, *The Pronunciation of English in the Atlantic States.* Ann Arbor: University of Michigan Press.

LABOV, WILLIAM 1966, *The Social Stratification of English in New York City.* Washington, DC: Centre for Applied Linguistics.

— 1972a, *Language in the Inner City.* Philadelphia: University of Pennsylvania Press.

— 1972b, *Sociolinguistic Patterns.* Philadelphia: University of Pennsylvania Press.

MACAULAY, RONALD K.S. 1977, *Language, Social Class and Education.* Edinburgh: Edinburgh University Press.

— 1978, Variation and consistency in Glaswegian English. In PETER TRUDGILL (ed.), *Sociolinguistic Patterns in British English* (pp. 132–43). London: Edward Arnold.

MACLAGAN, MARGARET A. 1982, An acoustic study of New Zealand vowels. *The New Zealand Speech Therapists' Journal* 37 (1), 20–6.

MITCHELL, A.G. and DELBRIDGE, ARTHUR 1965, *The Speech of Australian Adolescents.* Sydney: Angus and Robertson.

TRUDGILL, PETER 1974, *The Social Differentiation of English in Norwich.* Cambridge: Cambridge University Press.

TRUDGILL, PETER and HANNAH, JEAN 1982, *International English.* London: Edward Arnold.

TURNER, G.W. 1966, *The English Language in Australia and New Zealand.* London: Longman.

WALL, ARNOLD 1938, *New Zealand English: How it Should be Spoken.* Christchurch: Whitcombe & Tombs.

WELLS, J.C. 1982, *Accents of English.* Cambridge: Cambridge University Press.

8   Minder, Mork and Mindy? (-t) glottalisation and post-vocalic (-r) in younger New Zealand English speakers

DONN BAYARD

Background

In 1984–85 I carried out a Labovian study of sociolinguistic variation in 141 New Zealand English (NZE) speakers (Bayard, 1987; in press d). During the analysis, I noted sporadic to common occurrences of two phonological phenomena not usually associated with NZE: a fully glottalised realisation of word-final /-t/, and occasional post-vocalic /-r/ and rhoticised NURSE vowels.

Outside the Southland region, NZE is presumed to be completely non-rhotic, and I found its sporadic occurrence among my younger NZE informants of interest, even though many of the examples appear to have been stimulated by spelling pronunciations of word-list items. (-t) glottalisation was considerably more common, although most general surveys of NZE phonology (Turner, 1970; Wells, 1982; Trudgill & Hannah, 1985) make no mention of the presence of (-t) glottalisation in NZE. However, Bauer, in his more recent thorough survey of NZE phonetics and phonology, is clearly aware of the phenomenon:

> Word-finally and syllable-finally before another consonant all the voiceless plosives are frequently glottalised, and may also be unreleased. Often the oral closure is entirely missing, and only a glottal stop remains. This type of pronunciation is also found

149

utterance-finally, where it is in variation with an aspirated oral stop. Glottalisation appears to be less frequent in this environment. No study of this subject has, to my knowledge, been carried out, so no information is available on whether glottalisation is affected by the nature of the following consonant or the place of articulation of the stop. (Bauer, 1986: 15)

My observations seem to confirm that glottalisation is indeed much less common in utterance-final contexts, and suggest that glottalised /-k/ is rare and /-p/ even more so (I encountered no cases). However, this study is concerned with the effects of social rather than phonological constraints on glottalisation and rhoticity, particularly as my initial results suggested that youth was the most significant variable associated with both variables (once rhotic Southland accents were excluded from consideration). To test this, I re-analysed the speech samples of those speakers exhibiting clear cases of one or both phenomena, and quantified occurrences in each sample.

Procedure

The samples analysed were the 170-word reading passage and word lists employed in the earlier Labovian study (Bayard, 1987; see also Bayard, this volume); these provided 26 and 25 occurrences of (-r) and (-t) respectively in the reading passage (which was read twice), and 26 possible environments for rhoticity in the word lists. The total (-t) and (-r) scores for each informant were the larger of the glottalised (-t) and rhotic (-r) counts for each of the two readings, with the rhotic (-r) score for the word lists added to the second value. For economy '-r' rather than 'rhotic (-r)' and '-t' rather than 'glottalised (-t)' are used in the tables below.

Rhoticity (including degree of r-colouring of the NURSE vowel) is obviously a continuum, and only cases exhibiting clear r-coloration in this environment and in Wells' START, NEAR, SQUARE, NORTH/FORCE, CURE, and LETTER lexical sets (Wells, 1982: 123–68) were counted in scoring. Linking and intrusive (-r) were of course ignored in scoring. Four values of word-final (-t) were observed: unaspirated unreleased; unaspirated released; simultaneous glottal-apicoalveolar closure; and glottal closure only. Only the last was counted in scoring glottalised (-t).[1] Of course speakers of many English accents employ a glottal allophone of /-t/ in at least some environments (Wells, 1982: 260–1); e.g. my own North American (NAm) accent in contexts like 'don't go, can't go'. As only a relatively small number of tokens of (-t) were present in the fairly short texts, I arbitrarily assigned a score of 12% (i.e. three occurrences of [-?]) to all speakers. This was done to avoid giving the heavy glottalisers undue weight when running correlations, even though many of the older speakers scored below 12% (the actual unweighted percentages appear in Table 8.1).

The sample of 36 NZE speakers (Table 8.1) in which I had previously observed rhotic (-r) and/or (-t) glottalisation appears to fall into three fairly clear-cut groups as far as (-r) is concerned:

(1) children and young adults with rhotic (mainly NAm) parents (10; age range 6–23)
(2) older speakers from Southland and Dunedin (9; age range 24–71)
(3) other children of definitely non-rhotic parents (17; age range 7–19).

With respect to (-t), the relevant contrast is between younger Groups A and C on the one hand, and older Group B on the other. The data are combined in Table 8.1 for the sake of economy only, not to imply any relationship between the two variables, which in fact are not correlated (see Conclusion).

I analysed the results using groups t-tests to search for significant differences between the two younger groups, and rank-order correlations of (-r) or (-t) with several linguistic and social variables used in my earlier study (Bayard, 1985; 1987). As the title of this paper suggests, I am tentatively hypothesising that the spoken media are influential in the introduction or at least the possible spread of the two variables under consideration. Hence I was curious to see how occurrences of innovative values of these variables correlated with innovation in other phonological and lexical variables in the two younger groups. By 'innovative' in the phonological sense I refer to 'broad' variants of the four diphthongs (ei) (au) (ai) (ou), diphthongisation of (i), (-l) vocalisation, and the like (see Bayard, 1987). Lexical innovation on the other hand refers to use of or preference for American lexical items like 'elevator', 'eraser', 'gas' and 'flashlight' over older NZE/SEE[2] 'lift', 'rubber', 'petrol' and 'torch'. Twenty-seven such pairs of words were investigated as part of my 1984–85 study (Bayard, 1985; 1989). Rather than refer to the individual pairs of words, I employ here several overall indices from the earlier study:

LEXUSE: a scale measuring the continuum of reported *use* of one or the other of the 27 pairs of words, ranging from the 40s for North American informants to the

TABLE 8.1 *Informants analysed for pre-consonantal -r and -t glottalisation*

Sex	Age	Geog. Region[a]	N -r in text-list	Total -r (%)	Total glottal -t (%)	LEXUSE	LEXPREF	CONSIND
Group A: With one or both parents non-NZE rhotic (N = 9); listed by ascending age								
M	6	DN	11—23	65	0	62	61	−1
F	8	DN	7—9	31	24	68	67	−1
M	8	DN	0—2	4	32	62	65	3
M	8	DN	4—7	21	44	55	57	2
M	9	DN	7—14	40	8	67	71	4
F	11	DN	0—5	10	64	61	67	6
M	19	DN	0—0	0	24	63	65	2
M	20	SL	9—18	52	20	61	59	−2
M	23	SL	18—25	83	28	65	66	1
Mean	12.4		6.2—11.4	34.0	27.1	62.7	64.2	1.56
Group B: Older Southland and Dunedin, parents NZE (N = 10); listed by ascending age								
M	24	SL	11—18	56	4	73	77	4
F	24	SL	3—16	37	36	70	67	−3
M	27	DN	4—4	15	4	72	71	−1
F	44	DN	1—4	10	0	77	75	−2
F	53	DN	7—13	25	0	75	67	−8
F	58	SL	7—15	42	0	80	80	0
F	67	DN	0—2	4	0	72	70	−2
M	67	DN	9—19	54	8	71	73	2
M	68	SL	12—15	52	0	80	61	−19
F	71	SL	10—10	38	0	75	79	4
Mean	50.3		5.7—11.6	33.3	5.2	74.5	72.0	−2.5

Group C: Remaining rhotic/glottalised sample (N = 17); listed by ascending age

Sex	Age	Loc						
M	7	DN	0—1	2	24	68	65	-2
F	7	DN	0—5	10	64	67	57	-10
F	7	DN	5—10	35	28	72	74	2
F	7	DN	0—3	6	20	75	59	-16
M	7	DN	0—6	15	24	69	63	-6
M	8	DN	0—2	4	20	63	60	-3
M	8	DN	2—3	13	44	64	65	1
F	8	DN	2—4	12	32	67	69	2
M	9	DN	3—17	38	20	73	69	-4
M	10	DN	0—0	0	28	72	66	-6
F	10	DN	0—0	0	20	77	75	-2
M	12	OT	2—0	4	32	66	77	11
F	13	DN	0—1	2	24	73	73	0
F	13	DN	0—0	0	40	73	63	-10
M	17	DN	0—0	0	56	73	71	-2
M	18	SL	5—4	17	4	63	67	4
M	19	DN	0—9	17	16	72	73	1
Mean	10.6		1.1—3.8	10.3	29.2	69.8	67.4	-2.35

a. DN = Dunedin; SL = Southland; OT = rural Otago.

80s for SEE speakers, with most of the 141 NZE informants in the high 60s and 70s (mean value 72.3).

LEXPREF: a similar scale based on reported *preference* as 'better English' (mean 69.0).

SECIND: a 'lexical security index' based on the absolute (unsigned) difference between LEXUSE and LEXPREF, ranging from 0 ('completely secure') to 20 ('very insecure') (mean 5.5).

CONSIND: a 'conservative-innovative' index derived by subtracting LEXUSE from LEXPREF, negative for those whose 'insecurity' deviates from usage toward US models ('innovative') and positive for those preferring more SEE models than they use ('conservative') (range −20 to +11; mean −3.3).

Results: (-r)

Turning firstly to the post-vocalic (-r) variable, it is clear from the results given for Group B in Table 8.1 that the famous 'Southland r' is still quite alive there. The number of older speakers in Group B (mean age 50, with only three under 40) may perhaps suggest that it is becoming confined to them. The mean age of the nine other Southland informants in my sample who were non-rhotic and hence not included in Group B is 37. Somewhat stronger evidence for this is provided by a very brief survey carried out by a student from Invercargill (Richardson, 1986). Although based on a small sample (30), her results indicate a drop in (-r) from over 80% rhotic to approximately 65% in speakers under 50. Much more marked, however, was the preponderance of rhotic (-r) in working- as opposed to middle-class informants (94% *versus* 26%), and in rural *versus* urban dwellers (95% and 50%). Informants' statements made it clear that rhotic (-r) is stigmatised among urban middle-class Southlanders, although it appears to have some measure of covert prestige among working-class Invercargillites.[3] Obviously not all Southlanders are affected by this stigma (e.g. three of my informants, a retired minister, a graduate student and a 71-year-old middle-class returning student).

The situation with the children and young adults in groups A and C (Table 8.1, A and C) appears to be quite different. My ten-year-old son reports no stigma at all attached to rhoticism among his peers, one of whom is a child of NZE-speaking parents who retains a marked use of

(-r) even three years after returning from an early childhood in America. On the other hand, I have encountered two students born and raised in North America who remember well having their NAm accents so ridiculed in high school that they quickly abandoned them, and now have almost flawless non-rhotic NZE accents. This may indicate an increasing stigma as speakers enter adolescence, but attitudes may also have changed over the decade or more since these two students underwent their conversion.

As would be expected, the rhotic-parent group of children (Group A) exhibits a much higher mean percentage of rhotic (-r) than those with non-rhotic parents (Group C; 34% *versus* 10%); this is one of several statistically significant differences between the two groups. Obviously stylistic context and register would have some effect on the degree of rhoticity present, and the samples analysed were of course all in formal reading-passage and word-list registers, which would tend to encourage spelling pronunciations and increase rhoticism in both groups. On the other hand, a brief experiment carried out with my son at the age of eight would suggest that accentual context or 'accommodation' (Giles & Powesland, 1975: 157ff) is considerably more important than formal *versus* informal register.[4] However, the question obviously requires further investigation. Based on my knowledge of the family backgrounds of the Group A children, degree of rhotic (-r) retention would appear to depend on the amount of verbal interaction with rhotic parents, and on the degree of isolation and lack of contact with non-rhotic peers.

Oddly enough, the negative CONSIND average of the less rhotic children in Group C suggests that these children *prefer* somewhat more US words than they use. On the other hand, the more rhotic children in Group A, with a positive CONSIND mean, *use* more US items than they prefer (hardly surprising given their parents' dialect). Perhaps the children of non-rhotic parents (Group C) are aiming toward a usage pattern already held by Group A.

Rank-order coefficients indicate that rhotic values of (-r) are very significantly correlated with youth, lower SEI, innovative lexical use, and a tendency to prefer conservative lexical models (CONSIND; this last is probably explained by the presence of the older Southlanders in Group B). Less marked but still significant correlations are also present with female gender, mother's accent and degree of lexical insecurity (SECIND).

While the 10% overall figure for rhotic values of (-r) in Group C is not a large one, it is nonetheless noteworthy in a largely non-rhotic speech community. The difference between the 15% figure for rhotic (-r) in word lists and 4% for (-r) in the reading passage makes it clear

TABLE 8.2 Changes in mean values of -t, -r and other variables over two-year period: 19 young NZE speakers

| | -t (%) | -r[a] (%) | ei | au | ai | -l[b] | Mergers: | | | |
							EAR[c]	AEL[d]	SKED[e]	ZED[f]
1985–86	28.8	6.8	2.74	2.16	2.16	2.84	2.00	2.35	1.75	2.4
1987–88	23.4	4.0	2.58	1.90	2.00	1.84	3.05	1.78	1.19	3.1
Change	−5.4	−2.8	−0.16	−0.26	−0.16	−1.00	+1.05	−0.57	−0.56	+0.6

[a] -r means based on texts only; see Note 6.
[b] -l = (-l) vocalisation.
[c] EAR = /iə/–/eə/ merger.
[d] AEL = /æl/–/el/ merger.
[e] SKED = 'skedule'/'shedule'.
[f] ZED = 'zee'/'zed'.
Variables ei–zed scored from 1 = 'broad/innovative' to 4 = 'cultivated/conservative'.

that orthographic influences are probably responsible for a high percentage of rhotic (-r) occurrences. On the other hand, in the full sample of 141, 12 of the 30 NZE informants under the age of 20 with non-rhotic parents featured at least one occurrence of rhotic (-r), and one informant had a total of 17 out of 26 possible rhotic (-r)s in the word lists. Hence I think it is of some interest to ask if the phenomenon is a permanent one, or whether this sporadic rhoticity will tend to disappear as children in both Groups A and C become older.

I was able to effect a tentative test of this by arranging retesting interviews with 19 of the children in my original sample approximately two years after their first session (age ranges 6–13, 8–15). A new text was used, featuring not only occurrences of (-r) in all environments, but also a number of (-t) slots and several alternative pronunciation items, including some not used in the first test.[5] I was hoping to ascertain tentatively whether (-r) is following the same course as several other innovative phonological and lexical features. The sample is not a randomly selected one, relying on the continuation of social networks and contacts over the two-year period, but some of the results are worth comment.

The overall trend in this admittedly small sample seems to be toward more innovative phonological values of the three diphthongs, (-l) vocalisation, and /æl/–/el/ merger listed in Table 8.2. I found the increase in (-l) vocalisation particularly striking when listening to the tapes, but some of this is quite likely due to the use of word lists rather than a reading passage to score the variable in the original tests. With less merger in the later sample, /eə/–/iə/ merger appears to go against this trend. In terms of the alternative pronunciation variables 'schedule'/ 'skedule' and 'zed'/'zee', agreement is almost universal on 'schedule', but 'zed' appears to be putting up a fairly successful struggle. But in terms of the permanence of rhotic (-r), there is a noticeable decrease in the initially small percentage of rhotic values in the reading passages. This plus internal negative correlations of -0.46 (first test) and -0.50 (second test; $p < 0.05$ in both cases) between age and rhotic (-r) within this group of 19 children alone tentatively suggest that (-r) is not following the pattern exhibited by the other variables, and that rhoticity is indeed a temporary phenomenon which tends to decrease as children grow older. Obviously further study will be needed to confirm this.[6]

Results: (-t)

(-t) glottalisation appears to be much more firmly entrenched among younger NZE speakers, with young Groups A and C using 27% and 29%, while the older Group B average only 5%. Glottalised (-t) is thus very highly correlated with youth (-0.47 with age for the total sample of 141; $p = 0.000$). Thus its significant correlation with the use and preference of 'innovative' US lexical items comes as no surprise. Even when the effect of socio-economic index (SEI) is held constant, the correlation with age is almost as marked (-0.41; $p = 0.000$). On the other hand, if the effect of age is held constant, a correlation with SEI of -0.21 ($p = 0.008$) suggests some ties between amount of (-t) glottalisation and lower SEI, but this is not as strong as with youth.

Finally, the figures for the sample of 19 retested after two years (Table 8.2) also suggest that (-t) glottalisation will prove to be a fairly enduring phenomenon. Although percentage of glottalisation declined from 29 to 23%, almost a quarter of possible occurrences of /-t/ were fully glottalised. Obviously further work needs to be done to establish phonological probabilistic rules for glottalisation in NZE which are beyond the scope of this paper, but in the interim it appears that it is here to stay for quite some time.

Discussion and Conclusions

It would be interesting to attempt to find at least tentative causes for the appearance of these two phonological features, even though one of them may prove to be quite ephemeral. Given my previous arguments for the effect of the spoken media on NZE (Bayard, 1987: 21–5), it is not surprising that I see their influence at work here.

In terms of (-r) there is an interesting set of correlations which appear to run against the more dominant tendencies of younger NZE speakers to use disyllabic pronunciations of 'grown', 'known', etc. and a zero plural of 'woman' along with innovative 'American' pronunciations of certain lexical items. In my twice-tested sample of 19, significant positive correlations are present between a *mono*syllabic pronunciation of <-own> participles and *marked* plural of 'woman' on the one hand, and innovative American pronunciations of 'garage', 'dynasty', 'missile' and 'Z' on the other. The 'own/owen' and 'women/woman' variables are in turn positively correlated but of only marginal significance ($+0.42$, $p = 0.077$). I would tentatively interpret this as reflecting two groups, one the more 'normal' NZE speakers who accept 'growen' and 'two woman' but are more conservative about American-style pronunciations of 'missile', 'z', etc.; and a second, more 'Yank-influenced' group who tend toward American standards in 'women', 'grown' and other lexical items.

It is clear that some of this pattern (e.g. that exhibited by Group A subjects) may well be due to the influence of NAm-speaking parents; similarly, much of the scant rhoticity of the Group C speakers is probably due to spelling pronunciations of items in the word lists. However, a residuum of rhotic values remains in the texts (6.8% and 4.0% respectively; see Table 8.2). These are often in relatively unstressed and non-utterance-final environments like '. . . took off for a far planet . . .', 'commander was a woman too', '. . . boarded a spaceship . . .', and 'they were now often . . .' used by children whose parents are non-rhotic NZE speakers (and in one case Cantonese; the examples are from my two-year retest text). A glance at the after-school and Saturday morning television listings in the *New Zealand Listener*[7] provides a plausible but admittedly very inconclusive *prima facie* argument for the source of such sporadic rhoticity. However, arriving at a definitive correlation is far more difficult.

The same is obviously the case with (-t) glottalisation. I can of course offer the same argument for *Minder, EastEnders* and other non-Standard English programmes which feature accents with glottal allophones as I imply for *Mork and Mindy, Sesame Street*, etc., in accounting for sporadic rhoticity. But clear quantitative evidence is lacking. However, one possible avenue of approach was suggested to me by Trudgill's interesting excursion into the changing phonology of pop music (1983). I transcribed the texts of four songs recorded by three New Zealand (and NZE-speaking, as far as I could ascertain) punk rock groups in 1979 and 1986; a total of 114 tokens of (-t) were present (ignoring unstressed 'ain't', 'can't', etc).[8] The outcome is summarised in Table 8.3.

The increase in glottalised (-t) over time seems clear, as is the presence of other features obviously patterned on non-standard London English (final /-k/ glottalisation), although these need to be checked against a much larger sample. The phonology of the singers was predictably innovative throughout, with 'broad' values of the five diphthongs and marked (-l) vocalisation (and also an American pronunciation of 'missiles' in the third song). I think the approach merits further investigation, but the difficulty in establishing a direct connection between (-t) glottalisation and this or any other popular spoken medium obviously remains.

TABLE 8.3 -*t Glottalisation in punk rock lyrics*

Song title	Band	Year rec.	N tokens -t	[-ʔ] (%)
'I am a Rabbit'	Proud Scum	1979	25	20
'You're Gonna Get Done'	Primmers	1979	34	26[a]
'Get it Together'	No Idea	1986	41	34
'Like You'	No Idea	1986	14	50[b]

[a] plus two inter-vocalic glottalisations.
[b] plus seven cases of of /-k/ as [-ʔ].

Indeed, a case can be made for the view that the popular media have very little influence in effecting phonological change. Accepting Giles' interactional 'accommodation' theory referred to above, Trudgill has recently stated that 'the electronic media are not very instrumental in the diffusion of linguistic innovations, in spite of widespread popular notions to the contrary' (1986: 40). Face-to-face interaction is necessary for 'accommodation' to operate, and people do not hold conversations with their televisions or cassette players! Hence Trudgill believes that while the media may be influential in the diffusion of new words, alternative pronunciations and idioms by *imitation* or *copying* ('schlock', 'zee' and 'have a nice day' are good NZE examples), they have little or no influence on phonological innovations. If they did, Trudgill believes, 'then the whole of Britain would be influenced by a particular innovation simultaneously', rather than the innovation spreading from city to city (although I should note that the NZE speech community is of course far more homogeneous than Britain).

However, I think it is possible to view such diffusion as a two-step process. Individuals can certainly *imitate* or *copy* phonological features as well as lexicon,[9] albeit perhaps imperfectly, as British bands did with (-r) in the 1960s (Trudgill, 1983), or the bands in Table 8.3 have done with (-t). Following Le Page, Trudgill himself also suggests that pop singers adopt such innovations in an attempt to more closely resemble a group or groups[10] with which they wish to identify in a process with obvious similarities to accommodation (1983: 144). It thus seems possible that an innovation may appear first through simple copying and what might be called 'one-way accommodation', and then subsequently spread among peers (e.g. pop band fans) through more normal face-to-face interaction. As Trudgill says of the possible relation of the very rapid spread of the London /f/–/θ/ merger among Norwich teenagers to London

English television programmes such as the very popular *Minder*: 'Television *may* be part of a "softening-up" process leading to the adoption of the merger, but it does not *cause* it' (1986: 54–5). However, I suspect that it may prove difficult to draw any firm boundary between copying on the one hand and accommodation on the other.

In the scenario I envision, the sporadic occurrences of (-r) described here could be put down to simple copying, but I think the evidence suggests that (-t) has moved beyond this stage, and is now spreading by face-to-face interaction. Nonetheless, I freely admit the tentativeness of the argument and the extreme difficulty involved in attempting to test such a hypothesis or arrive at a definite correlation.

However, Chambers (1981) has attempted to establish just such a correlation between American media influence and the spread of fronted allophones of the 'raised' variants of Canadian NAm /aʊ/ among younger Canadians. He settled on a three-pronged approach, surveying indices based on 'Head' (degree of exposure to media), 'Lips' (degree of usage of specifically American vocabulary) and 'Heart' (overtly elicited attitudes toward America *vis-à-vis* Canada). While he was able to arrive at a 'gross correlation' between the three indices and degree of fronting in the three age groups surveyed, he had to conclude that:

> The failure to find a fine correlation reduces the confidence in the hypothesis . . . Still, it is not likely to lay it to rest completely, so strong is the intuition that [Americanisation] is a real factor. (Chambers, 1981: 33)

I would not wish to claim as strong an intuitive feeling for either of the two variables considered here, and offer this contribution only as a series of hypotheses to stimulate further investigation. In particular, the case for American media influence encouraging sporadic rhoticity, as opposed to spelling pronunciations and influence of rhotic parents, is not at all a strong one. I think it highly unlikely that younger NZE speakers will acquire phonemic rhoticism, a task which strikes me (as a fully rhotic speaker) as a difficult one in an almost wholly non-rhotic speech community.[11] If there is any trend toward sporadic rhoticity among NZE children in general, I suspect instead that it is an age-graded phenomenon stimulated in most cases by imitation, copying and orthography rather than accommodation; it will probably tend to disappear as these speakers move into adolescence. This may account for the absence of any direct correlation between (-r) and (-t) either in the sample of 19 children or in the full sample of 36 considered here.

However, I think the case for and future of (-t) glottalisation in NZE is considerably brighter. Casual observation, as well as the data presented above, suggests to me that it is spreading rapidly among younger NZE speakers, perhaps as quickly as its apparent spread in Britain earlier in this century (Wells, 1982: 261). Like (-l) vocalisation and (i) diphthongisation (Bauer, 1986: 20, 24–5), glottalised realisations of /-t/ may be destined to become as 'standard' in NZE in the near future as the previously 'foreign' American pronunciations of 'schedule', 'lieutenant' and 'clerk' (Bayard, 1989: 18–19) are currently becoming right now.

Notes

1. The original version of this paper was presented at the 7th New Zealand Linguistics Conference in August 1987. At that time a colleague remarked to me on the apparent difficulty involved in auditory detection of this range of closures. While I would not wish to claim 100% accuracy in my determinations, I was perhaps aided by the fact that the only language I am fluent in aside from English is Thai, which has phonemic contrasts in word-final position between unaspirated unreleased /-p/, /-t/, /-k/ and /-ʔ/ (e.g. /càp/ 'catch', /càt/ 'arrange', /càk/ 'split, notch', /càʔ/ 'future part.', etc.). I thus feel fairly confident about the quantitative scoring of the fourth of my categories vis-à-vis the first three, which is what I concentrated on for the question under investigation here. Finally, I am grateful to the editors of this volume for much constructive advice which I hope has made this article more digestible than it was initially; obviously the responsibility for any remaining inedible bits is my own.
2. Standard English English.
3. Southland students in my linguistic anthropology class have also expressed worry about ridicule (or at least frequent comments) from non-Southlanders as the reason for their hasty eradication of rhotic (-r) on arrival at the University of Otago (most of whose students are not from Otago or Southland).
4. The experiment involved quantification of post-vocalic (-r) and NURSE vowels in a fifteen minute taped segment of my son talking with his mother versus a forty minute segment taped while playing with a non-rhotic friend; he was unaware of the taping in both cases. The results were: conversation with mother, 69% rhotic (-r), 75% rhotic NURSE; with friend, 25% rhotic (-r), 50% NURSE. Obviously such 'accommodation' is not limited to children. My NAm-speaking wife is about 95–100% rhotic when talking to me but only about 80% when talking to NZE-speaking children.
5. Lexical items used in both tests include 'women', 'schedule', 'lieutenant', 'interesting/ed', 'garage', 'often', 'dynasty', and 'Z'. 'Missile', 'clerk', and 'NZ' were added in the second text.
6. I have excluded my son from calculations of the mean for rhotic (-r) in Table 8.2, as his rhoticity has continued to increase markedly (particularly

after a visit to relatives in Hawaii); the figures including him are 1985–86, 8.7%; 1987–88, 7.3%; change, −1.4%.

7. The preponderance of NAm-accent programmes on New Zealand television is not limited to these time slots. US material — almost wholly in a standard NAm accent — has dominated New Zealand programming since the early 1960s (Bayard, 1987: 22–4).

8. I am grateful to Warren Gumbley and Matthew Campbell for confirming the general accuracy of the transcriptions, although a few passages remained unintelligible even to those familiar with the recordings.

9. The disyllabic pronunciation of strong past participles ('knowen', 'growen', 'strewen') by insertion of a schwa at the morpheme boundary may be a good case in point. This innovation, apparently beginning in Australian English (G.W. Turner, personal communication) is now widespread there, and according to Bradley & Bradley is 'very frequently used by politicians, journalists, and media announcers' (1985: 337). They believe that lexical diffusion seems not to be involved. The innovation is spreading rapidly in NZE as well; my data suggest its use by almost 30% of NZE speakers (Bayard, 1987: 32–3). It is very frequently heard on the media here, and to my recollection it was much more common there than in face-to-face interaction for several years.

10. This can be taken to the point where they exhibit features of both NAm and non-standard British English simultaneously (Trudgill, 1983: 157). It may also have occurred to the reader that accommodation to my rhotic accent may well have been a factor accounting for some of the rhotic output of the younger Group C in particular. This is an important question, as about half of the interviews were conducted either by myself or my rhotic wife. However, an 'interviewer's accent' variable was also included in scoring (1 = NAm; 4 = NZE) and no significant correlation was present between it and number of occurrences of /-r/ with either the total sample of 141 or the group of 19 children retested.

11. The acquisition of rhoticity (or perhaps better competence in both rhotic and non-rhotic vowel systems) may not be as difficult or rare as I imply. The speech of my brother-in-law (a Hawaiian Creole English speaker) is completely non-rhotic in normal conversational register, but when taping the same passage used by my full NZE sample he was 79% rhotic. Although I know little about such phenomena, I would suspect that such cases are very common in creole-standard dialect continua. I might add parenthetically that as with many other non-rhotic accents spoken in America (New York City, the Southeast, etc.), rhoticism is proceeding at full speed in Hawaiian English. For example, my 12-year-old nephew is fully rhotic in all registers.

References

BAUER, LAURIE 1986, Notes on New Zealand English phonetics and phonology. Expanded version of paper published in *English World Wide* 7 (2), 225–58.
BAYARD, DONN 1985, Class and change in New Zealand English: a pilot study. Paper presented at 7th NZ Linguistics Conference, Wellington.

—1987, Class and change in New Zealand English: a summary report. *Te Reo* 30, 3–36.

—1988, Variation in and attitudes toward New Zealand English: a quantitative approach. *New Zealand English Newsletter* 2, 13–16.

—1989, 'Me say that? No way!': the social correlates of American lexical diffusion in New Zealand English. *Te Reo* 32, 17–60.

—In press. Social constraints on the phonology of New Zealand English. In JENNY CHESHIRE (ed.) *English Around the World: Sociolinguistic Perspectives*. Cambridge: Cambridge University Press.

BRADLEY, DAVID and BRADLEY, MAYA 1985, The phonetic realisation of a morpheme boundary in Australian English. *Festschrift in Honour of Arthur Delbridge, Beiträge zur Phonetik und Linguistik* 48, 333–40.

CHAMBERS, J. K. 1981, The Americanization of Canadian Raising. In CARRIE S. MASEK, ROBERTA A. HENDRICK and MARY FRANCES MILLER (eds) *Papers from the Parasession on Language and Behavior* (pp. 20–35). Chicago: Chicago Linguistic Society.

GILES, HOWARD and POWESLAND, PETER F. 1975, *Speech Style and Social Evaluation*. London: Academic Press.

RICHARDSON, LOUISE 1986, Regional dialectical variation: Southland area. Unpublished term paper. Dunedin: Anthropology Department, University of Otago.

TRUDGILL, PETER 1983, Acts of conflicting identity: the sociolinguistics of British pop-song production. In PETER TRUDGILL, *On Dialect: Social and Geographical Perspectives* (pp. 141–60). Oxford: Blackwell.

—1986, *Dialects in Contact*. Oxford: Blackwell.

TRUDGILL, PETER and HANNAH, JEAN 1985, *International English: a Guide to Varieties of Standard English (2nd edn)*. London: Arnold.

TURNER, GEORGE W. 1970, New Zealand English today. In W.S. RAMSON (ed.) *English Transported: Essays on Australasian English* (pp. 84–101). Canberra: Australian National University Press.

WELLS, JOHN C. 1982, *Accents of English. Vol. 1: An Introduction*. Cambridge: Cambridge University Press.

9 Audience and referee design in New Zealand media language[1]

ALLAN BELL

Responding to the Audience

Style shift is variation within the speech of an individual speaking a single language. That intra-speaker variation can occur on many linguistic levels, from the 'micro-variables' studied by sociolinguists to larger scale manifestations such as turn-taking and politeness strategies, which are not so amenable to quantitative research. Talk is always embedded in a social situation, and situations differ according to such things as where they occur (setting), who is present (participants), and what is being talked about (topic: cf. Fishman *et al.*, 1971). Speakers have numerous resources at their disposal for talking differently on different occasions. The sociolinguist's ultimate interest in examining style shift and related language phenomena is to ask the question *why*: what has caused this speaker to use this style on this occasion?

The Audience Design framework proposed in Bell (1984; cf. Milroy, 1987: 171ff) was developed in an attempt to account for this intra-speaker variation. I suggested that style shift occurs in response to a change in the extra-linguistic situation, primarily among the speaker's audience. The essence of style is that speakers are responding to their audience. It is generally manifested in a speaker shifting her style to be more like that of the person to whom she is talking. This is 'convergence' in the terms of the Speech Accommodation Theory developed by Howard Giles (Giles & Powesland, 1975; Giles *et al.*, 1987). The basic dimension on which we can examine a speaker's style is therefore a responsive one, and that response is primarily to the speaker's audience (Figure 9.1).

Sociolinguists have been accustomed since Labov's pioneering work (1966) to differentiating the inter-speaker and intra-speaker dimensions

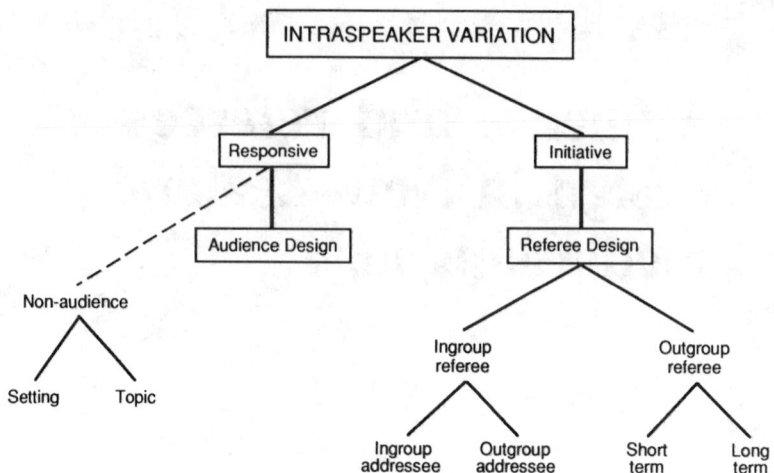

FIGURE 9.1 *Style as responsive and initiative: audience design and referee design*

of language variation. The inter-speaker or 'social' dimension has been correlated with differences in the measurable social characteristics (such as age, gender or social class) of a person — the speaker. Audience design proposes that the intra-speaker or stylistic dimension of language variation — differences within the speech of a single speaker — can be primarily correlated with the attributes of the hearers. That is, speakers design their talk for their hearers (the term 'design' is not meant to imply detailed awareness of individual language choices).

Audience design informs all levels of a speaker's linguistic choices — the switch from one complete language to another in bilingual situations (Gal, 1979; Dorian, 1981), choice of personal pronouns or address terms (Brown & Gilman, 1960; Ervin-Tripp, 1972), politeness strategies (Brown & Levinson, 1987), use of pragmatic particles (Holmes, 1986; in press), and quantitative style shift (Coupland, 1980; 1984).

Much work has been done in this field in the accommodation model. Crudely characterised, speech accommodation theory proposes that speakers accommodate their speech style to their hearers in order to win approval (Giles & Powesland, 1975). In the past decade the theory has been extensively developed, expanded and revised (e.g. Thakerar, Giles & Cheshire, 1982; Giles et al., 1987; Coupland et al., 1988). The proliferation of complexities is at times in danger of obscuring the framework's principal insight. Nevertheless the main findings within this field make it clear that speakers respond primarily to their audience in designing their talk.

Taking the initiative

Audience design is a strategy by which speakers draw on the variation which is available in their speech community to respond to different kinds of audiences. Their style shifts are an echo of the range of speech which they hear around them from other speakers (Bell, 1984). The first set of data I shall present in this chapter is drawn from a study of radio news styles in New Zealand (Bell, 1977; 1982a; in press), demonstrating how newsreading styles largely respond to their audiences' expectations.

As well as this 'responsive' dimension (Figure 9.1), there is another dimension of style, which I term the 'initiative' dimension. Here the style shift itself *initiates* a change in the situation rather than *resulting from* such a change. Communicators' strategies will sometimes be responsive and sometimes initiative. Sociolinguists have drawn attention to this distinction at least since Blom & Gumperz (1972) coined the terms 'situational' and 'metaphorical' switching. In situational switching there is a regular association between language and social situation. The entry of outsiders to a local group, for example, triggers a switch from local dialect to standard speech. These situational switches reflect the speech community's norms of what is appropriate speech for certain audiences. Initiative style trades on such regular associations, infusing the flavour of one setting into another, alien context. Here language becomes an independent variable which itself influences the situation (as Giles has long insisted, e.g. 1973).

Initiative style shift is essentially a redefinition, by the speaker, of the relationship between speaker and audience. The baseline from which initiative shifts operate is the style normally designed for a particular kind of addressee. So, speakers can persuade or convince someone intimate to them by shifting to the style or language one would normally address to strangers. With strangers the reverse tactic achieves the same effect: speakers can persuade a stranger by shifting to the style normally reserved for intimates. Such shifts appear to be powerful just because they treat addressees as if they were someone else.

This 'someone else' I term the 'referee'. In referee design, speakers diverge away from the style appropriate to their addressee and towards that of a third party. Referees are third persons not physically present at an interaction but possessing such salience for a speaker that they influence style even in their absence.

Response and initiative are to be understood as poles of a continuum rather than a dichotomy. Response always has an element of speaker initiative, and initiative is invariably in part a response to one's audience. Initiative strategies are usually to be regarded as instances of 'referee design'. They focus on an absent reference group, for example by adopting a non-native accent, rather than the present addressee. They are therefore always directed towards a stereotyped rather than actual recipient (cf. Coupland *et al.*, 1988), as we shall see below in analysis of the varieties of English used in New Zealand television advertisements.

Audience Design: News Talk in New Zealand

Mass media define a different communication situation from face-to-face interaction. Mass communication involves a disjunction of place, and often of time, between communicator and audience. This fracture in the process means that the feedback which is an integral factor in most speech situations is delayed, reduced or completely absent. Media can, however, also throw into sharper relief factors which operate less obviously face-to-face. The media audience is large, and the communicator's prime need — professional as well as personal — is to win and hold that audience (McQuail, 1969). So the motivation of seeking approval, traditionally the core of accommodation theory explanations of speech style (Giles, 1973), is strengthened accordingly.

News is the archetypal 'responsive' format of the media. In an earlier study on news styles of Auckland radio (Bell, 1977; 1982a), I analysed a number of phonological and syntactic variables. Although I have updated aspects of this data from time to time since, the original research remains the most compelling illustration of audience design in media language (cf. Milroy, 1987: 181).

At the time of the original sample (1974), five radio stations broadcast news in Auckland city.[2] Three were operated by the public corporation, Radio New Zealand, which networked much of its news from the capital, Wellington, for re-transmission by local stations. Private radio was legalised in New Zealand in 1968, which permitted the pirate station Radio Hauraki (1XA) to set up on shore after several years of broadcasting to the youth of Auckland from a barge of doubtful seaworthiness anchored in the Hauraki Gulf beyond the twelve-mile territorial limit (Blackburn, 1974).

The five stations were differentiated by both programme content and audience membership (Bell, 1982a; in press carry further detail). 1YA was (and still is) the Auckland repeater station of Radio New Zealand's National Radio network originating in Wellington. It is the Corporation's flagship, the prestige station of public radio, carrying much solid news, current affairs programmes, in-depth interviews and other talk programmes. Its audience is among older people and the higher education and professional levels. 1ZB was Radio NZ's general-audience commercial station in Auckland. It was the city's chief service and information station, carried a lot of advertising, cultivating a homely relationship with its audience. (In 1989 the station has taken its role even further, to become 'News Talk 1ZB', devoted to news and information.) The audience was middle New Zealand, in age and class, and their families. Station 1ZM was Radio NZ's rock music station, with a young, largely male audience to match. The private rock station, 1XA, was similar in tone and appeal, but with a larger audience. Finally, the other private station, Radio i (1XI), at the time offered mainly telephone talkback programming to a middle audience similar in composition to 1ZB's, but with more women listeners. All stations except 1YA carried advertising.

The five stations broadcast eight distinct sets of news. National Radio at this time broadcast a dozen bulletins daily from Wellington (coded YA). The local Auckland repeater station broke out of the network once daily for a bulletin of regional news (YAR). And in addition, three to four bulletins daily (coded BBC) were carried live from the BBC Overseas Service in London (now transmitted on the 'Concert Programme' network). Station 1ZB also carried news networked from Radio NZ in Wellington to the 22 local community stations throughout New Zealand (coded ZB). 1ZB itself also produced bulletins of local news (coded ZBR), broadcast immediately after many network bulletins. These five sets of news (YA, YAR, BBC, ZB, ZBR) were treated as separate and distinct for the language analysis. The situation on the other three stations was much more straightforward. ZM, XA and XI each compiled and presented its own news bulletins.

The multiple stations of New Zealand public broadcasting made possible a controlled comparison of news styles. YA and ZB news originated in the same suite of studios in Wellington, with the same individual newsreaders heard on both networks. Similarly, YAR, ZBR and ZM also shared a common pool of announcers reading the news in Auckland. This enabled a comparison of the different styles used by a single newsreader when recorded on more than one station.

The random language sample consisted of about seventeen hours of newsreader speech from the eight news outlets. All news was recorded on all stations from 6 a.m. to 12 midnight on five weekdays, selected according to the 'constructed week' design developed in content analysis research (Jones & Carter, 1959). Content such as headlines, repeated news items (up to five times during 'breakfast' sessions), speech by reporters or interviewees and non-news matter such as station identification was excluded. The sample yielded 80–200 tokens of phonological variables for between four and nine newsreaders each on all stations except YAR. An additional non-random sample was collected during the months following the main sample period. This focused on gathering more speech by those newsreaders who were heard on two or three different stations.

Quantitative sociolinguistics since Labov (1966) has looked to correlate linguistic variation with a number of extra-linguistic factors (cf. Figure 9.1):

(1) Primarily these have been characteristics of the speakers recorded. Potentially news style differences could correlate with differences in the social attributes of the communicators. However, the news genre is the classic case of language with multiple originators, with journalist, several copy editors and newsreader all contributing. The effect of personal characteristics such as age, gender, ethnicity and social class on speech patterns is one of the confirmed findings of sociolinguistic research in the past twenty years. We might thus anticipate that there may be differences between the styles of different individual newsreaders.

(2) As well as individuals, it is possible that the broadcasting institution as a whole moulds language style. One aspect of this involves the structures, management and control mechanisms of media organisations (Gerbner, 1969). The structure of New Zealand public broadcasting provides an ideal site to test this. The structures (and often the personnel) which produced and influenced news at the time of this study were identical for YA and ZB in Wellington, and YAR, ZBR and ZM in Auckland. This could result in news styles which are similar between YA and ZB, and between YAR, ZBR and ZM.

(3) Attention paid to speech has been adopted by many researchers, following Labov (1972), as the one factor which affects style shift. However, Bell (1984) and others have argued against the adequacy and usefulness of this explanation, motivated largely by the findings to be presented here.

(4) Topic is well established as a variable which can result in style shift (for example in the early interview methodology of Labov, 1966). I did not subject the language sample to detailed content analysis, but it was classified for local *versus* national *versus* international origin. Stations YA and ZB have similar mixes of news on this classification, with 90% of their stories originating nationally or internationally. Again, YAR and ZBR carry almost entirely local news. We could expect these two pairs of stations to have similar news styles if these topic dimensions are significant.

(5) Physical setting is also seen as an important variable affecting style. For radio, the setting for the communicator is a studio, and for the audience is almost anywhere. There are no systematic differences in setting between the different stations in this study.

(6) The audience is the final variable we will consider. It proved to be the primary dimension in this study.

Who are the audience?

The Auckland radio audience was described by surveys of the social characteristics of a random sample of Aucklanders. Surveys were conducted in the months of the language sample, questioning 586 respondents over the age of 15 on their demographic characteristics and media reception habits.[3]

For the age variable (Table 9.1), the five stations divided clearly into three groups, as one would expect from the outline of their programming presented above. ZM and XA were very similar, with two-thirds of their audiences in the 15–24-year-old age bracket and a mean age of 25.6 and 26.6 years respectively. (Doubtless these mean ages would have been lower if under-15-year-olds had been included in the population.) ZB and ZBR (coded ZB/R) (mean age 43.1 years) and XI (41.5 years) have the middle age audiences. YA's audience has very few in the youngest age group, a large proportion for the over-55-year-olds, and a mean age of 47.4 years.

Education differences between stations' audiences were not strongly marked (Table 9.1). YA has the generally highest education level, followed by ZM, with ZB/R, XI and XA grouped below. The stratification for occupation is more evident, as we might expect from the use of occupation as a measure of social stratification in New Zealand (Pitt,

TABLE 9.1 *Profiles of audiences for Auckland radio stations (1974) by age, education and occupation (as a percentage of station's audience)*

	YA (%)	ZB/R (%)	ZM (%)	XA (%)	XI (%)
Age					
15–24	4	12	67	65	20
25–34	13	22	17	18	20
35–44	26	19	11	9	15
45–54	20	16	4	3	16
55+	37	31	1	5	29
Education					
Primary or secondary school	42	55	43	54	62
School qualification	20	25	33	32	15
Post-school qualification	23	14	11	10	17
University	15	6	13	4	6
Occupation					
Manual	8	10	27	27	9
Skilled	11	22	33	28	20
Office/sales	31	32	22	25	36
Professional	50	36	18	20	35

1977). YA is clearly the highest status station on the measure. It has 50% 'professionals' in its working audience, and the least manual workers. ZM and XA share similar occupation profiles to each other, weighted to the low-status end of the audience. ZB/R and XI also have similar-occupation audiences, with profiles close to that of the general population: that is, they are the mid-status stations.

These survey findings reveal three distinct groupings of stations. We have YA with the older listeners and highest education and occupation levels, ZB/R and XI in the middle rank for occupation and age, and ZM and XA with the young male audience and low occupation levels. We will expect then that if news styles are related to audience characteristics, the stations will rank in the same order.[4]

The diversity of news styles

I will take just one linguistic variable of news English to exemplify the stratification of styles in Auckland radio news. The rule by which the negative 'not' is contracted to 'n't' and attached to a preceding auxiliary or modal (Negcon) is a salient marker of style in English. In general, uncontracted negatives are the norm in most written language, and contractions the norm in most speech, to the extent that the use of the alternative form can be stylistically very marked.

Radio news, as language scripted to be read aloud, offers an area of potential variability in application of this rule. Negcon has been largely ignored in the study of linguistic variation, partly because it is so subject to conscious control. In addition, contraction or non-contraction must be specified in any written text, making it unsuitable for a Labovian comparison between scripted and *ad lib* styles. Negcon also has a rather low frequency of occurrence — only about once every two minutes of broadcast speech. Nearly the entire seventeen hour sample of news language had to be scanned to produce sufficient tokens for analysis ($N = 551$).

The Negcon rule was discussed in early transformational literature (e.g. Chomsky, 1957), but has since received only spasmodic attention (Zwicky & Pullum, 1982). By the rule, the item 'not' may be variably contracted and adjoined to an immediately preceding finite modal, 'do' (auxiliary), 'be' or 'have'. Contraction cannot apply unless one of these items appears to the immediate left of the negative. The 'n't' may attach to the auxiliary (which I use here as a cover term for all the items permitting contraction) either without further phonological change (e.g. 'aren't', 'haven't') or with a vowel change ('don't', 'can't'). Regular phonological rules can account for the deletion of the final liquid in 'will' and 'shall', and for reduction of the consonant cluster in 'must'. Of the closed set of 23 items to which 'not' may attach, only 'am not' has no negative contraction in Standard English, although it is one of the forms covered by non-standard 'ain't' (which, of course, does not apear in news language). 'May not' produces the disfavoured disyllabic 'mayn't', which did not occur in the sample (cf. Zwicky & Pullum, 1982).

The obvious candidate for a variable linguistic constraint affecting the frequency of application of Negcon would appear to be the phonetic nature of the preceding segment. These are of six kinds: vowel, stop, sibilant, liquid, nasal and labiodental. However, the data broken down by these six preceding environments gives an entirely confusing picture, making it impossible to order them in any convincing way. All that can be said is that on most stations preceding nasal ('can') favours Negcon most, and preceding sibilant least. The likely grouping of environments by phonological features would be preceding sonorant (vowel, liquid, nasal) resulting in a monosyllabic contraction, *versus* preceding obstruent (stop, sibilant, labiodental) giving a disyllabic contracted form. However, the vowel environment, which one might have expected to favour contraction at similar frequencies to nasal, inhibits it as much as does a preceding sibilant. The lack of explicable pattern in these figures may well reflect the low N in some cells of the cross-classification.

Classifying according to auxiliary type (distinguishing 'be', 'have', 'do' and modals) gives a clearer pattern (Table 9.2). Although ordering of the auxiliaries is inconsistent, 'be' is clearly the least favoured environment. A cross-classification of auxiliary type by preceding phonetic segment shows that some of the deviance for the preceding phonetic environment is really a reflection of auxiliary type. The sibilant forms 'does' and 'has' favour contraction up to 100%, but 'is' contributes most of the tokens to the preceding-sibilant cell and takes a maximum of only 35% contraction. The vowel form 'do' occurs rarely but takes contracted negative on each occasion. By contrast, 'are' and 'were' — which provide most of the tokens in the preceding-vowel cell — contract at similarly low levels to the obstruent forms 'is' and 'was'.

However, while the effect of linguistic factors may seem inconsistent, the stratification of the stations themselves is quite clear. The relative frequencies with which stations applied the variable Negcon rule in all linguistic environments are displayed in Figure 9.2. The most notable feature of the array is that BBC never contracts negatives — a surprising

TABLE 9.2 *Percentage of negative contraction on seven Auckland radio stations, by four preceding auxiliary types*

	Be (%)	Modal (%)	Have (%)	Do (%)
YA	4.8	33.3	25.0	63.6
ZB	39.1	69.6	57.9	77.8
ZBR	14.3	66.7	81.8	62.5
ZM	22.2	76.1	58.3	100
XA	51.5	76.7	92.3	86.7
XI	25.0	70.3	70.0	54.5
BBC	0	0	0	0
$N = $	21	24	16	11
	23	23	19	9
	28	36	11	8
	36	46	12	11
	33	30	13	15
	20	37	20	11
	10	20	4	4

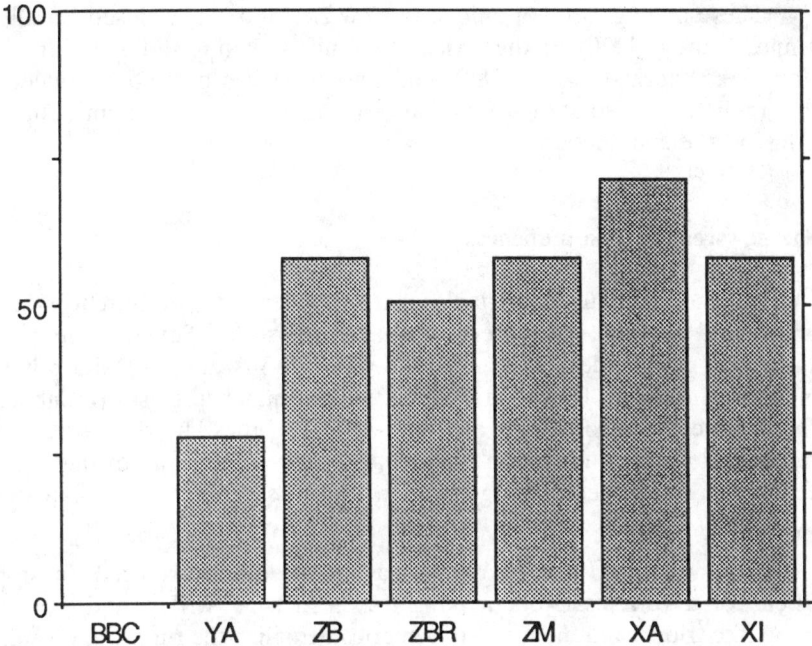

FIGURE 9.2 *Percentage of negative contraction on seven radio stations, summing all linguistic environments*

non-application of a very frequent rule of spoken English. This reflects the susceptibility of Negcon to conscious control, and probably arose from an explicit style ruling for newsreading on the BBC World Service. YA falls closest to the BBC, with a total mean contraction of 27.8%. ZBR, ZB, XI and ZM are beyond YA, and XA contracts most negatives of all at 71.4%.

The external station BBC appears to be functioning as a formal standard of non-contraction, a reflection of the prestige of BBC English both world-wide and in the New Zealand speech community (Bell, 1982b). There then follow — in three clear groupings — the New Zealand station with the highest status audience, YA; the mid-status stations ZB, ZBR and XI; and the low-status XA. Only ZM has any suggestion of deviating from the rank its audience status indicates it should occupy. At 58.1% it is nearer to the middle stations than to its expected companion, XA. The stations thus appear to be designing their style, as reflected in this particular variable, to suit their audience.

These findings are not unique to New Zealand. They closely parallel Brunel's study (1970) of the styles of French-speaking radio stations in Montreal. Yaeger-Dror's (1988) analysis of the use of Hebrew dialects on Israeli radio also shows a similar pattern, which she accounts for in terms of audience design.

One newsreader: two audiences

A second linguistic variable sharpens these style differences still further and confirms the patterns we have seen so far. Several individual Radio NZ newsreaders were recorded on both YA and ZB, and others on YAR and ZBR. These are in effect natural matched guises (Lambert, 1967). Listeners record their approval of one of these by their presence in the audience of the station that broadcasts it rather than of the other station. The prestige of the guise then ranks according to the status of the audience who received it.

Inter-vocalic /t/ can be realised as an alveolar voiced flap or stop instead of a voiceless stop, making words such as 'writer' and 'better' sound like 'rider' and 'bedder'. In American English the rule is now semi-categorical (applied more than 90%), and the merger with inter-vocalic /d/ is approaching completion (Fisher & Hirsh, 1976). In New Zealand, however, it is a genuinely variable rule, such that /t/ may be voiced when it follows a vowel and precedes an unstressed vowel. There is a gradient of realisation from a voiceless alveolar stop followed by aspiration [tʰ], through degrees of fricativisation and voicing, to a full-voiced alveolar stop [d].

The rankings of stations for their application of the /t/ voicing rule confirm much of what has already been shown above for Negcon. In addition, we have with this phonological variable evidence on how individual newsreaders performed. Newsreaders were surveyed with a demographic questionnaire, yielding an individual social status ranking similar to that used for the audience survey. Table 9.3 orders the speakers from top to bottom for decreasing speaker status and increasing /t/ voicing. Most strikingly, all five YA newsreaders for whom /t/ voicing was analysed rank above the four ZB newsreaders analysed. This is despite the fact that, in every case but one, the data come from the same four newsreaders heard on both stations. The rankings bear little relationship to the newsreaders' individual social-status rankings.

The detail of these style shifts is presented in Figure 9.3, together with data for two YAR/ZBR newsreaders. Three linguistic constraints on

TABLE 9.3 *YA and ZB newsreaders ranked (from top to bottom) for social status against their rank for inter-vocalic /t/ voicing*

Status		/t/ voicing	
YA	ZB	YA	ZB
OJ	OJ	VG	
PB	PB	OJ	
		SD	
SD	SD	PB	
		RK	
			OJ
RK	RK	PB	
			RK
VG			SD

the rule are distinguished: presence of a word boundary after the /t/ ('but##*if*'), following morpheme boundary ('creat#ing'), or no boundary ('letter'). While these environments do not order with complete consistency, the shift by individual speakers between stations is very regular. The six newsreaders shift on average 20% in each environment between YA and ZB or YAR and ZBR.

Audience design is the only tenable explanation for the individual speaker shifts shown in Figure 9.3. Of the six extra-linguistic factors I suggested above as possible influences on news style, only the audience correlates with the individual speaker shifts. All five other variables remain constant. There is just one individual speaker producing two divergent styles. The institution is the same in both cases. The topic mix of the news is similar. The studio setting is the same. And it is implausible to suggest that the amount of attention paid to speech is being systematically varied.

These graphs display 18 pairwise comparisons of station rankings for newsreader by linguistic environment. None deviates from the style which one would predict from audience design.[5] Single newsreaders heard on two different stations show a remarkable and consistent ability to make considerable style shifts to suit the audience. These switches between stations are at times very rapid: at off-peak hours a single newsreader may alternate between YA and ZB news with as little as ten minutes between bulletins on the different stations.

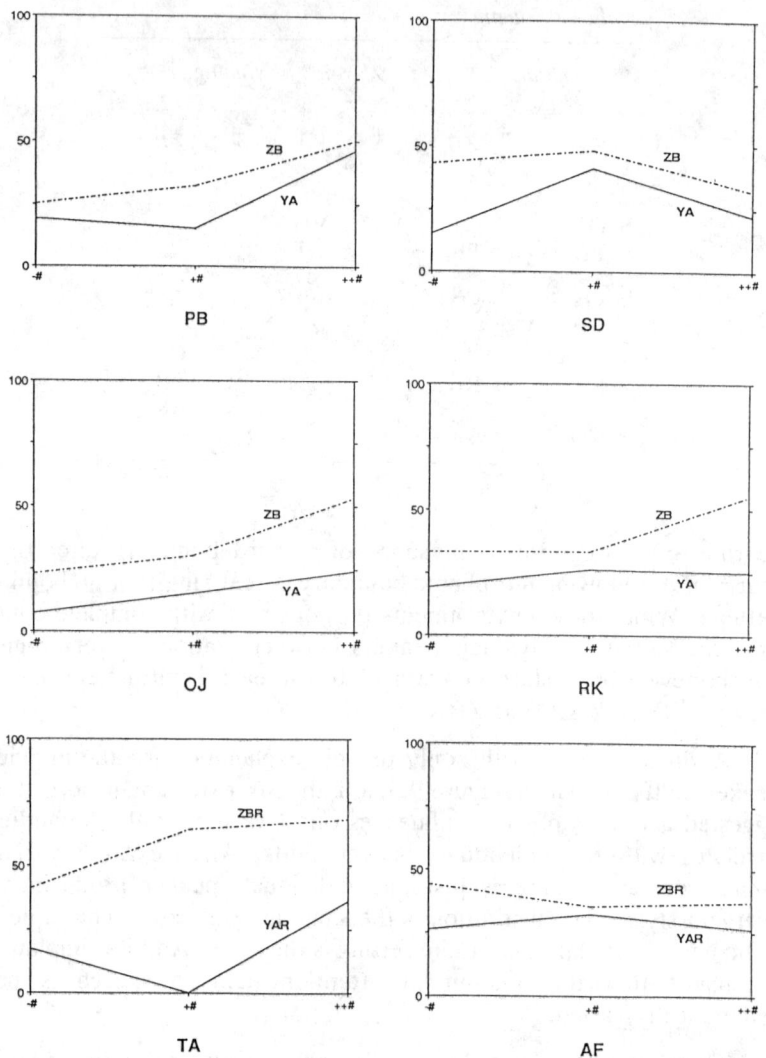

FIGURE 9.3 *Percentage of inter-vocalic /t/ voicing for four YA/ZB news-casters (PB, SD, OJ, RK), and two YAR/ZBR newscasters (TA, AF), in three linguistic environments. −#, no following boundary; +#, following morpheme boundary; +##, following word boundary*

What we see here is individual newsreaders converging towards a common style of speech targeted at their audience. Individual differences are minimised, and speakers tend to cluster around the station mean frequency for the variable, giving content to the notion of a 'station style' which is accommodated to its audience. Whether we take the social or the linguistic variables as independent, therefore, the same relationships show up. The natural grouping of newsreaders on stations, and of stations according to audience, undeniably stratifies news language styles.

Our analysis of audience design in the mass media indicates a number of conclusions. While the one newsreader/two audiences comparison is the clearest case, the other evidence also points overwhelmingly to the operation of audience design in newsreading. For negative contraction, stations rank precisely according to their audience's status, with the external prestige norm, BBC, contracting no negatives at all. Not only do stations with different audiences differ systematically in their styles, those with similar audiences (ZM/XA and ZBR/XI) tend to share similar styles. News is thus clearly on the responsive dimension posited by audience design.

Referee Design

Referee design is on the complementary 'initiative' dimension of intra-speaker variation. The effect of referee design is to make a speaker style-shift in the same manner as if she was actually talking to a member of the referee group rather than to the addressee in front of her. We expect the shift to be in the same direction — but not necessarily to the same degree — as if the referee were in fact the addressee. Referee design is a rhetorical strategy by which speakers use the resources available to them from their speech community. These strategies may be confined to initiative and creative use of the linguistic repertoire of styles or languages which they themselves normally employ. Or the strategies may draw on a wider speech community — socially, in adopting features from the speech of other socio-economic, ethnic or age groups; geographically in the dialects of other regions or continents; and historically, in the forms of the language spoken (or supposed to have been spoken) at an earlier period. We may examine referee design from several aspects:

(1) The speaker may be a member of the referee group (in-group referee design: Figure 9.1), producing for an occasion heightened use of her usual speech patterns. Or she may not be a member

of the referee group (out-group referee design). The addressee may, likewise, be a member of the in-group or out-group.

(2) Referee shift is basically a short-term phenomenon, occurring for very short stretches of speech. But it may in some circumstances be long term. Referee design may occur in isolated situations or more widely across a group and its interactions with another group.

(3) Referee design is generally linguistically divergent, with the language style shifted away from the addressee's own speech patterns. But it may in some situations converge towards the addressee's speech.

(4) The language code may be monolingual, diglossic or bilingual, and accordingly be affected in different ways by referee design.

(5) The shift towards the referee's language code may be accurate, correctly reproducing the referee's own linguistic patterns. Or it may be inaccurate, missing the target variety in a number of ways.

(6) The shift may be reciprocated by the addressee in his own speaking turn, accepting the speaker's shift as establishing a new norm for the conversation. Alternatively, the addressee may reject the speaker's attempt to redefine the language code for the situation.

In-group referees

The division into in-group and out-group referees is fundamental. In-group referee design sees you as speaker shifting to an extreme level of the style of your own in-group. This may occur when the addressee is either also a member of your in-group, or a member of an out-group. With an out-group addressee, a speaker is reacting to that addressee by shifting towards an enhanced style of the speaker's own absent in-group. Such a speaker is taking the initiative to deliberately reject identification with the immediate addressee, in order to identify instead with a referee not actually present.

A wealth of research in the accommodation framework documents the social psychological processses which cause in-group referee design (e.g. Giles, 1977). If a Welsh bilingual speaks Welsh to an English monolingual, that is in-group referee design to an out-group addressee. Such a shift is essentially short-lived. It represents a confrontation, challenging your interlocutor's use of a given language code. A successful challenge will usually spell an end to the interaction. Conversations tend not to last when one interlocutor deliberately switches to a language that the other cannot understand.

The second type of in-group referee design is where the addressee is from your own in-group. You as speaker appeal to your solidarity with the addressee, to the common ground which you have as speakers of a language or dialect which is not shared with the out-group. When two Swiss people are conversing in High German, if one switches to their shared 'Low' language, Swiss German, this represents a claim to its associations of solidarity in order to persuade or challenge the addressee.

Out-group referee design

Out-group design is similar to in-group in its sociopsychological processes, but rather different in its sociological structure and linguistic effects. Here speakers lay claim to a speech and identity which is not their own but which holds prestige for them. They diverge from the language code of their in-group — and thus from their own usual speech — towards an out-group with whom they wish to identify. Thus, in an otherwise standard-language conversation, local dialect forms can be introduced to provide anecdotal colour. Conversely, standard language features may surface as a claim to intellectual authority during a conversation conducted in local dialect (Blom & Gumperz, 1972). As with in-group design to an in-group addressee, both speaker and addressee agree on the prestige of the out-group language for the purpose, and that fact makes its use powerful. But such a switch is essentially short term. Continued use of that code would violate the norm of conversation between intimates, or in the extreme case redefine the relationship as no longer intimate.

However, while all other classes of initiative shift are by nature brief, out-group referee design can be long term, even institutionalised. Diglossia is the classic case. In Ferguson's original definition (1959), the prestige or 'High' form in diglossia is not native to any group in the speech community. Rather, it is the dialect of an external referee. In the critical cases Ferguson presents, the dialect is distanced either by space (e.g. France for Haitian creole) or time (classical Arabic or Greek). The common factor in all such situations is an orientation which regards the referee society and culture as superior, either generally or on some particular dimension. This is often the fruit of a colonial past, reflected in a linguistic colonialism (Bell, 1982b) which has frozen the momentary phenomenon of initiative shift into a norm in which the speech community acknowledges the status of the external, referee code. Because both speakers and addressees share the same reference point, the shift to the referee code can be widespread and prolonged, but it may also be confined to certain genres, settings or topics.

The linguistic consequences

Common to all referee design (except that with an in-group addressee) is the absence of direct feedback, because referees are not present in a speaker's actual audience. For in-group shift, the lack of feedback is not important. The speaker is a member of the in-group and knows its language as well as any other member. But for out-group design, absence of feedback has crucial consequences for a speaker's performance. The speaker lacks access to the out-group, and therefore has no adequate model of out-group speech. The result, even in the long-term situation of diglossia, is that speakers never acquire full fluency in the High language (Ferguson, 1959), although they may use it regularly.

Le Page (McEntegart & Le Page, 1982) has pointed out the formidable obstacles which impede successful referee design. Before speakers' ability to modify their speech even becomes an issue, they have to overcome ignorance both of a model speech community to which they may have no access, and of a target variety which they may never have heard spoken natively. Linguistically, refereee design raises interesting questions on how such identification with external reference groups can be expressed:

(1) What kinds of linguistic entities are used to represent referee design?
(2) What aspects of language do they come from — discourse, phonology, syntax, lexicon, etc.?
(3) What is the minimum necessary shift for successful referee design?
(4) Is there a maximum allowable shift?
(5) And what in fact constitutes successful referee design? Is it native-like competence in the target code, or something less than that, or even something more or something different?

Referee Design: The Case of Television Advertisements

Initiative style shift is much harder to research than responsive. In face-to-face interaction, such shifts are by nature brief, sporadic and unpredictable, and have therefore not been much researched. But there is a more readily available data source in mass communication, where the forces of initiative shift are also operating. The structure of broadcast advertising provides a laboratory-like simulation of referee design conditions. Like face-to-face referee shifts, advertisements are very short (average thirty seconds). Their function is an initiative one — to persuade, challenge, seize the audience's attention, tell an anecdote. The language in them is used to simulate distance or intimacy of relationship. While data from mass communication cannot be automatically extrapolated to face-to-face interaction, I shall show that in referee design the parallels are good and the findings give a fair indication of what we might expect in face-to-face situations.

The data for this study (drawn from Bell, 1986) is a sample of advertisements screened on New Zealand television, mostly in 1986. At the time New Zealand had two channels, both operated by the public corporation, Television New Zealand.[6] Both channels carry advertising, often a total of ten or more minutes per hour. Estimates vary on where the mix of programmes screened on New Zealand television come from, but probably only some 25% of programming is fully locally made and therefore uses speakers of New Zealand English (NZE). About another 25% is imported from Britain, mostly with speakers of Received Pronunciation (RP), but also with other urban and rural British dialects. About 45% of programming is imported from the United States, and the remaining 5% comes mainly from Australia and Europe. New Zealanders are therefore exposed in the principal mass medium to nearly double the amount of American English as of NZE, and to about the same amount of British as NZE.

The use of language in this sample of advertisements illustrates three of the four categories of referee design:

(1) As in-group referee design to the in-group audience, there are a number of advertisements which adopt a strong New Zealand local dialect in order to associate their product with in-group values.
(2) Short-term out-group referee design occurs in a large proportion of advertisements, with non-native dialects such as British or American varieties used.

(3) Long-term out-group design occurs in one specific genre: all singing has traces of an American accent.

(4) The fourth category, in-group design to out-group addressees, is logically impossible here because the audience for New Zealand television is by definition a NZE in-group. An example would be the use of a distinctive NZE dialect overseas to advertise New Zealand goods to consumers in other countries.

The targeted varieties

The principal data are some 150 television advertisements recorded in 1986. About half of these contained referee designed speech (Table 9.4). Forty-two per cent were audience designed, using what I would class as mainstream New Zealand media speech — labelled 'Middle New Zealand' (MNZ) in Table 9.4.[7] 'Upper New Zealand' (UNZ) is the speech of traditional national newsreaders on Television New Zealand, and National Radio, and a number of other media personalities. This is an intermediate accent which both mixes RP and NZE variants, sometimes of the same vowel, and in other cases uses phonetically intermediate vowel values. It is not categorised for audience or referee design because I am frankly undecided whether it should be treated as a normal New Zealand variety (like Middle NZ) or as an out-group referee dialect. It falls between the two and shares features of both. My indecision reflects the real linguistic and cultural ambiguity of this variety.

TABLE 9.4 *Varieties of English used in New Zealand television advertisements (1986)*

Category	Variety	42%
Audience design	Middle New Zealand	
Indeterminate	Upper New Zealand	9
In-group referee, in-group addressee	Lower New Zealand Maori	7 2
Out-group referee, short-term	Upper British Lower British American spoken Other	6 4 5 10
Out-group referee, long-term	American sung	15
		100%

In-group referee design is heard in the 9% of advertisements which used markedly local in-group speech. These I term 'Lower New Zealand'. A few use the ethnically marked variety distinctive to some Maori speakers.[8] The products these two varieties advertise are linked to the two kinds of values usually associated with strongly in-group dialect — solidarity, home and friendship, for example in an advertisement for long-distance telephone calls; and macho male values, used to advertise home-building products and 'utes' (pick-up trucks).

Short-term out-group referee design is represented by a number of dialects not native to New Zealand. Upper British (UB: 6% of advertisements) is associated with gracious, upper-class living. The advertisements tend to contain stereotype visuals of people getting into Rolls Royces or being waited on by butlers. Both UB and UNZ are used in advertisements to make authoritative statements, particularly voice-overs. Most of the 'Lower British' category (4%) were marked as lower-class British, especially London dialects. Five per cent of the spoken out-group dialects were American. All these appeared to be produced by native speakers (as was UB), many of them American media personalities. There is an assortment of other overseas dialects — Scottish, Australian, Singaporean — and a number of non-native accents such as Spanish- and French-accented English.

Long-term out-group referee design is evidenced (apart from the indeterminate UNZ class) only in the use of American forms in singing. This provides the largest single category of referee designed language in television advertisements — 15%. American features appear in all singing in advertisements, just as they do in New Zealand music generally, reflecting the American origins and continuing dominance of most popular music styles.

Linguistic analysis

Even from the preliminary analysis conducted, it is clear that referee design can be manifested at any level of linguistic structure. Phonological, lexical, syntactic and discourse features are all used, but these resources are not employed equally. Distinctive discourse and syntactic markers were rare. Notable was the tag 'eh?', as in 'not long to go now, eh?'. This is stereotypical of Maori English, and embedded in one of a series of advertisements for Air New Zealand in which (Maori) entertainer Billy T. James speaks in a caricatured Maori teenage accent. The infrequent use of syntactic markers is not surprising. Dialects differ less in their syntax than their phonology, and syntactic variation often involves non-standard features — which are deliberately invoked in the above example.

The lexicon is the most obvious source of referee markers. In the UB advertisements we hear expressions which New Zealanders associate with the stereotype of the upper-class Britisher — 'positively terrific', 'absolutely super', 'truly spiffing'. These are even more obviously in the realm of stereotype than most referee-designed speech, as are the visuals which tend to accompany them. The other main group of advertisements using lexical strategies is those with LNZ and Maori dialect. Here we hear the greeting 'G'day', the solidarity term 'mate', abbreviations such as 'beaut', and 'cuzzies' (for 'cousins'), and 'decent', 'choice' and 'neat' as adjectives meaning 'good'. These lexical items are used to claim in-group identity and establish solidarity.

The most common referee design strategy is to use phonological marking. Since the phonology is the major area of inter-dialectal difference, this is not surprising. Further, it is the vowel systems where most dialect differences are manifest rather than the consonants. But at this point the strategies of referee design are skewed: the consonants do much more than their share of the work. For example, most of the LB advertisements seem to have working-class London dialects as their target variety. They concentrate on four features associated with Cockney:

(1) /h/-dropping
(2) glottalised inter-vocalic /t/
(3) vocalised final /l/
(4) labiodental [f] for dental /th/.

This list of features is, unsurprisingly, similar to that which Trudgill (1983) found as markers of British working-class identity in pop songs. They are favoured as strategies in advertisements because the sounds themselves are already present in NZE, although not necessarily in the same environment, and certainly at lower frequencies. In one ten-second advertisement, the speakers succeeded in producing three [f] for /th/, three vocalised /l/, and one glottalised inter-vocalic /t/. Those seven tokens are more than enough to mark the speech as LB. Moreover, the advertisement shows signs of being scripted just so as to maximise the occurrence of these features, for example in the choice of the name 'Nigel' (spoken with vocalised /l/) for one of its characters. It thus deliberately displays the dialect at its points of obvious difference to NZE, a device frequently used in everyday anecdote or narrative.

The vowels are, on first consideration, the obvious resource for someone trying to imitate an out-group dialect. But the salience of vowels as markers of another dialect is counter-balanced by the difficulty of achieving native-like control of an alien vowel system (Payne, 1980; Trudgill, 1981; Shockey, 1984). So for some target dialects, genuine native speakers are usually used. The advertising profession seems to recognise that the risk of inaccurately imitating spoken American and UB is too great given New Zealanders' exposure to these varieties through other television programming. For UB, the native speaker's vowels can be used to display the accent, with a particular vowel repeated many times in a short advertisement.

But where NZE speakers hardly ever attempt to speak American, in song American must always be attempted (cf. Trudgill, 1983). The stability of the norm is highlighted by the fact that even advertisements which appeal to New Zealand nationalism always have American features in their singing. The use of American phonology can extend to the import of American cultural symbols. A patriotically toned advertisement for the high-circulation magazine, the *NZ Woman's Weekly*, used the expression 'from coast to coast' to convey its nationwide appeal. In New Zealand's long, narrow islands the normal geographic reference to encompass the whole country is 'north to south'.

Referee design is more a matter of individual occurrences of salient variants than of quantitative summings of actual over potential occurrences. It is more important that a marked variant occurred once out of ten possible occurrences than that the unmarked variant occurred nine times. One of the strategies of successful referee design is to focus on few variants (or even one) to the exclusion of others and keep on repeating them. Copywriters produce scripts to maximise the occurrence of sounds which will highlight the reference group and the product name. In one thirty-second UB advertisement, the vowel /i:/ is repeated thirteen times. Three of those occurrences are in the product name ('Reach' toothbrush). Another four each occur in 'clean', and 'teeth', setting up a nice, quasi-poetic assonance between the product and the description of its function.

It seems from the television data that in certain conditions as little as one dialect-marked variant could be enough for successful referee design. In a three-second, ten-word stretch of speech, two occurrences of the RP /ou/ vowel in the word 'motorshow' were enough to establish the accent as UB. In other cases, three marked variants (two inter-vocalic glottal stops and a lexical item) were enough to claim a London identity. For longer stretches of speech, marked variants have to keep on occurring at regular intervals for referee design to be convincing.

Accuracy *versus* success

Assessing accuracy in the execution of referee strategies means measuring the speaker's performance against the standard of native speakers. But the essence of referee design is not the accuracy of the speaker's production but the audience's perception of that production. Success depends on who your audience is and whether your speech puts them in mind of the intended reference group. Apart from the American and UB varieties produced by native speakers, all of the varieties in this sample of advertisements were more or less inaccurately imitated. The advertisements included Scottish, Australian, Singaporean and various LB accents. Not one was reproduced with full accuracy. The most inaccurate in the sample were the attempts at LB. There is even one advertisement where I have been quite unable to decide what target accent the advertisers were aiming at. Few of the vowels approach the values of the target, and most remained identifiably New Zealand.

A television advertisement provides optimal conditions for accurate referee design — maximum rehearsal, minimum speaking time and a recorded product. Even so, the vowel system of the target accent is not produced. The limits on consistent production of an alien dialect seem to be quite severe. Two speakers successfully maintained a ten-second LB dialogue, but a twenty-second monologue produced an indeterminate mixture of London and NZ speech. Although London dialects are often heard on New Zealand television, the crucial condition of the presence of these varieties in the New Zealand speech community is lacking (cf. Trudgill, 1986). No amount of passive media reception compensates for the fact that NZE speakers rarely have the chance to interact with addressees who speak these dialects (but cf. Bayard, this volume).

Even Australian dialect is inaccurately reproduced, in spite of the fact that the two countries are close neighbours and their accents are so similar that usually only native speakers can tell them apart. One of the salient differences between the two is /ɪ/ — centralised in NZE, close front in Australian. An advertisement for Australian 'Riverland' oranges produced the first vowel of the name with [i:] — qualitatively accurate, but inaccurately lengthened. This hypercorrection might be a reflection of the actor's inability to produce the Australian variant (which is phonetically very similar to New Zealand /e/). Or it may well function as a deliberate part of the referee design, exaggerating one of the most salient differences between Australian and NZE.

Success in referee design depends on who your audience is. The exact condition which obstructs accurate referee design — an absent target variety — also restricts the goal and mitigates the cost of failure. The more distant the referee out-group, the less a NZE speaker may know their code. But, happily, the audience knows the out-group code just as imperfectly, and may therefore be in no position to question the performance. Testing accuracy requires evaluation of speech by native speakers of the referee dialect. But testing success requires evaluation by fellow-members of the speaker's own community.

Conclusion

The preponderance of foreign dialect advertisements in New Zealand broadcasting is initially surprising. But it reflects, first, a small nation's focus on the prestige of other culturally powerful nations such as the United States and Britain (Bell, 1982b; 1988; Bayard, this volume). Linguistically, it reflects the comparative lack of diversity within NZE, which has less regional, social and ethnic variation than many other countries. New Zealanders therefore reach beyond the linguistic resources available in their own immediate speech community and draw language strategies from the vast array of English dialects world wide.

The referee phenomenon is a rich field for social and cultural analysis. For example, 75% of the spoken American dialect advertisements were associated with American products or spoken by American media stars. For British dialects, the figure was only 30% associated with British products or personalities. The other 70% of British dialects were freely chosen by the advertisers to associate with their product. This implies that a British image is the target of more deliberately selected associations, whereas the American associations are less intentionally chosen. That seems to reflect, perhaps surprisingly, continued high prestige for British rather than American cultural norms.

Such reaching beyond the speech community's normal repertoire in order to achieve certain effects has been found in a number of other studies of media language. Coupland (1985) describes a Cardiff music-show presenter who shifted from a stigmatised local dialect (in itself an initiative style) to adopt American phonological features in announcing certain kinds of songs. Haarmann (1984) demonstrates in detail how Japanese advertising makes extensive use of foreign language material (as New Zealand has also recently begun to do).

In this chapter I have presented complementary data sets from the two principal genres of mass media: news and advertising. It is clear that while the first operates largely on the responsive dimension of style, the second is primarily initiative-oriented. Newsreading proves to be a case where linguistic style is stratified in a way which can only be explained as audience design. By contrast, advertising shows a predominance of referee design as a means of evoking cultural associations. Advertisers make creative use of the resources of language variation to catch audience attention and evoke desirable images for their product. In both cases the mass media situation throws into sharper relief the strategies which operate in everyday interaction. And at the same time, it illuminates the social and cultural forces which operate to shape language in use in New Zealand.

Notes

1. This paper brings together data and theory developed over a number of years. Some of the material has appeared in different forms in the interim (e.g. Bell, 1982a). I am grateful to the many people whose suggestions improved this research, including Nikolas Coupland, Derek Davy, Joy Kreeft, William Labov, Gillian Sankoff, Walt Wolfram, the late Colin Bowley, and my co-editor, Janet Holmes.

2. The time at which I first studied Auckland radio proved to be optimal for an examination of language style. Five stations provide enough differentiation to be interesting stylistically. Two or three stations would not give sufficient variety. There are now ten stations — too many to offer clear stratification among their audiences and language styles. I describe here the situation as it was at the time of the main language sample used in this research (1974), while updating some labels which have changed in the interim. Much of the basic programming and character of the stations remains remarkably unchanged despite several re-organisations of public broadcasting and the addition of several more stations (mostly FM). News programming, formats, sources and networking have altered more, yet the accommodative patterns are largely constant. Several resamplings of specific linguistic variables at intervals since the original sample indicate that the basic patterns to be described here have remained very stable. In tables and lists, the stations are always given in the order of their medium wave frequences: 1YA, 1ZB, 1ZM, 1XA, 1XI.

3. These surveys were conducted every two months by the National Research Bureau. The basic questionnaire and data-processing methods were designed by Brian Murphy of the Economics Department, University of Auckland, a director of NRB. I owe him thanks for giving access to the surveys and allowing me to include additional questions.

4. This presentation limits itself to the central factors in explaining the style variation. In other presentations of aspects of this data (Bell, 1982a; in press), I have also included the 'local' or 'solidarity' dimension necessary to explain some of the behaviour of other linguistic variables.

5. A similar comparison on another variable — consonant cluster reduction — patterns in the same way (Bell, 1977; in press). Of 20 pairwise comparisons (four environments for five speakers), only one environment deviates from the pattern expected from the operation of audience design.

6. A third, privately owned channel started up in late 1989. With broadcasting deregulation, other contenders are proposing additional channels in the near future.
7. I use the labels 'Upper', 'Middle' and 'Lower' New Zealand in preference to the trichotomy imported from Australia of Cultivated, General and Broad (Mitchell & Delbridge, 1965; cf. Bayard, Gordon & Abell, this volume). The Australian classification is of doubtful applicability to New Zealand, and in any case I am dealing here with media language only, which does not necessarily correspond to everyday speech. As Bayard indicates, the varieties of NZE are best regarded as a continuum. The term 'Upper British' means RP or an acceptable approximation of it, and 'Lower British' other urban and rural dialects of England, especially London-based.
8. The fact that 'Maori English' can be used as an advertising stereotype lends substance to the existence of such a variety, despite sociolinguists' inability as yet to define its features or even agree on its existence (Benton, in press; Bell & Holmes, in press). Note also that no Maori language is used in advertising, a reflection and reinforcement of its low consumer status (cf. Vaughan & Huygens, this volume). By contrast, in 1989 a number of advertisements appeared (most without sub-titles) in European languages, especially German.

References

BELL, ALLAN 1977, The language of radio news in Auckland: a sociolinguistic study of style, audience and subediting variation. Unpublished PhD thesis. Auckland: University of Auckland.

—1982a, Radio: the style of news language. *Journal of Communication* 32 (1), 150–64.

—1982b, This isn't the BBC: colonialism in New Zealand English. *Applied Linguistics* 3 (3), 246–58.

—1984, Language style as audience design. *Language in Society* 13 (2), 145–204.

—1986, Responding to your audience: taking the initiative. Paper presented to the Minnesota Conference on Linguistic Accommodation and Style-Shifting, Minneapolis, Minnesota.

—1988, The British base and the American connection in New Zealand media English. *American Speech* 63 (4) 326–44.

—Audience accommodation in the mass media. To appear in NIKOLAS COUPLAND, HOWARD GILES and JUSTINE COUPLAND (eds) *Contexts of Accommodation: Developments in Applied Sociolinguistics*. Cambridge: Cambridge University Press.

BELL, ALLAN and HOLMES, JANET Sociolinguistic research on New Zealand English. To appear in JENNY CHESHIRE (ed.), *English Around the World: Sociolinguistic Perspectives*. Cambridge: Cambridge University Press.

BENTON, RICHARD A. Maori English: a New Zealand myth? To appear in JENNY CHESHIRE (ed.), *English Around the World: Sociolinguistic Perspectives*. Cambridge: Cambridge University Press.

BLACKBURN, ADRIAN 1974, *The Shoestring Pirates*. Auckland: Hodder and Stoughton.

BLOM, JAN-PETTER and GUMPERZ, JOHN J. 1972, Social meaning in linguistic structure: code-switching in Norway. In JOHN J. GUMPERZ and DELL HYMES (eds) *Directions in Sociolinguistics* (pp. 407–34). New York: Holt, Rinehart and Winston.

BROWN, PENELOPE and LEVINSON, STEPHEN C. 1987, *Politeness: Some Universals in Language Usage*. Cambridge: Cambridge University Press.

BROWN, ROGER and GILMAN, ALBERT 1960, The pronouns of power and solidarity. In THOMAS A. SEBEOK (ed.) *Style in Language* (pp. 253–76). Cambridge, Massachusetts: MIT Press.

BRUNEL, GILLES 1970, Le français radiophonique à Montréal. Unpublished MA dissertation. Montreal: University of Montreal.

CHOMSKY, NOAM 1957, *Syntactic Structures*. The Hague: Mouton.

COUPLAND, NIKOLAS 1980, Style-shifting in a Cardiff work-setting. *Language in Society* 9 (1), 1–12.

—1984, Accommodation at work: some phonological data and their implications. *International Journal of the Sociology of Language* 46, 49–70.

—1985, 'Hark, hark, the lark': social motivations for phonological style-shifting. *Language and Communication* 5 (3), 153–71.

COUPLAND, NIKOLAS, COUPLAND, JUSTINE, GILES, HOWARD and HENWOOD, KAREN 1988, Accommodating the elderly: invoking and extending a theory. *Language in Society* 17 (1), 1–41.

COUPLAND, NIKOLAS and GILES, HOWARD (eds) 1988, *Communicative Accommodation: Recent Developments* (*Language and Communication* 8/3–4). Oxford: Pergamon Press.

COUPLAND, NIKOLAS, GILES, HOWARD and COUPLAND, JUSTINE (eds) In press, *Contexts of Accommodation: Developments in Applied Sociolinguistics*. Cambridge: Cambridge University Press.

DORIAN, NANCY C. 1981, *Language Death: The Life Cycle of a Scottish Gaelic Dialect*. Philadelphia: University of Pennsylvania Press.

ERVIN-TRIPP, SUSAN M. 1972, On sociolinguistic rules: alternation and co-occurrence. In JOHN J. GUMPERZ and DELL HYMES (eds) *Directions in Sociolinguistics* (pp. 213–50). New York: Holt, Rinehart and Winston.

FERGUSON, CHARLES A. 1959, Diglossia. *Word* 15 (2), 325–40.

FISHER, WILLIAM M. and HIRSH, IRA J. 1976, Intervocalic flapping in English. In SALIKOKO S. MUFWENE, CAROL A. WALKER and SANFORD B. STEEVER (eds) *Papers from the Twelfth Regional Meeting* (pp. 183–98). Chicago: Chicago Linguistic Society.

FISHMAN, JOSHUA A., COOPER, ROBERT L., MA, ROXANA, *et al.* 1971, *Bilingualism in the Barrio*. Bloomington, Indiana: Indiana University.

GAL, SUSAN 1979, *Language Shift: Social Determinants of Linguistic Change in Bilingual Austria*. New York: Academic Press.

GERBNER, GEORGE 1969, Institutional pressures upon mass communicators. In PAUL HALMOS (ed.) *The Sociology of Mass-Media Communicators* (*Sociological Review Monograph No. 13*) (pp. 205–48). Keele: University of Keele.

GILES, HOWARD 1973, Accent mobility: a model and some data. *Anthropological Linguistics* 15 (2), 87–105.

—(ed.) 1977, *Language, Ethnicity and Intergroup Relations*. London: Academic Press.

—1984, *The Dynamics of Speech Accommodation* (*International Journal of the*

Sociology of Language 46). Amsterdam: Mouton.

GILES, HOWARD, MULAC, ANTHONY, BRADAC, JAMES J. and JOHNSON, PATRICIA 1987, Speech accommodation theory: the first decade and beyond. In MARGARET L. MCLAUGHLIN (ed.), *Communication Yearbook 10* (pp. 13–48). Beverly Hills: Sage.

GILES, HOWARD and POWESLAND, PETER F. 1975, *Speech Style and Social Evaluation*. London: Academic Press.

HAARMAN, HARALD 1984, The role of ethnocultural stereotypes and foreign languages in Japanese commercials. *International Journal of the Sociology of Language* 50, 101–21.

HOLMES, JANET 1986, Functions of *you know* in women's and men's speech. *Language in Society* 15 (1), 1–21.

—New Zealand women are good to talk to: an analysis of politeness strategies in interaction. To appear in *Journal of Pragmatics* 13 (4).

JONES, ROBERT L. and CARTER, ROY E. Jr 1959, Some procedures for estimating 'news hole' in content analysis. *Public Opinion Quarterly* 23 (3), 399–403.

LABOV, WILLIAM 1966, *The Social Stratification of English in New York City*. Washington, DC: Center for Applied Linguistics.

—1972, *Sociolinguistic Patterns*. Philadelphia: University of Pennsylvania Press.

LAMBERT, WALLACE E. 1967, A social psychology of bilingualism. *Journal of Social Issues* 23 (2), 91–109.

MCENTEGART, DAMIAN and LE PAGE, R. B. 1982, An appraisal of the statistical techniques used in the Sociolinguistic Survey of Multilingual Communities. In SUZANNE ROMAINE (ed.) *Sociolinguistic Variation in Speech Communities* (pp. 105–24). London: Edward Arnold.

MCQUAIL, DENIS 1969, Uncertainty about the audience and the organization of mass communications. In PAUL HALMOS (ed.) *The Sociology of Mass-Media Communicators* (*Sociological Review Monograph No. 13*) (pp. 75–84). Keele: University of Keele.

MILROY, LESLEY 1987, *Observing and Analysing Natural Language: A Critical Account of Sociolinguistic Method*. Oxford: Basil Blackwell.

MITCHELL, A. G. and DELBRIDGE, ARTHUR 1965, *The Speech of Australian Adolescents*. Sydney: Angus & Robertson.

PAYNE, ARVILLA C. 1980, Factors controlling the acquisition of the Philadelphia dialect by out-of-state children. In WILLIAM LABOV (ed.) *Locating Language in Time and Space* (pp. 143–78). New York: Academic Press.

PITT, DAVID (ed.) 1977, *Social Class in New Zealand*. Auckland: Longman Paul.

SHOCKEY, LINDA 1984, All in a flap: long-term accommodation in phonology. *International Journal of the Sociology of Language* 46, 87–95.

THAKERAR, JITENDRA N., GILES, HOWARD and CHESHIRE, JENNY 1982, Psychological and linguistic parameters of speech accommodation theory. In COLIN FRASER and KLAUS R. SCHERER (eds) *Advances in the Social Psychology of Language* (pp. 205–55). Cambridge: Cambridge University Press.

TRUDGILL, PETER 1981, Linguistic accommodation: sociolinguistic observations on a sociopsychological theory. In CARRIE S. MASEK, ROBERTA A. HENDRICK and MARY FRANCES MILLER (eds) *Papers from the Parasession on Language and Behavior* (pp. 218–37). Chicago: Chicago Linguistic Society.

—1983, *On Dialect*. Oxford: Basil Blackwell.

—1986, *Dialects in Contact*. Oxford: Basil Blackwell.

YAEGER-DROR, MALCAH 1988, The influence of changing group vitality on convergence toward a dominant linguistic norm: an Israeli example. *Language & Communication* 8(3–4), 285–305.

ZWICKY, ARNOLD M. and PULLUM, GEOFFREY K. 1982, Cliticization versus inflection: English *n't*. Bloomington: Indiana University Linguistics Club.

10 They're off and racing now: the speech of the New Zealand race caller[1]

KOENRAAD KUIPER and PADDY AUSTIN

Introduction

Oral-formulaic performance is normally the research province of those who are interested in oral literature, that is in the artifacts of what might be called high culture. High culture is typified by considerations of value, particularly by aesthetic considerations. Consider, for instance, the place of opera in western cultures. Opera is granted status in a number of ways. It is regarded as inherently more valuable than popular songs by members of ruling elites. Operas themselves are compared with each other, some being regarded as better than others. Performances and performers are compared and so forth.

Products of popular culture, are not so much seen in terms of aesthetic or cultural value. For this reason amongst others, oral-formulaic varieties in contemporary popular culture have not received much attention. But that does not mean that such varieties do not exist or that they are without interest. Furthermore the study of such varieties has much to tell us about the nature of oral-formulaic performance particularly since our judgements of such performances need not be affected by aesthetic considerations. The performances of the auctioneer and the sports commentator are cases in point (Kuiper & Haggo, 1984; 1985; Kuiper & Tillis, 1986).

Why should oral-formulaic speech be of interest to linguists? Let us suppose that native speakers of a language have in their heads as part of their linguistic competence a dictionary of the language they speak. This dictionary contains some of the words of the language and also some of its idioms or formulae. Idioms are the kind of set phrases which speakers of the language use as set pieces rather than building them up out of words from scratch. Part of a speaker's ability to communicate using language has to do with the ability to sound native-like, i.e. using expressions which other speakers recognise as being the way native speakers of their language say that sort of thing.

For example one greets people in a native-like way in New Zealand by saying things like 'Gidday', or 'How are you?' or 'Hi'. One does not say 'Are you in good health?' or, as a Chinese speaker might say in similar circumstances, 'Have you eaten?'. This means that a native speaker must know which expressions are native-like. It follows that they must be in the native speaker's internal dictionary. That makes such expressions the province of the linguist.

Such expressions also make the business of speaking and hearing easier since linguistic performance is reduced, at the moment of selecting such an expression from the dictionary, to saying it rather than building it as a complex function of its parts in the case of the speaker, and looking up what it means in the case of the hearer. For this reason oral-formulaic performance is of interest to a linguist because it is a theory of linguistic performance in the Chomskyan sense.

Lastly since all such formulae are commonly used expressions for common social functions, such as greetings and apologies, they have a social aspect which can provide an insight into the society in which they are used. Their selection is triggered by the speaker's desire to accomplish particular social ends. So when they appear in speech, the social matrix which led to their being selected is manifest to native speakers since such speakers have been similarly enculturated.

The particular aspect of New Zealand culture which forms the focus of this study is horse racing. Horse racing may not itself be remarkable but the circumstances in which a race caller finds himself are somewhat unusual and it is this unusual performance situation which gives rise to the particular oral formulaic performance of which such commentators are masters. This means that the study or oral-formulaic performance is relevant to the study of communicative competence (Hymes, 1974: 75) and as such of interest to the sociolinguist and ethnolinguist. Lest it be thought that we are using sexist terminology above we should say that, to our knowledge, there are no women race callers in New Zealand, or anywhere else. The same can be said for auctioneers in New Zealand although there are women auctioneers in the USA. It appears that a very large number of oral formulaic traditions are dominated by men.

The chant of the race caller is a familiar sound in suburbia on weekends in both Australia and New Zealand. Coming over the airwaves and emitting from transistor radios it mingles with the sound of motor mowers and alternates with the more tranquil tones of the cricket commentator. Like much of popular culture it passes as, in itself, uneventful and therefore uninteresting. However appearances can be and often are deceiving. Race calling is a fertile field for testing predictions made by Kuiper & Haggo (1984) about the nature of oral-formulaic varieties of speech and we will show that these predictions are corroborated by the facts of race-calling speech.

Kuiper & Haggo (1984) give a description of the speech of New Zealand livestock auctioneers and suggest that it has four particular properties which, as a cluster, make it different from 'ordinary speech'. These four properties are: being abnormally fluent; being intoned with an unusual prosodics in the form of droned intonation; having local discourse structures rules which can be formalised as context-free rewrite rules; and using lexicalised syntactic fragments termed 'oral formulae' which can be formalised as finite-state grammars. Kuiper & Haggo theorise that these four properties are each, independently, a function of constraints on speech processing occasioned by heavy loading on short-term memory (STM). The extreme fluency of oral-formulaic speech is both a requirement on the speaker which adds to STM loading and an outcome of its particular character.[2] Kuiper & Haggo also show that oral-formulaic speech is learned through a three-stage process from listener to master performer and that it is passed on as an oral tradition from masters to initiates. This is again in line with Lord's description of the way singers of tales learn their craft (Lord, 1960: 21–6).

This explanation is well and good but operates only to explain in one direction, i.e. the phenomena are explained but the explanation is not used to make predictions. But such predictions can be made. A prediction would be that where similar constraints on STM operate on other speakers, similar features of speech will tend to appear. It can be shown that similar constraints on memory to those that operate on livestock auctioneers operate on race callers. Their speech also has the linguistic properties which were found in the speech of New Zealand livestock auctioneers. This finding therefore corroborates the hypothesis that if speakers are under STM pressure then they will tend to utilise the speech production mechanisms afforded by oral-formulaic performance.[3]

Our discussion of race calling is based on that of New Zealand race callers, particularly Reon Murtha who is the local caller in Christchurch.

The speech of overseas callers we have heard also shares some linguistic properties with that of New Zealand callers. We would predict, since callers the world over are under similar pressures on STM, that this would be so. But there are individual idiosyncracies. We doubt that there are national styles because the oral traditions by which callers learn are not really national. A caller may model himself on anyone. In the days of international radio broadcasts, that may even be an overseas someone although it is more likely that the modelling will be on a provincial basis.

Short-Term Memory Constraints on Race Callers

Race callers provide commentaries of horse racing in two different modes. Before and after a race the commentary is in what Kuiper & Haggo (1985) refer to as 'colour commentary'. It is fluent in normal ways, has normal intonation, does not have entirely fixed discourse rules but does use formulae although not in a very concentrated fashion. Race commentators also relate the events of the race as it happens, in what Kuiper & Haggo (1985) call 'play-by-play commentary'. Play-by-play mode involves relaying abnormally fluently, although not necessarily rapidly, the events which the commentator is seeing. We shall show that play-by-play commentary is oral formulaic. Colour commentary is not. The reason is that STM is not nearly so heavily engaged while the commentator is in colour mode because the race has either not yet begun, or because it is over. However while the commentator is in play-by-play mode the race is being run. This involves (minimally) the following things stored in the speaker's long-term memory (LTM):

(1) a list of the names of all the horses which are running;
(2) linked with this list and for each horse, its colours, i.e. the colours of the owner or trainer;
(3) linked with list 1, the jockey/driver of each horse;
(4) linked with list 1, the name(s) of the owner(s);
(5) linked with list 1, the name(s) of the trainer(s);
(6) linked with list 1, a list of the favourite(s) for the race;
(7) the length of the race;
(8) the physical nature of the track and the names of its topographical features;
(9) the current state of the track.

It involves, minimally, the following actions and associated STM and processing operations:

(1) watching the race through field glasses;
(2) on the basis of the colours and possibly physical features of each horse, recalling the name of the horse and when required the name of its jockey, trainer and owner from LTM;
(3) discerning for each horse its relative and absolute position both in a linear sequence if horses are one behind the other and in two dimensions if horses are travelling one outside the other (absolute position is given in specialist dimensions such as lengths, necks, noses);
(4) discerning the current location of each horse (note that position is both position on the track as a physical (elliptical) entity and position in the race as a linear entity with a beginning, middle and end);
(5) discerning changes in relative and absolute position;
(6) noting any unusual happenings such as horses or riders falling, infringements of good racing behaviour and the like.

Let us suppose that commentators have, at any one time, a perceptual window in which the salient items are: a horse under current scrutiny, the horses immediately in front, beside and behind it, and the location of each horse relative to the others in two dimensions and in both relative and absolute terms. In the perceptual window too is the location on the track, for example, in the back straight, or on the showground's bend, and the location in the race dimensions, for example, at the 1,500 m mark. What is in the perceptual window changes in two ways. The commentator changes what is in the window by moving the window through the field from the first horse to the last and then back to the first horse again, i.e. the window is moved cyclically through the field of runners. But what is in the window changes while the commentator is speaking. First the relative location of the whole field changes in two ways, it moves round the track and from the start to the finish of the race. That is always the case. And at any time the participants in the window may change their relative positions in two dimensions. At the same time events outside the current window may be significant enough to override the attention on the current window and the commentator must be able to switch at a split second's notice to describing some event outside the current window.[4]

Continuously as the commentator is speaking, the names of the runners must be accessed from LTM as required. It should be clear that in such a performance situation STM is heavily engaged in non-linguistic activities. Yet the commentator is speaking fluently all the while. Speaking also requires STM space. It is exactly in such circumstances that

Kuiper & Haggo show that auctioneers have recourse to oral-formulaic performance.

Learning to Call Races

Kuiper & Haggo (1984) show that livestock auctioneers, like Serbo-Croatian oral poets, go through a three-phase process in acquiring their variety. These poets and the process of acquisition of their tradition are described in detail in Albert B. Lord's seminal book on oral-formulaic performance, *The Singer of Tales* (Lord, 1960). The first phase is a period of listening only, followed by a period of apprenticeship and journeymanship where the performer starts speaking in a stereotypical fashion following discourse rules closely and using a relatively small inventory of formulae. At the end of this period the performer is able to perform fluently as a native speaker of the variety with a full inventory of formulae and with a flexible response to situational variation. The last phase is that of the virtuoso or master when the performer is able to make a contribution to the variety by constructing his own formulae and having apprentices use him as a model.

Race commentators learn their variety of English in this way. There is no official training for race calling, most of the early practice, modelled on the local oral tradition, being done at informal Sunday workouts, where the numbers of horses in a race is comparatively small, and the consequences of inefficiency relatively unimportant. A race caller may then, if fortunate and able, go on to call races at small country meetings, after which he may graduate to the status of stand-in for the main commentator of the area.

One master commentator is responsible for a large area; for instance, in the Canterbury area, one person calls the races for all meetings (harness racing and galloping) in Christchurch, Ashburton, Rangiora and Methven, an area within about an hour's drive from Christchurch. In the main cities this person is often a semi-professional race caller and broadcaster, while others who may stand in for him are often part-timers being employed by livestock firms as auctioneers. Dave Clarkson who used to call races in Canterbury was originally an auctioneer. However, Reg Clapp who calls harness races in Auckland works as a menswear retailer.

Reon Murtha, who is the main Christchurch race caller, has a history which is a good example of the education of a race caller. As a young boy he always had his heart set on becoming a race caller. He describes setting up games with improvised objects as horses and calling his own backyard races. After he left school he joined the local radio station initially as a technician and later became an announcer but always with the intention of becoming a race caller. At age 19 he called his first race in his home town of Reefton on the West Coast of the South Island of New Zealand. He was initially appointed by the Reefton Jockey Club as its on-course commentator and with that came the possibility of also being the radio commentator. A few years later the race caller who had covered the race meetings in Greymouth moved house and Reon was appointed by his radio station as the West Coast caller. On the West Coast he called about ten to fifteen race meetings a year. After he had called races for ten years on the Coast the Christchurch commentator, Dave Clarkson, who had been the model for Reon, changed occupations and Reon was appointed to the position of race caller for Radio New Zealand in Christchurch.

One aspect of race calling which differentiates it from livestock auctioneering is that of broadcasting. The main race caller for an area not only has many of his commentaries broadcast live on the national radio and television network, but also frequently has programmes on either or both media, in which he previews race meetings, interviews horse owners and trainers, and gives predictions on possible winners. In this respect race callers are like ice-hockey commentators in being entertainers as well as informers.

Do Race Callers Use Oral-Formulaic Performance?

If it is the case that heavy pressure on the limited STM of speakers causes them to use oral-formulaic speech, then we would expect the speech of race callers to have the four characteristics of oral-formulaic speech: abnormal fluency, doned prosodics, discourse structure rules and oral formulae.

Abnormal fluency

Kuiper & Haggo (1984) suggest that oral-formulaic varieties exist in situations where fluency is of great importance. As a result of using the particular performance strategy afforded by oral-formulaic performance, speakers achieve not just conventional fluency but abnormal fluency. Kuiper & Haggo (1984) suggest that this abnormal fluency has a number of aspects. The first is the steady articulation rate. Non-oral-formulaic speech usually starts slowly at the beginning of a clause, builds up speed in the middle and then slows at the end. Oral-formulaic speech, on the other hand, has a more steady articulation rate. The second is the absence of hesitation phenomena and fillers. Clause boundaries are usually places where there is in normal speech, a concentration of hesitation phenomena like pausing, voiced pausing, including 'ums' and 'ers' and filler phrases like 'ye know' and 'like'. A typical (manufactured) example might be a sentence such as 'Er he's er going to be coming when, ye know, he's er like finished er painting his car'. Those who have transcribed spoken text will be familiar with these normal hesitation and filler phenomena.[5] Such phenomena are absent from oral-formulaic speech. The third area of difference is false starts. In normal speech speakers not infrequently make false starts, i.e. fail to complete a sentence on which they have embarked. They then switch in mid-stream to another sentence. In the case of oral-formulaic performance false starts are, for the most part, absent. These three differences from normal speech create a sense of abnormal fluency.

There are good practical reasons for wanting to be particularly fluent in the situations where oral-formulaic performance is used. In the case of racing commentaries a caller, unlike the horses he is describing, cannot break down.[6] Therefore fluency is essential. Kuiper & Haggo (1984) show how oral-formulaic performance facilitates fluency. Race calling, with its high demand for fluency, again provides a good reason for the speech of race callers to be an oral-formulaic variety. The fact that race commentaries are broadcast both at the track and on radio (and sometimes television) makes high levels of fluency important. An oral-formulaic mode of performance facilitates fluency by allowing most speech production to take place more automatically. Oral formulae, being accessed from LTM, allow the speaker to produce formulae in the right order on the basis of their discourse indexing, as we will show later. All that has to be 'filled in' is the name of a horse. Since formulae are used frequently, their production is automated, resulting in abnormal fluency. Kuiper & Haggo (1984) indicate that livestock auctioneers articulate at a steady rate of about six syllables per second. Reon Murtha runs at between four and five syllables a second. American tobacco auctioneers range from about six syllables a second to an incredible nine to ten syllables a second in the case of Harry Crisp from Pine Tops, Virginia. Crisp manages to achieve this pace for the central bid-calling phase of each sale.

At the end of a race after the horses have passed the winning post, the caller is no longer under the kind of memory pressure we outlined earlier. His speech can therefore revert to a more normal mode and consequently disfluencies of the normal kind occur. Fluency is also no longer at such a premium because the vital part of the race which must be fluently and accurately relayed is over. Hesitation phenomena increase as is illustrated in the epilogue of the sample text given below. The syntax becomes disfluent as well, as the two false starts in the epilogue section of the sample text below. 'He actually decided to, once he'd got loose from his driver, he bounded away by himself.' 'He ah this sort of thing happened . . .' This can be contrasted with an example from a different commentary where disfluency is masked during a play-by-play section. In this example there are no hesitations and only two formulae juxtaposed while the commentator searches for the correct name of a horse. 'They were followed through there now by as they make their way on to the top end of the course by Bahrein.' The formula which is interrupted is: 'They were followed through there now by X', where X is the name of a horse. The formula which is seamlessly inserted is: 'as they make their way on to the top end of the course'. This formula is a field-locator formula rather than a horse-locator formula. We can tell that Reon Murtha is having processing trouble, i.e. cannot pick up the horse he is looking for, either in memory or in the field, by the fact that he seldom uses a formula which locates the field of horses while he himself is running through the field. Yet here such a formula is interpolated into a horse-locator formula to create processing space. The use of the formula clearly enables him to remain fluent.

Drone prosodics

Racing commentaries in play-by-play mode are droned in a way which is similar to that of ice-hockey commentators (Kuiper & Haggo, 1985), that is, they are basically on a monotone. What we mean by that is that the normal rules of English intonation which lay an intonation contour over what a person is saying, do not operate. That is not to say that there is no pitch variation at all. The relative pitch of the drone is matched in ice-hockey to the perceived excitement of the events being relayed. This varies from moment to moment, and the commentator often manages to match the rise and fall of the crowd roar. In racing commentaries the drone usually rises in semitones to a high point at the finishing post and then gradually comes down as the commentator moves through the last cycle. On the way down the commentator also moves out of drone mode back into colour mode with normal speech intonation. The movement up the scale is usually accomplished in a stepwise sequence starting slowly and moving rapidly at the end of the race. At the end of the race when the pitch moves rapidly upward, some commentators move stepwise while others move on a sliding scale so that one cannot tell exactly on which syllable the rise in pitch takes place. The climb down in pitch after the horses have passed winning post is usually also a slide rather than a set of steps and it is accomplished in a straight line rather than a curve.[7]

While this is a description of the archetypal drone there are variations. If a particularly exciting event takes place there will be a larger jump. In the sample text below this takes place at the point where one of the drivers is pitched out of the sulkie.[8] At that point in his commentary Reon Murtha jumps up three semitones in pitch and stays at that note for longer than he normally would. The reason for this is that having an octave span in most of his commentaries and having, as it were, spent three semitones early on, Reon rations himself for the rest of the race with the steep part of the curve coming at about the same distance from the end of the race as it would have come had the untoward incident not taken place. We show this drone and a normal one for comparison in Figure 10.1.

There are a number of variations among callers in the way they perform the drone. Drones may in fact be chanted. We distinguish in the following way between droning and chanting. In a drone a speaker consistently speaks on a monotone with little or no normal speech intonation (although drone may be accompanied by various kinds of prosodic ornamentation). Chant is what happens when drone is sung. It appears that speakers and hearers alike make categorical distinctions between whether people are singing or speaking. Drone is a kind of speech and chant is a kind of singing. What drone and chant share is a strong tonal centre, rather like the pedal base in baroque music, with some room for ornamentation. While New Zealand livestock auctioneers generally drone, tobacco auctioneers of the American South described by Kuiper & Tillis (1986) chant. In the case of race callers some chant and some drone. Reon Murtha, Lachie Marshall from Oamaru, and Dave McDonald from Gore all chant while Keith Haub from Auckland drones.[9] Whether one drones or chants appears to be in part a matter of oral tradition. Those callers who follow in the tradition of the great Dave Clarkson, such as Reon Murtha, chant because Dave Clarkson chanted. Reon Murtha believes that unchanted droning is an Australian oral tradition while the indigenous tradition is for chant. To judge from the few examples we have heard, this seems to be so, although Sid Tonks

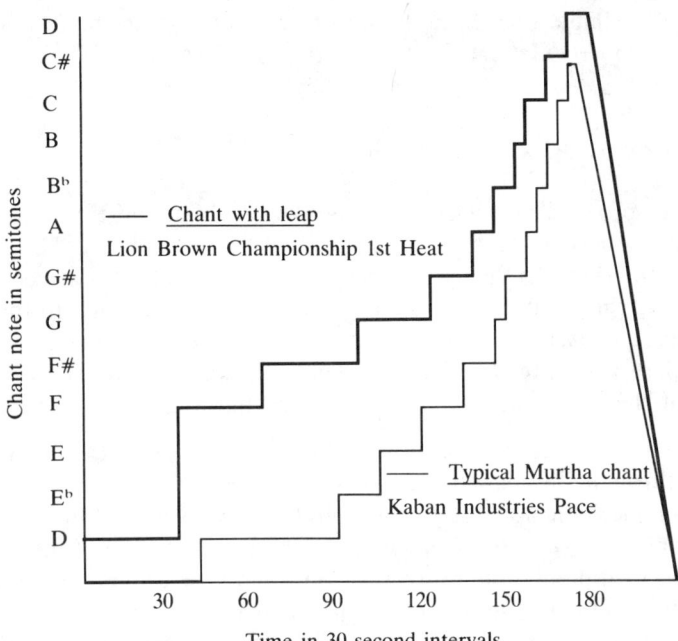

FIGURE 10.1 *Comparison of normal chant with a leap chant showing curve adjustment (recorded at the Addington raceway 15th October 1986)*

who used to call races in Auckland seems more of a droner than a chanter. The chant also appears to be a New Zealand tradition in that BBC race callers do not chant. The BBC race callers we have heard managed to postpone droning until quite late into the race. They were also disfluent.

A second way callers vary their drone is the actual pitch range. For any particular commentator this tends to be unique. Reon Murtha, as we have said, typically covers one complete octave from D to D while calling a single race. We have annotated this in Figure 10.1. One race called by Keith Haub had a range of C# to G, a much smaller range.

Commentators also have prosodic ornaments of various kinds. Reon Murtha uses a fall contour at the end of particular formulae. His fall tones tend to come at the end of particular discourse nodes, for example, at the completion of a cycle, but this is not invariably the case. He might produce six fall tunes in a race where four come at cycle boundaries and two do not. In another it might be two at cycle boundaries and two at random. Dave McDonald will on occasion drop a half tone on the first syllable of a formula before returning to the base tone. He also has a very regular fall contour at the end of a cycle.

The discourse structure of race calling

Races proceed in a particularly obvious fashion and this leaves few options as to how matters are to be relayed to the listeners. The horses line up at the start. In the case of galloping races the horses are confined in cages and the front door to the cage is opened at the start. In the case of trotting and pacing the horses may be lined up at a standing start or at a mobile start. After the start, the field of runners makes one or more circuits of the track and then finishes at the finishing post.

The commentator's task is to indicate the order of the runners as they go through this banally simple process. But the process is not as banally simple as it appears to the uninitiated viewer. Before the start, it is possible to take note of salient facts about some or all of the horses, sometimes with number and driver, or rider, and the trainer, and perhaps the owner(s). One can note the starting place of the horse, details about individual idiosyncrasies in starts, such as the behaviour of unruly, difficult or good starters. Then there are the gambling odds associated with the race: the favourites for the race and what they and all the runners are currently paying. All this is relayed in colour mode.

The race itself is also a complex activity which we have already mentioned in the section on STM loading. Horses run on what is effectively a two-dimensional track, as if they are seen from the air. They also run in a linear race which is treated as though it were a straight line. Their positions may change at any time in both absolute and relative terms. The finish of the race is crucial since money hangs on it and horses pass the finishing post in order before the crowd and the commentator.

The commentator's task is to relate these events in the most informative way possible. The discourse structure, once the race is underway, consists of as many passes through the field as can be managed in the time. Since the activity before the start is leisurely, a commentator will always relate events in colour commentary mode, that is with normal intonation, and without fixed discourse rules. The commentary in play-by-play mode begins with the start of the race. That start is almost always signalled by a single formula. At that point the on-course public address system also switches the commentator's voice on for the on-course patrons. There are idiosyncratic variations in the exact time of the switch from colour into play-by-play mode. Some commentators take a few seconds to switch from colour to play-by-play mode. Others switch into play-by-play mode at the moment the race commences.

Each cycle of the race commentary indicates the position of the runners starting at the leading horse and ending with the horse at the tail of the field. In the process, horses are either described as being closest to the rail or further out or behind other horses. This is done until the last horse is reached after which there is usually a loop formula which tells the audience that the cycle is about to begin again. Such loop formulae often indicate the relative and absolute location of the field in the race.

Late passes through the cycle are often incomplete in that the whole field is not covered. The cycle then becomes a naming of the leading contenders often without clear locations for them being specified. After the horses pass the finishing post there is a last pass through the whole cycle, towards the end of which the commentator moves from play-by-play mode back into colour mode.

That cycle complete, there is a colour description of various further features of the race such as whether there is a photo called[10] and also often including the gambling consequences of the final placings. During this colour commentary the on-course public address system relaying the commentary is switched off. An idealised discourse structure rule for the play-by-play commentary is given in Figure 10.2 from which it is clear then, that race callers use discourse structure rules in order to perform.

There are idiosyncrasies among race callers in implementing this set of rules. For example in the middle phase of the race, some callers call every horse while others call only the leading contenders. For example, Lachie Marshall who calls races in Oamaru will run through the leaders again in a short cycle if he has just called the leaders and found there to be a change. He will then go on to give the whole field. In the pre-finish phase of the commentary the number of horses covered and the number of cycles varies from caller to caller. Reon Murtha will cover about six horses and cycle only a few times with a reduced field.[11] Allan Bright from Wellington, on the other hand, will cover between three and six horses in the pre-finish phase and may loop about half a dozen times.

Oral formulae

In order for race calling to qualify as an oral-formulaic variety it has to be constructed of oral formulae. Oral formulae have the following properties:

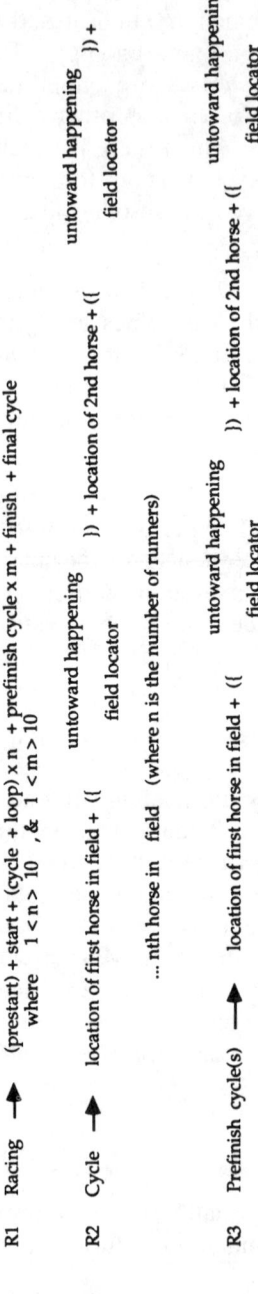

R1 Racing $\longrightarrow$ (prestart) + start + (cycle + loop) x n + prefinish cycle x m + finish + final cycle
where $1 < n > 10$, & $1 < m > 10$

R2 Cycle $\longrightarrow$ location of first horse in field + ((untoward happening / field locator)) + location of 2nd horse + ((
...nth horse in field   (where n is the number of runners)

R3 Prefinish cycle(s) $\longrightarrow$ location of first horse in field + ((untoward happening / field locator)) + location of 2nd horse + ((untoward happening / field locator)) +
... mth horse in field   (where m < n)

R4 Loop $\longrightarrow$ (track location) + (race location)

FIGURE 10.2 *Discourse structure rules for racing commentary in play-by-play mode based on the call of Reon Murtha*

(1) They have syntactic structure which can be given by a finite-state representation. Finite-state grammars are a very simple form of grammar which can be thought of as a machine which moves through a finite sequence of states emitting a word as it moves from state to state. Such grammars are informally discussed in Chomsky (1957) and formally in Aho & Ullman (1972). Haggo & Kuiper (1983) and Austin & Kuiper (1988) discuss the syntactic properties of idioms and formulae at some length.

(2) They consist of a (not necessarily unbroken) sequence of words.

(3) Each formula is indexed for use to a particular part of the discourse structure as it is given by the discourse structure rules.

This last property requires some additional explanation since it is not a commonly recognised property. In oral-formulaic varieties, formulae are always used in specific parts of the discourse. In homeric poems, for example, there are specific formulae used for specific episodes of the discourse sequence in which warriors are armed (Thornton, 1984: 100–1). In livestock auctions in North Canterbury, particular formulae are used to indicate the provenance of the stock being sold. The place in the auction where the provenance of the stock is mentioned is dictated by the discourse structure rules. So it is our hypothesis that all formulae are associated with an index which indicates where in discourse they may appropriately be used. We can think of this as a tag on the formula's file card in memory which indicates its appropriate conditions of use.

What of 'normal speech' which is not strictly oral-formulaic? Speakers use formulae all the time to apologise, greet each other and so forth. Examples and discussions of these more everyday formulae can be found in Coulmas (1979). In such non-oral-formulaic varieties of speech the index of each formula refers also to its conditions of use. But here those conditions of use are not given by discourse structure rules but by sociolinguistic parameters such as politeness level, age of participants and so forth. In some cases these conditions of use are very narrowly circumscribed as is shown in the description of the conditions of use of the English formula: 'He's old enough to be your father' in Kuiper & Tan (1989).

Given such a definition of oral formulae, we can now see that racing commentaries are constructed almost wholly of oral formulae. In the sample commentary, the whole of the play-by-play portion of the text appears to consist of formulae. This commentary has been used not because it is particularly unusual but because it is normal. We might have chosen any commentary but this suffices for the purpose. It does have one oddity which was used earlier to illustrate a further property of oral-formulaic speech, namely its unusual prosodic character. The text is taken from a race meeting where it was the fourth race of the day ('the fourth race on the card'). The race took place at the Addington raceway in Christchurch, New Zealand which is used for harness racing. The start for this race is a mobile start where the horses line up behind a barrier carried on the back of a vehicle. The vehicle picks up speed and the horses behind follow and as the vehicle and the following horses approach the start, the barrier folds away and the vehicle speeds up and moves out of the way of the horses. This is unlike galloping races where each horse is separately caged at the barrier and leaves the cage from a standing start. Lion Brown is a New Zealand beer and the company which manufactures this beer is the sponsor for this race.

Sample Racing Commentary

The authors' annotations of the text in braces show the discourse structure. Duration of the commentary is given in ten-second intervals and is indicated by a vertical slash (l).

Race 4 on the card: Lion Brown Championship first heat.
Age: 3 year olds.
Start: Mobile start.
Length: 2,000 metres.
Commentator: Reon Murtha.

This is the first heat of the Lion Brown Rising Star Three Year Old championships and the first four that are placed in this qualify for the grand final here in just a week, l Friday week. Thirty thousand dollar race, the final. The favourite is number five, Race Ruler, although you wouldn't think it if the dividends on the board are anything to go by. l At the moment it's paying eleven dollars but that's not quite true. It was two dollars before and I just think something's wrong with those dividends that are showing up on our screen. They've got Speedy Cheval the favourite but l I'm not exactly sure that that's correct but anyway they're in behind the mobile going towards the starting point now for the first heat of the Lion Brown Rising Star Three Year Old Championship just about there. l
(*End of colour commentary; beginning of play-by-play*)

They're off and racing now.

And one of the best out was Speedy Cheval   (*1st cycle*)
coming out at number two
from El Red
and also Florlis Fella's away fairly well l
a little wider on the track the favourite Race Ruler.
Twilight Time is in behind those.

Breaking up behind is Noodlum's Fella
and he went down
and one tipped out was My Dalrae |
and the driver's out of the sulkie.
The horse actually went down on its nose and cartwheeled,
sulkie over the top.

They race their way down the far side   (*Loop*)
1,600 to go

and El Red stoked up | to go to the lead now.   (*2nd cycle*)
Race Ruler's going to be caught without cover
followed by Speedy Cheval in the trail.
Florlis Fella was next
followed then by Twilight Time.
Little River's got a nice passage | through over on the outside.
Megatrend next along the rail
followed then by Lone Eagle.
About two lengths away is Belvedere.
Belvedere was followed by False Image |
and one buried on the inside of those two was Catarina.

But they race through the straight in a bunch now   (*Loop*)
with 1,300 metres left to go.

El Red the leader by two lengths from Speedy Cheval. | (*3rd cycle*)
the favourite Race Ruler parked on the outside
followed by Florlis Fella.
Twilight Time's up against the rail.
Megatrend the inside is joined on the outside by Little River.
Lone Eagle and Catarina were next. |
They were followed then by Belvedere
and last of all would have been False Image.

They race their way around the showground's bend into the back   (*Loop*)
1,100 metres to go

and El Red the leader | by two lengths from Speedy Cheval
and Race Ruler.   (*4th cycle*)
On the rails to Twilight Time.
Belvedere is going up three wide.
Florlis Fella in the centre.
False Image attacking around three wide. |
In between them is Little River.
Lone Eagle is up three wide
and Megatrend and Catarina.

Down to the 800 metres goes El Red the leader.   (*Loop*)

It's El Red in front now | (*5th cycle*)
being joined by Belvedere half a length away.

Race Ruler right in behind them.
Speedy Cheval's up against the rail.
They were followed by False Image getting closer. |
Twilight Time on the inside of Florlis Fella.
Then Little River.
Lone Eagle around those pretty wide
and back behind them Megatrend and Catarina.

They travel off the back | (*Loop*)
500 metres to run

and the big chestnut El Red by half a length the leader.   (*1st pre-finish cycle*)
They're attacking him now though
and False Image has gone round in a couple of strides to take the lead.
It's False Image from El Red |
and Belvedere
and Race Ruler
and Florlis Fella is about four wide.
Speedy Cheval is locked up in the inside
and further out to Little River.

They turn for home   (*Loop*)
240 to go. |

False Image scampers clear by a couple of lengths.   (*2nd pre-finish cycle*)
Here's Florlis Fella unwinding
and through the middle Race Ruler.
He's coming home great guns.
Up the centre then Little River
and Catarina's flying home |
too late perhaps.

                                                            (*Loop*)
False Image.   (*3rd pre-finish*)
But Race Ruler's got to him.
Race Ruler in front now
from Florlis Fella and False Image.
False Image will hold second down to the post.

                                                            (*Loop*)
Race Ruler won it. | (*Final cycle*)
False Image followed by Florlis Fella,
Catarina.
Then Megatrend.
It was followed home over on the inside of those by Little River.
Then Twilight Time,
Belvedere,
Speedy Cheval, |
El Red,
and Lone Eagle.

(End of play-by-play and return to colour commentary)

And the other one that didn't complete the journey or two of them: Noodlum's Fella was one, and the other one over on the far side of the course I ah also catapaulted and let's have a look to see how he is, number seven over there, My Dalrae. I What a spectacular spill. He actually decided to, once he got loose from his driver, he bounded away by himself. The sulkie was on its side and just as the sulkie tipped over on its wheels I ah he missed his footing ah he went into a break, tripped, fell, went down on his nose and then absolutely catapaulted with the sulkie right over on top of him and ah I he's back on his feet so luckily, I suppose, he's come away with a few abrasions but it the horse looks as though he is walking OK so he hasn't done any serious damage to himself and the driver I is quite OK, Tony Robb, My Dalrae. Noodlum's Fella was the one that broke. He ah this sort of thing happened to him on Saturday I out at Banks Peninsula when he was another, he was one who came down in that race. So two in a row.

Here's the call, Number five the winner. Good performance. I Five. So five, nine, four, thirteen, the judge's call. A close photo for fourth. Number five, Race Ruler, the winner I and Race Ruler I can give you all the details now. He's paid a dollar ninety and a dollar thirty. A dollar ninety and a dollar thirty. Number nine is second. False Image has paid four dollars twenty five. I And the third one to pass, number four, Florlis Fella, who paid two dollars fifty. A dollar ninety, a dollar thirty, four dollars twenty five, two dollars fifty. The quinella, I seventeen dollars forty five. Seventeen forty five. The trifecta, two hundred and forty six dollars. Two forty six dollars, the trifecta and the double on races three and four, one, Bronze Tiger I and number five, Race Ruler, sixty nine dollars seventy. Sixty nine dollars seventy. And the concession, seventy nine dollars sixty five. Seventy nine sixty five. I

He's a good horse, Race Ruler. He's proved that he's possibly the best three year old in the country at the moment and was one of the top two year olds last year. Didn't ah start in all of the classics I because he wasn't ah entered for them. But won the major ones ah and ah he's certainly a very fine looking three year old this season. I

Glossary

The card: The racing card is the list of races for a particular day at a race meeting.
Concession double or *concession* for short: The concession is a bet on the horse which was first in the first race of the double and the horse which was second in the second leg of the double.
Dividends: A horse may be bet on for a win or a place. Therefore there are two dividends for the winner, namely, what the horse paid for a win and what it paid for a place. The other two place getters pay only the single dividend for a place.
The double: The double is a set of two designated races at a race meeting. A bet on the double is a bet as to which two horses are going to come first in each leg of the double.

Jockey club: Horse racing is organised in New Zealand by jockey clubs which are, in fact, not clubs of or for jockeys but merely the local group of people who organise race meetings and take care of race tracks.

Quinella: The quinella is a bet on which horses will be placed first and second but not in order.

Trifecta: The trifecta is a bet on which horses will be placed first, second and third and in that order.

We can now address the question of whether the formulae of race callers have the three properties which we said were characteristic of oral formulae? It seems that they do. They can be generated by finite-state grammars (Figure 10.3). It is clear from the finite-state diagrams that some or all of the words of the formula are given. Each formula has a role(s) in the discourse of racing commentaries. It is indexed to appear as a pre-start formula or a finish formula or a locator formula.[12] We could illustrate these three properties with numerous other formulae which appear regularly in racing commentaries.

The formulae of racing commentaries have syntactic properties similar to those which have been noted in the speech of auctioneers (Kuiper & Haggo, 1984). One of these properties, also noted by Green in the case of basketball commentaries (Green, 1980), is post-position of subject, sometimes called right dislocation. In auction speech many formulae have resumptive pronoun subjects with the full Noun Phrase appearing in a post-posed position. For example, 'They should make the 50 dollar mark, those in that pen'. In racing commentaries this post-position pattern takes the form of preposing around 'be'. This form of post-position of subject is very common as the following examples taken from the sample commentary show:

Pre-posing around 'be'
1. *With* 'be' *present*
   one of the best out was Speedy Cheval
   breaking up behind is Noodlum's Fella
   and one tipped out was My Dalrae
   about two lengths away is Belvedere
   last of all would have been False Image
   and one buried on the inside of those two was Catarina
   In between them is Little River

2. *With* 'be' *elided*
   A little wider on the track the favourite, Race Ruler
   and through the middle, Race Ruler
   and back behind them, Megatrend and Catarina
   up the centre then, Little River

1. Prestart formula

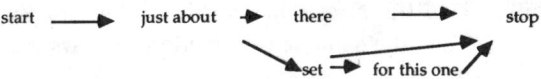

2. Start formula

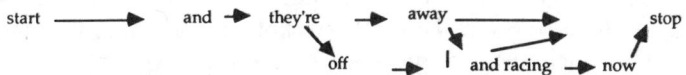

3. Horse locator formula

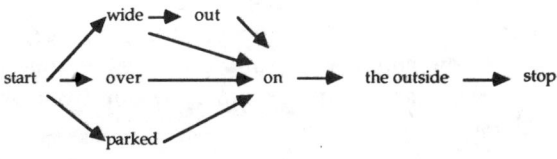

4. Race locator formula   (these often function as loop formulae)

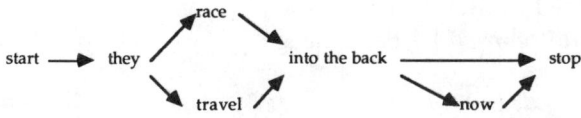

5. Finishing formulae

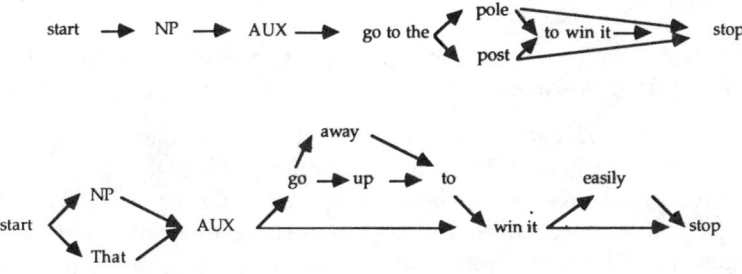

FIGURE 10.3 *Some formulae of race calling*

Passives are also common particularly where the active form of the same sentence would place the horses in an order which is not the one they adopt in the race. Thus the sentence 'Belvedere follows Race Ruler' has 'Belvedere' appearing in the sentence before 'Race Ruler'. But in the race Belvedere comes after Race Ruler. We have suggested that the perceptual window which the commentator uses moves down the field and therefore the active form of such a sentence would require more STM to hold both horses in one order while the syntactic processor is using the reverse order. Note we are not claiming here that the syntactic processor which encodes speech is reversing the order, just that it has a non-isomorphic representation of the order to that held by the visual processor. We take it, following Jackendoff (1987), that visual and linguistic processors both make representations available to the human mind. Note the passive is also a way of post-posing the subject. So using the passive saves the commentator reversing the order of the horses from the order in which they come. Also the passive is longer, two words longer, and thus gives the commentator more processing time to pick up the second horse. Here are some examples taken from the sample commentary:

Passives
1. *With* 'be' *present*
   Belvedere was followed by False Image
   Megatrend the inside is joined on the outside by Race Ruler
   They were followed then by Belvedere
   being joined by Belvedere
   They were followed by False Image

2. *With* 'be' *elided*
   followed by Speedy Cheval
   followed then by Twilight Time
   followed then by Lone Eagle
   followed by Florlis Fella

If the word 'precede' were in common use we would predict that this would be used in some formulae indicating relative location of horses.

Kuiper & Haggo (1984) suggest that these syntactic patterns are a product of STM load since such constructions, when they are formulaic, allow for processing time to be made available during the production of the formula because the Noun Phrase subject can be processed while the formula is being said. Note that the Noun Phrase subject is what the commentator must process since it is accessible only from a visual source. The formula, however, comes from LTM. So the formula which has a post-posed subject slot gives the commentator until the last possible moment to pick up which horse is next in the sequence. Clear evidence in favour of this explanation comes from the fact that left dislocation or subject pre-posing is very rare in oral-formulaic varieties. For example we would predict that formulae such as 'Noun Phrase$_1$, he is followed by Noun Phrase$_2$, Noun Phrase$_1$, he's on the rails', with subject pre-posing, or left dislocation would be rare or non-existent in race commentaries. That seems to be the case.

As with the discourse structure rules there are idiosyncrasies of both formula inventory and use. In his formula inventory Reon Murtha has the formula 'past the judge you'll have to go' which is not said by other commentators we have listened to. Reon Murtha uses field-locator formulae which locate the field on the track and in the race to loop and does not use them as locators in the cycle very often. Lachie Marshall, on the other hand, often uses a field-locator formula within the cycle. What this means is that the discourse structure index on the formula can vary from one commentator to another so that while one commentator may use a particular formula in one part of the discourse, another may use what looks like the same formula in a different place in the discourse.[13]

Is race calling an oral-formulaic variety?

We are safe to conclude on the strength of the above evidence that race calling is an oral-formulaic variety in that it has the essential features of such a variety: abnormal fluency, droned prosodics, discourse structure rules and oral formulae indexed to these rules.

Conclusion

For those who frequent New Zealand's betting shops or listen to their transistor radios on a Saturday afternoon, none of what has been said about the oral-formulaic nature of race calling speech is of direct concern. But all audiences of an oral-formulaic performer are heirs to the tradition within which the performer performs. They are the passive beneficiaries of it. It provides them with fluent, clear accounts of races so they may follow the fortunes of their favourite horses. They are able to do so because all that they hear, they have heard before. This is because the formulae which race callers use are familiar also to their audiences.

But it is the pressures on the race caller himself that cause oral-formulaic performance to be as it is, since it is the pressures on the caller which create the necessity to find a way to speak fluently while at the same time allowing the caller to keep his mind on the action he sees through his binoculars. The process of acquiring the formulaic tradition is a long one and yet the rewards are clear. Great callers are folk heroes to their audiences. They are invited to speak as after-dinner speakers. Everyone knows their names and their opinions on racing matters are frequently sought. So we have to conclude that in popular culture too, questions of value are not absent. In this case the popular culture is that of racing and the traditions are New Zealand traditions. Given where New Zealand is as a culture, it is not surprising that we should find both indigenous elements as in the case of the chanted calling of Dave Clarkson and Reon Murtha, but also Australian elements in the case of Keith Haub's drone.

Notes

1. The research reported in this paper was supported by research grants from the New Zealand University Grants Committee and the University of Canterbury. We are grateful to Peter Kane who transcribed much of our sample of commentaries, to Reon Murtha who was prepared to talk about his craft, to Radio NZ who allowed us to listen to taped recordings of race callers from inside and outside New Zealand, and for Radio New Zealand's permission to publish the transcript of Reon Murtha's commentary of the Lion Brown Championship first heat of 1986. We are also grateful to Sonya Kuiper who looked after the piano and dictated some of the texts, and Miranda Kuiper who looked after the stopwatch during part of the investigation of the prosodics of racing commentators.

2. This hypothesis is not in the broad sense, an original one. Lord (1960: 4) puts the general case this way: 'he (the singer) is forced by the rapidity of composition in performance to use these traditional elements'. Kuiper & Haggo's hypothesis that STM pressure is responsible for the use of 'traditional elements', is a more specific version of the general Lord hypothesis.

3. We do not wish to make this a universal prediction for a number of reasons. First the features or oral-formulaic speech are individually found in other kinds of speech. For example a playscript which has been perfectly memorised could be performed with the kind of abnormal fluency we later discuss. Normal routine speech also contains many formulae. Secondly it may be that even under STM pressure, some speakers perform without all of these features. For example, some race callers in the UK do not drone until near the end of the race, and have normal disfluencies during this non-droned phase of the race. However they do utilise discourse rules and formulae throughout their commentary.

4. Reon Murtha described to us a situation in which he was concentrating on the last few hundred yards of the race, calling only the first few horses. At

this point two horses fell at the back of the field, an occurrence which he did not see but which was seen by most other people on the course. It must be, then, that the perceptual window does at times occlude peripheral events.

5. For an account of hesitation phenomena and the rate of articulation in normal speech see Kuiper & Haggo (1984) and the literature cited therein.

6. This can be contrasted with slow sports such as cricket and baseball. Here there are also many formulae in common use but they have the same function as such formulae have in ordinary speech, namely to code significant repetitive events. But a cricket commentary can be, and usually is, entirely in colour mode. A horse-racing commentary could not be without losing the commentator's ability to relay information with the fluency and at the rate required to fully inform the audience of what they want to know.

7. Musically such slid tonal movements are *glissando*. In computational terms the movement is analogue as opposed to the digital step-wise movement. We currently have no explanation as to why the change from analogue-to-digital pitch change takes place.

8. A sulkie is a kind of two-wheeled cart in which drivers in harness races sit when they are driving.

9. Reon Murtha has told us that Keith Haub has modelled himself on the call of Bill Collins who calls races in Melbourne, Australia. It seems, on listening to both of them, that there is a close resemblance in their calling styles.

10. Photos are called when the finish is particularly close. The judges then use the photo of the finishing post at the time the first horse passes it to separate the place getters in the photofinish.

11. He explains his strategy this way: all of the horses have someone betting on them so everyone has a right to hear how their horse is doing until the last possible moment when only a few horses still have some chance of being 'in the money', i.e. able to pay a dividend.

12. Unlike most treatments of formulae which take them just to be a form of words, we take it that the finite-state diagram is the formula. Thus each diagram can yield a finite number of outputs which are its surface manifestations. We suppose this because it is the finite-state diagram which is discourse indexed, and if we are right about the way formulae are stored in memory then it is the finite state diagram which is so stored. (See Haggo & Kuiper (1983) and Kuiper & Haggo (1984) for a more extensive treatment of this suggestion.) It is also the case that a single line of words with no bifurcations is generable by a finite-state grammar. Thus such formulae also meet the requirement of being generable by finite-state grammars.

13. Having said earlier that a formula is a finite-state grammar, we can now add that any adequate definition of the formula must also include its discourse structure index. This is quite clear when one comes to look at the social function of formulae in ordinary language. A form of words which functions as an apology for one group of speakers can be considered a deliberate insult by another group. This can happen when the same expression has different conditions of use for the two groups. Thus for a formula to be a formula its conditions of use must be an integral part of it. Sociolinguists such as Coulmas (1979; 1981), and those interested in second language learning such as Gläser (1981) are commonly interested in formulae for this property.

References

AHO, ALFRED J. and ULLMAN, JEFFREY D. 1972, *The Theory of Parsing, Translation and Compiling*. Englewood Cliffs, New Jersey: Prentice Hall.

AUSTIN, PADDY and KUIPER, KOENRAAD 1988, Constraints on coordinated idioms. *Te Reo* 31, 3–17.

CHOMSKY, NOAM 1957, *Syntactic Structures*. The Hague: Mouton.

COULMAS, FLORIAN 1979, On the sociolinguistic relevance of routine formulae. *Journal of Pragmatics* 3 (3–4), 239–66.

—1981, *Conversational Routine*. The Hague: Mouton.

GLÄSER, ROSEMARIE 1981, *Phrasiologie der Englischen Sprache*. Potsdam: Wissen-schaftlich-Technisches Zentrum der Pädagogischen Hochschule 'Karl Lieb-knecht'.

GREEN, GEORGIA 1980, Some wherefores of English inversions. *Language* 56 (3), 582–602.

HAGGO, DOUGLAS and KUIPER, KOENRAAD 1983, Review of Florian Coulmas (ed.) *Conversational Routine*. (The Hague: Mouton, 1981). *Linguistics* 21 (3), 531–51.

—1985, Stock auction speech in Canada and New Zealand. In REGINALD BERRY and JAMES ACHESON (eds) *Regionalism and National Identity: Multidisciplinary Essays on Canada, Australia and New Zealand* (pp. 189–97). Christchurch: Association for Canadian Studies in Australia and New Zealand.

HYMES, DELL 1974, *Foundations in Sociolinguistics*. Philadelphia: University of Pennsylvania Press.

JACKENDOFF, RAY S. 1987, *Consciousness and the Computational Mind*. Cambridge, Mass.: MIT Press.

KUIPER, KOENRAAD (to appear), The English oral tradition in auction speech. *American Speech*.

KUIPER, KOENRAAD and HAGGO, DOUGLAS 1984, Livestock auctions, oral poetry and ordinary language. *Language in Society* 13 (2), 205–34.

KUIPER, KOENRAAD and TAN, DAPHNE 1989, Cultural congruence and conflict: acquiring formulae in second language learning. In OFELIA GARCIA and RICARDO OTHEGUY (eds) *English across Cultures: Cultures across English* (pp. 281–304). Berlin: Mouton.

KUIPER, KOENRAAD and TILLIS, FREDERICK 1986, The chant of the tobacco auctioneer. *American Speech* 60 (2), 141–9.

LORD, ALBERT B. 1960, *The Singer of Tales*. Cambridge, Mass.: Harvard University Press.

THORNTON, AGATHE 1984, *Homer's Iliad: Its Composition and the Motif of Supplication*. Göttingen: Vandenhoek & Ruprecht.

11 The sociolinguistics of questioning in district court trials

CHRIS LANE

Introduction

The courtroom is a distinctive social context in which distinctive patterns of language use occur. In particular, lawyers' questions in the courtroom contrast strikingly with questions used in everyday conversation, and provide both problems and rich material for sociolinguistic and pragmatic analysis. This study focuses on lawyers' questioning of witnesses in criminal trials at the Auckland District Court. Details of the particular courtroom context and of the data used will be given in the next section.

The New Zealand legal system and its court procedures are based on an English model, and closely resemble those of other English-speaking countries, such as Britain, the United States and Australia. In particular, trials are normally conducted on an 'adversarial' basis (in which advocates of opposing parties present cases to a jury or judge(s)) rather than an 'inquisitorial' procedure of the kind common in continental Europe (in which a judge questions witnesses and examines the evidence directly). Thus one would expect to find similarities rather than differences in language use between New Zealand and other English-language courtrooms. Such an expectation is borne out in the research reported here. The major differences in the way English is used in courtrooms appear not to be between legal systems, but rather within them, between different types of hearing, and between different procedures within a hearing. One such difference will be highlighted here.

The stages of trials in which lawyers question witnesses are referred to as 'examinations'. Three sub-types of examination are recognised by legal practitioners: 'examination-in-chief' and 're-examination' are co-operative encounters, and I subsume them under the general category 'co-examination'. On the other hand, 'cross-examination' generally has an adversary character. The major difference in patterns of questioning is between co-examination and cross-examination. Different legal and procedural rules govern these two types of questioning, and lead to different pragmatic and syntactic possibilities.

Accordingly it will be necessary to describe in more detail the nature of examination and its sub-types, in the third section, before discussing the pragmatic and syntactic complexities of questions in co-examination and cross-examination, in the fourth and fifth sections. Lawyers' questions are constrained by the possibility of objections by other counsel or vetoes by the judge, based on legal and procedural rules. Courtroom questions thus initiate distinctive discourse sequences, which will be discussed in the sixth section.

These sections (1 to 6) provide a basis for discussing an issue which has been of particular concern to social scientists studying questions and/ or courtroom interaction. It is readily apparent that lawyers exercise control over witnesses by asking questions, and that questioning in cross-examinations in particular frequently has a coercive or aggressive character. Nevertheless, how such control or coercion is achieved is a complex matter. A number of contributing factors will be discussed in the seventh section, in particular the management of 'face'.

Auckland District Court Trials

Many different kinds of court hearing take place in New Zealand. This study is concerned *in the main*[1] with trials of one particular type, defined by the following features:

(1) They took place in a *District Court*. District Courts form the lowest level of the New Zealand court system, which has essentially four tiers: District Courts, High Courts, the Court of Appeal, and the Privy Council.

(2) They involved *summary jurisdiction*, that is, the cases were tried by a judge alone, without a jury.

(3) They were *criminal* trials, i.e. trials of persons charged with criminal offences, rather than civil hearings of lawsuits.

(4) They were *defended hearings*: the defendants had previously entered pleas of 'not guilty'.

(5) There was a *single defendant* (or *accused*) in each trial.

The corpus of data used for this study consists of (records of) 24 trials. The trials are numbered 1–21, because they arose from 21 sets of charges.[2] Trials 1–10 took place between 1970 and 1983. The only information I have on these trials is the official stenographers' transcripts.[3] Trials 11–21 were heard in the Auckland District Court during a two-week period in 1983. I was given permission to observe, take notes and make audio tape recordings of these trials. The Court Registrar's staff later provided me with copies of the complete official stenographers' transcripts.[4] Trials 11–21 provided approximately ten hours of tape recordings. For a fuller description of the data and the data-collection methodology, see Lane (1988).

In quoting from transcripts (the court's or my own), all names of participants have been disguised. Witnesses and defendants have been given a pair of fictitious initials representing given and family names. Judges, prosecutors and defence counsel have been referred to as J, P and D respectively, plus a distinguishing lower case letter. All other details that might identify the trials and participants — such as addresses and other locations, dates, makes of vehicle, etc. — have been disguised.

The Genre of Examination

The prosecution or defence evidence consists generally of a series of testimonies by different witnesses. Each testimony itself consists of a series of communicative events, as set out in Table 11.1. Cross-examination and re-examination are optional, that is, the opposing counsel may or may not elect to initiate cross-examination following an examination-in-

TABLE 11.1 *Communicative events in a witness's testimony*

Event	Main participants (*Initiator* of the event)
1. Opening: witness called and brought into courtroom	$CC \longrightarrow R \longrightarrow O \longrightarrow W$
2. Swearing of oath or affirmation	$R \longleftrightarrow W$
3. Examination-in-chief	$CC \longleftrightarrow W \longrightarrow J$
4. Cross-examination	$OC \longleftrightarrow W \longrightarrow J$
5. Re-examination	$CC \longleftrightarrow W \longrightarrow J$
6. Closing (e.g. 'Thank you')	$J \longrightarrow W$

Abbreviations: *CC*: calling counsel. *OC*: opposing counsel. W: witness. *J*: judge. *R*: registrar. O: orderly. $X \longrightarrow Y$: X speaks to Y. $X \longleftrightarrow Y$: X and Y speak to each other.

chief and, similarly, the calling counsel may or may not opt to conduct a re-examination following a cross-examination.

Instances of examination-in-chief, cross-examination and re-examination can be seen as belonging to one overall *genre* of 'examination'. The term *genre* is used in the ethnography of communication not just for a type of communicative event, but typically for a type of event that is recognised and oriented to by members of the speech community where it occurs. The category 'examination' is indeed recognised and oriented to, at least by 'insiders' (i.e. court personnel), although instances are more often referred to in terms of which of the three sub-categories they belong to. Note that 'examination' is distinct from 'testimony', at least in my usage of the terms, since I include the call and the oath or affirmation as part of the testimony, but they are not part of the genre of examination.

'Examination' is distinguished from other genres which occur in the courtroom (such as 'submissions', the legal arguments that the counsel present to the judge) by at least the following combination of factors. 'Examination' is concerned with 'the facts' or 'evidence' rather than 'the law' or legal interpretation. The primary speakers are a witness and one of the counsel, who initiates the examination. The judge and the other counsel also have speaking rights, and the judge is also an addressee of the witness's utterances. Turns are 'pre-allocated' to the initiating counsel and the witness, and turn order is in general fixed, in the pattern C–W–C–W . . ., with the proviso that the judge or other counsel can disrupt this pattern (see Atkinson & Drew (1979: 61ff) for a more detailed consideration of these points). The initiating counsel's turns are meant to be hearable as 'questions', and the witness's turns as 'answers', though this is only a first approximation to the actual pragmatics and discourse structure, which is discussed in more detail below.

Co-examination and cross-examination

Examination-in-chief and re-examination may be grouped together as one sub-genre of examination, which I call 'co-examination' because of its more co-operative nature, in opposition to the sub-genre of cross-examination. Co-examination therefore comprises all examinations by counsel of witnesses they have called, with the exception of witnesses declared 'hostile'. Cross-examination comprises all examinations of witnesses called by other counsel, as well as examinations of hostile witnesses by their calling counsel.

The two sub-genres are distinguished by a number of features. One is the relationship between the initiating counsel and the witness. In co-examination, it is generally co-operative, and the two may well have rehearsed the event together — Valdés (1986: 278) refers to the two as a 'performance team'. The counsel prompts the witness to present to the judge a prepared account of the incident(s) that have given rise to the charge(s). In cross-examination the relationship is generally an adversary one. The counsel and witness are unlikely to have met before, unless the witness appears regularly in court (e.g. an 'expert' witness) or unless there has been an earlier hearing of the case.

The two sub-genres also differ crucially in terms of the legal rules governing interaction. In particular, 'leading questions' are in general not allowed in co-examination, while they are allowed and are frequently used in cross-examination. The purposes of questioning are also entirely different in the two sub-genres, as explained succinctly by Willis (1960) in a text on evidence and procedure:

Examination-in-chief
After a witness has been sworn or has affirmed, the party calling him examines him in chief or directly, in order to elicit from the witness all the facts he can prove in support of that party's case . . . the witness may give evidence-in-chief of facts in issue or relevant to the issue, also in certain cases, hearsay, or opinion as to such facts; also facts showing any special means of knowledge, opportunities of observation, reasons for recollection or belief, or other circumstances increasing his competency to speak on the particular case . . . (Willis, 1960: 221)

Cross-examination
By cross-examination is meant an examination of a party's witness by the other side at the conclusion of the examination-in-chief. The purpose of cross-examination is to weaken, qualify or destroy the case of the opponent and to establish the party's case by the opponent's witnesses. (Willis, 1960: 225)

Re-examination is subject to the same rules as examination-in-chief. However, the purpose of the questions is somewhat different: in re-examination it is to prompt evidence to counter impressions given in the course of cross-examination. Re-examination is an attenuated version of co-examination, compared to examination-in-chief; usually much shorter and referring to just one or two 'points of fact'.

The Pragmatics of Courtroom Questions

Trial participants speak of lawyers' 'questions' in examinations. I will generally use instead the term 'initiation' (to be defined more precisely in a later section; cf Mead, 1985). Initiations are not always 'questions' in the sense of having interrogative or other particular syntactic forms, nor are they always 'questions' in the pragmatic sense of requesting information. When they *are* intended (at least in part) to elicit information, I will call them 'elicitations' (following Sinclair & Coulthard, 1975).

One of the things that make most courtroom elicitations odd in comparison with ordinary conversational requests for information is that the intended recipient of the information is not the questioner (the counsel) but rather a third party, the judge. On occasion, witnesses are explicitly asked to address their responses to the judge:[5]

EXAMPLE 1 *Trial 13: Examination-in-chief of witness RM by prosecutor Pp before judge Je*

Prosec:	now —— at about six o'clock on [day, date] this year — can you tell the Court where you were at that time
Witness:	in the shoe shop — which is adjacent to — the main shop of the — X's
→ **Prosec:**	just — speak up and address your answers to His Honour — everything's gotta be
	⎡ taken ( ) ⎤
→ **Judge:**	⎣ speak up this way⎦— er — the stenographer has to — hear you —— what time was it — again
Witness:	— six o'clock — round about approximately six p.m.
Judge:	yes — thank you
Prosec:	and — what were you doing at the shoe shop
Witness:	I was working there

Witnesses were sometimes merely told that they should speak up so that the judge and stenographer could hear. This admonition also seemed to draw the witness's attention to the judge as (candidate) addressee. Witnesses in fact regularly appear to have a problem in working out who to address their responses to, since both the judge and the questioning counsel seem to be candidates for the role of addressee.[6] In particular, witnesses often appear to have difficulty deciding which way to face: in the settings I observed, the counsel was to the witness's left and the judge to the witness's right, and it was not possible to face both the judge and counsel at the same time. Witnesses needed to see the counsel to attend to the elicitation, but were either already aware or became aware that they should address their responses to the judge.

Many witnesses (especially more experienced ones) adopted a compromise of facing neither judge nor counsel, but halfway in between, over the head of the court registrar. Police witnesses in examinations-in-chief did not have this problem, since they gave most of their evidence-in-chief as a monologue directly to the judge.

Standard elicitation 'prefaces' (such as 'Can you tell the Court X', 'Please tell the Court X') in fact can be understood (transparently) as asking the witness to tell X to the *judge*, since the judge is the personification of the court, and the expression 'the Court' is used (for instance in stenographers' transcripts) to refer to the judge. This, together with the explicit instruction mentioned above, clearly identifies the judge as the officially intended addressee for the witnesses' responses. In the following example, the elicitation preface makes the situation quite clear:

EXAMPLE 2 *Trial 3: Examination-in-chief of the accused DS by defence counsel Dc*

→ **Counsel:** Tell His Worship in your words what happened when you got to the intersection of G Street and F Road?
Accused: We were going up to the 'Stop' sign there when I applied the brakes and there was nothing.

Nevertheless, counsel sometimes slip into expressions which include themselves as addressees. The situation is rather like that of formal meetings where participants are supposed to address all their utterances to the chair, but in fact often talk directly to each other.

EXAMPLE 3 *Trial 16: Examination-in-chief of witness ZV by prosecutor Pt*

→ **Prosec:** and — can you tell us who was in the motor-car — at that time please
Witness: um — MX — and — G and Q
Prosec: MX
[*two exchanges omitted*]
Prosec: is he here today — 's he here now
Witness: yes
→ **Prosec:** could you tell us please where — then

For a formal pragmatic analysis I will adopt the experienced witness's solution and regard judge and questioning counsel as joint addressees of the witness's responses. Felicity conditions on courtroom elicitations can then be given on this basis.[7] There is a contrast in every condition with the felicity conditions on a conversational request for information:

Conditions for a conversational request for information

If speaker S makes an utterance U addressed to addressee A and

(a) U gives A evidence for believing that S wishes A to provide S with information I, for the benefit of S,

and A believes that S believes that

(b) S needs I for some reason or purpose,

(c) A would not provide I in the absence of U,

(d) S does not have I already, or is uncertain about the validity of I,

(e) A is likely to have I,

(f) A is willing or obliged to provide S with I, and

(g) S has the right to ask A for I,

then U is heard (by A) as a valid (conversational) request for information.

Note that in the following conditions, the utterance is assessed as a valid or invalid courtroom elicitation by the judge — an 'auditor' in Bell's (1984) terms, or 'side-participant' in Clark and Carlson's (1982) terms — and not by the addressee, the witness.[8]

Conditions on a courtroom elicitation

If the counsel makes an utterance U addressed to the witness and

(a) U gives the witness (and the judge) evidence for believing that the counsel wishes the witness to provide the judge (and the counsel) with information I, for the judge's benefit,

and the judge believes that

(b) the counsel believes that the judge needs I as evidence in the trial, and/or the counsel needs I for confirmation, and to prepare for the next elicitation;

(c) the witness would not provide I in the absence of U;

(d) the counsel has I (or an approximation to it), but the judge does not have I already, or is uncertain of the validity of I;

(e) it is reasonable for the counsel to expect the witness to have I;

(f) the witness is obliged to provide the judge with I, under threat of legal sanction;

(g) the counsel has the right to ask for I, subject to restrictions on 'leading questions' and rules on the admissibility of evidence;

then U is heard (by the judge) as a valid courtroom elicitation.

The legal sanction mentioned in condition (f) is provided, for summary trials, by Section 39 of the Summary Proceedings Act 1957, which specifies a penalty of up to seven days' imprisonment each time a witness refuses to answer questions put.

Note also that decisions on the validity of elicitations are 'locally managed' in the terms of conversational analysis (cf. Atkinson & Drew, 1979: 36ff). The validity is decided by the judge at the time, and an utterance of the same form, in the same kind of context, might conceivably count as valid or admissible on one occasion but not on another. This is provided for in the set of conditions by reference to the judge's beliefs, that is the judge's beliefs at the time of utterance.

The appropriateness of the conditions given above for a conversational request for information can be questioned, since the validity of requests for information is rarely made an issue (even if the conditions are not met). However, the formulation of the conditions on a courtroom elicitation seems particularly appropriate, since the validity of elicitations is a constant issue which is frequently raised in the form of vetoes and objections (see pp. 238–40).

Although counsel are constrained in general to meet these conditions in order to have their utterances recognised as 'questions', there is a strong expectation that what counsel will produce in their turns *will* be 'questions'. This in fact gives counsel a certain latitude, allowing them to produce initiations that would be normally read in informal conversation as assertions or claims or accusations, etc. In the courtroom however, the witness, judge and other counsel are pre-disposed to look for a 'question' interpretation (whatever other interpretations they might make as well). Nevertheless, in the following example, it is difficult to interpret the second initiation as an elicitation:

EXAMPLE 4 *Trial 13: Defence counsel Dk cross-examining witness RM*

> **Counsel:** there were quite a few people there on the [date] who had (1.0) beards weren't there (1.0)
> **Witness:** yes but I wouldn't mistake him (1.5)
> → **Counsel:** well that's precisely what I'm suggesting to you (1.0) that — if this language was used Mrs M it certainly wasn't used by this man [*ends on mid pitch and falling tone*]
> **Witness:** — it was

Atkinson & Drew (1979: 105ff) point out that it is inadequate to treat the counsel's utterances simply as questions, and that they do other 'work' as well, especially in cross-examinations. Atkinson & Drew mention in particular 'work' as accusation or blaming and as pre-accusation. Harris (1984: 18–22) similarly shows how magistrates' questions can function as accusations. This 'bivalence/plurivalence' (in the terms of Thomas, 1985) creates a fundamental problem for discourse analyses which assign *single* act and move categories to (part) utterances (for example, those of Sinclair & Coulthard, 1975; subsequent 'Birmingham school' analyses; and of Edmondson 1981).

Initiations in co-examinations

Willis (1960: 221–2) makes the following comments on questions in examinations-in-chief:

> Leading questions are not allowed in examination-in-chief (unless with the Court's permission). The rule is intended merely to prevent the examination from being conducted unfairly. The judge has a discretion in the matter, and his discretion is not open to review.
> Leading questions are questions which suggest the required answer, or which put disputed matter to the witness in the form permitting of the simple reply of 'Yes' or 'No'. The question is said to be leading when the words which the witness is expected and required to utter are put into his mouth, or when the question suggests to the witness the answer which the examiner wishes or expects to have . . .

Leading questions are allowable, however, in a number of specified circumstances.

Though the restrictions on leading questions are usually put in terms of not putting words in the witness's mouth, they also have the effect of preventing the counsel from foreshadowing or presenting evidence to the judge through initiations. Compare the use of initiations for this purpose in cross-examinations, discussed below.

The examinations-in-chief in the corpus appeared to consist of three stages or phases. The first one to three exchanges are concerned with identifying the witness by name, address and occupation (typically the elicitations are declaratives which merely ask the witness for confirmation of these details). The main body of the examination-in-chief consists of what I call 'elicited narrative' — the elicitations prompt the witness to produce (for the judge) components of a narrative reporting the witness's involvement in the incident(s) giving rise to the charge(s), or in their aftermath. This 'elicited narrative' displays some of the components of narrative identified by Labov (1972). Thus the first elicitations after the identification of the witness typically ask for 'orientation' to the narrative — identifying time, place and people involved in the narrative. Then the elicitations usually prompt telling of the 'complicating action' in chronological order. The typical elicitation in an examination-in-chief is 'What happened next?' or 'What did you do (then)?'. The following excerpt is an example of the beginning of an examination-in-chief, including the identification of the witness, and part of the elicited narrative:

EXAMPLE 5 *Trial 21: Examination-in-chief of the accused UD by defence counsel Dz*

Counsel:	your name is UD — and you live at [*address*] — that right
Accused:	yes
Counsel:	and — you're employed now as a [*occupation*] full time — and you've had that work for the last [*period of time*]
Accused:	that's correct
	(7.0)
Counsel:	in [month, year] did you have an accident
	(1.0)
Accused:	that's correct yes
Counsel:	what was that
Accused:	— um — while — working in a hotel (1.0) ah — I broke my hand — and — I's [= I was] off work — for x weeks (1.0)
Counsel:	yes which hotel were you working at then
Accused:	[*name*]
Counsel:	yes — what were you doing (1.0)
Accused:	(well) evicting a d — unruly patron
Counsel:	mhm (1.0) and what happened as a result of that injury (2.0)
Accused:	ah (1.5) well I got broken hand — I was — un — well — I lost my job (1.5) and was unable to work for x weeks
Counsel:	you went to the hospital
Accused:	yes
Counsel:	— and did you — do anything else about income (1.0)

Accused: ah — I obtained a medical certificate — and — necessary
forms from ACC (1.0)

⌈ (   )
Counsel: ⌊ who's ACC
Accused: Accident Compensation
Counsel: yes
Accused: to make a claim — for — income lost — through injury

The elicited narratives are peculiar in comparison with the conversational narratives analysed by Labov, in that the elicited narratives
display little 'evaluation' — that is they contain relatively little that
dramatises the narrative, that explains the 'point' of actions, that tells
how the witness felt, etc. This results from the focus on 'facts' and from
the restrictions on the kinds of questions that may be asked. It
gives examinations-in-chief a rather 'flat', 'unemotional' and sometimes
disjointed quality. Following the elicited narrative, the counsel sometimes
asks a number of 'supplementary' elicitations to prompt the witness to
provide information not mentioned in the elicited narrative. Initiations
in re-examination are typically designed to counter an impression given
in cross-examination, and usually concern only one or two points or
issues.

Initiations in cross-examinations

Willis (1960: 225–6) makes the following observations on questions
in cross-examinations:

A witness may be asked in cross-examination questions as to facts
in issue and relevant to the issue. Leading questions are also allowed;
also questions tending:
  (a)   To test his means of knowledge, opportunities of obser-
        vation, reasons for his recollection or belief, and his
        powers of memory and perception.
  (b)   To expose the errors, omissions, inconsistencies, or
        improbabilities in his testimony.
To impeach his credit by attacking his character, antecedants,
associations, and mode of life, and by eliciting:
    (i) Previous contradictory statements.
   (ii) Previous conviction for crime.
  (iii) Bias or partiality . . .

My own observations of District Court trials suggest the following functions as important (some of these confirming Willis):

(1) clarifying aspects of the examination-in-chief;
(2) challenging the witness's evidence as inaccurate;
(3) blaming the witness for some or all of the offence;
(4) trying to get the witness to agree to propositions that contradict or cast doubt on the rest of the witness's testimony or on other witnesses' testimonies;
(5) presenting directly to the judge aspects of the client's case;
(6) 'putting' the client's evidence to the witness.

These are functions that initiations *may* have. Individual initiations differ in their functions and typically have several but not all of these functions at once.

The last two posited functions require a little more explanation. Initiations in cross-examination are typically 'leading', and frequently declaratives or tag-questions. Thus they clearly indicate a position or point of view and therefore convey an assertion to the judge (and to other participants), as well as having an illocutionary force (such as elicitation or accusation) addressed to the witness. That is, they are 'multivalent' in Thomas's (1985) terms. This function of conveying an assertion to the judge is particularly important in New Zealand courtrooms, since defence counsel do not make opening addresses at the beginning of the trial summarising the elements of their case (as their counterparts may do in United States courtrooms).[9] Hence it is only through initiations in cross-examinations that the defence counsel can foreshadow to the judge the elements of the defence case. The prosecutor can use initiations in cross-examinations of defence witnesses to reiterate points made in the prosecution case.[10]

Counsel are expected to use initiations in cross-examination to give the opposition witness an opportunity to comment on evidence that the counsel's witnesses have already put forward or will put forward later in the trial. Judges in the trial corpus paid considerable attention to whether or not aspects of one party's case had in this way been 'put to' witnesses appearing for the other party. In summing up the evidence in Trial 15, judge Jm commented on the defendant's failure to put evidence to the constable she was alleged to have assaulted:

It is one of those cases which is somewhat unsatisfactory I cannot help but feel if the defendant had been represented by counsel then the defence would have been better put, or what the defendant had to say would have been better presented to the Court because none of the very relevant matters that arose from the evidence of the defendant were put to the constable and that does lead to a certain degree of uncertainty in these matters.

A frequent initiation 'preface' is 'I put it to you that . . .'. This can be understood, literally, as putting the client's claims to the witness for the witness's reaction (which almost invariably is to contradict them). One of the peculiar features of cross-examinations is that a non-answer, e.g. 'I don't know', 'I can't remember', or evasion or inconsistency can represent success for the questioner. This is allowed for in the formulation of condition (e) in the conditions for a valid courtroom elicitation.

Syntactic Features of Courtroom Questions

Danet & Kermish (1978) surveyed a number of American manuals of trial procedure, looking particularly for explanations of the kinds of questions which may be objected to, especially leading questions. Most manuals were very inexplicit, but Danet & Kermish were able to note several correlations between 'leading questions' and particular syntactic forms. Tag-questions and complex embedded forms with a negative interrogative main cluase were clearly recognised as leading, while declaratives, negative interrogatives and 'alternative questions' were implicitly regarded as leading in most cases. Polar (i.e. Yes/No) interrogatives were not clearly indicated as leading (in spite of Willis's comments quoted above) and WH-interrogatives were considered less likely to be leading.

The forms generally counted as leading are ones correlated with a function (superficially, at least) of requesting confirmation or acknowledge-ment. That is, they are forms which generally indicate the speaker's point of view on the questioned proposition. Negative interrogatives generally come into the category of request for confirmation or 'leading question', because they typically have positive or negative 'orientation' (Quirk *et al.*, 1972: 388–92). That is, they typically assume a positive or a negative answer.

Danet and her colleagues (Danet & Kermish, 1978; Danet & Bog-och, 1980; Danet *et al.*, 1980) have ranked syntactic forms according to a scale of 'coerciveness', where a 'coercive' elicitation is one that gives the witness fewer options for response. In order from most to least coercive, their categories (in Danet *et al.*, 1980) are: tag-questions and declaratives; Yes/No and alternative questions; WH-questions; 'requestions' and 'imperatives' (i.e. embedded forms with interrogative and imperative main clauses respectively). In that this scale of 'coerciveness' is based essentially on syntactic form, without reference to the particular context of use, it can only be a crude measure of the actual coerciveness in context. Dunstan (1980) strongly criticises Danet & Bogoch's approach, pointing out the importance of the sequential position of a 'question' in the unfolding discourse.

The functions of initiations in co- and cross-examination, together with the restrictions on leading questions in co-examination, lead to a distinct distribution of syntactic forms in the two sub-genres. In Table 11.2 I set out the figures derived from Danet *et al.*'s (1980) statistics for two trials in Boston, and the corresponding figures for Trials 3 and 4 in my Auckland corpus (based on official *verbatim* transcripts). The general similarity of profiles in the Boston and Auckland trials is remarkable, and may reflect the similarity of courtroom procedure in the two places.[11]

A notable feature of courtroom initiations is that they are frequently syntactically complex, in the sense of consisting of two or more finite clauses. There are two major types of construction which contribute to this frequency. One occurs because elicitations are frequently concerned with temporal relations — whether one event occurred after, before or at the same time as another. This concern is typically shown in complex elicitations, with subordinate temporal clauses introduced by subordinators

TABLE 11.2 *Initiation syntax in co- and cross-examination*

| | Boston | | Auckland | |
| | co | cross | co | cross |
Initiation forms:	(%)	(%)	(%)	(%)
Declaratives and tags	11	45	10	40
Yes/no and alternative	26	28	34	25
WH-questions	42	13	43	25
Requestions and imperatives	17	6	10	1
Others	4	9	2	10
Total: (%)	100	101	99	101
(*N*)	(1,085)	(1,891)	(173)	(415)

such as 'when', 'while', 'before', 'after', 'until', 'once', 'immediately'. There are several such elicitations in the following extract:

EXAMPLE 6 *Trial 21: Cross-examination of the accused UD by prosecutor Pz*

→	**Prosec:**	You were aware were you not that your account was in overdraft at the time you wrote the first cheque?
	Accused:	I had insufficient funds to cover the cheque.
→	**Prosec:**	Your account was overdrawn when you wrote the first cheque wasn't it?
	Accused:	I am not absolutely sure.
	Prosec:	Didn't you so state in your statement to the police?
	Accused:	I said there was insufficient funds to cover the cheque.
→	**Prosec:**	When you rang the bank they told you they would not give you an overdraft so you must have known any subsequent cheque at least would be dishonoured?
	Accused:	I was expecting payment from some people.
	Prosec:	But the bank had told you that they would not give you an overdraft facility?
	Accused	That is correct.
→	**Prosec:**	So you knew when you wrote the second cheque out that it must be dishonoured?
	Accused:	No.

See also Examples 8 and 16 below.

The other major type of complex elicitation is embedded forms (Danet *et al.*'s 'requestions' and 'imperatives' come into this category). Here the clause indicating what information is required is a subordinate noun clause (or complement clause), and the main clause acts as a kind of preface. These prefaces are frequently formulae (cf. Coulmas, 1981) or lexicalised clause stems (Pawley & Syder, 1983). For example: 'Do you know . . .', 'Can you remember . . .', 'Are you saying that . . .', which also occur with some frequency in ordinary conversation. The following prefaces are specific to the courtroom: 'Can you tell the Court . . .', 'Can you describe to the Court . . .', 'I put it to you that . . .'.[12]

Exchange Structures in Examinations

Examination is usually regarded as having a recurrent 'question–answer' structure (for example by Atkinson & Drew, 1979: 61ff). However, the questioner sometimes responds to the witness's response, giving a three-part exchange. I refer to the three parts, following Coulthard & Brazil (1981) and Mead (1985), as 'initiation' (I), 'response' (R), and 'follow-up' (F). Initiations are usually interpretable, minimally, as elicitations or contingent queries (Garvey, 1977; 1979), and are spoken by counsel or judge. Responses are spoken by the witness, and follow-up by the counsel or judge. Mead (1985: 56–64) discusses these IR(F) structures in courtroom discourse in considerable detail.

The follow-up is often just an acknowledgement of the response, but in co-examination can be a way for the counsel to convey encouragement to the witness, as in Example 7, and in cross-examination a way to indicate surprise, disbelief etc. to the witness and to the courtroom audience, as in Example 8.

EXAMPLE 7 *Trial 4: Examination-in-chief of witness GB by prosecutor Pd*

I	**Prosec:**	Now which seat did the defendant get into?
R	**Witness:**	In the front seat of my patrol vehicle on the lefthand side.
→ F	**Prosec:**	Yes,
I		and what was the reason for this?
R	**Witness:**	I intended to give him a breath test and then take him into Auckland City Council administration building if the test proved positive.

EXAMPLE 8 *Trial 4: Beginning of cross-examination of witness HC by defence counsel Dc*

I	**Counsel:**	Mr C, do you know whether his [the defendant's] nose was broken?
R	**Witness:**	No.
I	**Counsel:**	He sustained two black eyes?
R	**Witness:**	No.
I	**Counsel:**	A cut in his mouth?
R	**Witness:**	No.
→ F	**Counsel:**	You didn't know that.
I		When he got to the Auckland City Council building is it not true that he asked for the police to be called?
R	**Witness:**	Yes he asked for the police to be called.

	Counsel:	What did he say when the police arrived?
I	Witness:	What did?
	Counsel:	What did he say when the police arrived?
R	Witness:	He just wanted to tell the police, he reckoned that he had been assaulted.
→ F	Counsel:	He did, did he.
I		Now going back to the point where you and traffic officer B. were in P. Road by [*name*] school, at one stage a police vehicle pulled up?
R	Witness:	Yes.

A negative follow-up (e.g. 'no') can be used to clearly indicate that the questioner regards the response as inadequate or unacceptable:

EXAMPLE 9 *Trial 2B: Judge Jc questioning the accused SW (second-language speaker of English)*

I	Judge:	But you didn't let go the can opener, you held on to it?
R	Accused:	I move my arms like this.
→ F	Judge:	No,
I		just a minute while you were lying on the ground and he was kicking and punching you, you still held on to the can opener?
R	Accused:	Yes.[13]

IR(F) is the normal (unmarked) exchange structure in examination. However, two other (marked) exchange structures occasionally occur. The judge may 'stop' a counsel's initiation from being responded to — I call this a 'veto'. This produces an exchange structure:

I	initiation (by counsel)
Ve **veto**	(by judge);
to	

as in the following example, which also illustrates the confusing complexity that some initiations have:

EXAMPLE 10 *Trial 1: Defence counsel Dc cross-examining witness CM before judge Ja*

| Counsel: | When he gave evidence in this courtroom half an hour ago R said when I asked him whether he had said it could be him and it could be another fellow, he said that he had said that. |

	Judge:	Well the question is did you hear him say that?
	Witness:	I cannot remember hearing anything like that.
I	**Counsel:**	That would not be a positive identification would it?
→ Veto	**Judge:**	That is a question for me. The question for you to him is did he say it. The difference is enormous.
I	**Counsel:**	You would remember him saying any such thing?
R	**Witness:**	No sir.

Alternatively, the other counsel may object to the initiation on such grounds as the following:

(1) that the questioning counsel has used a leading question during co-examination;
(2) that the elicitation is asking for information that is irrelevant to the case;
(3) that the elicitation is asking for evidence that is relevant but inadmissible according to the law of evidence;
(4) that the questioning counsel is misrepresenting other evidence.

The judge will then usually make a ruling, upholding or overruling the objection (in the corpus, objections were usually upheld).[14] This procedure produces an exchange structure:

I	initiation (by counsel)
Obj	objection (by other counsel)
Rul	ruling (by judge).

Rulings normally terminate exchanges — even if the judge overrules an objection, the initiation is usually made again, commencing a new exchange:

EXAMPLE 11 *Trial 8: Prosecutor Pj cross-examining the accused, TH, in presence of judge Jg and defence counsel Dm*

I	**Prosec:**	The Constable said that he saw you strike the other man but he did not see the other man lift up the bottle towards you, what do you say to that?
Obj	**Counsel:**	It is not quite the Constable's evidence, Sir.
Rul	**Judge:**	That was the evidence he gave and then he further went on to say there was a time that he could not see what the actions of the complainant were and the defendant were, what prior actions there had been.
I	**Prosec:**	Constable said he saw you striking the complainant, that he had not seen him lift any bottle towards you, what do you say to that?

R **Accused:** The police officer came well afterwards. I saw his car come into the carpark when I picked the guy up.

The fact that initiations are subject to the possibility of being vetoed or objected to provides a powerful practical constraint on the content and the form of initiations.

Control, Coercion and Face

A recurrent issue in studies of courtroom questioning has been the perception of questions as techniques of control, coercion or aggression. The coerciveness scale of Danet and her colleagues is one reflection of a concern with this issue. It has also been discussed by Adelswärd *et al.* (1987), Adelswärd, Aronsson & Linell (1985), Atkinson & Drew (1979), Drew (1984; 1985), Dunstan (1980), Harris (1984), Liebes-Plesner (1984) and Mead (1985).

Elicitations can be seen as controlling in that they constrain the addressee's possible contribution to the interaction (in terms of both topic and timing). This view thus involves an implicit contrast with the possibility of an unconstrained contribution. I see this 'controlling' character not as an inherent feature of questions but as a combination of a number of contextual factors. A major one in the courtroom is the existence of institutional sanctions, such as imprisonment, for failing to answer. A more immediate sanction, which counsel frequently use in cross-examination, is repetition or rephrasing of the question. Another factor is the existence of set questioner (lawyer or judge) and respondent (witness) roles, which means that witnesses are effectively prevented from initiating topics or exercising control over the counsel. That is, there is an asymmetry of initiation and control. A further feature of 'controlling' initiations is the expectation and enforcement of a close topical match between the initiation and the response (with the main sanction again being repetitive questioning). In other words, there are 'tight' topic constraints.

On the other hand, questions may be seen in an entirely different light, as 'facilitative' (the term is borrowed from Holmes, 1985). Such questions facilitate the addressee's contributing to the interaction. This function is especially noticeable when there are reasons why the addressee might not contribute — shyness, unwillingness, not being a native speaker. Seeing questions as facilitative involves an implicit contrast with the possibility of silence. Kearsley (1976: 362–3) rather disparagingly uses the term 'verbosity' for this kind of function. Facilitative questions are common in informal conversation. In this context there are no set questioner and respondent roles. There are loose topic constraints, that is, addressees are not necessarily expected to provide the precise information requested. Questions are often used as a kind of prompt to get the addressee to start talking about a particular topic, or tell a story or joke, etc. Studies that show women asking more questions in conversation than men (e.g. Fishman, 1978) reflect women's use of facilitative rather than controlling questions (Holmes, 1984; 1985). Similarly, the tendency of native speakers to adopt a questioner role in interaction with non-native speakers (Hatch, 1978) should be seen as reflecting a desire to facilitate rather than control the interaction.

Elicitations in examinations-in-chief are facilitative in that they assist the witness in presenting testimony — otherwise the witness might well have difficulty in speaking at all, or in constructing a coherent account. They are controlling in that they are meant to restrict the witness to providing admissible evidence. If allowed to present evidence directly to the judge (as are some witnesses, usually law enforcement officers) the witness might well produce evidence that is not legally admissible. One case I have observed (but which is not included in the corpus) clearly illustrated this. A traffic officer was allowed to give monologue evidence to the judge, in the usual manner of law enforcement officers. After three or four instances of mentioning inadmissible matters, the prosecutor reverted to using elicitations to prompt the witness's evidence, and this seemed to solve the problem.

Counsel can also control the witness's presentation of evidence by interrupting the witness to ask for clarification or elaboration:

EXAMPLE 12 *Trial 14: Examination-in-chief of the accused GD by defence counsel Dn*

    Counsel: so what did you do then
                (2.0)
    Accused: so I hopped into the back seat (1.0) Mr K hopped into the front — and we drove up to — ah — [*suburb*] to get some gas (3.0) we drove into — ah —
→ **Counsel:** I — I'm sorry — on — on the way to the station (1.0) did you see the police car — at any stage
    Accused: — oh no — it wasn't visible to us at all and we were —
→ **Counsel:** were you looking for it
    Accused: we were looking for it because [. . .]

In cross-examination, the controlling use outweighs any facilitative character.

One of the main tactics used in cross-examination, as mentioned above, is repetitive questioning. A repeated or rephrased question, or a contingent query, conveys the implication that the questioner does not accept the preceding response, and in specific circumstances may imply that the witness is lying, or being evasive or unclear or inconsistent. Repetitive questioning sequences are a common feature of cross-examination and are discussed in some detail in Lane (1988).[15]

Another aspect of cross-examination which can contribute to its coercive or aggressive character is the portrayal of a defendant or witness as being of a particular character and/or as conforming to a particular stereotype. A prime example is the portrayal of rape victims as promiscuous or masochistic. This aspect of cross-examination is discussed in detail by Drew (1984; 1985) and by Liebes-Plesner (1984). Such portrayal can be achieved in cross-examination because the initiations can convey claims to the judge and the rest of the courtroom audience, and to a certain extent counsel can use follow-ups to reinforce such lines of questioning.

Initiations in co-examination can be seen as face-threatening acts (Brown & Levinson, 1987). They ask the witness to perform in public before a large audience of strangers (see Austin, this volume, on the effect of audiences in magnifying problems of face maintenance or loss). They are additionally face-threatening if for example they ask the witness to admit wrongdoing or negligence, or ask for embarrassing information, as is sometimes necessary in co-examination:

EXAMPLE 13 *Trial 13: Examination-in-chief of witness RM by prosecutor Pp*

Prosec: do you recall what sort of language was being used (1.0)

Witness: um (yeah) — um — (he) said — don't let those effing scabs serve you (5.0) and — he used that word on a number of occasions —⌈( )

Prosec: ⌊(now) you've — you've said — effing

Witness: — yes

Prosec: (ha)ve you shortened that word

Witnes: — yes (3.0)

Prosec: d'you know who — those words were directed to

Witness: ah — JP and myself (1.0) and to the customers (1.5) that were in the shop at the time.

In Brown & Levinson's theory, the degree or 'weight' (W) of face threat is a function of the variables P (power or status of hearer compared to speaker), D (social distance between speaker and hearer) and R (ranking of degree of imposition of the act). Here there is low P, but high D and relatively high R, and hence relatively high W. Therefore the theory would predict that off-record or negative politeness strategies would tend to be used. To some extent off-record strategies are required by the restriction on leading questions in co-examinations: counsel know what information they want witnesses to present but cannot simply request confirmation of it — see Examples 5 and 13 above.

Many of the initiation prefaces can be seen as negative politeness devices. They come both under the strategy 'be conventionally indirect', and the general negative politeness maxim of providing options. Most of these embedded forms specifically allow that the witness may not know or remember, and they make it easier for the witness to provide such an account for not supplying the requested information. An indication of their frequency is given by the figures for 'requestions and imperatives' in Table 11.2. Examples which occur in Example 13 above are 'do you recall' (what . . .), and 'd'you know' (who . . .). There are several examples (indicated by the arrows) in the following extract:

EXAMPLE 14 *Trial 13: Examination-in-chief of witness RM by prosecutor Pp before judge Je*

	Prosec:	is your full name RM
	Witness:	yes
→	Prosec:	— (can you) tell the Court where you reside please
	Witness:	— [*address*]
	Prosec:	and — where are you employed
	Witness:	— X's store (in) [*suburb*]
→	Prosec:	— can you — say where X's premises are in [*suburb*]
	Witness:	corner of J Road and K Street
	Prosec:	now — at about six o'clock on [*day, date*] this year —
→		can you tell the Court where you were at that time
	Witness:	in the shoe shop — which is adjacent to — the main shop of the — X's

[*10 turns omitted*]

	Prosec:	now — I understand something was going on outside the
→		shop can you tell the Court — what was happening there
	Witness:	yes um — we had um — picketers — picketing X's store

Initiations in cross-examination frequently have the force of challenges, criticisms, accusations or complaints (I will use 'challenge' as a cover-all term for this general category of act). Such initiations can clearly be seen as face-threatening acts, in this case threatening positive face in particular. D (social distance) is higher than in co-examination; counsel and witness are likely to be complete strangers meeting for the first time, and are in general on opposing sides in the trial. R (ranking of imposition) is higher in general since the kinds of challenges issued in cross-examination clearly threaten a greater loss of status (as a competent witness) than the kinds of elicitations asked in co-examinations. Thus on the basis of Brown & Levinson's theory, one would expect greater use of negative politeness and off-record strategies than in co-examination. However, the reverse is the case. Fewer negative politeness question prefaces are used, and bald-on-record strategies are in frequent use.

In Brown & Levinson's theory, on-record face-threatening acts which carry a significant threat to face require politeness strategies to redress the potential face loss. However, one of the main purposes of questioning in cross-examination is to undermine or destroy the credibility (or 'impeach the credit' as Willis puts it) of the witness in the eyes of the courtroom audience. In other words, challenges in cross-examination are uttered with the goal of maximising face loss rather than redressing or minimising it. Thus they are better seen as 'face attack acts' (Austin, this volume) than as face-threatening acts. Seen in this light, the use of bald-on-record strategies and the relative lack of politeness strategies is less surprising.

The only apparent exception is the greater use of address terms in cross-examination than in co-examinations. The address terms are always of the form 'Title' or 'Title + Last Name' (here abbreviated T (+ LN)). Brown & Levinson treat the use of such address terms as a particular example of their general negative politeness strategy 'give deference', and specifically mention their use in courtrooms (1987: 184): 'Such usages are also typical in legal proceedings, the title and name accompanying questions that are intended to nail the defendant, for instance, rather than small clarifications of fact'. However, one would expect address terms to co-occur with other negative politeness devices, e.g. with elicitation prefaces in co-examinations. The lack of co-occurrence suggests that the address terms have a different function from the elicitation prefaces.

It could simply be the case that the greater frequency in cross-examination reflects the greater social distance between counsel and witness. However, the address terms appear to be strategically placed. They occur at the beginning of cross-examinations, where they appear to function as boundary markers.[16] They also occur, as Brown & Levinson suggest, as part of strong or repeated challenges (see Example 4 above for an example). This suggests that they have greater pragmatic significance than just reflecting the relationship in general.

My intuition is that the address terms are distancing devices which accentuate the adversary nature of the cross-examination. When they occur with particular challenges, it is to aggravate rather than mitigate the face attack. This impression can be accounted for in the following way. The relative absence of address terms in co-examination suggests that no-naming is the most appropriate address usage in co-operative interaction in this context. T (+ LN) is thus a relatively marked usage, and since it reflects a relatively high P and/or D, it can be interpreted as *emphasising* the high D (since the P factor can be taken to be constant across the different sub-genres of examination). Liebes-Plesner (1984: 178–9), in an analysis of a trial conducted in Hebrew, discusses an analogous use of apparently deferential address terms as an aggressive tactic in cross-examination.

With most witnesses, the only possible appropriate address term is of the form 'Mr/Mrs/Miss/Ms' + LN. However, with law enforcement officers, a wider range of forms is possible, allowing greater potential for pragmatic exploitation. The following examples involve traffic officers.[17] The normal respectful address to a traffic officer is 'officer', and this form is found in one examination-in-chief. In the following excerpt from a cross-examination the defence counsel repeatedly uses the form 'Mr' + LN. In addition to possibly accentuating the social distance between the counsel and the witness, this form appears to deny the witness's status as a law enforcement officer:

EXAMPLE 15 *Trial 4: Defence counsel Dc cross-examining traffic officer GB*

> Counsel: He [the defendant] will give evidence that you were abusing him in similar terms to the terms he was using to you?
>
> Witness: I would call him a liar.
>
> → Counsel: In fact when he gives evidence Mr B he will tell the Court the car never left where it was stationary on the side of the road?
>
> Witness: As I say again I would call him a liar. We hit the footpath and hit the kerb and went up onto the footpath.
>
> → Counsel: He will say when he gives evidence Mr B that in fact he was abusive to you, he used foul language to you; he will say that you used language back to him of a similar kind?

> **Witness:** That would be incorrect.
→ **Counsel:** And he will say Mr B that you struck him three times in the face, breaking his nose, blackening his eyes, cutting his mouth; he then put his foot up to protect himself from you?
> **Witness:** That would be incorrect.

However, in the following extract the same defence counsel uses the expanded forms 'traffic officer' and 'traffic officer' + LN:

EXAMPLE 16 *Trial 4: Defence counsel Dc cross-examining traffic officer HC*

> **Counsel:** And what was the next thing?
> **Witness:** The next minute the defendant was kicking around and traffic officer B was fending [*sic*] himself . . .
→ **Counsel:** Look, I put it to you traffic officer C that when this struggle so to speak started in this car that is what you would have been looking at? That is what you were there for?
> **Witness:** It was just to help keep an observation on the defendant.
> **Counsel:** Yes,
> so as soon as something started in the car you would have taken note of what was going on wouldn't you?
> **Witness:** Well I didn't think anything would happen. He was just going to put the seat belt on him.
→ **Counsel:** When the alleged struggle happened traffic officer, you would have taken careful note of what was going on. That is what you were there for?
> **Witness:** No.

If we take 'officer' as the unmarked form, then these are clearly marked forms, which in this instance convey disparagement. This implication may arise because they explicitly draw attention to the traffic officer's status as being lower than the lawyer's. However, it is perhaps more likely that the implication is ironic (roughly equivalent to 'so-called traffic officer').[18]

Conclusion

Cross-examination, as a kind of ritualised verbal dispute, is one of the most dramatic aspects of British-based court systems. Consequently it is not surprising that it has received much more attention than co-examination has from researchers (as well as dramatists). One of the aims of this paper has been to redress the balance somewhat, and show that co-examination also has interesting features. However, more than that, I have aimed to show that the *contrast* between co-examination and cross-examination is of particular interest. Given that the major difference (in general) between co- and cross-examination is one between co-operation and conflict, the courtroom provides a context approaching laboratory conditions for comparing the sociolinguistic features of co-operative and adversary interaction.[19]

One of the other aims has been to demonstrate the syntactic and pragmatic complexity of many courtroom questions. This complexity can create difficulties for witnesses in terms of framing responses. The syntactic complexity can make the questions difficult to process and the responses accordingly difficult to formulate. The pragmatic complexity can mean that the witness is faced with a 'question' which is not only requesting information, but also conveying other illocutionary forces such as accusation or pre-accusation, while simultaneously providing a commentary on the witness's testimony to the courtroom audience. Atkinson & Drew (1979: 148) comment on the difficulty of responding to such questions. A successful response needs not only to counter the indirect challenge and the impression being given to the audience, but must also appear to provide a factual, informative answer.

The complexity of lawyers' questions poses considerable difficulties for witnesses who are second-language speakers of English, even if they are reasonably competent in everyday interaction. In earlier work (Lane, 1985; 1988) I have concluded that the major problem facing witnesses who are second-language speakers of English (in the absence of interpreters) is in comprehending and hence responding appropriately to lawyers' questions.

Where comparison is possible the characteristics of the New Zealand lawyer's questions match closely those of lawyers in other English-speaking countries. However, differences in language use may be found where there are differences in laws or procedures governing trials of a given type. An example is the difference in follow-ups between New Zealand and Malaysian courts. Whether other features noted here are peculiar to New Zealand courts is as yet unclear. Is the apparent lack of standard expressions for vetoes, objections and rulings a peculiarly New Zealand characteristic? Do lawyers in other jurisdictions use the same negative politeness question prefaces? Do they use terms of address in the way outlined in the previous section? Answers to these questions await comparable research in other countries.

Notes

1. There are a number of exceptions. Four of the 24 trials (Trials 2A, 2B, 6B and 7B) were High Court jury trials, four (Trials 5, 6A, 6B and 18) had more than one defendant, and one (Trial 12) was a trial following a guilty plea.
2. Three sets of charges were heard twice.
3. These record cross-examinations and re-examinations with reasonable, though by no means perfect, accuracy. Transcripts of examinations-in-chief are frequently unusable as data because the dialogue has been transformed into a notional monologue by the witness. These points are discussed in detail in Lane (1988).
4. I am especially grateful to those who assisted me in obtaining the transcripts and recordings of trials which provided the material for this study. Because it is my policy to keep the identities of people involved in those trials anonymous, it is not possible to mention the names of all who helped me in this way. I am grateful to the two lawyers who allowed me access to transcripts of Trials 1–7 from their files (subject to a guarantee of anonymity). I am also grateful to Auckland District Court chief judges Blackwood and Nicholson, and to the presiding judges in each trial, for giving me permission to observe and record in their courtrooms. I was greatly assisted in this fieldwork by the Auckland District Court Registrar's staff, particularly Bob Kelly and Ika Tameifuna, and Cynthia Singh and her team of stenographers who typed the transcripts of Trials 8–21 at my request.
5. Two styles of transcription are used in presenting excerpts from the trials. Extracts from stenographers' transcripts are presented in standard punctuation. In transcripts from tape recordings of trials, the following conventions are used:

(yeah)	Parentheses around a word or string of words indicate that the transcription is uncertain.
( )	Empty parentheses indicate untranscribable speech or noise.
[	indicates the beginning of simultaneous speech.
[ ]	enclose simultaneous speech.
—	indicates a short pause of up to about 0.5 s.
——	indicates a pause of approximately 1.0 s.
(1.5)	pause of indicated length in seconds (to nearest 0.5 s).
→	indicates a line or utterance of particular interest (in both styles of transcription).

6. Mead (1985: 36–7, 93), describing practice in English magistrates' courts, notes that witnesses are expected to 'refer [their] responses to the magistrate', and quotes Carlen (1976) on the confusion consequently experienced by defendants.
7. These conditions are based on similar conditions proposed by Labov and Fanshel (1977), Searle (1969) and Edmondson (1981). Like Levinson (1983: 105) I am inclined to treat these conditions as conversational implicatures carried by the utterance in the appropriate context.
8. Similar conditions have been proposed by Hoffmann (1983; quoted in Dechert, 1985: 541) for questions in German courts.
9. In fact in summary trials, neither prosecution nor defence make opening addresses. In jury trials, only the prosecution may make an opening address.
10. See Examples 15 and 11 for instances of such foreshadowing and reiteration.

11. There are some noticeable differences between the two sets of figures as well. For instance, the frequency of WH-questions in cross-examination in the Auckland trials is twice that in the Boston trials. However, these differences may not be due to any difference in procedure. Both sets of figures are based on the questioning of a small number of witnesses in only two trials. The Boston figures are from jury trials on homicide charges, while the Auckland figures are from summary trials on relatively minor charges. The Boston figures reflect questioning mainly of defendants, while the Auckland figures reflect questioning mainly of non-defendants.

12. See Examples 2, 3, 13, 14 and 16 for further instances. Such prefaces are discussed further in the penultimate section.

13. Mead (1985: 24–7, 69–80) also discusses types and uses of follow-ups in Malaysian magistrates' courts in great detail. One type which does not occur in New Zealand courts arises from differences in recording procedures. Whereas the New Zealand trials reported here were recorded by stenographers, Malaysian magistrates make the official record of proceedings themselves, and many of their utterances are follow-ups which indicate what they are recording and allow for corrections by counsel.

14. In my data, counsel never said 'Objection Your Honour', and the judge never said 'Objection sustained' or 'Objection overruled': rather the actual expressions used for these functions were quite variable.

15. See Examples 6, 15 and 16 for instances.

16. See Example 8 above for an instance. Compare Sinclair & Coulthard's (1975) 'markers' in classroom interaction, and Blum-Kulka's (1983) observation of a similar use of terms of address in Israeli television interviews.

17. In New Zealand, the function of enforcing traffic laws is exercised by a number of authorities separate from the police. The law enforcement officers employed by these authorities are known as traffic officers.

18. Unfortunately, as I have only a transcript of this trial, information on intonation, which would be particularly interesting in this instance, is lacking.

19. It is possible to compare co- and cross-examination of the same witness (by different questioners) or co- and cross-examination by the same questioner (of different witnesses), while other variables in the context are essentially held constant.

References

ADELSWÄRD, VIVEKA, ARONSSON, KARIN, JÖNSSON, LINDA and LINELL, PER 1987, The unequal distribution of interactional space: dominance and control in courtroom interaction. *Text* 7(4), 313–46.

ADELSWÄRD, VIVEKA, ARONSSON, KARIN and LINELL, PER 1985, Discourse of blame: courtroom construction of social identity from the perspective of the defendant. Mimeo. Linköping: Linköping University.

ATKINSON, J. MAXWELL and DREW, PAUL 1979, *Order in Court: The Organization of Verbal Interaction in Judicial Settings*. London: Macmillan.

BELL, ALLAN 1984, Language style as audience design. *Language in Society* 13(2), 145–204.

BLUM-KULKA, SHOSHANA 1983, The dynamics of political interviews. *Text* 3(2), 131–53.

BROWN, PENELOPE and LEVINSON, STEPHEN C. 1987, *Politeness: Some Universals in Language Usage*. Cambridge: Cambridge University Press.

CARLEN, PAT 1976, *Magistrates' Justice*. London: Martin Robinson.

CLARK, HERBERT H. and CARLSON, THOMAS B. 1982, Hearers and speech acts. *Language* 58(2), 332–73.

COULMAS, FLORIAN (ed.) 1981, *Conversational Routine: Explorations in Standardized Communication Situations and Prepatterned Speech*. The Hague: Mouton.

COULTHARD, MALCOLM and BRAZIL, DAVID 1981, Exchange structure. In MALCOLM COULTHARD and MARTIN MONTGOMERY (eds) *Studies in Discourse Analysis* (pp. 82–106). London: Routledge & Kegan Paul.

DANET, BRENDA and BOGOCH, BRYNA 1980, Fixed fight or free-for-all? An empirical study of combativeness in the adversary system of justice. *British Journal of Law and Society* 7(1), 36–60.

DANET, BRENDA, HOFFMAN, KENNETH B., KERMISH, NICOLE C., RAFN, H. JEFFREY and STAYMAN, DEBORAH G. 1980, An ethnography of questioning in the courtroom. In ROGER W. SHUY and ANNA SHNUKAL (eds) *Language Use and the Uses of Language* (pp. 222–34). Washington, DC: Georgetown University Press.

DANET, BRENDA and KERMISH, NICOLE C. 1978, Courtroom questioning: a sociolinguistic perspective. In L. MASSERY (ed.) *Psychology and Persuasion in Advocacy* (pp. 412–41). Washington, DC: Association of Trial Lawyers of America, National College of Advocacy. 412–41.

DECHERT, CHRISTIANE 1985, Review of Ludger Hoffmann, *Kommunikation vor Gericht* (Tübingen: Gunter Narr, 1983). *Language in Society* 14(4), 540–6.

DREW, PAUL 1984, Disputes in courtroom cross-examination: 'contrasting versions' in a rape trial. Mimeo. York: University of York.

—1985, Analyzing the use of language in courtroom interaction. In TEUN A. VAN DIJK (ed.) *Handbook of Discourse Analysis* (volume 3, pp. 133–47). London: Academic Press.

DUNSTAN, ROBERT 1980, Context for coercion: analyzing properties of courtroom 'questions'. *British Journal of Law and Society* 7(1), 61–77.

EDMONDSON, WILLIS 1981, *Spoken Discourse: A Model for Analysis*. London: Longman.

FISHMAN, PAMELA 1978, Interaction: the work women do. *Social Problems* 25(4), 397–406.

GARVEY, CATHERINE 1977, The contingent query: a dependent act in conversation. In MICHAEL LEWIS and LEONARD A. ROSENBLUM (eds) *Interaction, Conversation and the Development of Language* (pp. 63–93). New York: Wiley.

—1979, Contingent queries and their relations in discourse. In ELINOR OCHS and BAMBI B. SCHIEFFELIN (eds) *Developmental Pragmatics* (pp. 363–72). New York: Academic Press.

HARRIS, SANDRA J. 1984, Questions as a mode of control in magistrates' courts. *International Journal of the Sociology of Language* 49, 5–27.

HATCH, EVELYN M. 1978, Discourse analysis and second language acquisition. In EVELYN M. HATCH (ed.) *Second Language Acquisition: A Book of Readings* (pp. 401–35). Rowley, Mass.: Newbury House.

HOFFMANN, LUDGER,1983, *Kommunikation vor Gericht*. Tübingen: Gunter Narr.

HOLMES, JANET 1984, Women's language: a functional approach. *General Linguistics* 24(3), 149–78.

—1985, Sex differences and mis-communication: some data from New Zealand. In JOHN B. PRIDE (ed.) *Cross-cultural Encounters: Communication and Mis-communication* (pp. 24–43). Melbourne: River Seine.

KEARSLEY, GREG P. 1976, Questions and question-asking in verbal discourse: a cross-disciplinary review. *Journal of Psycholinguistic Research* 5(4), 355–75.

LABOV, WILLIAM 1972, The transformation of experience in narrative syntax. In WILLIAM LABOV, *Language in the Inner City: Studies in the Black English Vernacular* (pp. 354–96). Philadelphia: University of Pennsylvania Press.

LABOV, WILLIAM and FANSHEL, DAVID 1977, *Therapeutic Discourse: Psychotherapy as Conversation*. New York: Academic Press.

LANE, CHRISTOPHER L. 1985, Mis-communication in cross-examinations. In JOHN B. PRIDE (ed.) *Cross-cultural Encounters: Communication and Mis-communication* (pp. 196–211). Melbourne: River Seine.

—1988, Language on trial: questioning strategies and European–Polynesian mis-communication in New Zealand courtrooms. Unpublished PhD thesis. Auckland: University of Auckland.

LEVINSON, STEPHEN C. 1983, *Pragmatics*. Cambridge: Cambridge University Press.

LIEBES-PLESNER, TAMAR 1984, Rhetoric in the service of justice: the sociolinguistic construction of stereotypes in an Israeli rape trial. *Text* 4(1–3), 173–92.

MEAD, RICHARD 1985, *Courtroom Discourse*. Birmingham: University of Birmingham, English Language Research.

PAWLEY, ANDREW K. and SYDER, FRANCES H. 1983, Two puzzles for linguistic theory: nativelike selection and nativelike fluency. In JACK C. RICHARDS and RICHARD W. SCHMIDT (eds) *Language and Communication* (pp. 191–225). London/New York: Longman.

QUIRK, RANDOLPH, GREENBAUM, SIDNEY, LEECH, GEOFFREY N. and SVARTVIK, JAN 1972, *A Grammar of Contemporary English*. London: Longman.

SEARLE, JOHN R. 1969, *Speech Acts: An Essay in the Philosophy of Language*. Cambridge: Cambridge University Press.

SINCLAIR, JOHN McH. and COULTHARD, R. MALCOLM 1975, *Towards an Analysis of Discourse: The English Used by Teachers and Pupils*. London: Oxford University Press.

THOMAS, JENNY 1985, Complex illocutionary acts and the analysis of discourse. *Lancaster Papers in Linguistics* 11.

VALDÉS, GUADALUPE 1986, Analyzing the demands that courtroom interaction makes upon speakers of ordinary English: toward the development of a coherent descriptive framework. *Discourse Processes* 9(3), 269–303.

WILLIS, J. D. 1960, *Garrow and Willis's Principles of the Law of Evidence in New Zealand* (4th edn). Wellington: Butterworth.

12 Politeness strategies in New Zealand women's speech[1]

JANET HOLMES

> A: That meeting I had to go to today was just awful.
> B: Where was it?
> A: In the NLC building. People were just so aggressive.
> B: Mm. Who was there?
> A: Oh the usual representatives of all the government departments.
> I felt really put down at one point, you know, just so humiliated.
> B: You should be more assertive dear. Don't let people trample all over you and ignore what you say.

This conversation took place between a woman (A) and her husband (B) after dinner one evening. It looks like a pleasant and polite interchange — and in some respects it was. The woman, however, felt at the end of it that she had not really been heard, and that her husband had missed her point. He had undoubtedly been responsive — asking about where, and who, and proffering advice to help resolve her problem. But she had been conveying another message and was not simply exchanging information. She was sharing how she had felt at the meeting, wanting to elicit sympathy and understanding from her spouse. He, on the other hand, heard only the informative content of what she said, and asked for more information to fill out his picture of her experience. This pattern of male orientation to information, compared to female orientation to 'affective meaning' (Holmes, 1983; 1984) is remarkably widespread. It is a pattern which I intend to explore in some detail in this paper, using a range of evidence from interactions between New Zealand women and men to support my arguments. It seems that women and men may weight linguistic politeness differently.

I will begin by outlining a model of interaction which takes account of these different types of meaning. In subsequent sections I will use the model to describe a number of differences in women's and men's verbal behaviour and, in particular, to explore the claim that women express linguistic politeness differently from men.

A Model for Analysing Women's and Men's Interaction

In a discussion of features of politeness extending over almost ten years, Robin Lakoff (1972; 1973a; 1973b; 1975; 1977; 1979; 1980) developed a model of interaction which has stimulated considerable research into sex differences in varieties of English. She introduced three Rules of Politeness (1973b), or Rules of Rapport (1975):

(1) Don't impose (Distance).
(2) Give options (Deference).
(3) Be friendly (Camaraderie).

It is obvious that these rules focus on the same factors as Brown & Levinson's concepts of negative politeness (Rules 1 and 2) and positive politeness (Rule 3) (Brown & Levinson 1978; 1987: passim, 257).[2] They were incorporated ultimately by Lakoff (1977; 1979) into a model which analysed interaction along a stylistic continuum extending from strategies based on Gricean maxims at one end (Lakoff's Rules of Clarity) to strategies of camaraderie at the other, with distance and deference as points in between (Figure 12.1).[3]

Just as the continuum is an improvement on the notion of mutually exclusive rules or categories, a graphed square or two-dimensional plot provides an even more satisfactory model of the interdependence of elements in interaction (see Figure 12.2). The area within the four quadrants of the square represents interactional space. Any utterance, expression or interaction, may be located in that space according to the extent to which it expresses both referential content, on a scale from 0 to 100%, and affective meaning on a scale running from high solidarity at one end to maximum social distance or deference at the other.[4]

CLARITY ------> DISTANCE ------> DIFFERENCE ------> CAMARADERIE
Least relationship   Most relationship
between participants   between participants

FIGURE 12.1 *Lakoff's model of interaction (1979: 62)*

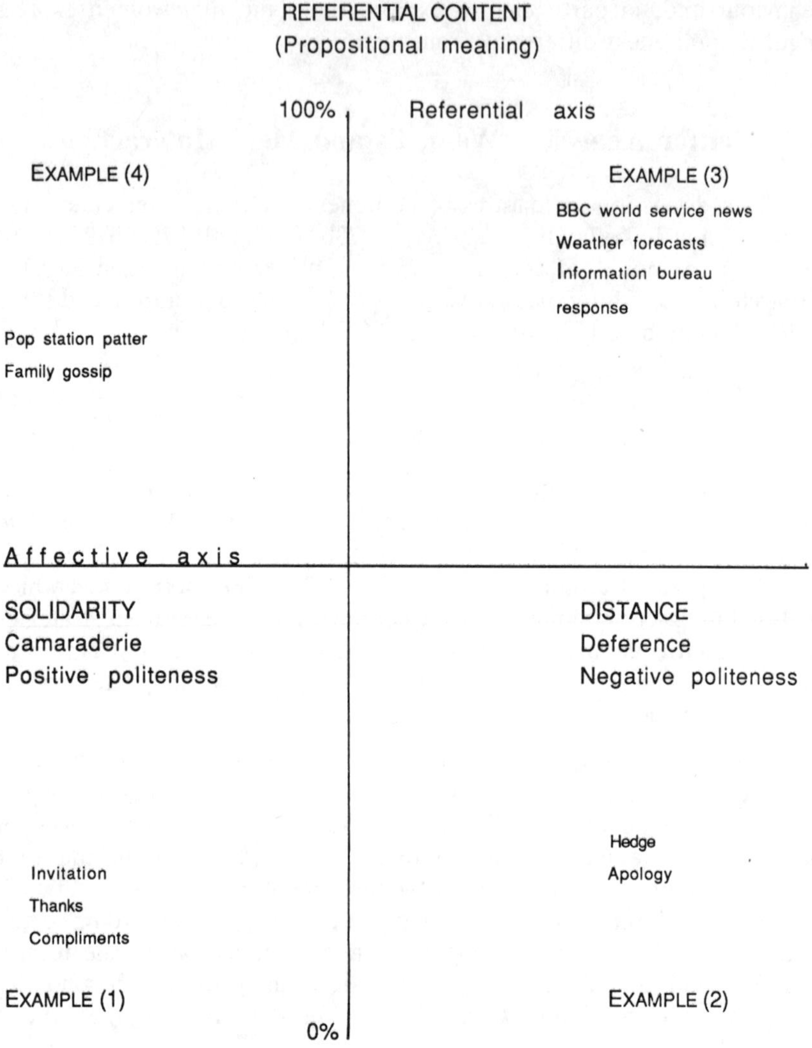

REFERENTIAL CONTENT
(Propositional meaning)

100%   Referential   axis

EXAMPLE (4)   EXAMPLE (3)

                                                              BBC world service news

                                                              Weather forecasts

                                                              Information bureau

                                                              response

Pop station patter

Family gossip

Affective   axis

SOLIDARITY   DISTANCE

Camaraderie   Deference

Positive politeness   Negative politeness

                                                              Hedge

Invitation   Apology

Thanks

Compliments

EXAMPLE (1)   EXAMPLE (2)

                        0%

FIGURE 12.2 *Model of interaction*

Such a model not only allows but requires analysis of interaction as
simultaneously expressing both propositional content and affective meaning. But it also recognises that the attention paid to each will differ in
degree in any particular situation.

A couple of examples may be useful, though they are inevitably simplified. A greeting such as Example 1 between friends in the pub, will be located towards the solidarity end of the affective axis.

EXAMPLE 1

'Gidday Fred me old mate.'[5]

Since it conveys little referential content or propositional meaning, it will be positioned towards the bottom of the referential scale. A very formal greeting such as Example 2 similarly conveys little new information, but has a high affective content, in this case expressing maximum social distance or deference.

EXAMPLE 2

'Good afternoon madam.'

Information about the weather provided by the telephone weather service, exemplified in Example 3, is high on the referential scale but would be located towards the social distance end of the affective axis.

EXAMPLE 3 *Context: Wellington meteorological service telephone broadcast*

mostly cloudy and cool today/ with light southerlies//

Finally, Example 4 is an interaction between a mother and her daughter which provides an example which illustrates a high level of information while also expressing great solidarity.

EXAMPLE 4 *Context: telephone call from mother to daughter*

Mother: hello love/ look sweetheart I'm very sorry/ but/ I've got some bad news for you
Daughter: oh mum no/ what is it/
Mother: I'm afraid your Uncle Tom has had a stroke dear//

These examples illustrate the four extreme points of the model, as shown in Figure 12.2.

Figure 12.2 also includes a number of suggestions about where an analyst might locate a range of different types of interaction or expressions on the model. Invitations, for instance, generally convey at least a little information along with high solidarity: 'Why don't you come out and visit us at our bach at the weekend?'. Apologies are generally low on information content but high on affect: 'I'm terribly sorry. I didn't mean to hurt you'. An apology's main point is to restore social harmony and equilibrium (Holmes, 1990a) and it achieves this effect by paying attention to the addressee's 'negative face needs' for distance and deference (Brown & Levinson, 1987: 187–90).

Speech functions such as compliments, thanks, jokes and, in some of their meanings, pragmatic particles such as 'you know' and tag-questions often express a predominantly affective positive politeness meaning (see below, and also Holmes, 1986a; 1986b).[6] Deference, distance or negative politeness, on the other hand, are most obviously and frequently expressed not so much through particular speech functions as by the modification and modulation of 'face threatening acts' or FTAs (Brown & Levinson, 1987: 60). Hedges, impersonalisation strategies and indirectness devices generally serve this purpose.

Family gossip frequently conveys both solidarity and information, and the patter of pop station disc jockeys is another example where the information content as well as the positive politeness functions may be relatively high. Weather forecasts and news broadcasts tend to be very high on information but, as Bell (1984; this volume) demonstrates, one would position different news readers at different points along the solidarity–distance dimension according to the audience aimed at by the particular radio or TV station involved. As such examples suggest, it is impossible to position utterances or interactions out of context.

Even where one might consider a speaker was primarily concerned to express referential content or propositional meaning (i.e. where the utterance seems predominantly content-oriented), the affective axis will always be relevant. Affect is always expressed, even when it takes the form of maximum formality and social distance. Indeed the purpose of the model is to emphasise that speakers cannot avoid encoding messages in ways which convey some information about the speaker-hearer relationship. Every utterance provides some affective information of this kind. Even those who record answer-phone messages make some assumptions about their relationship to their listeners, and these assumptions are inevitably reflected in features of their language (see Bell, 1984).

The range of linguistic features which may convey this affective meaning is very wide. Different types of speech act such as greeting and apology clearly serve this purpose, as illustrated above, but a variety of other features can also be analysed within this model of interaction. Semantic content and topic selection, for instance, may express the speaker's concern to involve others in the discussion. Interactive patterns, such as the number and distribution of interruptions and feedback, often reflect the relationship between participants. Lexical and syntactic choices, pragmatic particles and pronunciation features may all express affective meaning. A speaker's level of h-dropping or l-vocalisation may express solidarity or social distance with their addressee. Indeed the model can account for speech accommodation or divergence (Giles, 1984) at any linguistic level, including code-switching patterns between different varieties of a language or even between languages where these are used as strategies for expressing positive or negative politeness (see also Giles, Taylor & Bourhis, 1973).[7]

Thus the form of the model has quite specific implications. The referential axis represents a scale which extends from minimum referential or propositional content at its base (0%), to maximum referential content (100%) at the top. The affective axis, on the other hand, does not represent a scale of minimum to maximum affect. Rather, different points along the axis represent different kinds of affect, or the degree to which the speaker takes account of the addressee's positive *versus* negative face needs. The affective axis thus combines Brown & Levinson's (1987) concepts of power (*P*) and distance (*D*), or Brown & Gilman's (1960) concepts, power and solidarity. The scale makes it possible to account for utterances which express predominantly solidarity or distance/deference, while also reflecting the fact that a particular utterance may have elements of each. As Brown & Levinson point out, the various techniques of positive politeness and negative politeness 'operate, respectively, as a kind of social accelerator and social brake for decreasing or increasing social distance in relationships, regardless of FTAs' (1987: 93). Placement on the scale reflects a judgement of the result of their interaction.

The affective scale reflects the fact that an expression of solidarity or positive politeness reduces social distance, just as an expression of deference increases distance, or at least inhibits the development of solidarity. It is true that a particular interaction may illustrate a wonderful balance of solidarity and deferential devices (see Brown & Levinson, 1987: 17), but the model permits an analysis which plots each independently if appropriate. Hence the overall description of an interaction may be built up from an accumulation of information on the placement of components, if necessary, on a number of graphed squares.

The following interaction between a woman and her secretary illustrates the point. The conversation expresses varying degrees of information and affect at different points. The stages of the interaction can be represented by different graphic representations. The coding of utterances (A1, B1, etc.) allows them to be identified on Figure 12.3.

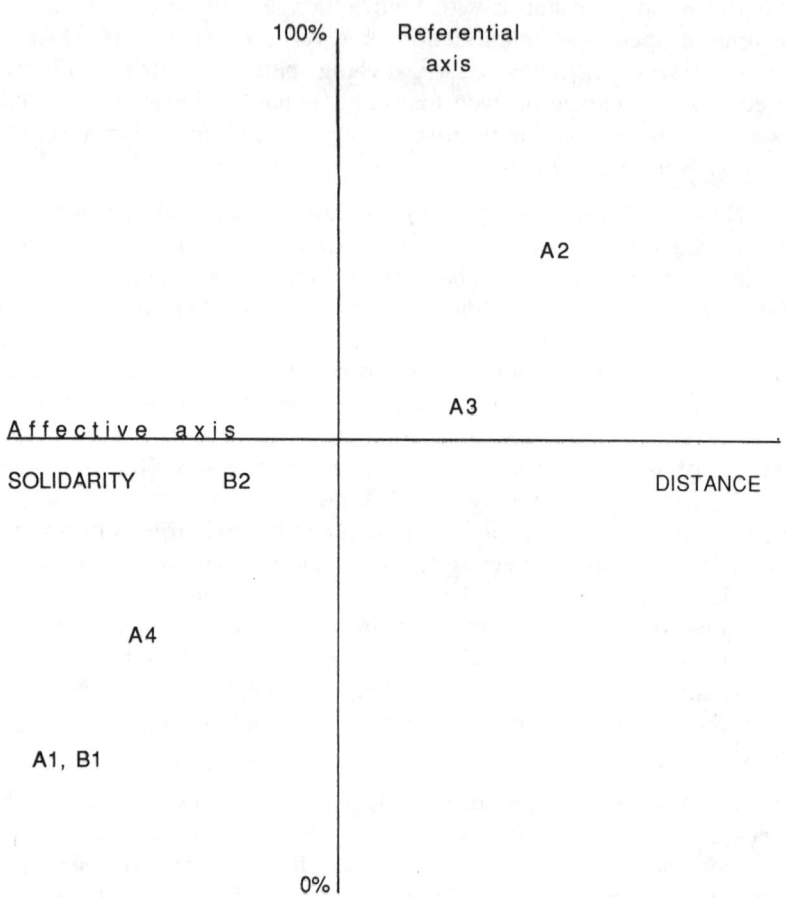

FIGURE 12.3 *Example of exchange plotted on model*

EXAMPLE 5 *Context: boss and secretary's first encounter of the day*

A1: good mörning Sue/ lovely day/
                              [*Positively polite, low information*]
B1: yes it's beautiful// makes you wonder what we're doing here
         doesn't it//   [*Positively polite, low information*]
A2: mm/ that's right// look I wonder if you could possibly
                                               [*High information,*
         sort this lot out by ten//   *negatively polite*]

A3: I need them for a meeting//
                    [*High information, mid-point affective*]
B2: yes sure/ no problem   [*High information, positively polite*]
A4: thanks that's great//   [*Positively polite, low information*]

The development of the interaction from a largely phatic exchange serving to reinforce solidarity, to an information-oriented or transactional exchange where relative roles become relevant, with some movement back towards the former position at the conclusion, can be reflected in the plotting of its components as a sequence of positions within the model. This pattern seems likely to be typical of workplace interactions.

Negative politeness usually relates to a particular FTA, while positive politeness is not so constrained (Scollon & Scollon, 1981; Coupland, Grainger & Coupland, 1988). However, the fact that negative politeness and positive politeness are thus rather different in kind presents no problem for this model.[8] While a whole exchange (such as a greeting routine) may be classified simply as high on positive politeness, low on information, it is also possible to classify any and every expression or utterance appropriately on the positive-negative politeness scale. One is not forced to make an absolute single final placement 'summing' the effects of different politeness devices — any more than the addressee does when interpreting the affective meaning of the relevant communication.

Different components of a single complex utterance may be best separated out. The contribution of each component to the overall effect of the utterance may be described by several independent placements within the interactional space represented by the model, rather than by one overall placement. Correspondingly the analysis of any particular interaction may involve a 'mapping' by means of a number of accumulated graphs. One obvious advantage of this approach is that, while not being overly complex, it more accurately reflects the dynamic nature of interaction (see Giles, 1984; Thomas, 1985; Coupland *et al.*, 1988; Coupland, Grainger & Coupland, 1988). Moreover since this approach documents the relative effect of linguistic devices at different points in an interaction, it also allows the analyst to show how identities and relationships may be constantly negotiated and renegotiated throughout (see, for example, Harris, 1981; Gumperz, 1982; Cameron, 1985: 142). As in Example 5 the use of positive politeness devices may increase or decrease during the progress of an interaction. Consequently the interactional effect of a positive politeness device (and even of the 'same' form) may vary from one point to another in the course of an interaction.

The model I have outlined cannot represent all aspects of interaction. Its strengths are that it incorporates both referential and affective meaning within one framework of analysis,[9] that it emphasises the relevance of both aspects of meaning in any interaction, and that it allows for a dynamic interpretation. It is, however, clearly hearer-oriented in that it reflects the face needs of the hearer rather than the speaker. A different model would be needed to represent those of the speaker. In the model represented in Figure 12.2 an apology, for example, expresses attention to the hearer's negative face needs. In a speaker-oriented model it would be classified as an utterance which threatens the speaker's positive face, since it admits deficiency (Brown & Levinson, 1987: 68).

Finally, as I will illustrate below, the model is concerned with accounting for the expression of positive affect (or what Brown & Levinson include in their use of the term 'politeness') rather than negative affect. In other words it is concerned with the analysis of essentially co-operative communication between interactants who are well-disposed towards each other. An interaction which involved coercive or challenging behaviour, as described for instance by Lane (this volume), or insulting behaviour, such as that described by Austin (this volume), would require a rather different model. Challenges and insults would need to be graphed on a scale of negative affect. Both negative politeness and positive politeness essentially express positive affect. A model taking account of negative affect is needed to account for expressions designed to deliberately reduce solidarity or positive politeness without expressing deference or negative politeness. For a more complete analysis of any interaction these factors among others would need to be considered and integrated with the information accounted for by this model.

In sum the model of interaction presented here provides for an analysis of positive affect from the addressee's point of view. It provides a useful framework for a discussion of linguistically expressed politeness. In what follows I will examine a number of ways in which the speech of New Zealand middle-class Pakeha women and men seems to differ in politeness. I will first describe differences in the emphasis which women and men appear to place on the affective axis *versus* the referential axis in interaction. Then I will discuss differences in their use of some specific positive and negative politeness strategies.

Referential and Affective Meaning

There is a considerable body of evidence that women put more emphasis than men on the importance of talk in establishing and maintaining relationships, whereas men more often regard talk as a means of communicating information (Kalcik, 1975; Aries, 1982; Wodak, 1981; Maltz & Borker, 1982; Turner & Henzl, 1982). This does not necessarily mean that talk actually serves exclusively different purposes for each sex — talk expresses both types of meaning at once, as the model discussed above illustrates. Moreover the context and type of talk involved is clearly relevant to such perceptions. One would not want to argue that the way women talk can always be characterised as emphasising affective meaning regardless of the type of discourse involved.[10] In formal situations such as law courts, lectures and news interviews, all participants will recognise that the informative function appropriately predominates in most cases. Nevertheless it appears that women and men may perceive the primary functions of particular types of talk differently. It is in less formal contexts that different perceptions seem to become relevant.[11] Let me give an example.

It has been claimed by a number of New Zealand women that they are frequently misunderstood when they describe a problem or a worry in the course of a casual conversation with a man (Holmes, 1985). The woman presents her problem to elicit sympathy and understanding. The male's reaction is typically to analyse the problem and propose a solution, or even a variety of solutions, treating the utterance as a request for information and advice. Both partners feel misunderstood after an exchange which follows this pattern. The woman seeks a reaction that responds to the expression of how she feels, rather than simply to the information content of her utterance. Her male addressee feels equally misunderstoood because his proposed solutions are not appreciated, and the woman dismisses them with scarcely any attention. He feels his attempts at assistance have been rejected and his suggestions under-valued (see also Wodak, 1981; Maltz & Borker, 1982: 213).

The dialogue at the beginning of this paper, which appears harmonious and co-operative enough on the surface, nevertheless illustrates a similar kind of pattern. The man's questions, which reflect his concern for getting the facts straight, could be interpreted by the woman as evidence of lack of interest in her main point — namely how she is feeling as a result of the meeting. One explanation for these minor and often undiagnosed miscommunications appears to be the different degrees of importance attached by women and men in such informal interactions to affective *versus* referential meaning.

Maltz & Borker suggest that the reasons for this difference in priorities lies in the different socialisation of girls and boys which results in 'different cultural rules for friendly conversation' (1982: 212). Research is needed to establish whether New Zealand girls and boys value different sociolinguistic skills which might account for the different emphases that adults appear to give to different types of meaning in informal talk. But given what we know of the socialisation process, this explanation is certainly plausible (e.g. Ritchie & Ritchie, 1978; Phillips, 1980; 1987).

The way women and men use some pragmatic particles also provides evidence for the claim that women and men often place a different emphasis on affective *versus* referential meaning in different uses of language. Pragmatic particles, such as 'you know' and 'of course', are very clear examples of linguistic devices which simultaneously express both referential and affective meaning. The referential meaning involves epistemic modality or degrees of certainty (Holmes, 1983; James, 1983; Coates, 1987), while the affective meaning can generally be analysed as an expression of solidarity or positive politeness, though in some cases (such as 'of course') it may express negative politeness or social distance. Let me illustrate with the tag-question, a syntactic device which clearly expresses both types of meaning, and where it is generally possible to categorise one type of meaning as primary in a particular context (Holmes, 1984).

Tag-questions may be used as epistemic devices to express uncertainty. In other words their primary meaning may be referential indicating that the proposition asserted in the main clause is subject to doubt. In Example 6 the speaker is uncertain about the date and she indicates this with the tag which signals doubt about the validity of the proposition being asserted.

EXAMPLE 6 *Context: one friend to another recounting her school experiences (/ indicates rising intonation)*

/

I did my exams in sixty three was it

In terms of the interactive model described above this utterance relates primarily to the referential axis. The degree of positive or negative politeness involved is determined more by the context and surrounding discourse than by anything expressed explicitly in the utterance.

But tags may also express primarily affective meaning. They may function as facilitative devices, providing an addressee with an easy entrée into a conversation, as illustrated in Example 7.

EXAMPLE 7 *Context: teacher to pupil looking at a picture in a book* (\
indicates falling intonation)

    T: what's this called Sam?
    P: [*No answer*].
                  \
    T: it's a cocoon isn't it?

Teachers, interviewers, hosts and, in general, those responsible for the success of an interaction tend to use tags in this way (Johnson, 1980; Holmes, 1984; Cameron, McAlinden & O'Leary, 1988). In such cases the tag serves a predominantly affective function. The teacher makes it easy for the child to participate. The referential content is low and the utterance expresses positive rather than negative politeness.

By attenuating or hedging the force of a directive or softening a criticism, a tag may serve as a negative politeness strategy (Brown & Levinson, 1987: 147), as in Example 8.

EXAMPLE 8 *Context: mother to child who has emptied her shopping out all over the floor*

                                \
that was a bit of a daft thing to do wasn't it

Once again the information conveyed is minimal: the primary message is affective.

It is also possible for tags to be used affectively as confrontational and coercive devices marking an utterance as a 'face attack act' (Austin, 1988; this volume; Lane, 1988; this volume). Example 9 shows a tag used to 'force feedback when it is not forthcoming' (Thomas, 1988: 27).

EXAMPLE 9 *Context: Superintendent to Detective Constable during interview criticising the Constable's performance*

    A: . . . you'll probably find yourself um before the Chief Constable, okay?
    B: Yes, Sir, yes, understood.
    A: Now you er fully understand that, don't you?
    B: Yes, Sir, indeed, yeah.

                              (Example from Thomas, 1988: 28)

The tag functions not to attenuate but rather to strengthen the negative illocutionary force of a face attack act. (As mentioned in the discussion above, the model of interaction used in this paper focuses on positive affect or politeness rather than negative affect. Hence the aggressive function of tags illustrated here is not accounted for in this model since this function involves the expression of negative affect, i.e. is not 'polite'.)

Table 12.1 summarises the patterns found in a 60,000 word corpus containing equal amounts of female and male speech collected in a range of matched contexts. The patterns clearly support the claim that women tend to put more emphasis on affective functions of language while men emphasise its referential function. In this corpus New Zealand women used tags most often as positive politeness facilitative devices, encouraging the addressee to contribute to the conversation rather than as devices expressing uncertainty. Moreover they used tags in this way more often than men, who tended to use more epistemic modal tags requesting confirmation or expressing doubt.

Data on other particles such as 'I think' (Holmes, 1985), 'you know' (Holmes, 1986b), 'of course' (Holmes, 1988a), and 'sort of' (Holmes, 1989b; Meyerhoff, 1986), reveals a similar picture, though with variations, such as the extent to which particular particles express positive *versus* negative politeness functions. Moreover it is possible that if one turned attention to devices used to express negative rather than positive *affect* the picture might be quite different, as Example 9 suggests (see also

TABLE 12.1 *Distribution of tag-questions by function and sex of speaker*

Function of tag		Female % (N)	Male % (N)
Epistemic modal (expressing uncertainty)		39 (23)	57 (27)
Positive politeness (facilitative)	p = 0.001	56 (33)	28 (13)
Negative politeness (softening)		5 (3)	11 (5)
Face attack marker (challenging)		–	4 (2)
Total		56	44

Cameron, McAlinden & O'Leary, 1988). Overall, however, focusing on the politeness devices accounted for in the model described above, the picture is clear. The distribution of pragmatic particles in women's and men's speech supports the claim that in informal contexts women emphasise affective meaning while men tend to focus on the referential function of language.

Positive and Negative Politeness

As the model makes clear, one can distinguish within affective meaning between devices which effectively establish or increase rapport and solidarity between participants, on the one hand, and devices which maintain distance or express deference on the other, i.e. positive *versus* negative politeness strategies (Brown & Levinson, 1987). In this section I will examine the evidence that New Zealand women and men use these politeness devices differently. I will first consider a positive politeness device, the compliment, and secondly, I will look at the way women and men use a negative politeness device, the apology.

Compliments

There is not a great deal of research which focuses on sex differences in the realisation of specific speech functions or speech acts. One study by Goodwin (1980) demonstrated that black girls and boys in Philadelphia expressed directives differently in same-sex interactions. The boys tended to use unmodified imperatives reflecting the hierarchical organisation of their groups, while the girls used utterances introduced by 'let's' or 'we gonna', and modalised declaratives, reflecting their more participatory decision-making styles. Though Goodwin does not use these terms, it is clear that the girls used more positive politeness devices than the boys — devices such as the inclusive pronouns 'we' and 'us' which explicitly pay attention to the addressee's need to be noticed. In New Zealand the data I have analysed on the distribution of compliments in women's and men's speech certainly reveals a similar pattern (Holmes, 1988b).

Compliments clearly function as positively affective speech acts which serve to increase or consolidate solidarity between the speaker and addressee. They are social lubricants serving to 'create or maintain rapport' (Wolfson, 1983: 86). An analysis of nearly 500 compliments demonstrated that New Zealand women give and receive significantly more compliments than New Zealand men do.[12] Table 12.2 shows that women gave 68% of all the compliments recorded and received 74% of

TABLE 12.2 *Compliments according to sex of participants*

Complimenter–Recipient		Number	%
Female–Female	(F–F)	248	51.2
Female–Male	(F–M)	80	16.5
Male–Female	(M–F)	112	23.2
Male–Male	(M–M)	44	9.1
	Total	484	100

them. It is also clear that compliments between men were relatively rare (only 9%), and that even taking account of women's compliments to men, men received overall considerably fewer compliments than women (only 26%). Complimenting appears to be a speech behaviour occurring much more frequently in interactions involving women than men.

The frequency patterns identified are consistent with the hypothesis that women generally perceive compliments as positively affective speech acts. The between-women complimenting patterns are also consistent with research which interprets women's linguistic behaviour as 'affiliative' or co-operative, rather than competitive or control-oriented (Cameron, 1985; Kalcik, 1975; Smith, 1985). However, the patterns in Table 12.2 suggest that men may perceive these speech acts differently. Men do not give compliments to each other or receive compliments from each other very often, and women do not compliment men as often as they compliment women.

It is interesting to speculate on the reasons why people do not compliment men as often as they do women. It appears to be much more acceptable and socially appropriate to compliment a woman than a man. Wolfson (1984) takes the view that compliments act as socialising devices, and thus one would expect more of them to be addressed 'downwards'. The pattern is thus explained by referring to women's socially subordinate status in society. She says:

> women because of their role in the social order, are seen as appropriate recipients of all manner of social judgments in the form of compliments . . . the way a woman is spoken to is, no matter what her status, a subtle and powerful way of perpetuating her subordinate role in society. (Wolfson, 1984: 243)

In my view compliments are appropriately regarded not as put-down or socialisation devices, nor as patronising linguistic strategies, but rather as positively affective speech acts. They serve as signals of solidarity and, as such, one might expect them more frequently in same-sex interactions than cross-sex interactions. While this is clearly true for women, supporting my interpretation of their function, it is not the case for men. It may be, however, that males do not consider compliments the most appropriate way of expressing solidarity. They may use other linguistic and non-linguistic strategies for this purpose (see Phillips, 1980; Kuiper, in press).

If, for instance, men regard compliments as FTAs, experiencing them as embarrassing and discomfiting speech acts, then it would not be surprising that the fewest compliments occur between men. And the lower frequency of compliments from women to men as opposed to from women to women could then be interpreted as evidence of women's sensitivity to men's feelings about compliments. A more detailed analysis of the contexts in which they occur could throw further light on these speculations. Whatever the reasons for the observed patterns, however, there is no doubt that they reveal women as more positively polite than men. Overall in their use of compliments, women express solidarity and take acount of their addressee's positive face needs, such as the need to be admired, more frequently than men do.

Apologies

Apologies are utterances aimed at remedying the effects of an offence or FTA and restoring social harmony and equilibrium. They are examples of negative politeness strategies or utterances concerned with maintaining or supporting the addressee's negative face. Apologies may be expressed by a range of strategies, with some variant of 'sorry' the form most frequently used (e.g. Olshtain & Cohen, 1983; Owen, 1983; Trosborg, 1987). There are no significant differences between women and men in the preferred strategies for expressing apologies (Holmes, 1989a). As with compliments, the differences which arise in women's and men's apology usage relate rather to the distribution of apologies in their speech.

In a corpus of 183 apologies produced by New Zealand women and men there were significant differences between the sexes in the distribution of apologies (see Table 12.3). Women gave 75% of all the apologies recorded and received 73% of them. Hence in this corpus at least, over a range of contexts, New Zealand women apologised more than New

TABLE 12.3 *Apologies analysed according to sex of participants*

Apologiser–Victim		Number	%
Female–Female	(F–F)	99	56.3
Female–Male	(F–M)	32	18.2
Male–Female	(M–F)	30	17.0
Male–Male	(M–M)	15	8.5
	Total	176	100

Zealand men did, and they were apologised to more frequently than the men were. The table also illustrates the fact that, as with compliments, apologies were most frequent between women, while apologies between males were relatively rare (only 9%).

It is superficially surprising that apologies to males are so much less frequent than apologies to females (27% *versus* 73%). One might expect negative politeness strategies, as expressions of deference and social distance, to be used more to those with power and status in the society. Apologies signal the speaker's concern for having offended another or for having interfered with their freedom of action. Hence they could be expected to occur most often 'upwards'. In western culture males are generally recognised as the dominant and powerful group and one would therefore expect more apologies to men from women. But the number of apologies from women to men and *vice versa* is remarkably evenly distributed.

As with compliments, part of the answer to this puzzle may lie in differential perceptions by women and men of verbal politeness devices. The contexts, types of relationship and kinds of offence which elicit apologies appear to differ between the sexes (Holmes, 1989a). It seems likely that women regard explicit apologies for offences as more important in maintaining relationships than men do. The very low frequency of apologies between males provides support for this hypothesis. Apologies, it seems, function differently for women and men. Women perceive them as important face-support strategies while men appear to regard them as more dispensable. (An alternative explanation, discussed in Holmes (1989a), accounts for the lower number of male apologies in terms of the threat which apologies represent to speaker's face. Men may use them less because they regard them as uncomfortably threatening to their own self-esteem.)

Once again the overall pattern shows New Zealand women using more linguistic politeness devices than men, but in this case they are negative politeness devices. Hence women appear to give greater weight to affective aspects of interaction than men do. Women clearly regard overt linguistic politeness strategies, such as compliments and apologies, as important components of interaction, while men apparently do not. Do men, perhaps, have alternative ways of paying attention to the face needs of their addressees?

Conclusion

In the predominantly informal contexts examined, the evidence surveyed in this paper suggests that New Zealand women pay more attention to the feelings and 'wants' of their conversational partners than New Zealand men do. In other words they are more 'polite', in Brown & Levinson's sense of the term, which includes both positively polite and negatively polite behaviour.[13] This reflects the fact that, at least in informal contexts, women appear to give more weight to interpersonal or affective factors than men do. In terms of the model described in the first section, women are more likely to emphasise the affective axis and men the referential axis. The data discussed has provided a range of empirical support for this claim.

There is further interactional data which paints the same picture. On a range of· measures women appear to make more attractive conversational partners than men, simply because they take more account of their addressee's face needs. In terms of negative politeness they do not intrude by dominating the talking time, for example, and they interrupt less frequently than men.[14] In terms of positive politeness strategies, women provide more encouraging and facilitative feedback than men do (e.g. Edelsky, 1981; Fishman, 1983; Holmes, 1984; 1986b; 1988b). Study after study supports the view of women as 'affiliative' and co-operative conversational partners (e.g. Eakins & Eakins, 1979; Cameron, 1985; Smith, 1985; Preisler, 1986; Coates, 1988). The little New Zealand research there is in this area suggests that the patterns of conversational interaction in New Zealand women's speech are similar (Holmes, 1990b; Meyerhoff, 1987).

In this paper I have examined a number of ways in which New Zealand women's usage reflects their concern for affective aspects of interaction, including positive and negative politeness devices. New Zealand women use tag-questions more often than men as a facilitative positive politeness device. They use both compliments, which are clearly positive politeness strategies, and apologies, which realise negative politeness strategies, more often than men. These patterns clearly support the view that New Zealand women place more emphasis than men on affective aspects of interaction.

It has been suggested that the reasons for these patterns relate to the subordinate status of women in western culture. While it is obvious that women's status needs drastic improvement in New Zealand (as in other countries), I have argued in more detail elsewhere (Holmes, 1990b) that the fact that women use politeness devices can be regarded positively, as evidence of their concern for their conversational partners, rather than negatively, as a reflection of their lack of power or status. The strategies examined include ones which entail the speaker taking the initiative, and ones which are commonly used by those in leadership roles. What unites them is the fact that they reflect concern for the face needs of the addressee or conversational partner. In other words, rather than seeing this data as evidence of women's inferior status, one could regard it as evidence of women's interactional maturity relative to men.

Another explanation addresses the source of the patterns. Maltz & Borker (1982) point to the different socialisation patterns of girls and boys in order to account for the miscommunications and misinterpretations which often occur between the sexes in adulthood. They suggest that girls develop co-operative strategies of interaction and supportive ways of speaking. Boys, on the other hand, are more likely to compete for the floor, challenge and insult other speakers, and to express themselves 'bald on record' (Brown & Levinson, 1987: 60), presumably regarding the use of politeness devices as superfluous (Maltz & Borker, 1982: 205–9). Their account of the reasons why women's and men's ways of speaking differ is quite compatible with the New Zealand data described above. Research which examined the sociolinguistic skills which character-ise the interactions of New Zealand girls and boys would undoubtedly be a valuable contribution to our understanding in this area.

It seems, then, that women and men may view interaction rather differently. White middle-class culture attaches a high value to informativeness or referential aspects of communication. This cultural norm has been discussed by a number of researchers (e.g. Hymes, 1979; Lakoff, 1979; Brown & Levinson, 1987). Lakoff (1979: 63), for example, labels this aspect of communication Clarity (see Figure 12.1), and says 'Clarity is often thought of as the ideal mode of discourse, at least in this culture at the present time'. She further suggests that Clarity is a male norm (Lakoff, 1979: 71); and the data in this paper certainly supports that claim.[15] At least in informal contexts women value politeness highly and use a range of devices which take account of their addressees' politeness needs as they perceive them. Men presumably interpret these situations differently. They do not see them as contexts where one needs to adopt interaction patterns which are very different from those appropriate in more public, formal contexts.

But where does this interpretation lead? Is linguistic politeness a solely female prerogative? Is it even perhaps a sexist concept? Brown & Levinson characterised British culture as a 'negative politeness culture' (1987: 245). They suggested that at a gross level a speech community might be described in terms of preferred ways of interacting politely. I have provided evidence that New Zealand middle-class Pakeha women appear to have preferred ways of interacting (with consideration for the 'face' or feelings of others) which differ from those of New Zealand men — at least in private informal contexts. The politeness strategies examined to date are most certainly those used predominantly by women. The question of how New Zealand men express solidarity and deference in private informal contexts remains.

Notes

1. I would like to thank Allan Bell for his helpful comments on an earlier draft of this paper and in particular for his contribution to the development of the model of interaction.
2. Page numbers refer to the 1987 edition. I have generally referred to this edition since it is now the most accessible one.
3. Lakoff's model distinguishes between distance and deference. I have not done so since the strategies which express each appear to substantially overlap. Moreover Lakoff (1979: 66) elaborates the continuum into a three-dimensional rhombus-shape but confines its value to a 'representation of style as a whole'.
4. Solidarity is Brown & Gilman's term (1960), while Lakoff (1975) uses 'camaraderie', and Brown & Levinson (1978, 1987) refer to 'positive politeness'. Similarly Brown & Gilman use 'power', where Lakoff refers to 'deference'. Brown & Levinson's 'negative politeness' relates to the expression of both distance and power.
5. Where examples are constructed or reconstructed after the event I have indicated this by the use of quotation marks and conventional orthography. Though the sense of such examples is accurate, the precise form of the linguistic expressions used cannot be guaranteed. Where examples are exact transcriptions of interactions recorded on tape or in writing at the time they occurred, / and // are used to record two degrees of pause length.
6. Note, for example Labov's statement that 'really can be described as a "cognitive zero"' (1984: 44).

7. Deuchar (1987) suggests that women's tendency to use more standard and prestigious phonological variants than men (a pattern found also in New Zealand (Bayard (1987)) reflects women's concern with protecting their own positive face, rather than with the addressee's face needs. One would need to examine in detail, however, the shifts involved according to different addressees. The reality seems likely to be very complex. See, for example, Bell (1984) on the complex effects of audience factors on speech style.

8. In the new introduction to the re-publication of their (1978) paper Brown & Levinson (1987: 18) acknowledge this point: 'positive politeness, which is relevant to all aspects of a person's positive face, is quite a different phenomenon from negative politeness which is specific for the particular FTA in hand'. They argue, however, that this difference is 'not . . . incompatible with a systematic use in once case vs. another' (Brown & Levinson 1987: 18).

9. Some linguists have included referential meaning in their analytical models, e.g. Halliday (1985), Crystal & Davy (1975) and Östmann (1981). Other researchers have paid it less attention. Brown & Gilman (1960), Brown & Levinson (1978, 1987), and Giles, Scherer & Taylor (1979) all tend to focus on social-psychological aspects of interaction, for example. James (1983) provides a useful review of the analysis of meaning from these two points of view.

10. Note, for example, Jones' (1980: 194) discussion of the functions of gossip defined as a 'way of talking between women in their roles as women, intimate in style, personal and domestic in topic and setting'.

11. I suspect this is the reason why Shimanoff (1977) found no difference in the level of politeness expressed by women and men in her study: i.e. she was analysing speech from relatively formal transactional exchanges.

12. The data was collected by observers noting down the exact words used in compliment exchanges together with full contextual details (see Holmes, 1986a).

13. Brown (1980) reports that women in the highly sex-segregated Tenajapan society also use more politeness devices, both positive and negative, than men. While in Tenajapan society the explanation appears to relate to the subordinate status of women, I suggest below (following Maltz & Borker, 1982) that the different socialisation patterns of girls and boys provide a more satisfactory explanation in western society.

14. See Section VB of the annotated bibliography in Thorne, Kramarae & Henley (1983) for studies dealing with amount of talk, and Section VC for studies on female–male interruption patterns.

15. As noted above (Note 3), Lakoff's model distinguishes distance from deference. She claims men use distance strategies more than women, and women use deference strategies more than men do. Since these strategies overlap extensively — for instance, both are included in Brown & Levinson's inventory of negative politeness strategies — it is difficult to see how one would investigate this claim. In the research reviewed in this paper, for instance, it is apparent that women use negative politeness strategies more often then men. My interpretation of the significance of this pattern is clearly different from Lakoff's.

References

ARIES, ELIZABETH J. 1982, Verbal and non-verbal behaviour in single-sex and mixed-sex groups: are traditional sex roles changing? *Psychological Reports* 51(1), 127–34.

AUSTIN, PADDY J. M. 1988, The dark side of politeness: a pragmatic analysis of non-cooperative communication. Unpublished PhD dissertation. Christchurch: University of Canterbury.

BAYARD, DONN 1987, Class and change in New Zealand English: a summary report. *Te Reo* 30, 3–36.

BELL, ALLAN 1984, Language style as audience design. *Language in Society* 13(1), 145–204.

BROWN, PENELOPE 1980, How and why are women more polite: some evidence from a Mayan community. In SALLY MCCONNELL-GINET, RUTH BORKER and NELLY FURMAN (eds) *Women and Language in Literature and Society* (pp. 111–36). New York: Praeger.

BROWN, PENELOPE and LEVINSON, STEPHEN 1978, Universals in language usage: politeness phenomena. In ESTHER N. GOODY (ed.) *Questions and Politeness: Strategies in Social Interaction* (pp. 56–289). Cambridge: Cambridge University Press.

—1987, *Politeness: Some Universals in Language Usage.* Cambridge: Cambridge University Press.

BROWN, ROGER W. and GILMAN, ALBERT 1960, The pronouns of power and solidarity. In THOMAS A. SEBEOK (ed.) *Style in Language* (pp. 253–76). Cambridge, Massachusetts: MIT Press.

CAMERON, DEBORAH 1985, *Feminism and Linguistic Theory.* London: Macmillan.

CAMERON, DEBORAH, MCALINDEN, FIONA and O'LEARY, KATHY 1988, Lakoff in context. In JENNIFER COATES and DEBORAH CAMERON (eds) *Women in their Speech Communities.* London: Longman.

COATES, JENNIFER 1987, Epistemic modality and spoken discourse. *Transactions of the Philological Society* 110–31.

—1988, Gossip revisited: language in all-female groups. In JENNIFER COATES and DEBORAH CAMERON (eds) *Women in their Speech Communities.* London: Longman.

COUPLAND, NIKOLAS, GRAINGER, KAREN and COUPLAND, JUSTINE 1988, Politeness in context: intergenerational issues. *Language in Society* 17(2), 253–62.

COUPLAND, NIKOLAS, COUPLAND, JUSTINE, GILES, HOWARD and HENWOOD, KAREN 1988, Accommodating the elderly: invoking and extending a theory. *Language in Society* 17(1), 1–41.

CRYSTAL, DAVID and DAVY, DEREK 1975, *Advanced Conversational English.* London: Longman.

DEUCHAR, MARGARET 1987, Sociolinguistics. In JOHN LYONS, RICHARD COATES, MARGARET DEUCHAR and GERALD GAZDAR (eds) *New Horizons in Linguistics 2* (pp. 296–310). Harmondsworth: Penguin.

EAKINS, BARBARA and EAKINS, GENE 1979, Verbal turn-taking and exchanges in faculty dialogue. In BETTY-LOU DUBOIS and ISOBEL CROUCH (eds) *The Sociology of the Languages of American Women* (pp. 53–62). San Antonio, Texas: Trinity University.

EDELSKY, CAROLE 1981, Who's got the floor? *Language in Society* 10(4), 383–421.

FISHMAN, PAMELA M. 1983, Interaction: the work women do. In BARRIE THORNE,

CHERIS KRAMARAE and NANCY HENLEY (eds) *Language, Gender and Society* (pp. 89–102). Rowley, Mass.: Newbury House.

GILES, HOWARD (ed.) 1984, *The Dynamics of Speech Accommodation. International Journal of the Sociology of Language* 46.

GILES, HOWARD, SCHERER, KLAUS R. and TAYLOR, DONALD M. 1979, Speech markers in social interaction. In KLAUS R. SCHERER and HOWARD GILES (eds) *Social Markers in Speech* (pp. 343–81). Cambridge: Cambridge University Press.

GILES, HOWARD, TAYLOR, DONALD M. and BOURHIS, RICHARD 1973, Towards a theory of interpersonal accommodation through language: some Canadian data. *Language in Society* 2(2), 177–92.

GOODWIN, MARJORIE HARNESS 1980, Directive response sequences in girls' and boys' task activities. In SALLY McCONNELL-GINET, RUTH BORKER and NELLY FURMAN (eds) *Women and Language in Literature and Society* (pp. 157–73). New York: Praeger.

GUMPERZ, JOHN J. 1982, *Discourse Strategies*. Cambridge: Cambridge University Press.

HALLIDAY, MICHAEL A. K. 1985, *An Introduction to Functional Grammar*. London: Arnold.

HARRIS, ROY 1981, *The Language Myth*. London: Duckworth.

HOLMES, JANET 1983, Speaking English with the appropriate degree of conviction. In CHRISTOPHER BRUMFIT (ed.) *Learning and Teaching Languages for Communication: Applied Linguistic Perspectives* (pp. 100–13). London: Centre for Information on Language Teaching and Research.

—1984, Hedging your bets and sitting on the fence: some evidence for hedges as support structures. *Te Reo* 27, 47–62.

—1985, Sex differences and miscommunication: some data from New Zealand. In JOHN B. PRIDE (ed.) *Cross-cultural Encounters: Communication and Miscommunication* (pp. 24–43). Melbourne: River Seine.

—1986a, Compliments and compliment responses in New Zealand English. *Anthropological Linguistics* 28(4), 485–508.

—1986b, Functions of *you know* in women's and men's speech. *Language in Society* 15(1), 1–22.

—1988a, *Of course*: a pragmatic particle in New Zealand women's and men's speech. *Australian Journal of Linguistics* 8(1), 49–74.

—1988b, Paying compliments: a sex-preferential positive politeness strategy. *Journal of Pragmatics* 12(3), 445–65.

—1989a, Sex differences and apologies: one aspect of communicative competence. *Applied Linguistics* 10(2), 82–101.

—1989b, *Sort of* in New Zealand women's and men's speech. *Studia Linguistica* 42(2), 85–121.

—1990a, Apologies in New Zealand English. *Language in Society* 19(2).

—1990b, New Zealand women are good to talk to. *Journal of Pragmatics*, 13(4).

HYMES, DELL 1979, Sapir, competence, voices. In CHARLES J. FILLMORE, DANIEL KEMPLER and WILLIAM S-Y. WANG (eds) *Individual Differences in Language Ability and Language Behaviour* (pp. 33–45). New York: Academic Press.

JAMES, ALLAN R. 1983, Compromisers in English: a cross-disciplinary approach to their interpersonal significance. *Journal of Pragmatics* 7(1), 191–206.

JOHNSON, JANET L. 1980, Questions and role responsibility in four professional meetings. *Anthropological Linguistics* 22(1), 66–76.

JONES, DEBBIE 1980, Gossip: notes on women's oral culture. In CHERIS KRAMARAE (ed.) *The Voices and Words of Women and Men* (pp. 193–8). Oxford: Pergamon Press.

KALCIK, SUSAN 1975, '. . . like Ann's gynaecologist or the time I was almost raped' — personal narratives in women's rap groups. *Journal of American Folklore* 88(1), 3–11.

KUIPER, KOENRAAD, Sporting formulae in New Zealand English; two models of male solidarity. In JENNY CHESHIRE (ed.) *English Around the World: Sociolinguistic Perspectives*. Cambridge: Cambridge University Press.

LABOV, WILLIAM 1984, Intensity. In DEBORAH SCHIFFRIN (ed.), *Meaning, Form and Use in Context: Linguistic Applications, Georgetown University Round Table on Languages and Linguistics* (pp. 43–70). Washington DC: Georgetown University Press.

LAKOFF, ROBIN T. 1972, Language in context. *Language* 48(4), 907–27.

—1973a, Language and woman's place. *Language in Society* 2(1), 45–79.

—1973b, The logic of politeness. In CLAUDIA CORUM, CEDRIC SMITH-STARK and ANN WEISER (eds), *Papers from the Ninth Regional Meeting of the Chicago Linguistic Society* (pp. 292–305). Chicago: Chicago Linguistic Society.

—1975, *Language and Woman's Place*. New York: Harper and Row.

—1977, Women's language. *Language and Style* 10(4), 222–48.

—1979, Stylistic strategies within a grammar of style. In JUDITH O. ORASANU, M. SLATER and LEONORE A. ADLER (eds) *Language, Sex and Gender. Annals of the New York Academy of Science* 327, 53–78.

—1980, Psychoanalytic discourse and ordinary conversation. In ROGER W. SHUY and ANNA SCHNUKAL (eds) *Language Use and the Uses of Language* (pp. 269–87). Washington, DC: Georgetown University Press.

LANE, CHRIS 1988, Language on trial: questioning strategies and European-Polynesian miscommunication in New Zealand courtrooms. Unpublished PhD dissertation. Auckland: University of Auckland.

MALTZ, DANIEL N. and BORKER, RUTH. A. 1982, A cultural approach to male-female miscommunication. In JOHN J. GUMPERZ (ed.) *Language and Social Identity* (pp. 196–216). Cambridge: Cambridge University Press.

MEYERHOFF, MIRIAM 1986, The kind of women who put '-ish' behind everything and 'sort of' in front of it — a study of sex differences in New Zealand English. Unpublished MA dissertation. Wellington: Victoria University.

—1987, A review of sex and language research in New Zealand. In ANNE PAUWELS (ed.) *Language, Gender and Society in Australia and New Zealand* (pp. 32–44). Melbourne: River Seine.

OLSHTAIN, ELITE and COHEN, ANDREW D. 1983, Apology: a speech act set. In NESSA WOLFSON and ELLIOT JUDD (eds) *Sociolinguistics and Language Acquisition* (pp. 18–35). Rowley, Mass.: Newbury House.

ÖSTMAN, JAN-OLA 1981, *'You know': a Discourse-Functional Approach*. Amsterdam: John Benjamins.

OWEN, MARION 1983, *Apologies and Remedial Interchanges: a Study of Language Use in Social Interaction*. Berlin: Mouton, Walter de Gruyter.

PHILLIPS, JOCK O. C. 1980, Mummy's boys: Pakeha men and male culture in New Zealand. In PHILLIDA BUNKLE and BERYL HUGHES (eds) *Women in New Zealand Society* (pp. 217–43). Sydney: George Allen & Unwin.

—1987, *A Man's Country — the Image of the Pakeha Male: a History*. Auckland: Penguin.

PREISLER, BENT 1986, *Linguistic Sex Roles in Conversation*. Berlin: Mouton de Gruyter.

RITCHIE, JANE and RITCHIE, JAMES 1978, *Growing Up in New Zealand*. Sydney: Allen & Unwin.

SCOLLON, RON and SCOLLON, SUZANNE B. K. 1981, *Narrative Literacy and Face in Interethnic Communication*. Norwood, New Jersey: Ablex.

SHIMANOFF, SUSAN B. 1977, Investigating politeness. In ELINOR O. KEENAN and DINA BENNET (eds) *Discourse across Time and Space* (pp. 213–41). Los Angeles: University of Southern California Press.

SMITH, PHILIP 1985, *Language, the Sexes and Society*. Oxford: Basil Blackwell.

THOMAS, JENNY 1985, The language of power: towards a dynamic pragmatics. *Journal of Pragmatics* 9(6), 765–83.

—1988, Discourse control in confrontational situations. In LESLIE HICKEY (ed.), *Pragmatics of Style*. London: Croom Helm.

THORNE, BARRIE, KRAMARAE, CHERIS and HENLEY, NANCY (eds) 1983, *Language, Gender and Society*. Rowley, Mass.: Newbury House.

TROSBORG, ANNA 1987, Apology strategies in natives/non-natives. *Journal of Pragmatics* 11(1), 147–67.

TURNER, LYNN H. and HENZL, SALLY A. 1982, Language utilised in rationalising conflict decisions: is there a different voice? *Research Report* 143: University of Illinois. ERIC document: ED 260467.

WODAK, RUTH 1981, Women relate, men report: sex differences in language behaviour in a therapeutic group. *Journal of Pragmatics* 5(2–3), 261–85.

WOLFSON, NESSA 1983, An empirically based analysis of complimenting in American English. In NESSA WOLFSON and ELLIOT JUDD (eds) *Sociolinguistics and Language Acquisition* (pp. 82–95). Rowley, Mass.: Newbury House.

—1984, Pretty is as pretty does. *Applied Linguistics* 5(3), 236–44.

13 Politeness revisited — the dark side

PADDY AUSTIN

Introduction

This paper examines non-co-operative[1] or impolite behaviour which is used in situations where the speaker has something to gain by maintaining power asymmetries or social distance in relation to the hearer. The variables which give rise to the choice of impolite over polite strategies are discussed, and some examples of face attack strategies are analysed.

The choice of the title 'the Dark Side' is drawn from the movie *Star Wars*, where there is a force for good which is taken and corrupted for the purposes of evil (Kuiper, 1988). The analogy is strong. Face attack is often, in fact, an application of the same principles which are used for face preservation, and many of the strategies for the one can be co-opted for the other. What causes utterances to be interpreted on the dark side is the context in which they are produced. This crucially includes the hearer's assumptions about the speaker's values, opinions and intentions, as well as other discernible clues like the physical environment, visual and kinesic clues from the speaker or other audience members.

Firstly, we consider a definition of face. Goffman (1967: 5) says:

> The term face may be defined as the positive social value a person effectively claims for himself by the line others assume he has taken during a particular contact.

Brown & Levinson (1987: 62), in their work on universals of politeness, define face in two ways:

> negative face: the want of every 'competent adult member' that his actions be unimpeded by others.

277

positive face: the want of every member that his wants be desirable to at least some others.

I distinguish between positive and negative face in the following way:

Positive face is the desire of the individual to have a recognised value in the society in which she lives. The individual needs to know about her standing in relation to others, including others' opinion of the individual, and the relative status of the individual and others. The derivative needs of this general desire are the need to be liked, to have one's needs appreciated, to have one's value ranked as highly as possible — in other words to maintain a self esteem.

Negative face constitutes the other element of the desire for a place in society. Here the desire is for an imposition-free space, wherein the individual can maintain self esteem and freedom of action within the general boundaries set by society. The individual needs to be able to assess her freedom to act or to refrain from acting, depending on preference, responsibility or external constraints. Derivative needs include the desire to be free from coercion, imposition and constraint within the space the individual claims for herself, or that society allows. (Austin, 1988: 3)

Face is a constant in interaction. There may be other, more immediate motivations for communicating, but considerations of face are always part of the social aspect of interaction. Goffman (1967: 36) states that face-orientation can be seen as the traffic rules of interaction; particularly in situations where there is some social reason why participants feel their face is at risk, or where they feel some face threat, they will find that considerations of face may well override the communicative purpose of the interaction. In such cases, extreme sensitivity to, and knowledge of, face-oriented strategies is indispensable to the hearer in maintenance of some degree of composure.

Face Attack

In the model of face attack[2] which I have constructed, I assume that the speaker intends to communicate, and rationally chooses a means to achieve the communicative end, but I do not assume that what the speaker wants to communicate is necessarily or always co-operative. There are many interactional situations where the basic assumption will be that the speaker may not, and probably will not, want to co-operate, as it is not necessarily mutual interest which governs the conduct of interaction, but can frequently be the interest of only one participant or group of participants.

The 'dark side' to politeness is characterised by acts which I have identified and call Face Attack Acts. I define Face Attack Acts as those communicative acts which are injurious to the hearer's positive or negative face, and are introduced in a situation which could have been avoided, but where their inclusion is perceived by the hearer to be intentional. This may or may not be true, as the speaker may just be being clumsy, but the perception of intentionality is readily accessible.

In my model of face attack, certain assumptions fundamental to Brown & Levinson's (1987) model of politeness cannot be held. These are that the speaker wants or needs to maintain the hearer's face, that the hearer poses a threat to the speaker's face, and that the speaker cares what the hearer does in retaliation. The more an act threatens either participant's face, the more the speaker will need to consider going off-record, or doing the Face Attack Act with redressive action which is inappropriate.

Power, Solidarity and Group Membership

The major variable involved in the decision whether or not to save face is power. The power variable is the one which, more than others, allows an individual to be humiliating and coercive without fear of retribution. People cannot always be expected to defend their face when threatened, since the consequences of this could be more damaging than the face attack in other areas such as job security, employment prospects and physical safety. In the case of sexual harassment, for instance, a verbal approximation of the physical threat involved will be immensely face threatening on a continuum ranging from flirtatious remarks to blackmail or coercion. In Example 1 below, the recipient will have to balance the potential threat to face and her possible retribution against several very real alternative threats which may cause her to suffer the insult in silence.

EXAMPLE 1

A: I was discussing my work in a public setting, when a professor cut me off and asked me if I had freckles all over my body.[3]

Because of the complete irrelevance of the professor's remark to the subject of the preceding discourse, the hearer has no choice but to assume that there is a message intended for her quite apart from the academic purpose of the meeting. That this is sexual is clear because of the reference to all of her body in a situation where this cannot be expected to be of any relevance at all. The fact that he has asked this overtly face-threatening question without any fear of retribution shows his awareness of his power. The power differential between the professor and A causes the latter to suffer the humiliation without retaliating, since the consequences of publicly challenging his remark are potentially damaging to her academic progress.

Solidarity, or the degree of intimacy which interactants share, is a variable in strategy choice. In some cases, solidarity is so great that the individuals concerned will tolerate Face Attack Acts which would otherwise cause a lot of hurt, particularly among groups such as families and participants in intimate relationships. An interesting case here is the group which is somehow differentiated from, and sometimes under threat by the outside world, so that solidarity is of the utmost importance. In this situation, members will go to great lengths to hold together the group membership, and will tolerate a great deal from other members. In other cases, solidarity may actually rest on the necessity of destroying the face of another person or group.[4]

Note that there is an interaction between the power and solidarity factors. A person with more power has greater freedom to adjust the solidarity variable up and down the scale, so that the less powerful person is unsure where that variable actually rests. This can be seen in situations where there is a certain amount of intimacy shown on one occasion, which the less powerful person might continue on the next occasion, only to be rebuffed by a redefinition of their intimacy towards distance again.

EXAMPLE 2

A: This is my associate, Jim.
B: Yes, Mrs Wright and I have worked together for some time now.

The message given by B in this constructed example is that A has misjudged the degree of intimacy between them, and that B is the one who is empowered to make the decisions about their degree of intimacy. B has publicly declared that A's judgement is wrong and that, no matter what the details of their professional relationship are, he is the one with the power to redefine that relationship. Given the exchange in Example 2 it is difficult to imagine A as the one who can make those decisions.

Group membership is particularly important from the perspective of sexist language, as language is a powerful tool available for use by men to keep women out of influential positions and membership of elites. There are many ways of reinforcing a woman's out-group status. They include differential naming practices, use of in-group jargon, and jokes. As I have mentioned, one group's very existence can sometimes depend on keeping a threatening person or group of people out, and sometimes a very useful way of consolidating one's own group membership is to push someone else publicly out of the group. In Example 2 above, Jim may well derive status in his group from being the powerful group member who determines who is to be accorded status within the group.

Types of Face Attack Acts

The rational speaker will choose the means to convey the face attack[5] most efficiently, including those strategies which redress or mitigate the attack if necessary. Redressive actions, whether polite or not, need not be verbal, and in face attack behaviour, they may often be suprasegmental or kinesic (intimate/warning tones; winks and leers). The more effort the speaker expends in face-saving strategies, in a face-saving framework, the more the speaker communicates the desire to satisfy the hearer's face wants. This is not true of face attack behaviour, where the use of ostensible face-saving strategies inappropriately is interpreted as a face attack. The speaker is trying to draw attention to the face-threatening aspects of the interaction, and to reinforce them in an indirect manner.

Bald on-record

This is the strategy which pays minimal attention to the hearer's face wants. The speaker recognises the hearer's positive face needs, but does not orient to them, therefore performs the Face Attack Act baldly, without redress. The effect of this is to insult the hearer or to appear to do so. It is more common in face-attack than in face-saving behaviour, but even so, there are likely to be more effective ways of attacking face than bald on-record attacks, which are the most likely of all the strategies to be seen as rude. They will appear only in situations where the risk to the speaker's face in the event of miscalculated situational variables is very small. However, they do occur, especially in asymmetric power groupings. Here, the need to minimise face threat will be seen as less important than the need to reinforce certain affective aspects of the interaction.

Bald on-record threats to positive face

The speaker attacks positive face by being irreverent, or talking on taboo topics. Here we include reference to sexual characteristics (especially derogatory references to the hearer's sexual characteristics). Bodily functions may be referred to, or beliefs and values which the hearer is known to hold may be introduced in a derogatory way. An example of this strategy is taken from an interaction I had with a member of the business community. Towards the end of what I had seen as a knowledgeable and informed discussion, the following exchange took place:

EXAMPLE 3

A: Now that will be Miss, won't it?
B: No, Ms.
A: Oh, one of *those*.

The hearer is likely to and, in fact, I did recover the following assumptions:

(1) I have said that my title is *Ms*.
(2) A has replied that I belong to a specific group.

The hearer accesses that particular utterance which is formulaic, and therefore indexed in the lexicon with information like this:[6]

(3) A has used a formula which has derogatory connotations.

This assumption leads to the following two assumptions:

(4) A would not use such a formula about a group he respected.
(5) A is indicating a lack of respect for people who use the title *Ms*.

The hearer's knowledge of interactional conventions such as politeness strategies leads her to the following assumptions:

(6) Furthermore, A is indicating this in a joking and blatant fashion.
(7) A is being overtly derogatory.

The hearer's knowledge of the interaction of the power variable with derogation and insult lead her to the conclusion:

(8) He would not do so unless he had sufficient power to be confident of freedom from risk of retribution.

Such an interpretation leads to discomfort in further interaction with that speaker, and therefore constrains the hearer's behaviour in some way. Either the hearer will feel uncomfortable in the future, or will feel obliged to avoid interactions with the speaker, in which case she may miss out on some other benefits which might accrue from interacting with him.

On-record without redress to negative face

The speaker does not orient to the hearer's negative face, although the speaker recognises the hearer's need. The speaker impinges, makes impositions, without redress. This is directly coercive behaviour, as seen in the following constructed example.

EXAMPLE 4 *A male executive says to an obviously busy female colleague*

Make the tea will you, Jill?

Since Jill is busy, and her male colleague knows this, there is no reason why she should be asked to make the tea. The male colleague may be known for getting others to do such things, or he may be known to hold views about gender roles in this respect. The hearer will then interpret the question as either a general coercion, or one that is linked to her gender. If the latter interpretation is made, this will be a multi-layered face attack, which involves coercion to a certain sort of behaviour, with the added coercion to conform to a stereotype, which may or may not be offensive to the hearer.

On-record with inappropriate redress

Here, the speaker uses redressive strategies, ostensibly to save the hearer's face in some way. However, the nature of the interaction, or the nature of the relationship between the speaker and the hearer should ordinarily preclude the need for such redress. This is a doubly face-attacking strategy, in that it not only causes the hearer to feel a decrease in self-esteem, but also invites conjecture as to the reason for the speaker's perceived concessions to the hearer's face. This points to facts about the social relationship between the speaker and the hearer which are obviously different from those perceived by the hearer, and the hearer's possible misinterpretation of the nature of that relationship can in itself be humiliating and/or coercive.

On-record with inappropriate redress to positive face

The speaker orients to the hearer's positive face where circumstances render such orientation inappropriate. This strategy involves the use of an ostensibly polite hedge or qualification to a face attack which should not have needed any redress. The speaker may go off-record (i.e. be indirect) where there is a genuine case for more direct, efficient communication. Any redress given by the speaker is marked and gives rise to assumptions about the affective nature of the relationship. The effect of this is patronising and condescending or perceived to be intended that way. Example 4 above, re-cast in a different way, exemplifies this:

EXAMPLE 5 *A male executive says to an obviously busy female colleague*

Would you mind making the tea today while Mrs B is away, Jill? You'd be much quicker at it than me.

The attack on face lies in the fact that the hearer is aware that the imposition is unjustified. In spite of this, he includes a redressive strategy which is not only inappropriate, but reinforces the sexist nature of the original face attack. If the speaker uses redressive strategies, the hearer will interpret such behaviour in one of the following ways:

(1) The speaker has different ideas from the hearer about appropriate behaviour — no offence.
(2) The speaker thinks that the hearer is not capable of withstanding bald on-record utterances.
(3) The speaker is trying to redefine the relationship in a way which is harmful to the hearer's interests.

The result of the hearer's interpretation in the second and third of these cases will be some loss in self-esteem or self-image and, as with the bald on-record stategies, this will modify the hearer's future behaviour with regard to the speaker, thus having a coercive side-effect. An example of this strategy can be seen when the speaker comments admiringly on the hearer's appearance, abilities or character where these are either already known or are irrelevant to the discourse in hand.

EXAMPLE 6

> You have been a capable and decorative chairman.
> (*Where the speaker is a local authority councillor, and the specific*
> *addressee is the female chairing that authority*.)

On the surface it seems like a straightforward compliment, and indeed
may have been both intended that way, and interpreted likewise.
Brown & Levinson's model of politeness would require that it is seen as
a positive politeness strategy. The insulting nature of the comment will
be recovered by an enrichment of the context. In this case, several other
factors are unavoidably brought to the hearer's attention and also to that
of the wider audience, the readers of the local newspaper reporting the
incident. The councillor is speaking in support of a vote of no confidence
in the chairperson, and the utterance quoted above is a preface to a list
of reasons why the chairperson should step down.

In this context, the interpretation is likely to follow this path:

(1) He is telling me that he has an opinion of me. ⸜

(2) The opinion is that I have certain qualities — capability and
decorativeness.

The assumption in (2) quite clearly causes difficulty in interpretation,
since the second epithet does not connect up with salient assumptions
about a council chairperson, and the first contradicts assumptions strongly
held and highly salient to the audience, who are aware of the power
struggle involved.

(3) If he thinks I am capable, then why the vote of no confidence?

At this point, the utterance fails to achieve relevance. The audience must
go to the rest of the utterance in the hope that there will be an increase
in contextual effects gained by doing so. The second part of the utterance
does provide much greater effect, in terms of a revelation of the speaker's
attitude to the specific audience.

(4) He has the opinion of me that I am also decorative.

Here, the audience accesses information about decorativeness, which
includes no immediate link between that quality and the function of
chairing a council.

(5) Decorativeness is not a necessary quality of a local authority
chairperson.

(6) Decorativeness is usually a quality of women, art, etc.

(7) He is drawing attention to the fact that I am a woman.

Here, the audience would have gained insufficient contextual enrichment owing to the lack of an immediate clue as to the relevance of 'woman' in this context. The most fruitful method of gaining that enrichment seems to be to pursue the speaker's likely reasons for making that link. The audience will search for any information available on the councillor's views about women, or the place of women in relation to that particular council (that they are under-represented, that they are often spoken about in humiliating ways, or other related information).

(8) My being a woman is a significant fact, apart from my being capable.

(9) He is suggesting that I am capable, for a woman; or that my capability lies in my decorativeness.

(10) He is diminishing my importance as a local body politician.

Since what is at stake is the woman's ability to continue in her position of power, the most likely conclusion must be:

(11) He is attacking my position of power and influence.

Notice that this is one possible interpretation of the utterance, which may or may not have been the one intended by the speaker, or accessed by the audience. The crucial deciding factor must be the contexts available to the audience, and there may be some cut-off points earlier in the analysis, dictated by the actual context available to individual audiences. However, the interpretation of the utterance as a straightforward compliment has to be unacceptable on the grounds that some information irrelevant to the situation was introduced.

The concept of salience is crucial in predicting the manner in which such an interpretation will proceed. If assumptions about the speaker's attitude to women, or to that particular woman, are highly salient, it is likely that some of the earlier steps in the above interpretation will be bypassed, and that the search will begin at a point like (7) above.

On-record with inappropriate redress to negative face

The speaker orients to the hearer's negative face where familiarity would be appropriate. This is distancing behaviour. Once again, this strategy has an off-record element, in that the ostensible politeness can be interpreted as genuine, especially as the features of negative politeness, as noted by Brown & Levinson (1987: 130), are those most typically associated with the social notion of 'politeness' as a whole, at least in some societies. As a face attack strategy, it is typically used in situations where the hearer has either good reason to believe that there is a sufficient level of intimacy or a small enough power asymmetry that a more casual, friendly style could have been expected. In other words, the speaker is redefining the social distance variable in particular, but as a consequence, also the power variable. The speaker is intimating, for instance, that although the hearer has good reason to assess distance as low, for some reason — possibly a situational increase in power for the speaker, or a miscalculation by the hearer of the level of imposition — the speaker needs to make a greater distance between them. Example 2 is a good example of such a strategy.

Another form of inappropriate redress to negative face is the avoidance of material, ostensibly to save the face of a hearer or group of hearers, where such avoidance is either unnecessary or draws attention to the characteristics which differentiate this hearer or group of hearers.

EXAMPLE 7 *At a social gathering organised by a men's service club for members of both genders, the after-dinner speaker says:*

> I was going to talk about (passage of technical jargon concerning electricity), but then I thought that the women won't be interested in anything past the switch on the wall, so . . .

The audience to that utterance are aware that there are few if any people in the room of either gender who know much about electricity. Therefore, the interpretation will go this way:

(1) The speaker has announced that he is avoiding a particular topic.
(2) The reason for this is that there are women in the audience.
(3) There are also men in the audience who have no knowledge about electricity.
(4) The speaker is not including them in the group of people without knowledge.
(5) This is because of some assumption he holds about women.

Given the knowledge of the speaker's area of expertise, and the sort of technical talk he is likely to give, the following assumptions are accessible:

(6) He assumes that women cannot understand technical language.
(7) He assumes that men are capable of understanding technical language.

Since there is nothing in the audience's encyclopaedic information which explains this disparity, the following assumption is readily accessed:

(8) He assumes that men are more intelligent than women.

Both of these forms of the strategy are coercive to the hearer, in that they give a warning that the hearer must adjust behaviour in order to meet the social requirements of the situation. They can also be humiliating, because the hearer has publicly calculated power and distance variables and has been publicly shown that the calculation is wrong.

Interestingly, the interpretation of Example 7 in the actual context of occurrence varied widely among the audience present. This variation nicely illustrates the importance of assumptions salient in the individual's cognitive environment. Some older women saw nothing strange in his utterance at all, since they had as some of their cultural assumptions that men are more capable of understanding technical language than women. Note that this strategy can be quite easily defended as politeness, given that our society has a perception that maintaining wide social distance is a polite way to behave. In Example 7 the speaker is ostensibly being careful not to exclude a group of people from the interaction, whereas in fact he is excluding them by the inapproriate redress.

Off-record

In selecting any of the strategies described above, the speaker begins with an estimation of risk. In a model of face attack, the speaker will be concerned with personal risk, rather than the risk of threatening the hearer's face. The more the speaker feels at risk from challenge or retribution, the more likely it is that the strategy chosen will in some way mask the face attack intention, or push it underground, as it were. The strategies decrease in riskiness the more they move towards ostensible redress (a form of off-recordness), and those which can be categorised as completely off-record.

Off-record face attacks rely on the hearer's ability to recover implicatures from what is said. The actual face attack is not recoverable from just the utterance itself, but relies heavily on the context, and the participants' mutual experience. In fact, there is no clear cut-off point between on-record and off-record face attacks, because even in on-record strategies, there are elements recovered from the context which determine whether or not the hearer will interpret them as attacks or not.

First, we examine some of the types of utterance which can be subsumed under the heading 'off-record'.

Hints, allusions

Here, the hints will draw attention to some fact or set of opinions/values about which the hearer is known to have strong opinions. The focusing of attention on these facts will be motivated by the desire to attack the hearer's face in some public or private way.

EXAMPLE 8

No danger of paternity suits now, huh?
(*Where the hearer is known to want to keep his recent vasectomy a secret.*)

Irony

Because of its echoic nature, irony is often expressed in a form which, if used sincerely, would be perfectly non-ironic. This gives a possible 'out' to the speaker.

EXAMPLE 9

No, no — go ahead. White carpet is boring and the red spots really improve it.
(*Where the carpet is new, and the hearer has just spilt red wine on it.*)

Co-Occurrence of Positive and Negative Face Behaviour

There is no mutual incompatibility between the effects of threats to positive face and those to negative face. All attacks on positive face (humiliation) have a secondary effect of coercion, as a humiliated hearer can be constrained to a small range of options for further behaviour. The hearer can ignore the attack, and attempt further interactions from the same starting point as before the attack, thus risking further attacks. The hearer can accept a redefined role in relation to the speaker for all further interactions, or until the speaker redefines the relationship again, thus surrendering the leading role completely to the speaker. The hearer can avoid interactions with the speaker, thus possibly sacrificing other rewards from situations in which the speaker is likely to be present.

The humiliation will increase, if the interaction is in a public situation (i.e. before an audience of others) because of the proportionate increase in face loss. An individual's perception of her acceptance by others is what constitutes positive face, so it follows that if face is lost, the degree of humiliation increases in proportion to the number of people who witness the face loss. Since the separation of positive and negative face is not possible, the coercive aspect of face loss is subject to similar effects. Attacks on negative face (coercion) involve humiliation, since they cause the hearer to lose at least some measure of self-esteem as a result of having to accept the attack without the possibility of retribution. In many cases the negative attack makes known to at least the hearer and possibly an audience that the hearer has miscalculated facts about the social relationship, like degrees of power, and social distance. Otherwise the attack will make public the real definition of those social facts in the speaker's estimation, and if the hearer does not retaliate for any reason, this makes public the fact that the hearer accepts the speaker's definition of the variables.

The Importance of Context

Notice that there will be some situations where what I have used to exemplify face attack is seen as quite unexceptionable in face terms. The fact is that there is no motivated and general way in which realisations of strategies can be assigned uniquely to one illocutionary force. The context in which the participants in a given interaction operate is what dictates the most fruitful direction of the interpretation process. This context will include some of the following information:

(1) previous interactions between these participants;
(2) immediately preceding utterances;
(3) encyclopaedic information available to the participants, mutual or otherwise;
(4) clues from the physical environment, including the physical behaviour of the participants.

The fact that many of the strategies used for co-operative means are equally appropriate for non-co-operative communication means that co-operation cannot be a principle constantly underlying interaction. Rather it is one of a number of assumptions, along with those assumptions which encode all the social facts about politeness and face attention, to which a hearer has access in determining the social implications of her interactions with others. Even in the weakest sense, Grice's (1975) Co-operative Principle, which requires a mutually accepted direction, cannot be upheld in a model of face attack, and we would not want to say as a result that face attack is not really communication.[7]

Elsewhere, (Austin, 1988) I have examined in depth the ways in which the function of the context can be formalised to account for face-oriented behaviour. I have applied the principles of Sperber & Wilson's (1986) Relevance Theory to these types of interactions, and have come up with an explanatory account of the way in which face-oriented discourse communicates information about the social relationships between interactants, and connects these relationships with wider social structures. Such an approach offers a motivated analysis of various manifestations of non-co-operative communication in society, and integrates the recovery of sociolinguistic information with the interpretive process.

Conclusion

Analysis of the interpretation of face attack in this way is of great value in providing justification for the continuing struggle to eliminate interactional phenomena such as sexist communication.[8] In showing how hearers recover information about their relative power and group-membership status in interactions, and in linking these perceptions to subsequent freedom to act, we can show how sexist communication has a negative effect on recipients.

In effect, what this approach shows about politeness and its dark side is that face attention exists on a continuum from polite to impolite, and realisations of impoliteness strategies cannot be regarded as uncommon aberrations. The construction of a model which attempts to impose a taxonomic structure on realisations of face attention is doomed to failure because of the resistance of utterances to categorisation in terms of illocutionary force. The importance of the context in assigning illocutionary force to individual utterances means that the explanation of face attention and its interpretation must be handled differently.

It is far more fruitful to approach the problem from the other angle, looking at the interpretation of utterances, and what causes hearers to arrive at the interpretations they do. Using Relevance Theory as a basis for this analysis, it is possible to predict not only what information hearers will extract from utterances, but also how they will relate the information to crucial facts about their face-status with regard to the relationship between themselves and others.

Notes

1. This paper originated as part of research for my PhD dissertation, written on a University Grants Committee Scholarship. I would like to express my thanks to Kon Kuiper whose support and guidance made it possible and enjoyable to pursue this fascinating line of enquiry.
2. In Austin (1987, 1988), I have formulated a model of face attack which mirrors Brown & Levinson's (1987) model of politeness. In this face attack model, I develop the notion of Face Attack Acts which are defined and exemplified in detail in Austin (1988).
3. From an unpublished Association of University Teachers report on sexual harassment in tertiary education.
4. Two examples of the importance of face attack for preservation of social structures by insult and humiliation are described in Kuiper (forthcoming) and Turnbull (1972).
5. These categories are devised by analogy with Brown & Levinson's (1987) politeness model, and show the close parellel between the dark side and its converse.
6. For a fuller definition of formulae, see Haggo & Kuiper (1983). For a discussion of the pragmatic indexing of formulae in the lexicon, see Austin & Kuiper (1988).
7. For a fuller discussion of the various interpretations of the Co-operative Principle, see Austin (1988: 8, 165).
8. There are situations in which women use strategies for humiliation and coercion, because they are experiencing situational power. However, because of the nature of our society, where women are under-represented in situations of power, it is likely that a quantitative study would reveal a greater occurrence of this communicative style among men than among women. A more serious fact is the institutional nature of the category of non-co-operative language as a whole, and in particular of sexist language.

References

AUSTIN, PADDY 1987, Review article of Dan Sperber and Deirdre Wilson, *Relevance* (Oxford: Basil Blackwell, 1986). *Australian Journal of Linguistics*, 7(1), 129–58.
—1988, The dark side of politeness: a pragmatic analysis of non-cooperative communication. Unpublished PhD Dissertation. Christchurch: University of Canterbury.
AUSTIN, PADDY and KUIPER, KOENRAAD 1988, Constraints on coordinated idioms. *Te Reo* 31, 3–17.

BROWN, PENELOPE and LEVINSON, STEPHEN C. 1987, *Politeness: Some Universals in Language Usage*. Cambridge: Cambridge University Press.

GOFFMAN, ERVING 1967, *Interaction Ritual*. Chicago: Aldine Publishing Company.

GRICE, PAUL 1975, Logic and conversation. In PETER COLE and JERRY MORGAN (eds), *Syntax and Semantics 3. Speech Acts* (pp. 41–58). New York: Academic Press.

HAGGO, DOUGLAS and KUIPER, KOENRAAD 1983, Review article of Florian Coulmas (ed.) *Conversational Routine: Explorations in Standardized Situations and Prepatterned Speech* (The Hague: Mouton, 1981). *Linguistics* 21(3), 531–51.

KUIPER, KOENRAAD 1988, Star Wars: An imperial myth. *Journal of Popular Culture* 22(1), 77–86.

—Forthcoming. New Zealand sporting formulae: two models of male socialisation. In JENNY CHESHIRE (ed.) *English Around the World: Sociolinguistic Perspectives*. Cambridge: Cambridge University Press.

SPERBER, DAN and WILSON, DEIRDRE 1986, *Relevance: Communication and Cognition*. Oxford: Basil Blackwell.

TURNBULL, COLIN 1972, *The Mountain People*. New York: Simon and Schuster.

Notes on Contributors

Marcia Abell studied linguistics in the Department of English Language and Literature, University of Canterbury, Christchurch.

Scott Allan is Lecturer in the Department of English, University of Auckland.

Paddy Austin studied linguistics in the Department of English Language and Literature, University of Canterbury. She works in the Education Review Office in Christchurch.

Donn Bayard teaches sociolinguistics in the Department of Anthropology, University of Otago, Dunedin.

Allan Bell works as a freelance journalist and researcher in sociolinguistics. He is an Honorary Research Fellow in the Department of Linguistics at Victoria University, Wellington.

Ross Clark is Senior Lecturer in Linguistics in the Department of Anthropology of the University of Auckland.

Elizabeth Gordon is Senior Lecturer in the Department of English Language and Literature, University of Canterbury, Christchurch.

Janet Holmes is Reader in Linguistics at Victoria University, Wellington.

Ingrid Huygens studied psychology and linguistics at the University of Auckland, and now works with Presbyterian Support Services in Auckland.

Koenraad Kuiper is Senior Lecturer in the Department of English Language and Literature, University of Canterbury, Christchurch.

Chris Lane lectures in the Departments of English and Linguistics at Victoria University, Wellington.

Margaret Maclagan teaches in the Speech-Language Therapy Department of Christchurch College of Education.

Graham Vaughan is Professor of Psychology at the University of Auckland.

295

Index

Note: Page references in italics indicate tables and figures. NZE = New Zealand English.

Abell, Marcia 36–47, 68–9, 71, 76, 86, 88, 91–3
Accent,
–American 68, 80, 184
–Australian 5, 64, *70*, 80, 83, 86, 88, 92–3, *see also* Australian English
–Canadian 80, 83, 86, 88, 91–3
–cultivated-general-broad 6, 36–47, *37, 38, 42*, 68–76, *70, 75*, 80–8, 91–3, 143
–and diphthong merger 133, 135, 142–5
–evaluation 3–4, 29, 34, 50, 54, 55–6, *56*, 67–8, 72, 76–94, *79, 87*
–history 35
–immigrants 50
–regional 5, 9, 23
see also dialect
Acceptability, and speech style 80, 83, 86, 89
Accommodation 155, 160–1, 165, 168–79, 257
Acker, Arch 34
Adams, R.N. 24
Address terms 244–6, 247
Adelswärd, Viveka *et al.* 240
Age,
–and audience design 171
–and diphthong merger 10, 138
–and glottalisation 150, 151, *156*, 158, 162
–and language attitude 43–4, 88, 91, 93
–and rhoticisation 150, 154–7, *156*, 158, 161

–and use of rising intonation 119–20, 122
Aho, Alfred J. & Ullman, Jeffrey D. 209
/ai/ 36
Aitchison, Jean 132, 139
Allan, Keith 113
Allan, Scott 2, 7–9, 12, 113–28
American English 6, 11, 68, 155, 158–61, 183–5, 187, 189
Analysis of variance (ANOVA) techniques 55, 57–61, 91
Andrews, E.W. 23, 25
Apology 15, 267–9, *268*, 270
Articulation 29–30, *31*, 37
–in horse race calling 202
Aspirate, omission 22–3, 186, 257
Atkinson, J. Maxwell & Drew, Paul 230, 240, 247
Attitudes to NZE 3–6, 21, 67–94
–changes in 43–4
–contemporary research 36–47, 68–94
–data 21–3, 35–6
–post-1900 23–8
–post-1930 32–5
–pre-1990 21–3
–and speech-training 28–31
Attractiveness, and speech style 5, 41, 44, 53, 64
Auckland,
–attitudes to NZE 3–4, 5
–courtroom questioning 221–47
–media speech styles 11, 168–79, *172, 174, 175*
–and rising intonation 119
–spoken Maori 49

Auctioneers, oral-formulaic performance 196, 197, 200, 202, 204, 209, 214
Audience design, and media speech styles 11, 165–79, *166*, 184, *184*, 190, 256, 272 n.7
Austin, Paddy 2, 13, 16, 260
Austin, Paddy & Kuiper, Koenraad 209
Australia, NZ influence on 12
Australian English 5, 8, 71, 113, 120, 122, 127, 188; *see also* accent
/aʊ/ 36
'ay-fever' 27–8, 33

Baines, William Mortimer 107
Baker, Sidney J. 97–8, 110–11
Bald on-record strategy 244, 270, 281–3
Barton, R.J. 105, 108, 111 n.8
Bauer, Laurie 12, 68–9, 83–5, 149–50
Bayard, Donn 2, 3–4, 5–6, 8, 9–12, 67–94, 149–64
Bell, Allan 3, 6, 11, 78, 93, 165–91, 228, 256, 271 n.1, 272 n.7
Benton, Richard 1, 8, 49
Bilingualism, among Maoris 65
Blom, Jan-Petter & Gumperz, John J. 167
Blum-Kulka, Shoshana 249 n.16
Borrowing 103, 111 n.2
Bracken, H.M. 33
Bradley, David & Bradley, Maya 163 n.9
Bright, Allan 207
British English, evaluation 56–61, *56*, *60*, 62–4, 185, 189
Brown, Gillian 124
Brown, Gillian, Currie, Karen & Kenworthy, Joanne 116–19, *117*, 127 n.2
Brown, Penelope 272 n.13
Brown, Penelope & Levinson, Stephen,
  –and face threat 243–5, 277–8
  –and interaction 272 n.9
  –and politeness 16, 244, 253, 257, 260, 269, 271, 272 n.8, 279, 286–7, 292 nn.2,5
Brown, Roger & Gilman, Albert 78, 257, 271 n.4, 272 n.9
Brunel, Gilles 176

Cameraderie 253, *254*
Cameron, Deborah 12
Campbell, Matt 163 n.8
Challenges 17, 180–1, 243–5, 247, 260
Chambers, J.K. 161
'chanting' 14, 197, 204–5, *205*, 218
Choice, language 100
Chomsky, Noam 209
Christchurch,
  –and attitudes to NZE 3, 27, 38–47
  –evidence of diphthong merger 133–46
  –horse race callers 197, 200–1, 210–13
Clapp, Reg 200
Clarity, interactional 253, 270–1
Clark, Herbert H. & Carlson, Thomas B. 228
Clark, Ross 2, 7, 97–112
Clarke, John 76
Clarkson, Dave 200, 201, 218
Class, socio-economic,
  –and diphthong merger 9–10, 133, 141, 142–5, *144*, 146
  –and glottalisation 158
  –and Maori English 50
  –and pronunciation 26, 27–8, 134–5
  –and rhoticisation 154
  –and sound change 132
  –and speech evaluation 39–46, 53, 69, 74, 77, *82*, 83, *84*, 86, 88–9, 93–4
Classification, ethnic 55–6, *56*, *57*, 58–60, 62–5, 77, 81–3, *82*, *84*, 88
Co-operative Principle 16, 290–1
Code-mixing 102–3
Code-switching 103, 257
  –situational/metaphorical 167
Coercion, *see* elicitation, coercive
Cognition, and speech 30
Cohen Commission on Education 23, 26–7

Cohen, Louis 26–7
Colenso, William 107, 109
Collins, Bill 219 n.9
Collins, David 102–3
Colonialism, linguistic 3, 11, 181–2
Commentary,
  –colour 13, 198, 204, 206–7, 210,
    213
  –play-by-play 13, 198, 206–7, *208*,
    209–12
  see also horse race commentators
Commercials, television, and speech
    styles 11, 168, 183–9, *184*, 190
Communication,
  –non-verbal 98–9
  –sexist 279–80, 282, 284, 287–8,
    291
Competence, communicative 196
Compliment 15, 265–7, *266*, 270,
    285–6
Confidence, in women's speech 15
Conservatism 74, 80, 84, 86, 88, 91,
    142–4, 154-5
Contact, language 98, 101–2
Content analysis 170, 171
Context,
  –and politeness strategies 14, 17,
    277, 285–6, 288, 290–1
  –social 15, 65, 165, 167, 171,
    221–47, 261
Contraction, in news broadcasting
    172–5, *174*, *175*, 179
Convergence 165, 180
Cook, James 98–9, 101
Correctness 25, 62, 80
Coulmas, Florian 209, 219 n.13
Coulthard, Malcolm & Brazil, David
    237
Coupland, Nikolas 189
Courtroom,
  –discourse structure 224
  –interaction 13, 14–15, 221–47
Crisp, Harry 202
Cruise, Richard A. 102, 105
Cruttenden, Alan 113, 123
Crystal, David & Davy, Derek 272
    n.9
Culture,
  –high 195
  –popular 195–7, 218

/d/, inter-vocalic 176
Danet, Brenda & Bogoch, Bryna
    235
Danet, Brenda & Kermish, Nicole
    C. 234, 235
Danet, Brenda *et al.* 235, 240
Data, collection 5, 51, 116–18,
    121–2, 134–6, 170, 183–4, 223
De Surville, Jean 98, 100
Declaratives 234–5
Deference 253–6, *254*, 260, 265, 268
  –and rising intonation 123, 127
Description, and intonation 121–2
Deuchar, Margaret 272 n.7
Deverson, Tony 93
Dialect,
  –British 11, 27–8, 187–9
  –literary 109–10
  –Maori, *see* Maori English
  –regional, *see* variation, regional
  –social 6, 10, 12, 17, 23–4, 34
  see also accent
Diffusion, lexical 10, 132, 133,
    139–41, 160
Diglossia 181, 182
Diphthongs 31, 33, 69, 71, 151, 157,
    162
  –/iə/ /eə/ 9–10, 33, 69, 129–46,
    137, *139*, *140*, 157
  –closing 24–5
Discourse analysis 12–17, 230
Dislocation, right/left 214, 217
Distance, social 15, 16, 243–5,
    253–7, *254*, *258*, 262, 265, 268,
    277, 286–8
Divergence, speech 257
Dominance, language 2
Drew, Paul 240, 242
Dunedin, and attitudes to NZE 3, 5,
    67–94, *85*
Dunstan, Robert 235, 240
Durkin, Mary 130, 132, 145
D'Urville, 104, 107
Dutch, evaluation 56–61, *56*, *60*,
    62–3, 68

/e/, raised 95 n.8
Edmondson, Willis 248 n.7
Education,
  –bilingual 1

–in Maori 49, 50
–and pronunciation 24, 26, 28, 31
Edwards, John R. 64
Effectiveness, communicative 3
Elicitation 116, 121, 226–8, 231–9
  –coercive 14, 222, 235, 240,
    242–4, 260, 263
  –conditions 228–30
  –facilitative 14, 240–1, 263–4
Elley-Irving Socio-Economic Index
    135, 143, 147 n.3
English,
  –distribution 2
  –as L2 15
  –Maori speakers 109–10
  see also American English;
    Australian English; British
    English; Maori English; NZE;
    Pacific English; Pidgin English
Ethnicity,
  –and speech evaluation 55–6, 56,
    57, 58–60, 62–5, 77, 81, 82, 83,
    84, 88, 91, 93–4
  –and use of rising intonation
    119–20, 122
Evaluation,
  –group/person centred 53
  –solidarity-stressing 53–4, 64,
    78–80, 81, 83, 86, 88–92
  –status-stressing 53–4, 63, 64,
    78–80, 81, 83, 86, 88, 91–3
Evaluation, social 50, 51, 52–65
Event, communicative 223–4, 223
Examination,
  –co-examination 14, 221–2, 224–5,
    230–2, 235, 235, 237–9, 242–5,
    247
  –cross-examination 14, 222, 223–4,
    225, 230, 232–4, 235, 235, 237,
    241–7
  –examination-in-chief 223–4,
    225–7, 230–2, 241
  –exchange structures 237–40
  –as genre 224
  –re-examination 223–4, 225, 232
Explanation, and intonation 121–2

Face,
  –definitions 277–8
  –positive/negative 16, 289–90

Face attack acts 2, 13, 14, 16,
    244–5, 263, 277, 278–80
  –types 281–9
Face saving strategies 281
Face threat acts 156, 242–4, 267,
    279–80
Fairburn, A.R.D. 33–4
False starts 202, 203
Feedback, positive 16, 168, 182, 269
Ferguson, Charles A. 181
Fishman, Joshua A. 53
Fluency, abnormal 13, 197, 198,
    201–3, 217
Formulae, linguistic 195–6, 282, see
    also performance, oral-formulaic
Friendliness, and speech style 5,
    41–2, 44–7, 53, 86
Fromkin, Victoria et al. 130–1
Fry, D.B. 132
Functions, distribution 15–16
Fussell, Alfred 29
Fussell, J.C. 109–10

Gender,
  –and diphthong mergers 9–10,
    133, 141–2, 142, 143–5, 146
  –and interaction 253, 260–71
  –and language attitude 91
  –and rhoticisation 155
Gibson, Harry 25–6
Giles, Howard 65 n.1, 90, 160, 165
Giles, Howard & Bourhis, Richard Y.
    76
Giles, Howard & Powesland, Peter
    36, 40–1, 53, 76, 80, 88
Giles, Howard & Ryan, Ellen
    Bouchard 53–4, 63–4
Giles, Howard, Scherer, Klaus R. &
    Taylor, Donald M. 272 n.9
Gläser, Rosemarie 219 n.13
Glottalisation 10–11, 74, 81–3,
    149–51, 152–3, 156, 158, 159–62,
    186
Goffman, Erving 16, 277–8
Goodwin, Marjorie Harness 265
Gordon, Elizabeth & Abell, Marcia
    2, 3–4, 6, 9, 21–47
Gordon, Elizabeth & Deverson,
    Tony 69
Gordon, Elizabeth & Maclagan,

Margaret 9–10, 129–47
Gordon, Philippa 4
Gould, Philip 5, 8–9
Grace, A.A. 109–10
Grammar, finite-state 197, 209, 214,
    215
Green, Georgia 214
Greenbaum, Sidney 17
Grice, Paul 16, 291
Gumbley, Warren 163 n.8
Guy, Gregory & Vonwiller, Julia
    113
Guy, Gregory *et al.* 8, 124

Haarmann, Harald 189
Haggo, Douglas & Kuiper,
    Koenraad 209
Hall, Moira 76
Halliday, Michael A. 272 n.9
Hamilton, Cynthia 4, 68, 80
Harassment, sexual 279–80
Harris, Sandra J. 230, 240
Haub, Keith 204, 205, 218
Havard-Williams, P. 105
Hawkins, Peter 130, 146
Health, and speech 30
Heine, Augustus 23, 27
Hesitation phenomena 202, 203
Hirsch, Walter 1
Hoffmann, Ludger 248 n.8
Holmes, Janet 2, 13, 15–16, 252–72
Holmes, Janet & Bell, Allan 1–18,
    123, 128, n.3, 147 n.2
Horse race commentators 13–14,
    196–218
  –discourse structure 206–7, *208*,
    209, 210
  –example 210–13
  –learning to call 200–1
  –oral-formulaic performance
    201–10, 214–18
  –short-term memory constraints
    197, 198–200
Horvath, Barbara M. 6, 71, 113,
    116, 119, 120–2, 123, 143
HRT, *see* intonation, High Rising
    Terminal
Humiliation 289–90
Humour, sense of, and speech style
    5, 41–2, 44–7, 78, 80, 86, 88

Huygens, Ingrid 41, 43, 65 n.1, 68,
    76, 83, 91–4
Huygens, Ingrid & Vaughan,
    Graham M. 58, 65 n.2, 74
Hypercorrection 142, 145–6, 147 n.6,
    188

/I/, centralised 8, 24–5, 33, 37, 188
/-i/, final 95 n.8
Identity, linguistic 11–12, 80
Immersion, pre-school education 1–2
in' endings 22–3
Initiations 14, 226, 229–34, 235, *235*,
    237–44
Innovativeness 74, 80–3, 85–6, 91,
    151, 154–7, 158–60
Insult 17, 260, 283
Intelligence, and speech style 63–4,
    80, 89, 91
Interaction,
  –and accommodation 160–1, 183,
    188
  –affective axis 15, 252–7, *254*, *256*,
    260–9
  –co-operative 13, 14, 16, 124–6,
    221–2, 224–5, 245, 247, 260,
    266, 269–70, 290–1
  –and high rising intonation 124–6
  –men-women 13, 15, 252, 253–71
  –negative 12–13, 16
  –non-co-operative 12–13, 16,
    277–92
  –referential axis 15, 253–7, *254*,
    258, 260–5, 270
Interference, language 110
Interrogatives, negative 234–5
Interruption 16, 269
Interview, Labovian techniques 116
Intonation, Australian Questioning
    124
Intonation, droned 197, 203–6
Intonation, High Rising Terminal 2,
    7–8, 113–27, *120*
  –function 123–7
  –and text types 120–2, *121*, 123,
    127
  –and turn length 122, *122*, 126–7

Jackendoff, Ray S. 216
Jacob, Jenny 12, 127 n.1

James, Allan R. 272 n.9
Jargon 7, 106–8, 109–11
Jarman, Eric & Cruttenden, Alan 113
Jones, Daniel 29, 31, 32
Jones, Debbie 272 n.10

/-k/, glottalised 150, 159
Kaiser, Julia et al. 119, 122, 128 n.4
Kearsley, Greg P. 240
King, Governor 102–3
kohanga reo (language nests) 1–2
Kuiper, Koenraad & Austin, Paddy 13–14, 195–219
Kuiper, Koenraad & Haggo, Douglas 13, 197, 198, 200, 201–2, 216
Kuiper, Koenraad & Tan, Daphne 209
Kuiper, Koenraad & Tillis, Frederick 204

/-l/ vocalisation 156, 157, 159, 162, 186, 257
Labov, William 131, 165, 170, 231–2, 271 n.6
Labov, William & Fanshel, David 248 n.7
Lakoff, Robin 15, 123, 253, 253, 270, 271 n.4
Lambert, Wallace E. 53, 76
Lane, Chris 13, 14–15, 221–49, 260
Language,
  –broken 105–6
  –contact 97, 105–8
  –sexist 16, 17, 95 n.11, 281
  –standard 25, 32, 47, 93
Language learning patterns 14
Le Page, R.B. 160, 182
Leadership, and speech style 89, 91
Levinson, Stephen C. 248 n.7
Lexical security index 154, 155
Liebes-Plesner, Tamar 240, 242, 245
Likeability, and speech style 80, 89, 91
Loanwords 97
Lord, Albert B. 197, 200, 218 n.2
Lynch, J.S. 33–4

McBurney, Samuel 22, 35
McDonald, Dave 204

Maclagan, Margaret 69, 71, 95 n.9, 133, 145
McLeod, Janet 29, 30
Maltz, Daniel N. & Borker, Ruth 261, 270
Maori,
  –distribution 1, 49
  –European use 99–102, 106–7, 109
  –as official language 2
  see also education; Pidgin Maori
Maori English 5, 7–9, 46, 50, 104, 111, 185, 191 n.8
  –compared with NZE 116, 119–27
  –evaluation 56–61, 56, 60, 62–5, 68, 93–4
Marion Du Fresne 98–9, 100–1
Markers,
  –lexical 186
  –phonological 186
  –syntactic 185–6
Marshall, Lachie 204, 207, 217
Matched guise technique 54, 68, 76, 90, 176
Mead, Richard 237, 240, 248 n.6, 249 n.13
Meaning, distorted, Pidgin English 104–5
Media,
  –influence on speech 10–11, 92, 151, 158, 159–61
  –and language accommodation 6, 160, 167, 168–79
  –public influence on 11, 165–79, 184, 190, 256, 272 n.7
  –speech samples 71, 72–3
Melanesian Pidgin 7, 106, 108
Memory,
  –long-term 198, 199, 202, 216
  –short-term 13, 197, 198–200, 201, 216
Men, referential orientation 15, 252, 260–71, 264
Merger,
  –/æl/-/el/ 69, 156, 157
  –diphthongs 9–10, 33, 69, 129–32, 133, 136–45, 137, 139, 140, 157
Methodology 12, 114–19, 133–5
Migrants, European, influence on speech 8
Miscommunication 15, 252, 261–2, 270

Mitchell, A.G. & Delbridge, Arthur
  6, 36, 68, 71, 83, 135, 142
Mitchell, Austin 34
Mix, language 102–3
Mühlhäuser, Peter 97
Murphy, Brian 190 n.3
Murtha, Reon 197, 200–1, 202–5,
  207, *208*, 210–13, 217, 218 n.4,
  218

Narrative,
  –elicited 13, 231–2
  –and intonation 121–2, 123–7
Negcon, in news broadcasting 172–5,
  174, 175, 179
News, and language styles 11,
  168–76, 256
Ng, S.H. 94 n.6
Nicholas, J.L. 97–8, 102, 103–5, 108,
  111 n.8, 111
Norwich (UK), diphthong mergers
  131–2
NZE,
  –compared with Maori English
    116, 119–27
  –cultivated 3–5
  –distinctiveness 17, 21, 22, 23–5,
    34–5
  –evaluation 56–64, *56, 61*, 68
  –pragmatic analyses 12–17
  –variation and change 7–12
  see also accent; attitudes to NZE

Off-record strategies 243–4, 279,
  288–9
On-record strategies 244, 283–8
Opinion, and intonation 121–2
Orthography,
  –and pronunciation 25–6, 35
  –US influence on 92
Östmann, Jan-Ola 272 n.9

/-p/, glottalised 150
Pacific English 94
Pacific Islanders 65
Pakeha English, *see* NZE
Parr, C.J. 29
Particles, pragmatic 15, 257, 262–5
Passive, in horse race commentaries
  14, 216
Pause, p. defined units 116–19, 121

Pearson, W.H. 112 n.9
Pellowe, John & Jones, Val 113
Performance, oral-formulaic 13–14,
  195–8, 200
  –and learning to call races 197,
    200–1
  –and memory constraints 198–200
Personality, and speech 38, 41, 53,
  89, 91–2
Petrie, D. 27–8
Pidgin 2, 7, 97–8, 106–9
  –New Zealand 103–4, 109–11
Pidgin English 97–8, 109–11
  –characteristics 104–5
  –and early contact 98–101
  –and jargon 105–8
  –later history 109–11
  –in pre-colonial period 101–5
Pidgin Maori 97–8, 100–4, 105,
  106–7
Pitch,
  –incremental increases 13–14,
    205–6
  see also intonation
Planning, speech 116–17, 126–7
Pleasantness, and accent 3, 80, 83,
  86, 89, 91
Politeness 2, 13, 15–16
  –negative 242–4, 247, 253, *254*,
    256–7, 259–60, 262–3, 267–71,
    277–92
  –positive 253, *254*, 256–7, 259–60,
    262–7, 269–70, 285
  –in women's speech 252–71
Pop music, changing phonology 11,
  159–60, *160*, 186
Power,
  –and face attack 16, 243, 279–81,
    282–3, 288, 291
  see also prestige
Pragmatic analysis 12–15
Preference, language 154–5
Prestige 43–6, 50, 57, 59–61, 63–4,
  78–80, 86, 88, 90–1, 181
  –and diphthong mergers 131–2,
    145–6
  –overt/covert 46, 78–80, 92–3, 154
  see also power; Received
    Pronunciation
Principal components analysis 80, 88
Pronunciation,

–/iə/ /eə/ 129–46, *137*
–attitudes to 21–31
–'colonial-genteel' 33
–monosyllabic/disyllabic 158–9, 163
  n.9
Prosodics, 'droned' 13–14, 197, 201,
  203–6, 217, 218

Questioning, courtroom 13, 221–47
–leading questions 225, 229,
  230–1, 232–3, 234–5, 239, 243
–repetitive 242
–syntactic features 234–6, *235*
see also elicitation; initiation
Quirk, Randolph *et al.* 234–5

/r/, post-vocalic 10, 85, 149–51,
  152–3, 154–7, *156*, 158, 159–61
Rampton, Ben 12
Received Pronunciation 3–5, 34, 36,
  37, 39–47, *42*
–and prestige 3, 40–3, 50, 63–4,
  67–8, 80, 83, 86, 91–2
Reduplication 101, 105
'referee' design,
–accuracy/success 188–9
–in-group 180–1, 182, 183–5
–and media speech styles 11, *166*,
  167–8, 179–82
–out-group 181–2, 183–5, 188–9
–and television commercials 11,
  183–9, *184*, 190
Register, formal/informal 155
Relevance Theory 16, 291–2
Reliability, and speech style 41–2,
  44–6, 80, 89
Renner, F. Martin 24
Rhoticisation 10, 85, 149–51, *152–3*,
  154–7, *156*, 158, 159, 159–61
Richardson, Louise 154
Romaine, Suzanne 97
Rules, discourse structure 13–14,
  197, 198, 200, 201, 206–7, *208*,
  209, 210, 217
Ryan, Ellen Bouchard, Giles,
  Howard & Sebastian, Richard J.
  64

Savage, John 102, 103, 106, 108
School inspectors, attitudes to
  language 21–6, 28–9, 31, 35

Searle, John R. 248 n.7
Self-confidence, and speech style
  60–1, 63–4, 78, 80, 89
Sharp, Andrew 104
Shimanoff, Susan B. 272 n.11
Sinclair, John McH. & Coulthard,
  Malcolm R. 249 n.16
Sinclaire, F. 30
Smith, John 26
Socialisation, effects on speech style
  261–2, 270
Solidarity,
–and politeness 16, 253–60, *254*,
  258, 262, 265–7, 280–1
–and speech evaluation 5
–and speech style 67, 78–80, *81*,
  83, 86, 88–92, 181, 185–6
South Seas jargon 7, 108
'Southland r' 10, 85, 149, 154–7
Speech,
–casual 12, 116, 123
–sampling 6, 51–2, 55, 71–8, *72–3*
Speech accommodation theory 6,
  160–1, 165, 168, 180
Speech Communication Association
  (NZ) Inc. 34
Speech styles, variation 11, 12,
  36–46, 50–65
Speech training 28–31, 50
Sperber, Daniel & Wilson, Deirdre
  16, 291
Status,
–language, *see* prestige, language
–socio-economic, *see* class, socio-
  economic
Stereotypes,
–language 36–41, 45, 49–65, 74–6,
  85, 93–4
–racial 7, 81, 110, 185–6
Stewart, Dorothy 25, 29
Stewart, Robert A.C. & Gorringe,
  Edith I. 52
Stigmatisation 4, 80–3, 93, 110,
  141–2, 145–6, 154–5
Strachan, D.A. 28–9
Strategy, discourse 12–13, 14–16,
  167, 179, 280
Strongman, Kenneth T. & Woosley,
  Janet 40
Style shift 165–7
–and media influence 168–79

–response/initiative 167–8, 179,
    181–2, 183, 189–90
Subject,
    –post-position 14, 214, 216–17
    –pre-posed 217

/t/,
    –glottalisation 10–140, 74, 81–3,
        149–51, *152–3*, *156*, 158,
        159–62, 186
    –inter-vocalic 176–7, *177*, *178*
Taborn, Stretton 4
Tag questions 15, 185, 234–5, 256,
    262–4, 269
Tahitian 111 n.3
Tajfel, Henri 63
Tasman, Abel 98
Text type, and rising intonation
    120–2, *121*, 123, 127
Thomas, Jenny 233, 263
Tone group boundaries 116–19, 121
Tonks, Sid 205
Topic,
    –constraint 240–1, 256
    –and style shift 171, 177
Transcriptions, and evaluation of
    speech 54–5
Trudgill, Peter 9, 131–2, 159–61, 186
Trudgill, Peter & Hannah, Jean 130
Turn length, and rising intonation
    120, 122, *122*, 126–7
Turner, George 34, 110–11, 130, 163
    n.9

Unit, pause defined 116–19, 121
Use, language 152–4

Valdés, Guadalupe 225
Variation,
    –inter-speaker 166

–intra-speaker 165–82, *166*
–paralinguistic 93
–regional 5, 49–50, 83–5, *85*, 189
–social 9–12, 68–94, *72–3*, *75*
Vaughan, Graham 65 n.1
Vaughan, Graham & Corballis,
    Michael C. 58
Vaughan, Graham & Huygens,
    Ingrid 2, 3, 4–5, 8–9, 49–65, 68,
    71, 92
Vernacular 12, 65
Vocabulary, Pidgin English 104

Wade, William Richard 106–7
Waitangi Treaty 2,.7, 109
Wall, Arnold 32, 95 n.8, 110–11,
    130
Ward, Ida 31
Warmth, in speech style 60–1, 63–4,
    65
Watts, Noel 68, 80
Wellington, and attitudes to NZE 3,
    4, 17
Wells, John 130, 150
Whinnom, Keith 106
Willis, J.D. 225, 230, 232–3, 234,
    244
Wolfson, Nessa 265, 266
Women,
    –affective orientation 15, 252–3,
        257–9, *258*, 260–71
    –facilitative questions 241
    –Maori/English 8, 116, 119–27
    –politeness strategies 13, 252,
        257–9, *258*
    –speech 2, 15–16
Word order, Pidgin English 105

Yaeger-Dror, Malcah 176